WITH A JUG OF WINE

An

UNUSUAL COLLECTION OF RECIPES

With

A JUG OF WINE

By Morrison Wood

FARRAR, STRAUS AND COMPANY · NEW YORK

First Printing, November 1949
Second Printing, December 1949
Third Printing, December 1950
Fourth Printing, June 1951
Fifth Printing, February 1952
Sixth Printing, October 1952
Seventh Printing, September 1953
Eighth Printing, February 1954
Ninth Printing, October 1954

Manufactured in the U.S.A.

Designed by Stefan Salter.

Some of the material for this book was taken from "FOR MEN ONLY!" a column which appears weekly in the *Chicago Daily Tribune* and other newspapers.

❯❯

Thanks are due the *Chicago Daily Tribune* for full permission to publish in book form.

CONTENTS

BY
RIC RICCARDO

I first met Morrison Wood under a truck.

It was during those rugged and lean depression years, when painting a truck meant one could eat.

Mr. Wood was somewhat better off than that. He and his father owned a large and profitable warehouse on Drexel Boulevard on Chicago's south side, and had not as yet felt the rumbling of banks' crashing all about them. They also owned several large moving vans, and I had been hired to paint them.

It was an unusually cold day around the middle of May. The concourse where the trucks were being painted was not heated and I was chilled, uncomfortable, and hungry. The paint dried slowly—I was preoccupied because my wife was expecting a baby and, in general, I was not in too cheerful a mood.

By contrast, when Morrison Wood walked out to inspect the work he seemed warm and protected. He was extremely well dressed and had a self-satisfied look of authority about him which for a moment might have made me seem rather cold toward him.

He introduced himself and, realizing my discomfort, he invited me into his office to get warm. Overlooking my paint-stained overalls, he offered me a soft chair near the radiator and a drink, and any antagonistic feelings I might have had were soon dissipated.

Three things attracted my attention as I sat there sipping my highball—a diminutive stage, a large and suspiciously inviting velvet couch, and in an alcove off his office a fully equipped miniature kitchen. When I inquired about them I learned that Mr. Wood was an excellent cook who enjoyed experimenting on new dishes and that he wrote plays and acted them out on his own stage with miniature puppets to preformulate the effect. As to the couch, I presumed, discreetly, that Mr. Wood was fond of afternoon siestas. I liked the man.

We had lunch together that day and I suggested an Italian

place I knew on the west side. Impecunious as I was in those de-
flationary times, no ordinary restaurant would do. It might be
only spaghetti, but it had to be the *best* spaghetti.

We repaired to the back room of a grocery store owned by one
Pescio Bonaguidi. Mr. Bonaguidi did many things to supplement
his income. He was an iceman, a trucker, a coal man, a grocer,
and he made some of the finest wine ever pressed out of grapes
by an Italian foot. Being a man of many good qualities, he had
also been blessed with a wife who was a very accomplished cook,
and in the manner of those never-to-be-forgotten speak-easy days,
they served, to an exclusive clientele, some very excellent food. Although it was simple, it was finely prepared; and although many
poor families were getting even poorer, and the depression was
beginning to set heavily upon us, Bonaguidi always insisted on
pure olive oil. He couldn't afford it, but "cottonseed oil," he said
emphatically, was "only for sows."

Pescio liked all men who enjoyed eating well. Morrison was one
of those; and before the second glass had been drained, the two
had found a common bond, namely, the camaraderie of gastronomic affinity.

They soon were in a huddle with Mrs. Bonaguidi, devising a
minestrone and a salad of such pungency and aroma as to make the
senses sing. We cut off large slices of capocollo and provalone
cheese and went down in the cellar to sample the Barbera while
the three of us murdered Rigoletto's quartet.

That was the beginning of a long friendship between Morrison
Wood and myself.

It was through Morrison Wood I first learned how good a lime
chiffon pie could really be. Like all accomplished gourmets he had
an inventive sense and a willingness to experiment even if the
results weren't always what he wanted. Occasionally we experimented together, to the despair of many a restaurant owner who
indulgently would put the facilities of his kitchen at our disposal.
No nuclear physicist ever worked more painstakingly for just the
right result.

In the dim past I had served as a cook on shipboard, mainly
because I wanted to see and sketch the far corners and distant
ports. I ran across every form of cooking from octopus *en bro-
chette* to fried iguanas. I believe a real thesis could be written

around the psychological effect of food on people and the manner
of serving it. The fact that cooking is often at such low ebb in
this age may account largely for the dyspeptic, psychotic condition of this world. Bad food and brutality are more akin than
many of us are willing to recognize.

A man with a platter of selected cheeses, grapes, English walnuts, fresh figs, and with a bottle of properly cooled Moselle from
a cool cellar isn't prone to be mad at anyone. I do not agree with
Allister McCauley who says in his *Book of Lies*: "We are Shrop-
shire geese; the tastiness of our talk comes from the disorder of
our body." Biliousness may produce heated arguments but never
great conversation.

I do see a vast improvement in the art of American cooking.
We are adventuring a little more, but it takes the Morrison Woods
and other proponents of the better and more leisurely life to lead
the way. I don't believe that with our advanced scientific knowledge in dietetics we shall ever return to the gluttony of Henry VIII,
nor, for that matter, shall we be like the Olympian warrior who
ate a whole ox for supper. More likely we shall exemplify the
highly selective taste of the Roman captain, who, on returning vic-
torious from battle and being told that he could ask for anything
he desired, threw down his shield and insisted it be filled with
the brains and tongues of hummingbirds.

The fact that the food columns of Lucius Beebe and Morrison
Wood are so widely read is in itself a wonderful advancement for
us Americans, who seem to run from any aestheticism or the
gentler aspects of life. We are fearful of a splash of color in our
clothes. We suspect the masculinity of anyone who sports a cane
and we sometimes question the honesty of those who are interested in wines and *apéritifs*. It is a self-consciousness that is lim-
iting and that may be one of the reasons why many of us are running away each year to soak up the atmosphere and tradition of
Capri, Paris, or Majorca.

As I am writing this preface I am in the midst of packing my
things for a trip to Europe—the main reason for this trip is that
I am actually *hungry*.

Any particular school of cooking largely identifies its practi-
tioners. The sauces and flavors of French cuisine show the imagination and gaiety of a spirited nation. The richness of the piquant

dishes served in Italy is the embodiment of a cultural and artistic race, while the unimaginative cooking in England is evidence of the stolid temperament of its people.

Good food and good wine embody great harmony, stimulate sparkling conversation, and promote good company. As Eric von Stroheim, the great movie director, once said to me, "In France the food is nearly always as good as the company—in America the company is seldom better than the food."

There is a bond and affection amongst those who, while nibbling at a slice of Prosciutto ham, watch the trout that is to be their supper being caught in the rapids of the Sesia (a river that flows through the city of Varallo in Italy). There is a glow as you mutually recall a serving of *Zuppa Inglese* (the king of all desserts), the specialty of some obscure inn on the Riviera. There is remembrance of a firm romantic attachment made over a fondue with just the right amount of properly sliced truffles.

Gaieties that follow a good supper have been the subject of many masterpieces simply because they are inspiring in their naturalness and spontaneity. Franz Hals, Manet, Monet, Renoir, just to mention a few, often painted eating and drinking scenes to catch the unaffected laughter of people.

I am not one to insist that the wife be chained to a stove, but if the modern woman would give more thought to preparing delectable dishes and less to the bridge table, perhaps the divorce courts wouldn't be so busy. The expression "Oh, if she could only cook," or "The way to a man's heart is through his stomach," have a psychosomatic meaning deeper than one would believe.

To duplicate a dish in the home is ofttimes to relive a particular experience that has carved deeply in our humble existence.

As a historian of cookery Mr. Wood becomes the owner of the Aladdin lamp—the lender of the Magic Carpet. A potato baked in rosin brings back memories of moonlit nights on the Tamiami Trail. Or we are sitting enthralled and peaceful on the high mountain that divides the valley of Aosta from the valley of Oropa in northern Italy, the grapes in full maturity. Strong smells of fermenting wine. We are having a *triglia* (a fresh water fish similar to perch) in aspic. Even the lowly but wonderful *pizza* with salty anchovy brings you back to Santa Lucia—silvery seas and fragrant midnights.

Morrison is an anxious, restless soul constantly searching out a better wine or a tastier sauce. I should like to pass a compliment on to him, which I received from my friend, the late John Barrymore, the celebrated actor. At a dinner party given in his honor on the opening night of *My Dear Children,* in New York, Mr. Barrymore was asked to say a few words. "In Chicago," he said, "I met a fellow who was an artist and a chef." Then after reflecting for several seconds, he went on, "No, I take that back—he was more than that. He was a snake charmer—he made me eat, and I had not touched food for thirty years." So much for Mr. Wood with this book—he is a snake charmer.

FOREWORD

Once upon a time there was a DELUXE young lad by the name of HORACE, who was classified 3F. He had family, FORTUNE, and fame.

The first he was BORN into.

The SECOND he acquired by not staying up with the OWLS at night. CONSEQUENTLY, he could fly with the EAGLES in the daytime.

The third was THRUST upon him, because he KNEW most of the ANSWERS, and, what is MORE important, all of the QUESTIONS.

But LOVE had passed him by. OR, perhaps he had passed LOVE by.

Then came the DAY when he FELL for a gorgeous BLONDE.

She was the KIND that when she walked into the STORK CLUB, all the oyster forks PAUSED in midair.

She had a CHASSIS that General Motors have been trying to get on a DRAWING board for years.

She had a BODY that would even make the FISHER brothers DROOL.

She was PRACTICALLY born in the RAINBOW Room at ROCKE-FELLER Center; she teethed on ESCOFFIER; and she was reared by the WINE and FOOD Society.

She was the PERFECT companion for the MAN about TOWN.

But, ALAS and ALACK!

HORACE, our hero, rated ABSOLUTE zero in the Man About Town DEPARTMENT.

He thought that SOUTHERN COMFORT meant lying in a HAM-MOCK under Magnolia trees in BILOXI.

He was SURE that Frogs' Legs PROVENÇALE was an affliction peculiar to FRENCHMEN.

He imagined BRUNSWICK stew was a GEORGIA drunk.

HOWEVER, his courtship of the GORGEOUS BLONDE was of the WHIRLWIND variety.

She thought his ERUDITION was terrific, to say NOTHING of his magnificent TORSO.

And then . . . . he INVITED her up to his apartment for DINNER.

KNOWING his Emily Post, he INCLUDED her mother in the INVITATION.

He gave COOK and the BUTLER the night off, for he WOULD not desecrate his LOVE by allowing ALIEN hands to prepare DREAM-BOAT's food.

The GORGEOUS BLONDE winced when HORACE served crème de MENTHE before dinner.

She SHUDDERED over the SOUP.

It would have made a PAPERHANGER's hands itch for a ROLL of wallpaper and a BRUSH.

She nearly FAINTED when our HERO brought in a BURNED steak surrounded by BOILED cabbage.

Mother had to LEAD her away in a STRAIT JACKET when HANDSOME HORACE poured Scotch OVER the slightly melted ICE CREAM and then tried to LIGHT it.

The NEXT day, the GORGEOUS BLONDE married a MAITRE d'.

The MORAL?

HELL, we haven't ANY. We're FRESH out of MORALS.

BUT . . . .

HANDOME HORACE would never have made his FATAL mistakes if he had FAMILIARIZED himself with delectable DISHES and their PREPARATION.

So . . . .

Let this be a WARNING!

WHO KNOWS? Someday, YOU, or one of your FRIENDS, may meet a GORGEOUS BLONDE!

APOLOGIA

I might as well be brazen right at the start. I think this is a damn good cook book. And all those who saw the original manuscript thought the same thing. It contains recipes for some of the best and most unusual concoctions that have ever passed your dentures, fixed or removable.

Most of the recipes contained herein have appeared in my weekly syndicated column in the *Chicago Daily Tribune*, and other newspapers. They are tried, tested, and true, and in over three years' time my rather large mail from bankers, industrialists, businessmen, mechanics, ministers, housewives, secretaries, and business women have been filled with praise for the recipes which they have tried and have found "out of this world."

If you are looking for recipes such as Miss Sally Arbuthnot's celebrated (in Round Corners, Nebraska) corn chowder, or Aunt Arbethera's escalloped chicken, or the chocolate meringue pie that won first prize at the Sulpha County Fair, don't waste your time going on. There are hundreds, or even thousands of recipes for ordinary dishes that you won't find in the following pages. If you are solely interested in the type of recipes that are to be found in women's magazines, in the columns of home economists, in standard cook books, in pamphlets put out monthly by various public utilities or by purveyors of foodstuffs, stop here, and try to salvage the price paid for this volume by trading it for something else you want, or chalk it up against foolish expenditures.

However, if you're seeking new taste thrills, if you'd like to become a renowned host or hostess, if you'd like to cook your way into a man's (or woman's) heart, or if you have an adventuresome spirit and yearn to experiment or to try something new— you've bought yourself a piece of goods!

Whether you're a neophyte or an old kitchen hand, you will have no trouble in following the recipes. If you can read the English language, if you can count up to twenty, with or without taking off your shoes, and if you can follow explicit directions, you can make anything mentioned in this book, and do it well.

I am not the repository of culinary secrets imparted to me by the master chefs of the Old or the New world. For twenty-five years I have collected recipes from all over the world. I have taken other unusual recipes, have experimented, and have come up with something that I thought was a little better than the original—at least, according to my taste and the tastes of discriminating friends. In some instances I have selected the best ingredients of several recipes for the same dish, have perhaps added a touch of my own, and again have come up with a very succulent concoction. And in some cases I've made up a dish that I thought would be good. If it turned out the way I thought it would—swell. If it didn't, I ate it (I'm against wasting food) and forgot about it.

Believe it or not, it was the United States Army which helped to make me a gourmet. I left college in April of 1917 to attend the first officers' training camp at Fort Sheridan, Illinois, and was commissioned a second lieutenant of infantry in the regular army on August 15, 1917. I joined my regiment at Fort Sam Houston, Texas, a week later. The following month, by dint of close attention to duty and by lending money to my regimental commander, I was made adjutant of the post. This rated me a striker, who pressed my uniforms, polished my boots, cleaned my quarters, and cooked my breakfasts. He could make, and did, one of the most delicious omelets I have ever tasted, and his coffee was worth waking up for, even at the crack of dawn.

From August 22 to November 1, 1917, it was a lovely war in San Antonio, Texas. Then came a rude awakening. My command was ordered to strike duty in the Texas oil fields, and for two months I starved, as everything tasted and smelled of crude petroleum. In the nick of time I was rescued from starvation by my regiment's being ordered to Galveston to guard the docks. For seven months I cleared ships in and out of the port, and between times partook of some of the finest southern cooking to be found south of the Mason and Dixon line.

Back in Camp Travis, in August of 1918, I trained with my division for overseas service. For a month I ate at the officers' mess, which was really pretty dreadful. Then an order was issued requiring one officer to eat at each company mess. Guided again by a strong sense of duty, and by the knowledge that my company cook had formerly been head cook for the Number 1 table in Ringling Brothers' Circus, I volunteered, and thereafter ate with L Company. The meals I had should only happen to a General of the Armies, and the things I learned about cooking, if laid end to end, would impel a more aggressive individual to start a restaurant. But instead, after leaving the army, I got married.

At this point I know what you're thinking—that I married a girl who couldn't even boil water! Quite the contrary, she was, and is, a terrific cook. She knows more tricks with food and pots and pans than a monkey does with a coconut. So . . . . for eighteen years I ate, not wisely, but well, and spent my spare time continuing to collect recipes, and occasionally whipping up a dish that she, or our cooks whom she had taught, were unfamiliar with.

Then World War II came along, and the Little Woman, burning with a desire to do her part, went into war work. She left the apartment each day at eight o'clock, and returned between five and six, completely frazzled. Our cook departed about the same time, correctly figuring that sixty dollars a week in a war plant was a hell of a lot more hay than slaving at the Maison Wood for fifteen dollars a week. Naturally, it doesn't take any I.Q. at all to guess who was left holding the bag!

So I graduated from an armchair cook to a practicing one . . . . and I do mean practicing!

Although my syndicated column is called "For Men Only!" this book is intended for anyone who likes to eat, and cook. I do not belong to the school which holds that only men are great cooks. I do believe it is true that most men approach cooking in an adventuresome spirit, simply because they are not obliged to cook day in and day out. It is to them first a game, then a pastime, and finally a hobby, all of which is swell. But to most women who have to cook three meals a day for husband and/or children, cooking is likely to be a sorry bit of drudgery. It's hard to find glamour or even fun in cooking three meals a day, seven days a week, fifty-two weeks a year. But I do believe some of the sting can be taken out of enslavement to pots and pans and stoves by occasionally experimenting with something old or common-place, or trying something new.

Why have I written this cook book? I believe there are many

women and a great number of male amateur cooks who would like to have a cook book which eliminates the ordinary, run-of-the-mill recipes and the very difficult recipes, and which presents unusual and delectable recipes that they can prepare and cook, and have their friends say, "Where on earth did you get that recipe?" or "How did you ever think of this wonderful dish?"

In other words, ladies and gentlemen, here is something upon which you can build reputation and fame. Your friends may laugh as they sit down at your table to partake of a meal you have prepared, but believe me, they'll applaud when the meal is over. Again, when the Little Woman has gone home to mother, either for a vacation or for a salutary effect, you won't have to eat out of cans, in expensive restaurants, or at Ptomaine Pete's lunch counter. As for the ladies, they can often make the approach to a new hat, an Easter outfit, or a new fur coat much less painless by serving the so-called "better half" with a superlative dish. You see, that old saw, "The way to a man's heart is through his stomach," can be amended to: "The way to a man's pocketbook is through a satisfied tummy."

Finally, for bachelors, cooking offers a new and better approach than that timeworn gag, "How would you like to come up and see my etchings?"

WITH A JUG OF WINE

(1) WINE

> Wine is, indeed, a living thing, brash in its youth, full-blossoming in its maturity, but subject, if not used in time, to senility, decay and death. It is gregarious, appearing at its best in the company of food, and as a constituent of food; and in the society of moderate men and women, priming their wit, assisting at their worship, and serving as a medicine for some of their ills.
>
> —*Encyclopedia Britannica*

It is, of course, entirely possible to cook without using wine. It is also possible to wear suits and dresses made out of flour or gunny sacks; to build a house out of milk bottles; to walk up to Joe Louis and slap him across the face without any provocation; or to win an argument from one's better half. But who wants to?

First, let's see what wine actually does for cooking. In wine cookery, it's not the flavor of the wine you taste, but a special goodness of the food itself that wine brings out. Wine balances food flavors and creates taste harmonies pleasing to the palate. (In case you don't know what taste harmonies are, they're what make ham and eggs, or mustard and frankfurters, or coffee and doughnuts go so well together.) To bland foods, wine adds flavor. Marinating (or soaking) some meats in wine before cooking makes them more tender and flavorsome. This is especially true of the less costly cuts, or of tough, stringy meats. Furthermore, wine supplies certain salts and sugars which improve flavors, and certain vitamins and other food values which enhance nourishment.

Throughout Europe, wine and food have been happily married for centuries. The humblest housewives, as well as the greatest chefs, know that wine, used intelligently, not only accents all the good natural flavors of foods, but adds a delightful fragrance and flavor of its own, and often raises a prosaic dish to undreamed-of heights of deliciousness. Of course, when heat is applied to wine, or other alcoholic beverages, the alcohol disappears in vapor (al-

3

cohol boils at 172.4 degrees Fahrenheit and water boils at 212 degrees Fahrenheit), leaving only the intrinsic flavor of the wine itself. It follows that what is left is no better than the flavor of the wine, and, naturally, the better the wine, the better the flavor.

There are some misconceptions about the use of wine in cooking. One is that it is difficult to cook with wine. As a matter of fact, cooking with wine is no more difficult than cooking with salt and pepper. Wine and its by-products, brandies and cordials, fill the same place for flavor as do vanilla, lemon, and almond extracts. It actually is easier to cook with wine than without it. With wine, left-overs become an opportunity rather than a problem.

"Cooking with wine must be terribly expensive," is a remark frequently made to me. It isn't. In the first place, expensive imported vintage or chateau-bottled wines are far less desirable in cooking than good American wines. The very qualities that make imported wines expensive—delicate bouquets and flavors—usually are lost at the first application of heat. With a few exceptions, good American wines equal or surpass 90 per cent of the imported wines, and at a fraction of their cost. You can purchase excellent American white or red wine or sherry for from one dollar to a dollar and a half a bottle. If a recipe calls for half a cup of wine, by the application of simple mathematics you find you have added only about twenty cents to the cost of your dish, and probably four or five dollars' worth of taste value.

What wine goes with what food? There has been a generalization that red wines belong with red meats and game, white wines with fish and poultry, appetizer wines in soups, and sweet wines and cordials in desserts. But time and ingenuity of cooks have outmoded such a generalization. There are fish dishes which utilize red wines. There are recipes for meat which even call for the use of the sweet dessert wines. And there are desserts which utilize white and red wines in their preparation. Sherry, of course, can be used to advantage in almost anything. So, the adventuresome chef may experiment with many different combinations of foods and wines.

The rules for the service of wines with dinner are more rigid. Dinner should begin with the appetizer wines, followed by the lighter white or red wines and building up to the heavier wines as the dinner progresses. For instance, a chilled dry sherry with the appetizer, a dry white wine with the fish, a full-bodied red wine with the meat, and a heavy sweet wine with the dessert. With coffee, of course, brandy or cordials. Champagne is one wine that can be served throughout an entire dinner.

There has been a great deal of balderdash put out by amateur gourmets and epicures about the service of wines, such as each particular wine should have its particular glass. That was all very well in the era of spacious homes, fat bank accounts, and competent servants, but it just isn't done any more in the average home.

Of course, wine is at its best when it is served in lovely crystal tulip-shaped glassware, just the same as food tastes better served on an attractively set table. But you don't have to have expensive glassware to enjoy wine. I have drunk a lovely vintage Burgundy out of an ordinary water tumbler (during the exigency of moving), and it tasted wonderful. So, in the interest of enjoying wine, don't let the lack of the proper glassware stop you from drinking wines with your meals.

I'd like to add a short remark about drinking the right wine with the right food. When the Little Woman and I were married, she liked a fairly sweet sauterne with her meals. I knew it was wrong, and she admitted that it might be. But who was I to insist that she immediately change her drinking habits? I chose the easier and much pleasanter way of subtly educating her. And it was not long before she came to appreciate the right wines with her meals. Today I don't know anyone who has a finer appreciation of wines, and their subtleties and flavors, than she has.

What kind of wines should one have in the home? That depends largely on the state of the exchequer and the space available to keep them. I should say the minimum requirements would be a bottle of good American sherry, an American dry white wine, an American dry red wine, a bottle of fine American port, and a bottle of good California brandy. If you can handle more than this, I should suggest a bottle of dry Madeira, a bottle of medium rum, a bottle of Marsala, and a bottle of imported curaçao. From there on you can add whatever you want. But with the above stock, you can cook almost any in this or any other cook book. At the end of this chapter, I shall have a buying guide on American wines and a list of the principal imported cordials.

For those who are not completely familiar with wines, it might help to briefly run through the different wine types. While there are hundreds of different names of wine, virtually all of them fit into five classes, and in these five classes are fourteen distinct wine types that are well known in the United States.

APPETIZER WINES
Sherry   Vermouth   Madeira   Marsala

WHITE TABLE WINES
Sauterne (dry and sweet)   Rhine Wines (Dry)

RED TABLE WINES
Burgundy (full bodied)   Claret (lighter bodied)

DESSERT WINES
Port   Muscatel   Tokay   White Port

SPARKLING WINES
Champagne   Sparkling Burgundy

Wine type names are of two main origins. About half of them, like Burgundy, Rhine wine, sauterne, and claret, came into use centuries ago as generic names of the wines of the Old World viticultural districts which were famous for those particular types of wines.

The other half are the varietal names, used when the wine type is named for the principal grape variety from which the wine is made. Examples are Pinot Noir, Gamay, and Isabella (Burgundy types); Cabernet and Zinfandel (claret types); Semillon, Sauvignon, Lake Niagara, and Isle St. George (sauterne types); and Riesling, Traminer, Sylvaner, Lake Erie Islands, and Lake Elvira (Rhine wine types).

There are three principal districts in the United States which produce fine wines: California (the areas north, east and south of San Francisco); New York State (the area around the Finger Lakes district); and Ohio (the Sandusky-Lake Erie Islands region of northern Ohio). There are other wine-producing areas in the United States, but the above three are the principal ones. The wines bottled in these districts are in many instances on a par with all except a very few of the great European wines. *You need never be ashamed to serve a fine American wine*—in fact, there is a growing tendency among the best eating places in America to feature fine American wines on the menus.

There are three guides for the buying of American wines: the varietal or generic name of the wine, the district in which the wine is made, and the vintner's name. As examples:

A DRY WHITE WINE
Livermore (district)   Sauvignon Blanc (variety)
Wente Brothers (vintner)

A DRY RED WINE (Burgundy type)
Napa (district)   Pinot Noir (variety)
L. M. Martini (vintner)

A DRY RED WINE (claret type)
Napa Valley (district)   Cabernet (variety)
Beaulieu Vineyards (vintner)

A DRY WHITE WINE (Moselle or Rhine wine type)
New York State (district)   Lake Elvira (variety)
Widmer's (vintner)

Throughout this book you will find designations such as "dry American white wine," "dry American red wine," "medium dry American wine," and so forth. There are also designations such as "Madeira," "Marsala," "port," and so on. I have not attempted to designate a particular varietal or generic wine for each recipe, because there are undoubtedly localities where such specific wines would be unobtainable. However, as I have said, at the end of this chapter I will list a buying guide for practically every fine American wine that is bottled in the United States today. If a recipe designates a dry American red wine, simply refer to the guide, and I am sure that out of the list you will find a wine that is obtainable in your town. You cannot go wrong with any of the varietal or generic names listed, the districts from which they come, and the vintners who bottle them. I have sampled all the wines that are listed, I am thoroughly familiar with the districts from which they come, and I know the reliability of the vintners. I can highly recommend everything on the list.

There are two wines appearing in my recipes which are not grown or bottled by American vintners, or, if they are, I am not familiar with and consequently cannot recommend them. These two wines are Madeira and Marsala. The former has a taste combination of sherry and port and is a fortified wine, that is, brandy has been added. There are two types of Madeira, the dry and the sweet. For use in cooking, outside of desserts, the dry (Sercial) is recommended.

Marsala is an amber colored, sweet wine with a mild sulphurous taste, and comes from Italy. The best type for cooking is the Florio Virgin Dry Marsala, which can now be obtained in the United States. The perfect Veal Scallopini Marsala cannot be made without it.

Vintners in California and New York are now putting out some excellent dessert wines and sherries. I have tasted wonderful sherries and ports from both California and New York—quite the equal of the imported varieties, except for certain rare vintage bottlings.

While California brandy is excellent to cook with, I must, in all fairness, confess that as an after-dinner drink it suffers from comparison with really good French or Spanish brandies. I do believe, however, that in the not-too-distant future California vintners will produce a creditable brandy.

American champagnes are not the equal of the great French champagnes. However, America does produce some very excellent champagnes. I think the consensus of opinion among experts is that the East produces a better champagne than that of California. I will list what I believe to be the best five champagnes bottled in America today.

In the matter of cordials, the imported are far superior to the domestic. For some reason, the great cordials just can't be made in America. This was demonstrated during the last war, when certain cordials, made in America apparently under the same formula as they were abroad, just didn't taste the same as they did when they came from Europe. There was a decided and easily distinguishable difference in the Grand Marnier, for instance, which was made in America during the war, and the Grand Marnier that was made in Europe. I am sorry to say that I cannot recommend any of the domestic cordials.

BUYING GUIDE FOR AMERICAN WINES

Again, let me caution you about buying American wines. Look for three things:

(1) The name, on the label, of the vintner

(2) The name, on the label, of this country's great wine districts. These names are gradually becoming famous; they are our own counterparts of the great wine names of France: Pommard, Chablis, Sauternes, Vouvray—all French towns or villages.

(3) The name, on the label, of an outstanding variety of grape. No producer will put the name of an inferior grape on his label. Nor will he put the generic name on his label if he is not proud of the wine.

Here are the names of fifteen leading winemakers in the United States today. Ten are located in California, four in New York State, and one in Ohio.

VINTNERS

Wente Brothers	Alameda	California
Beaulieu Vineyards	Napa	California
Louis Martini	Napa	California
Los Amigos Vineyards	Alameda	California
Almaden Vineyards	Santa Clara	California
Fountaingrove Vineyards	Sonoma	California
Inglenook Vineyard	Napa	California
Korbel and Bros.	Sonoma	California
Paul Masson	Santa Clara	California
Novitiati of Los Gatos	Santa Clara	California
Widmer's Wine Cellars	Naples	New York
Urbana Wine Company	Hammondsport	New York
Pleasant Valley Wine Company	Rheims	New York
Taylor Wine Company	Hammondsport	New York
Meiers Wine Cellars	Sandusky—Lake Erie Islands	Northern Ohio

In California, the names of the wine-growing districts are important. There are five to keep in mind: Alameda, Livermore Valley, Napa, Santa Clara, and Sonoma. These, with the exception of Livermore Valley, are names of counties.

In New York and Ohio, the districts are not so important. The vintner's name and the varietal or generic names are what really count.

And now, in closing, here are the varietal and/or generic names

of the leading wines bottled in the United States. California vintners' names do not appear after the varietal names, because there
may be two or three, or several, who bottle such a wine. For instance, Martini, Beaulieu Vineyard, Fountaingrove, and Wente all
bottle a Pinot Noir.

WHITE WINES
Rhine Wine Types (very dry and dry)

Name	District	Vintner
Riesling	California-New York	Widmer's, New York
Johannisberger Riesling	California	
Sylvaner	California	
Lake Delaware	New York	Widmer's
Lake Dutchess	New York	Widmer's
Lake Diana	New York	Widmer's
Delaware	Ohio	Meiers
Traminer	California	
Folle Blanche	California	
Sauvignon Blanc	California	
Chablis	California-New York	Widmer's, New York
Rhine Wine	California-New York	Widmer's, New York
Lake Erie Islands	Ohio	Meiers
Elvira	New York	Widmer's
Iona	New York	Widmer's

Sauterne Types (dry)

Pinot Chardonay	California	
Pinot Blanc	California	
Dry Semillon	California	
Chateau Beaulieu	California	
Isle St. George	Ohio	Meiers
Dry Sauterne	California-New York	Widmer's, New York

Sauterne Types (medium sweet to sweet)

Sauterne	California-New York	Widmer's, New York
Haut Sauterne	California-New York	Widmer's, New York
Lake Niagara	New York	Widmer's
Sweet Semillon	California	

RED WINES

Pinot Noir	California	
Gamay	California	
Cabernet	California	
Lake Isabella	New York	Widmer's
Barbera	California	
Charbono	California	
Zinfandel	California	
Burgundy	California-New York	Widmer's, New York
Claret	California-New York	Widmer's, New York

CHAMPAGNES

Gold Seal Brut	New York	Urbana Wine Company
Vindemy Brut Special	New York	Widmer's
Great Western Brut Special	New York	Pleasant Valley Wine Company
Almaden Brut	California	Almaden Vineyards
Korbel Brut	California	Korbel and Bros.

Liqueurs, or cordials, are very lovely things to look at, to sip slowly with your coffee after an excellent dinner, to use in cooking, or to use with ice creams. As a rule, they are expensive, but due to the fact that they are served and used in small portions, their cost is really not so high. And they do wonders for not only your taste buds, but your morale.

There are probably a hundred or more cordials on the market today, but some of them are special concoctions of some manufacturer and are known only in the locality where they are prepared. I should guess that there are about sixty really fine cordials, but many of these are unobtainable in the United States.

Cordials fall into two broad classifications: fruit cordials and plant cordials. It is said that some cordials, such as green chartreuse, contain up to 250 ingredients.

There is one cordial, Calisay, made in Spain, which is composed of more than 125 different herbs, plants and fruits.

A cordial is an artificial liquor or spirit prepared by one of two methods—maceration or infusion. In the first method, fruits and plants are steeped in brandy, or rectified spirit, for about six to eight months. Then other ingredients are added. In the second method, alcohol is mixed with the juices of fresh crushed fruit, then spiced and sweetened. Or alcohol is mixed with the oils of various plants, diluted with water, sweetened with sugar, and finally filtered. The best cordials are prepared by the maceration method.

APRICOT BRANDY or ABRICOTINE
This is an apricot cordial or brandy made from small French apricots.

ABSINTHE
The true absinthe is impossible to obtain today. Originally it contained wormwood, which is claimed to be a narcotic. If you

are old enough, you will remember Madame X, in the famous play of that name, who had become an absinthe fiend. One of the finest pick-me-ups used to be an absinthe frappe. Today absinthe can be obtained sans wormwood under such trade names as Herbsaint or Pernod, both of which are still wonderful flavoring agents.

ANISETTE
This is compounded from anise-seed oil and oil of bitter almonds, dissolved in strong spirits.

BENEDICTINE
This is made from a large variety of herbs and good cognac brandy. It was originated by a Benedictine monk in Fécamp, France, over four hundred years ago and is still made in the same town.

The initials D.O.M. on the label stand for *Deo Optimo Maximo* —To God, most good, most great.—the motto of the Benedictine Order.

CHARTREUSE, GREEN or YELLOW
This cordial is made in Tarragona, Spain, although it was originally made in France over three hundred years ago. The recipe is a secret of the Carthusian Fathers. The yellow chartreuse, made from 120 ingredients, is 86 proof and the green, prepared from about 250 ingredients, is 110 proof. These are two of the finest liqueurs obtainable.

CHERRY HEERING
This cordial is made in Copenhagen, Denmark, from fresh cherries, spice, sugar, and brandy.

COINTREAU
Cointreau, white curaçao, and triple *sec* are very similar, but Cointreau is sweeter than the other two. They are all prepared from fine brandy, with orange peel as their principal base. This is one of the ingredients of the famous Sidecar cocktail.

CRÈME DE CACAO
This cordial is prepared from cacao beans and fine brandy. In a cordial glass, with cream floating on the top, it is a favorite after-dinner drink of the gentler sex. It is also the base of the Alexander cocktail, which is another favorite with women.

CRÈME DE CASSIS

This cordial is made from black currants steeped in fine brandy and sweetened with syrup. One of the best known *aperitifs* in France is a *cassis vermouth,* which is made with equal parts of crème de cassis, dry vermouth, and sparkling water added. This is a deliciously cooling summer drink.

CRÈME DE MENTHE

This is prepared with cognac and fresh peppermint leaves. It may be white or green. White crème de menthe and brandy make up the well-known *Stinger* cocktail.

CRÈME DE NOYAU

This cordial is primarily used as a flavor in mixed drinks. It is compounded from brandy, bitter almonds, nutmeg, mace, and the kernels of apricot or peach pits.

CRÈME DE ROSE

This is made from aromatic seeds and brandy, and sweetened with rose petals. It is a wonderful flavoring agent in cooking.

CRÈME DE VIOLETTE

This cordial is made the same way as crème de rose, but violet petals are used instead of rose petals. It has an intriguing aroma and a beautiful color.

CURAÇAO

This is made from a variety of bitter green orange, mace, cloves, and cinnamon, and sweetened with wine brandy.

DRAMBUIE

This is a liqueur made from Scotch whiskey and wild honey.

FALERNUM

This is a West Indian flavoring agent prepared from herbs, limes, and rum. It has a low alcoholic content, about 6 per cent, but it adds the most unusual flavor to gin and rum drinks. It is rather sweet.

FLOR ALPINA

This is a sweet Italian cordial which is put out in a tall bottle, usually with a stalk of the crystalline tree in the bottle which is heavily encrusted with sugar.

FRAISETTE
This cordial is made from alcoholic syrup, white wine, and strawberries.

FRAMBOISE
This cordial, which has a high alcoholic content, is made from raspberries.

GOLDWASSER
This cordial is also known as *Eau de Vie de Dantzig,* which is the French name, or *Danzig Goldwasser,* which is the German name. The French cordial is a distillation of fruit peels, herbs, and spices with an alcohol base. The German has a caraway seed flavor. Both have flecks of gold leaf added to them. Goldwasser is reputed to be the oldest cordial made, and strangely enough, was first made by the Italians.

GRAND MARNIER
In the opinion of a great many people, this is one of the finest cordials made. It is composed of white curaçao and fine champagne (the finest type of brandy).

KÜMMEL
This cordial, which is flavored with caraway and cumin seeds, is believed to have originated in Russia. It is very popular in Germany. As a matter of fact, *kümmel* is German for caraway seed.

MARASCHINO
This cordial, made from sour cherries and honey, is white and is used largely as a flavoring agent. It is not to be confused with the red syrup contained in bottles of maraschino cherries.

PARFAIT AMOUR
This is a highly perfumed and very sweet cordial made from citron, cinnamon, coriander, and brandy. In French the name means "perfect love." Perhaps that is why it is a great favorite with *les belles filles* of France.

PRUNELLE
As the name indicates, this cordial is prepared from small Burgundian prunes and fine brandy.

SLIVOVITZ

This cordial is tremendously popular in Europe and has had some vogue in the United States. It is made from plums which are fermented and distilled. It is one of the few high-proof cordials.

STREGA

This is probably the best known Italian cordial and is very delicious. It is made from orange peel, spices, and strong spirits. Although very sweet, it is a delightful accompaniment for coffee.

SUZE LIQUEUR

This cordial has only recently been introduced in France and the United States. Its basis is gentian, a root with a bitter flavor and possessing some medicinal qualities. In the blending of the liqueur, the bitterness disappears, but the distinctive gentian flavor remains. This cordial is excellent in coffee. It can also be combined with equal parts of brandy and absinthe to make a very insidious cocktail called the "Suzy."

(2) HORS D'OEUVRES

Appetizers, canapés, or hors d'oeuvres have a very definite place in the gastronomical scheme of things entire, but I'd like to take my stand here and now. I am the bitter enemy of appetizers, canapés, or hors d'oeuvres *when they are served prior to a carefully thought out and prepared dinner.* They, together with strong cocktails, instead of whetting the appetite, invariably destroy it and anethetize one's delicate taste buds. Whenever I attend a dinner party where the host or hostess first serves trays loaded with canapés or hors d'oeuvres, accompanied by innumerable hard-liquor cocktails, I strongly suspect that the actual dinner will be very indifferent. And nine times out of ten I am right.

Hors d'oeuvres, as such, originated in the north countries, I believe, where appetites are lusty and liquor is strong. The Scandinavian *smörgåsbord* (which literally means "spread and covered bread") or the Russian *zakooskas* should be practically an entire meal in itself and not a prelude to dinner. Incidentally, the Chinese call their hors d'oeuvres *T'i Wei Ping,* the Italians, *antipasto* or *fritto misto,* the Hindus, *dumpoke,* and the Spanish, *gaspachio.* The favorite appetizer of the Spaniards is cloves of garlic crushed with salt and pepper and cumin seed, and worked to a smooth paste with olive oil, then spread on slices of peasant bread and topped with tomato paste. Like garlic soup, which you'll find in the following chapter, this appetizer is not for sissies. With a luncheon of *gaspachio* and *sopas de ajo,* it would seem to me that any bullfighter would be invincible, for his breath would surely asphyxiate the sturdiest bull!

Of course, when one is giving a cocktail party, and dinner is not indicated, hors d'oeuvres are almost a necessity, and, if a little ingenuity is used, delectable. There are hundreds of wonderful hors d'oeuvres. The standard French classic, *Larousse Gastronomique,* uses some thirty-odd pages to describe and list hors d'oeuvres.

16

The ideal prelude to a really excellent dinner accompanied by fine wines is a dry sherry, such as a manzanilla, a montilla, or an amontillado, among the imported sherries, or a fine American sherry of the dry type. An iced dry vermouth is also excellent. These *apéritifs* may be accompanied by a few unsalted crackers spread with *pâté de foie gras* or a reasonable facsimile thereof, or with one of the many savory butters, such as anchovy or Montpelier butter. However, if you want to serve cocktails and hors d'oeuvres, be sure that the cocktails are dry and that the hors d'oeuvres, few in number, really inspire a desire or relish for the food that is to follow.

Here is a marvelous spread for unsalted crackers or silver-dollar-thin slices of ice-box rye bread. But keep 'em few in number, for they'll go fast.

PÂTÉ OF CHICKEN LIVERS AND MADEIRA

½ *lb. chicken livers*	*Thyme*
1 *large Bermuda onion*	*Salt*
6 *tbsp. chicken fat*	*Pepper*
Madeira	

Slice a large Bermuda onion very thin and sauté it in 3 tablespoons of preheated chicken fat until it is golden brown. In another pan sauté for about 5 minutes ½ pound of chicken livers in 3 tablespoons of hot chicken fat, to which a pinch of thyme has been added, and salt and pepper to taste. Now mix the onion and the chicken livers together, and put them through a food grinder, using the finest blade. When the mixture has cooled, add enough Madeira to make a paste, spread on unsalted crackers or bread, and serve.

Pâté de foie gras is coming back on the market after a long absence, but its price makes it available only to those individuals whose incomes are listed in the public prints each year. However, here's a recipe for a paste that is every bit as good; and everyone except French counts and Russian princes (if there are any real ones left) will swear that you have served the real, old-time *pâté de foie gras*.

LIVERWURST PASTE

½ lb. liverwurst	1 tbsp. Worcestershire sauce
1 pkg. Philadelphia cream	1 tbsp. sherry
cheese	Salt
½ cup cream	Pepper
1 tbsp. melted butter	Curry powder

Mash ½ pound of liverwurst with 1 package of Philadelphia cream cheese. Add to the mixture ½ cup of cream, 1 tablespoon each of melted butter, Worcestershire sauce, and sherry; salt, pepper, and curry powder to taste (start with, say, ½ teaspoon of the curry powder, then add more, pinch by pinch, until you have the amount you want). Blend well, and serve on unsalted crackers.

At La Maison Wood, when we dine *en famille,* we always have two cocktails apiece an hour or so before dinner. With the cocktails we sometimes munch on a few nuts, sometimes on a little garlic cheese or anchovy cheese (these are packaged commercially, and are really excellent) spread on crackers, and sometimes on our own special canapés. They are the most taste-teasing, tantalizing, and terrific canapés I have ever tasted (I know I'm immodest, but please forgive me). But one needs real will power to keep from devouring several, and thereby spoiling one's dinner. Take my advice, and don't make more than three apiece.

CHUTNEY AND PEANUT BUTTER CANAPÉS

1 pkg. Philadelphia cream	4 ounces Major Gray's chutney
cheese	¼ tsp. Worcestershire sauce
½ lb. of peanut butter, chunky	¼ tsp. Lowry's salt
style	Dry red wine

Mix and blend the above ingredients together with a tablespoon, cutting the larger pieces in the chutney into smaller ones before adding. Use only enough dry red wine to moisten the mixture so that it can be spread easily. This paste is at its best when spread on Triscuits, although it can be spread on crackers, or silver-dollar-thin slices of ice-box rye bread. This spread can be kept in a covered jar in the refrigerator, and will remain in perfect condition for weeks.

Here's the second of the Wood Specials.

WILEWOOD CANAPÉS

1 *pkg. Philadelphia cream cheese*
Equal amount of Roquefort or blue cheese
1 *tsp. prepared horseradish*
1 *tbsp. mayonnaise (or Miracle Whip) salad dressing*

1 *tsp. finely chopped chives (or finely chopped little green onions)*
¼ *tsp. Worcestershire sauce*
¼ *tsp. Lowry's salt*
1 *tbsp. dry sherry*
1 *generous tbsp. whipped cream*

Mix and blend the two cheeses with a fork. Add the mayonnaise and stir. Then add the horseradish, and stir again. Add the chopped chives, and stir them in. Now add the Worcestershire sauce, Lowry's salt, and the sherry, and thoroughly blend. Finally, stir in the whipped cream and blend with the whole.

This mixture is at its best on salted crackers, but it is also excellent on ice-box rye bread cut silver-dollar thin. This paste can be kept in a bowl covered with wax paper in the refrigerator for two or three weeks.

Sooner or later, you'll be giving a cocktail party, or another cocktail party, or you'll be having open house on a birthday or other anniversary, or on a holiday, or you'll just get a few friends together to do a little left- and right-handed drinking, all of which I am heartily in favor of. And for such get-togethers I am the enthusiastic champion of appetizers, canapés, or hors d'oeuvres, provided they are not run-of-the-mill, or prepared wholesale by some caterer.

If you have any big, husky he-men coming to your cocktail party, or any of the outdoor type who like their meat raw, you'll probably ring the bell with them by serving Tartare canapés. However, I've seen dainty bits of femininity who look as if they'd have the old-fashioned vapors if they even looked upon pink meat, devour Tartare canapés with not only gusto but great glee.

TARTARE CANAPÉS

Round steak
Lime juice
Dry red wine
Garlic

Tabasco
Dry mustard
Salt
Capers

Put the raw round steak through the meat chopper twice. Then, in a bowl, mix with it a sprinkling of fresh lime juice, a little dry red wine, a finely minced clove of garlic, a dash of Tabasco, a little dry mustard, and salt to taste. Blend the mixture thoroughly, then make it into tiny cakes, just large enough to cover a slice of ice-box rye bread, and about half-inch thick. Put two or three capers on each patty and serve. I think that putting the patties in the refrigerator about an hour before serving improves this canapé.

I haven't given any measures or amounts of ingredients, because that will depend upon the number of canapés you want to make, and how hot you want them. Use enough wine to make the meat a little moist.

There are scores of ways of serving shrimps, all the way from just plain boiled ones dipped in any one of a number of sauces, to elaborate shrimp canapés. One of the most unusual ways of serving them is to bed them on ice-box rye bed covered with a very savory paste. For want of a better name, I call them Bedded Shrimps.

BEDDED SHRIMPS

2 *tbsp. peanut butter*	*Generous pinch of salt*
2 *tbsp. cream cheese*	1 *tbsp. dry red wine*
1 *tsp. curry powder*	6 *boiled shrimps*

Cream together the peanut butter and the cream cheese. Add the curry powder, a generous pinch of salt, and the dry red wine. Blend thoroughly, and spread this paste on slices of ice-box rye bread. Then split the shrimps lengthwise, and place half a shrimp on each slice. These should be served very cold, with a drop or so of fresh lime juice on each canapé.

One of the most delectable appetizers—a real whet to the appetite—is one of the easiest and simplest to make. I first tried it out at a meeting of the Streeterville and Sanitary Canal Gourmet and Study Society, a small group of serious eaters and drinkers which was organized in Chicago by Ward Walker, a former war correspondent for the *Chicago Tribune,* and myself. I'll tell you about that dinner, which was an early American one, in a later chapter on "Game"; but anyway, the dinner started out with what was called Hardtack and Bacon, just for atmosphere. But don't shy away—hardtack isn't used.

HARDTACK AND BACON

Very thin slices lean bacon   *Longbranch saltines*

Have your butcher slice some lean bacon as thin as possible. Split the Longbranch saltines in two lengthwise, and wrap a slice of bacon around each half, folding the ends of the bacon over. Then put them under the broiler. When the bacon is done on one side, turn them over, and when the bacon on the other side is done, serve quickly. You won't have to secure the bacon with toothpicks, because it will stay in place naturally. The crackers soak up just enough of the bacon fat to give the crackers flavor. I think I have had more raves over this exceedingly simple appetizer than any other. Again, leaning on the side of paucity, I advise serving not more than three apiece.

The number of hot hors d'oeuvres is legion. If you're a man-or a gal-about-town, you've probably shuddered many a time when confronted with the same old olives wrapped in bacon, little cocktail sausages, cheese straws, toasted sardines or oysters, hot crabmeat in various forms, etc., etc., etc. If you like 'em, fine. You'll find a guide to their preparation in dozens of cookbooks. But if you have a yen to startle (and overwhelmingly please) your guests, I'd like to oblige with a few out-of-the-ordinary delectables that make libations taste even better than usual.

Mushrooms are always a delicacy, and I am one of those people who feel that eating mushrooms is like making love to a young widow—you can't overdo it, particularly when the mushrooms are grilled with a Burgundy and garlic butter.

MUSHROOMS BOURGUIGNON

Large fresh mushrooms   *Freshly ground black pepper*
1 cup Burgundy   *1 tsp. minced parsley*
1 clove garlic   *⅓ cup salted butter*
1 little green onion   *Rounds of toast*

Over a hot flame, reduce to one half its volume 1 cup of Burgundy to which has been added 1 crushed clove of garlic and 1 little green onion, top and all, chopped very fine. Add a pinch of freshly ground black pepper and 1 teaspoon of minced parsley. Cool; then cream with ⅓ cup of salted butter.

Grill the mushrooms, from which the stems have been removed, under the broiler, or in a skillet with a little butter. Then mount each on a small round of toast, crowning each with a small pat of the Burgundy and garlic butter.

Another delightful hors d'oeuvre utilizing mushrooms is Mushroom Stuffed Eggs. These can be served either hot or cold, but I think they are more flavorsome hot.

MUSHROOM STUFFED EGGS

6 *hard-boiled eggs*	1 *tbsp. Madeira*
6 *large mushrooms*	*Salt*
1 *little green onion*	*Pepper*
1 *tbsp. butter*	*Breadcrumbs*
1 *tsp. chopped parsley*	*Rounds of toast*

Chop the mushrooms with 1 little green onion (top and all) and 1 teaspoon of chopped parsley. Mix in with this the yolks of the hard-boiled eggs, the whites of which have been cut in half ready for stuffing. In a saucepan melt 1 tablespoon of butter, then add the mushroom-onion-egg mixture, seasoning to taste with salt and freshly ground pepper, and moistening with 1 tablespoon of Madeira. Cook all together for a few minutes, until the mushrooms and onions are tender. Then stuff the egg whites with the mixture. Sprinkle them with fine breadcrumbs, dab with a little butter, place them on rounds of toast, and brown under the broiler.

If you want to serve these cold, allow the stuffing to cool, then stuff the egg whites and thoroughly chill in the refrigerator. Serve as is, without the rounds of toast.

Anchovies are one of the greatest whets to appetite known, not only for drinks, but for meat. Used in conjunction with certain fish and fowl, they heighten the flavor; and as a seasoning in sauces for cold meat, poultry, and game, they are tremendously effective. They are even used for larding of roasts, fowl, and game, and impart a tang of salt and a hidden flavor that can't be obtained in any other way.

As appetizers, fillets of anchovy rank right at the top. Fillets rolled around a caper, and eaten with unsalted crackers, really do things for your appetite, to say nothing of sharpening your zest for libations, just in case you haven't a zest for libations—God forbid!

For the following canapé, you should choose your guests very carefully. If they like garlic, they'll bless you for garlic anchovies. If they don't, they'll run, not walk, to the nearest exit.

ANCHOVIES AIOLI

6 *cloves garlic*　　　　　　1¼ *cups olive oil*
1 *raw egg yolk*　　　　　　1 *tbsp. red wine vinegar*
¼ *tsp. salt*　　　　　　　　*Tarragon*
¼ *tsp. freshly ground pepper*　*Lemon juice*
　　　　　Flat fillets of anchovy

You first make the *aioli,* a sauce which originated in Provence, France. Crush 6 cloves of garlic to a paste, add 1 raw egg yolk, ¼ teaspoon each of salt and freshly ground pepper, and a pinch of tarragon. Now add 1 cup of the finest olive oil, drop by drop at first, then increasing to a thin stream as the mixture begins to thicken, always stirring constantly. When blended, add 1 tablespoon of fine red wine vinegar and a few drops of lemon juice. Now, very slowly, add another ¼ cup of olive oil. Then chill thoroughly.

Now take your fillets of anchovy (the number depending on how many you are going to serve), mash them with a fork, and add enough *aioli* to the mashed anchovies to make a smooth purée of the whole. Spread this purée on rounds of toast, pressing it well down on them so that the sauce sinks in. Then grill them until they are brown. Serve very hot.

Cheese, of course, is always a delicious whet, but anchovy cheese is really something extra special. This recipe dates back many hundreds of years.

ANCHOVIES PARMESAN

Bread	*Parmesan cheese*
Butter	*Chopped parsley*
Anchovy fillets	*Sherry*
	Cayenne pepper

Fry pieces of bread, with the crusts trimmed off, in butter. Then cut them into fingers about 3 inches long and ¾ inch wide. On each finger lay a fillet of anchovy.

Grate some Parmesan cheese, mix it with the chopped parsley, and moisten with sherry to make a paste. Place the fingers of bread, with the anchovies on top, in a fireproof dish and spread the paste over the anchovies rather thick. Pour a little melted butter over the whole, and grill under the broiler until brown. Sprinkle with a dash of cayenne pepper and serve very hot.

Here's a combination of cheese, horseradish, and Madeira that will bring "ohs" and "ahs" from your guests, and why not! Let's call them Cheese and Horseradish *Croûtes. Croûtes,* by the way, is French for crusts.

CHEESE AND HORSERADISH CROÛTES

Bread cut in rounds	1 *tbsp. Madiera*
Butter	1 *tbsp. grated horseradish*
1 *ounce Gruyère cheese*	*Tarragon*
1 *ounce grated Parmesan*	*Paprika*
cheese	

Fry some thin slices of bread (with the crusts removed and cut in rounds) in butter, drain them, and keep them hot. Make a mixture of 1 ounce of soft Gruyère cheese and 1 ounce of grated Parmesan cheese, 1 tablespoon of Madeira, 1 tablespoon of finely grated horseradish, a dash of tarragon, and a sprinkling of paprika. Spread this paste over the previously fried rounds of bread, and put them in a 400-degree oven for about 5 minutes. Serve very hot.

The following canapé one might almost call an adaptation of a Welsh rabbit. It's very tangy, and cheese lovers will wax enthusiastic over it.

DEVILED CHEESE

1 *tbsp. butter*	*Tarragon*
2 *tsp. dry mustard*	*Pepper*
2 *tbsp. sherry*	*Cayenne pepper*
2 *tbsp. anchovy paste*	1 *cup diced Cheddar cheese*
	Rounds of toast

Put 1 tablespoon butter in a saucepan. Add 2 teaspoons of dry mustard, 2 tablespoons of sherry, 2 teaspoons of anchovy paste, a pinch of tarragon, pepper to taste, a pinch of cayenne pepper, and 1 cup of diced sharp Cheddar cheese. Stir well until melted, then spread on rounds of toast. Serve very hot. This can be made in a chafing dish, and served to all comers as they line up, which is very effective, but a little more work for the host or hostess.

One of my favorite varieties of shellfish is lobster. I can eat lobster, served either as a main course dish or in a salad, until it practically runs out of my ears. Half a tiny boiled lobster, very cold, makes an excellent first course appetizer when served with a tangy sauce, such as a cardinal sauce. But I had always shied away from any sort of lobster canapés until I was introduced to deviled lobster. That was love at first sight.

DEVILED LOBSTER CANAPÉS

1 *small can lobster meat*	2 *tbsp. breadcrumbs*
1 *tbsp. butter*	*Dry mustard*
1 *tbsp. rum*	*Cayenne pepper*
½ *lemon*	*Grated nutmeg*
	Rounds of toast or fried bread

Pound together in a mortar, or heavy bowl, the meat from a small can of lobster, 1 tablespoon of butter, 1 tablespoon of rum, the juice and grated rind of ½ lemon, and 2 tablespoons of fine breadcrumbs. Add a small pinch of dry mustard, a dash or two of cayenne pepper, and a sprinkling of grated nutmeg. Mix well, then spread the paste on rounds of toast, or rounds of fried bread, put under the broiler for a moment or so, and serve very hot.

I have heard Englishmen say that Angels on Horseback are the finest savories of all. I've never been able to discover how they got their name—if some reader knows, I'd appreciate the information, just to satisfy my own curiosity. I have, in my time, run across three different varieties—made with oysters, made with sardines, and made with kidneys.

They are simple to make, and they're good. You simply wrap oysters, sardines, or kidneys in bacon, skewer them, and grill. Come to think of it, olives wrapped in bacon and grilled might also be called Angels on Horseback. But they'd still be olives wrapped in bacon to me, and already I've eaten enough of them to last me the rest of my life.

The sardine Angels on Horseback require a little different treatment from the other two: The bacon is first half fried. Then the sardines are placed across the bacon slices. The bacon is then folded over, and fried until crisp, turning each "angel" over carefully with a fork once. A few grains of cayenne pepper or a few drops of Worcestershire sauce are sprinkled over each angel.

Caviar is the most exalted of all appetizers, and justly so. The flavor of fresh beluga or mollosol is so individual and piquant that it is a crime ever to mix it with any sort of dressing agent except sour cream. In my opinion, chopped onion, which is so often served with caviar, is too harsh, and should not accompany really fine caviar.

If there's any better way of eating caviar than with *blini,* I don't know of it. The real Russian *blini* are made with buckwheat flour, but you can make them very nicely with any of the ready-mixed pancake flours by following the directions on the package given for waffle-style pancakes made with eggs. The batter should be thin, and *blini* should be fried on a griddle with very hot butter, ladling out the batter in very small quantities and cooking until they are brown on both sides. They shouldn't exceed three inches in diameter. A generous tablespoon of caviar should be placed on each pancake, or *blini,* a little hard-boiled chopped egg sprinkled over the caviar, and the whole topped with a gob of sour cream.

Nearly all the appetizers, canapés, or hors d'oeuvres I've discussed have been *apéritif* or cocktail partners. However, there are many first-course appetizers, which are served at the table. Under this heading, and, for my money, heading the list, are oysters on the half shell (no cocktail sauce, please!) and clams on the half shell. Then there are the various shellfish cocktails (again I object to a pungent and sharp cocktail sauce, particularly if fine wines accompany the first course, or are to follow; better serve your fresh shellfish very plain and very cold, with perhaps a dash of lemon juice); and fruit cocktails, which to my mind, are an abomination of the devil.

In the course of my peregrinations I have come across a few first course appetizers which I think are notable, and worth passing on.

Highly regarded as an appetizer in both Russia and the Scandinavian countries, the herring is quite a fish. That it is a fish belonging to the genus *clupea* may not interest you, but one brief fact about its love life undoubtedly will. The female is terrifically prolific, and lays on an average of fifty million eggs a year. And brother, if you think that isn't a lot of eggs, ponder this fact: It has been estimated scientifically that if a single pair of herring got married and were allowed to produce, unmolested, successive generations of offspring for seven years, all the oceans, seas, and rivers of the world would be completely choked up with herring!

The herring is probably the only comestible, or at least the only fish, that ever had a battle named after it. In 1429 the English, under Sir John Falstolfe, were attempting to convey Lenten provisions, chiefly herrings, to the besiegers of Orleans, which was held by the French. The French (and Scots) tried to intercept the English supply train at Rouvray, and the resulting action was called the Battle of the Herrings, which, incidentally, the French lost.

One of my favorite first courses is pickled or marinated herring, topped with sour cream and a sprinkling of chives. Here again is a real appetite whet.

FILLET OF MARINATED HERRING

3 *fairly large salt herring*	2 *whole cloves*
1½ *cups vinegar*	½ *cup sugar*
½ *cup dry white wine*	2 *sprays of fresh dill*
10 *peppercorns*	*Onions*
1 *tbsp. allspice*	*Lemons*
3 *bay leaves*	*Grated fresh horseradish*
½ *tbsp. mustard seed*	*Sour cream*
½ *tbsp. celery seed*	*Chopped chives*

Wash and soak 3 fairly large salt herrings in cold water overnight. Then drain, split, skin and fillet them.

Heat in a saucepan 1½ cups of vinegar, ½ cup of dry white wine, adding 10 peppercorns, 1 tablespoon of allspice, 3 bay leaves, ½ tablespoon each of mustard seed and celery seed, 2 whole cloves, and ½ cup of sugar. As this mixture comes to the boiling point, remove from the fire and allow to cool.

Cut the herring fillets across into strips about one inch wide. Place a layer of them in a small crock, or glass dish. Cover the fillets with thin slices of peeled onions, two or three thin slices of unpeeled lemon, a sprinkling of grated fresh horseradish, and a couple of sprays of fresh dill. Then add another layer of the herring fillets, and repeat the onions, etc., and the fillets until the container is filled. Finally, pour the vinegar-wine-spice mixture over all, and weight down the whole with a plate. Let the marinated herring stand in the refrigerator for two or three days.

To serve, place two or three fillets on each plate with some of the spice mixture poured over, top with a generous blob of sour cream, and sprinkle some finely chopped chives over the sour cream. This can be served, of course, without the sour cream and chives.

A popular French dish is *Aubergines Caviare,* which is simply eggplant caviar. I'm not at all sure how it got its name, because I don't think it tastes like caviar, but I do know it is a mighty fine first course appetizer. Perhaps one might say that it's the poor man's caviar. If I recall correctly, I had it the last time I was in New York in that delightful French restaurant on East 62nd Street, La Cremaillère.

EGGPLANT CAVIAR

1 *large eggplant*	2 *fresh tomatoes*
1 *large onion*	½ *cup olive oil*
1 *green pepper*	*Salt*
1 *clove garlic*	*Pepper*

2 *tbsp. dry white wine*

Put a whole egglant in a 400-degree oven and bake until soft (about an hour).

While cooking the eggplant, peel and chop 1 large onion, chop 1 green pepper, having removed the seeds and white part, and peel and chop 2 tomatoes.

In a skillet put ½ cup of fine olive oil and 1 clove of crushed garlic. When the oil is hot, put in the chopped onion and green pepper, and simmer them until they are tender but not brown.

Now, cutting off the stem, peel the baked eggplant and chop it finely. Mix this with the chopped tomatoes, and add this mixture to the onions and green peppers in the skillet, along with salt and freshly ground black pepper to taste, and 2 tablespoons of dry white wine. Mix everything thoroughly, and continue to cook gently until the mixture is fairly thick. Cool, then place in the refrigerator. Serve very well chilled, with pumpernickel, or silver-dollar-thin pieces of ice-box rye bread.

During the summer, when melons are at their best, try cutting wedges and wrapping in tissue-thin slices of Prosciutto ham. The combination of flavors, sharpened by a little lemon juice, is quite intriguing, and most delicious. Either ripe honeydew or Persian melons (I prefer the latter) or cantaloupes can be used. Just cut the melons in about 2½-inch wedges, remove all the rind, and wrap in the Prosciutto ham.

If I were asked to name eight purveyors of delectable viands who are best known in this country from border to border and coast to coast, I should list Sherman Billingsley of New York, Ernest Byfield of Chicago, Roy Alciatore of New Orleans, Mike Romanoff of Hollywood, Ric Riccardo of Chicago, Dave Chasen of Hollywood, George Mardikian of San Francisco, and Mike Fritzel of Chicago. However, in addition to serving wonderful food, Mike Fritzel is also famous as a purveyor of outstanding entertainment. Sooner or later, every visiting fireman in Chicago ends up at the Chez Paree, an extraordinary night club, in that its food is as excellent and mouth-watering as its chorus line, known as the Chez Paree Adorables.

I've known Mike Fritzel for more years than either of us care to remember. However, when he opened his new restaurant in Chicago—Mike Fritzel's—I knew the food would be superlative, and would be served with an irresistible eye appeal. And I was right. The first night I ate there Jerry, the genial and attentive head of the dining room (which is beautifully paneled and furnished), suggested Sea Food à la Fritzel. When it was set before me, it was really a picture, and it would certainly stimulate the most jaded taste buds to joyful anticipation.

The preparation of Sea Food à la Fritzel is exceedingly simple, but I'll guarantee that your guests will get an eye and taste thrill from it, and that it will lend an air of swank to your next dinner party that nothing else will.

SEA FOOD À LA FRITZEL

1 *oyster on half shell*	*Cold boiled shrimps*
1 *clam on half shell*	*Cold lobster meat*
4 *empty oyster shells*	*Smoked salmon*
Crab meat	*Lemon wedges*

Sprigs fresh parsley

Fill a large soup plate with crushed ice (if you want to serve a cocktail sauce, bury a small glass container in the center of the ice and fill it with your favorite cocktail sauce). Then equally spaced around the plate place one oyster on its shell, one clam on its shell, and the four empty oyster shells. Fill one of the empty oyster shells with fresh crab meat, another with cold boiled shrimps, another with medium-sized chunks of cooked lobster meat, and the fourth with smoked salmon. Garnish with sprigs of fresh parsley and a couple of wedges of lemon. (Individual portion.)

I find, coming to the close of this chapter, that, in all fairness, I've got to eat crow. Earlier I said, and I quote, ". . . . fruit cocktails, which to my mind, are an abomination of the devil" . . .

As I was writing, the Little Woman, who has been perusing my manuscript, suddenly snorted. I looked up, startled, wondering what I could have written that would evoke even a mild snort.

"What's the matter, honey?" I asked.

"So you think fruit cocktails are an abomination of the devil, eh?" She cocked a cynical eye at me. "What about my minted fruit cup that you're so crazy about?" she asked.

And she had me!

The dish in question is a wonderful thing to start off a summer meal. It really is a favorite of mine, and I might as well go the whole hog and admit that it's delicious, marvelous, terrific, and that it certainly should not be passed by when the roll of first course appetizers is called. And, believe it or not, this is not being written under duress!

MINTED FRUIT CUP

1 *can pineapple chunks*	*Sugar*
Peeled segments of grapefruit	*Fresh lemon juice*
Sprigs of fresh mint	*Gin*
Maraschino cherries	

Empty a can of pineapple chunks and juice into a bowl, and add an equal amount of peeled segments of fresh grapefruit and several finely chopped mint leaves. Dredge all this with sugar, after having added some fresh lemon juice. Cover the bowl and put it in the refrigerator for at least 12 hours.

Serve in individual compotes, pouring over the fruit in each compote an ounce of gin, arranging two or three mint leaves in the center of each compote, and topping the whole with a large maraschino cherry. You'll have fun listening to your guests trying to figure out the flavor while they spoon with delight.

((3)) SOUPS, CHOWDERS, AND SUCH

Throughout the world "dinner" and "soup" are synonymous words for millions of people. As the main course of a light dinner, there's nothing more satisfying than a really good soup. On chill October nights, the riotous colors of autumn sunsets, and air redolent with smoke rising from burning leaves, bring back nostalgic memories of my grandmother's home in a small Michigan town. Coming in from a late afternoon hike, the softly lighted living room, with a crackling log fire, was the mort cheerful spot in the whole world, or at least, so it seemed. And what rich, savory smells drifted in from the kitchen, particularly on the night of a soup dinner. After we were seated at the dining-room table, the maid would bring in the big willow-pattern tureen, and then large, piping-hot soup bowls. Grandmother would remove the lid of the tureen and ladle the bowls brimming full. Emma would pass them without spilling so much as a single drop. With the soup came fresh, hot bread, or crisped corn bread, and a salad of chilled greens from which slivers of carrots, celery and parsnips peeped out. Dessert usually was apple pie accompanied by generous wedges of Herkimer County cheese, and strong, black coffee, with milk for me.

One of grandmother's pet soups was black bean soup, and to my mind it is one of the most delicious soups ever devised, particularly if it is made with Marsala instead of sherry.

BLACK BEAN SOUP

1 *cup black beans*	¼ *cup chopped onions*
1 *quart cold water*	4 *grains mustard seed*
2 *tbsp. butter*	1 *tsp. salt*
¼ *cup chopped celery leaves*	*Small clove garlic*
1 *medium-sized carrot,*	*Ham bone*
chopped	*Cayenne pepper*
1 *stalk celery, cut up*	¾ *cup scalded cream*
2 *whole cloves*	4 *tbsp. Marsala*
6 *peppercorns*	*Thin lemon slices*
1 *bay leaf*	*Sliced hard-boiled eggs*

Soak the black beans overnight in cold water. Drain, then add the beans to 1 quart cold water in a soup kettle, and bring to a boil. In the meantime, sauté in about 2 tablespoons of butter over a gentle flame ¼ cup of chopped celery leaves, 1 medium-sized carrot, chopped, 1 stalk of celery, cut up, and ¼ cup of chopped onion until they just begin to brown. Add these to the beans, as well as 2 whole cloves, 6 peppercorns gently bruised, 1 bay leaf, 4 grains of mustard seed, 1 teaspoon of salt, a small clove of garlic, and a ham bone. Now let the whole thing simmer until the beans are tender—about 3½ hours. Add a little more water if it cooks away too much, as it probably will. At the end of the cooking time, remove the ham bone, and press the soup through a sieve. Now reheat to the boiling point, taste for seasoning (a touch of cayenne pepper adds a great deal) and stir in ¾ cup of scalded cream and 4 tablespoons of Marsala. In serving, place a thin slice of lemon and a slice of hard-boiled egg in each soup plate or bowl, and pour the hot soup over them.

While we're on the subject of beans, have you ever tasted baked bean soup? Lowell and Whittier and Hawthorne, I am told, were very fond of it, but in their day it took a lot of doing to prepare it. But today you can make it very simply, and I'll wager it is just exactly as good as that served in grandmother's or great-grandmother's time.

BAKED BEAN SOUP

1 *tbsp. bacon fat*	1 *can baked beans*
1 *onion*	1 *stalk celery*
1 *clove garlic*	1 *sprig parsley*
1 *green pepper*	1 *bay leaf*
1 *cup chopped tomatoes*	*Madeira*
2 *cups consommé*	*Salt and pepper*

Lemon slices

In a tablespoon or so of bacon drippings fry together a sliced onion, a chopped clove of garlic, and a green pepper until tender.

Then add a cup of chopped tomatoes, 2 cups of consommé, a can of good baked beans *without tomato sauce,* 1 stalk of celery, cut up, 1 sprig of fresh parsley, cut up, 1 bay leaf, and salt and pepper to taste. Let all this simmer for about half an hour. Then press the beans, as well as the other vegetables, through a sieve, reheat, and, before serving, add a teaspoon of Madeira and a thin slice of lemon to each plate or bowl before serving, pouring the soup into the plates. After this dish, you'll speak only to the Cabots, Lowells or Lodges!

The onion is a Dr. Jekyll and Mr. Hyde among vegetables. On the other side of the tracks he is a lusty friend and companion, a highly prized mate of liver, hamburger, and steak. He is used generously as a flavoring agent, and is a favorite just plain boiled.

Among the stuffed shirt aristocracy, however, the onion is a low and vulgar lout, fit only for scullery maids or ditch diggers. To eat a raw onion is unthinkable. Masquerading as a shallot, however, the onion is tolerated in the cook books of the elite. And, as *soupe à l'oignon,* our friend is definitely "in"!

There are many recipes for onion soup. Some gourmets advocate cooking the onions until they are a dark brown, or even crisp and black. Others contend that the onions should not even be lightly browned. I belong to the latter school. Some people like their onion soup made very plain. Others prefer the addition of claret, sherry, or white wine. And I know of one recipe that calls for a cup of champagne!

In the center of Les Halles, Paris' great market place, there used to be a quaint workingmen's café called Au Père Tranquille. The hucksters (not advertising men, please!) ate and drank downstairs, but upstairs, where there was a funny little orchestra, you got what many claimed to be the best onion soup in Paris. It used to be a favorite hangout of Frank Fay, who, some four or five years ago, acquired a six-foot rabbit, and Tommy Manville, who has acquired almost as many wives as Henry VIII.

Perhaps Au Père Tranquille is no more, what with the war and the Germans. But here's the recipe for that café's famous onion soup, which you can make right in your own home, whether it's *tranquille* or not.

ONION SOUP

12 *to* 16 *red onions*	2 *tbsp. sugar*
¼ *cup olive oil*	6 *cups beef broth*
4 *tbsp. butter*	4 *tbsp. brandy*
Salt	*French bread*
Pepper	*Grated Parmesan cheese*

Peel and thinly slice the red onions (red onions make for strength, and you want plenty), cutting them on the bias to avoid rings. Put ¼ cup of olive oil in a casserole, and add the sliced onions. Cook them very gently, and when they begin to tender, add 4 tablespoons of butter, salt and pepper to taste, and 2 tablespoons of sugar. When the onions have attained the limpid state, add 6 cups or so of rich beef broth, or canned beef bouillon, and let the whole simmer for 15 to 20 minutes. While the simmering is going on, toast slices of French bread. When the bread is toasted and buttered, sprinkle the slices with plenty of grated Parmesan cheese (fresh, not the packaged commercial kind, please!) and pop them under the broiler for a moment so they will be slightly browned. When you put the toast under the broiler, add 4 tablespoons of brandy to the soup, stirring it in gently. Then take out the toasted bread, fill each soup plate with the soup, float the toasted bread on top, and serve quickly. If you like more cheese, grate it and serve it separately. This recipe should serve six. This onion soup is soul-satisfying, and really does things for one. Try it sometime for Sunday breakfast when the Saturday night libations have been *really* rugged.

Speaking of onion soup, and Saturday night libations, I am reminded of a bit of verse that was once dedicated to my father, who was a noble trencherman, and a good left- and right-handed drinker. A cook book is a hell of a place for poetry, but I'm including this, because it sort of points up one of the virtues of onion soup which Dad recognized.

> Sometimes, Old Pal, in the morning,
> When the dawn is cold and gray,
> And you lie mid the perfumed feathers,
> Thinking thoughts you dare not say;
> You think of the stunts of the night before,

And you smile with a feeble smile,
And you say to yourself for the hundredth time,
"Is it really worth the while?"

Then you pick up the morning paper,
And you read where some saintly man,
Who never was soused in all his life,
Who never said "hell" or "damn";
Who never stayed out till the wee small hours,
And jollied a gay soubrette,
But preached of the evils of drinking,
Of wine and the cigarette;

"Cut off in the prime of a useful life,"
The headlines glibly say,
Or "Snatched by Death's grim reaper,
He has crossed the great highway."
A few friends weep, and they bury him deep,
And the world moves on with a sigh,
But the saintly man is forgotten soon,
Even as you and I.

Then you say to yourself, "Well, Ralph, Old Scout,
When you're called to take the jump,
When you come to the place where the best and the worst
Must bump the Eternal Bump;
You can smile to yourself and chuckle,
Though the path be exceedingly hot,
When you were on earth you were moving some!"
Now is that an unholy thought?

Then you rise and attach a cracked-ice band
To the crown of your battered hat,
And you saunter forth for a cold gin fizz,
She's a great old world at that.
And you think, as you sip your onion soup,
What's the use to complain or sigh;
Go the route, Old Scout, and be merry,
For tomorrow you may die!

While there are many delicious soups, there are only a few real aristocrats of the soup tureen. You can almost count them on the fingers of one hand—the *Pot-au-Feu, Madrilène* and *Petite Marmite* of France; the Gumbos of America; the *Minestrone* of Italy, the Mulligatawny of India, the Lentil Soup of Arabia, Onion Soup, which is international, and Borscht, the national soup of Russia and Poland.

There are scores of recipes for *borscht,* but the essence of them all is the beet, which is a rather lowly vegetable in America. *Borscht* is made with meat stock, poultry stock, fish stock, game stock, or vegetable stock; it is served hot as the hinges of hell or cold as a jilted woman's heart. But however it is made or served, it is undeniably delicious, and it can well become a habit. The following recipe, while it may be rather a far cry from the *borscht* of the Russian peasant, is just about tops.

BORSCHT

2 *quarts beef stock or bouillon*	6 *medium-sized beets*
3 *tbsp. butter*	10 *peppercorns*
2 *cups shreddea cabbage*	2 *bay leaves*
1 *cup diced raw potatoes*	*Marjoram*
½ *cup diced raw carrots*	*Thyme*
½ *cup chopped celery*	*Salt*
1 *onion*	1 *cup canned tomatoes*
1 *green pepper*	1 *cup very dry white wine*
1 *leek*	*Sour cream*
1 *clove garlic*	3 *tbsp. Madeira*

In a soup pot or kettle heat 2 quarts of good beef stock or canned beef bouillon.

Melt 3 tablespoons of butter in a heavy skillet. Have ready 2 cups of shredded cabbage, 1 cup of diced raw potatoes, ½ cup of diced carrots, ½ cup of chopped celery, 1 small onion, peeled and chopped, 1 green pepper, chopped, 1 leek, cut up, 1 minced clove of garlic, and 6 medium-sized beets, peeled and shredded through a grater (save out 1 heaping tablespoon of the grated beets, mixed with 3 tablespoons of water). Put vegetables in the skillet, cover, turn the flame low, and sauté for about 5 minutes, shaking the pan constantly. Then add the sautéed vegetables to the boiling beef stock, together with 1 cup of canned tomatoes, 1 cup of very dry American white wine, 10 whole peppercorns, 2 bay leaves, a generous pinch each of marjoram and thyme, and salt to taste. Lower the flame and continue to cook until all the vegetables are tender—about 1½ to 2 hours. Shortly before serving add the grated beet in water, stir it in for coloring, and 3 tablespoons of Madeira. To each plate of borscht add a generous tablespoon of sour cream.

One of the most popular soups of Spain is *Sopas de Ajo,* and every province has its own special way of making it. But it is no soup for sissies, nor is it a soup to be eaten before going to the opera, theater, movies, or an evening of bridge, or before taking Dreamboat dancing, for *sopas de ajo* is, in plain American, garlic soup! But if you like that gastronomical gift of the Gods to mortal man, you'll find *sopas de ajo* a magnificent prelude to a meal, and well worth isolating yourself for.

Incidentally, garlic, an herb belonging to the lily family (believe it or not) was used by the early Egyptians and Romans quite extensively in cooking, and the Romans believed it to possess magical powers. I'm inclined to go along with the Romans today, because I've found, after one of my favorite lunches of French bread, raw garlic, and a glass of dry red wine, that no matter how crowded a conveyance may be, when I enter, I suddenly have plenty of room!

SOPAS DE AJO
(Garlic Soup)

5 *cups beef stock or bouillon*	*Salt*
1 *cup sherry*	*Pepper*
1 *pod of garlic*	*French bread*
¼ *cup olive oil*	*Parmesan cheese*

Heat 5 cups of meat stock or canned beef bouillon together with 1 cup of sherry.

Peel and slice 1 pod (not a clove, but a complete head) of garlic, and sauté it in ¼ cup of olive oil until golden brown. Add the garlic and the oil to the boiling stock, salt and pepper to taste, and let the whole thing simmer for about 30 minutes. Then strain out the garlic and reheat.

For each plate take a slice of toasted French bread, sprinkle it generously with grated Parmesan cheese, and place the slices in a hot oven for about 3 minutes. Then transfer the cheese slices to the soup plates, and fill the plates with the clear garlic soup.

It is only in comparatively recent years that lentils have become popular in the United States, and yet they are one of the most ancient of food plants, and have been used in Mediterranean countries for thousands of years. The first time I encountered lentils was in the home of a Syrian friend of mine in Detroit when he served *rishtaya,* which is sort of a lamb stew with lentils and noodles. Later, I became very fond of lentil soup, and it's rather a favorite of mine, particularly when I want a very light luncheon. A bowl of lentil soup, a couple of crusty rolls, and a glass of dry red wine not only makes a delicious midday meal, but a very healthful one, because lentils belong to the body-building, regulating, and protective food group.

Lentil soup is also called *Potage Esau,* and is mentioned in the Bible. Esau, as you may or may not recall, sold his birthright to his brother Jacob for a mess of pottage, or, as it is recorded in Genesis xxv:34, "Then Jacob gave Esau bread and pottage of lentiles; and he did eat and drink, and rose up, and went his way: thus Esau despised *his* birthright."

The following recipe closely approximates a 3,500-year-old recipe, although the Armenians do not garnish the soup with frankfurters, and the sherry is my own touch.

LENTIL SOUP

1 *pint of lentils*	*Thyme*
2 *quarts beef stock or bouillon*	*Bay leaf*
2 *slices bacon*	*Salt*
1 *large onion*	*Pepper*
½ *green pepper*	4 *mint leaves*
1 *clove garlic*	1 *tbsp. minced parsley*
1 *carrot*	*Sherry*
1 *stalk celery*	*Frankfurters*

Soak 1 pint of lentils in cold water overnight. Then pour off the water and add the lentils to 2 quarts of beef stock or canned beef bouillon.

In a skillet fry together, for about 3 minutes, 2 slices of bacon, chopped, 1 large onion, sliced, ½ green pepper, seeded and chopped, 1 crushed clove of garlic. Then add the contents of the skillet to the lentils and stock, together with 1 sliced carrot, 1 stalk of celery, chopped, a crumbled bay leaf, a pinch of thyme, and salt and pepper to taste. Simmer for 2 hours. During the last 10

minutes of simmering add 4 mint leaves, chopped fine, and 1 tablespoon minced parsley. When serving, add 1 teaspoon of sherry to
each plate, and about four ½-inch frankfurter slices that have
been sautéed for a few moments in butter.

Of all the so-called "peasant soups," I think the Italian
minestrone is the most imposing, zestful and satisfying. Just the
heavenly odors that emanate from the soup pot make my taste
buds do nip-ups, and to wait for its completion would try the
patience of Job himself.

It is possible to get the real Italian *minestrone* in authentic
Italian restaurants in this country, but don't count too heavily on
that statement. The basis for *minestrone* is a bean broth, and there
must be spicy meat in it along with lots of vegetables and *pasta*.
I personally like my *minestrone* to be thick enough so that the
spoon can stand upright in it.

Eating Italian bread (or bread of any kind) with *minestrone* is
definitely frowned upon by Italians when the soup contains any sort
of *pasta*. They say that it's like eating mashed potatoes with French
fried potatoes. But, natives to the contrary, I want plenty of grated
Parmesan cheese sprinkled over my *minestrone,* and a lot of hunks
of toasted garlic bread. The only discomfort this brings me is a
mental one—I am unhappy because my stomach can't hold more!

Don't begin an Italian dinner with *minestrone,* because you
won't be able to enjoy or contain anything else that follows this
nectar of the gods. Have an *antipasto* first, then the *minestrone.*
A green salad may or may not follow—I like a small one, with a
sharp dressing. For dessert, fruit and cheese. And here's a tip on
eating the fruit. Instead of having your Chianti served in a wine
glass, ask to have it served in a water tumbler. (I know this bor-
ders on heresy, and will make wine experts shudder, but what the
hell! we're after enjoyment.) Along about the time when the
minestrone is served, have the waiter bring you an apple and a
pear. Peel them and cut them into thin slices, and stuff your tumbler with them. Then pour in your Chianti. As you drink your
wine, and the glass empties, fill it up with more, leaving the fruit
in the glass. Then, after the *minestrone* has disappeared, eat the
wine-soaked fruit from your glass and nibble on some Gorgonzola,

provolone, or strachino de Milano cheese. Finish up with *caffe espresso,* which is black coffee with a twist of lemon peel in it, and a teaspoon of cognac added. But now let's get down to *minestrone.*

MINESTRONE

½ *cup kidney beans*	*Salt*
¼ *lb. bacon*	*Pepper*
¼ *lb. ham*	*Allspice*
¼ *lb. Italian sausage*	2 *quarts soup stock*
2 *cloves garlic*	2 *cups shredded cabbage*
1 *onion*	1 *cup Italian red wine*
2 *stalks celery*	1 *#2 can tomatoes*
1 *zucchini (Italian squash)*	½ *cup elbow macaroni*
1 *leek*	¼ *cup basil*
Parmesan cheese	

Soak ½ cup of kidney beans overnight in cold water (Roman beans are the best, if you can get them at an Italian grocery store; or lima beans can be used).

In a heavy skillet fry together until brown ¼ pound each of chopped bacon, chopped lean ham, chopped Italian sausage (*salsiccia*), and 2 crushed cloves of garlic. Then add 1 peeled and sliced onion, 2 stalks of celery, diced, 1 zucchini, sliced, 1 leek, sliced, salt and pepper to taste, and a pinch of allspice. Let simmer for 10 minutes.

In a soup kettle heat 2 quarts of consommé or soup stock. Put the contents of the skillet into the stock, and add the beans, which have been drained, 2 cups of shredded cabbage, and 1 cup of dry red wine. Simmer until the beans and vegetables are tender, about 1½ hours. Now add 1 #2 can of tomatoes (Italian if you can get it) and ½ cup of elbow macaroni. Cook about 15 minutes longer. About 3 minutes before the soup is to be served, add ¼ cup of finely minced basil (fresh if you have it, otherwise dried). If the soup is too thick for your taste, it can be thinned out to your preference with more hot consommé. Grated Parmesan cheese should be passed in a bowl, and generously sprinkled on each plate.

Up in the heart of the White Mountains, on U.S. Route 3 in North Woodstock, New Hampshire, is a delightful eating place called the Mount Adams Inn. The proprietors, Fred and Helen Kershner, make the Inn's slogan, "Where Hospitality Abounds," a very real fact, and their cuisine is something that every guest writes home about at great length. Some of their recipes have been handed down through the family for many generations; others are adaptations of dishes served in army messes, where Fred taught the proper preparation of food during the war. And I suspect that a few of their very special dishes are creations of Mr. and Mrs. Kerschner.

One of the most sought after specialties of the Mount Adams Inn is potato soup. If you live anywhere near the Inn, drop in, drive in, or fly in, and sample the food, particularly the potato soup. But if that's out of the question, don't despair, because here is exactly how they make it.

POTATO SOUP, MOUNT ADAMS INN

6 *medium-sized potatoes*	1 *pint milk*
½ *cup flour*	1 *cup light cream*
Salt	1 *large onion*
Pepper	*Bacon drippings*
Oregano	*Maggi's seasoning*
	¼ *cup sherry*

Pare and quarter 6 medium-sized potatoes. Boil and drain, reserving the liquid. Mash the potatoes add ½ cup of flour, and stir until well blended, adding salt and pepper to taste, and a pinch of oregano (the Spanish or Italian wild marjoram, which is packaged today and can be purchased in almost any good grocery store). Next, slowly blend in the potato water, add 1 pint of milk, 1 cup of light cream, and 1 large onion, peeled, chopped, and sautéd in bacon drippings. Add a generous dash of Maggi's seasoning; heat, and just before serving, add ¼ cup of sherry. I like a sprinkling of chopped chives over the soup, but that is optional and not in the original recipe.

Probably the most famous soup in the world is bouillabaisse. Your Provençal fishermen will swear that it is a national dish; certainly it is a favorite in many French seaports, and it reaches its peak of perfection in Marseilles. There are a great many legends about its creation, or origin. One I have heard was that it was created by Venus to further her progress in an affair with Vulcan. But why a gal with the charms and attributes of Venus should bother with a fish soup in trying to make the grade is beyond me. That would be like Rita Hayworth knitting a muffler to snare the Aly Khan!

It is impossible to get the real Marseilles Bouillabaisse in America, for the simple reason that the fish necessary to the dish are not available in this country. The original recipe calls for twelve different kinds of fish, five of which are unknown in the United States. You'll find recipes for bouillabaisse in at least every other cook book—I have over twenty in my files. But all the recipes call for substitutes, and many of them involve a lot of labor, so let's skip Marseilles Bouillabaisse, and, for the moment, make a little journey to Provincetown, on Cape Cod.

For centuries the rendezvous of pirates, freebooters, fishermen, smugglers, and adventurers of all nations, Provincetown has had a romantic past. It was the first place that the Pilgrims on the *Mayflower* (one of whom was a rather bashful ancestor of mine by the name of John Alden) landed in 1620. Someone once described Provincetown as a "village two miles long and two streets wide." Natives speak of the two ends of the village as "down-along" and "up-along." It is famous today as an artists' colony, and, in my opinion, for its bouillabaisse.

Provincetown Bouillabaise, made where the freshest sea food is obtainable, is hard to beat. It is an authentic bouillabaisse in that it contains at least one kind of fish, one bivalve, and one crustacean, in addition to other indispensable ingredients. And in these days of swift, refrigerated travel, all the principal ingredients can be obtained in almost any city in the United States. Of course, it's a one-dish meal, and I'd advise you to ignore Emily Post and tie a napkin under your chin before setting out on this wonderful gastronomic adventure.

BOUILLABAISSE PROVINCETOWN

2 *lbs. cod or haddock*   ½ *green pepper*
1 *qt. water*   2 *tbsp. minced parsley*
½ *cup olive oil*   8 *oysters*
Salt   8 *mussels*
Pepper   8 *small clams*
Thyme   1 *cup fresh crab meat*
Bay leaf   1 *cup lobster meat*
Juice 1 *lemon*   1 *cup shelled shrimps*
2 *onions*   ½ *cup sliced pimentos*
1 *clove garlic*   Saffron
2 *fresh tomatoes*   ¾ *cup very dry white wine*

Cut the heads, tails, and fins from 2 pounds of fresh cod or had, dock, place in a kettle with 1 quart of cold water, and bring to a boil, boiling until the liquid is reduced to 1 pint. Drain, and save the resulting broth. Cut the fish into serving pieces, brush with olive oil, sprinkle with salt, pepper, a generous pinch of thyme, a crumpled bay leaf, and let stand.

Now put the fish broth and ½ cup of olive oil in a pot. Add the juice of 1 lemon, 2 chopped onions, 1 crushed clove of garlic, 2 peeled tomatoes, ½ green pepper, seeded and chopped, and 2 tablespoons of minced parsley, and let the whole simmer for 1 hour, stirring just once.

Next add the cut-up fish, 8 oysters, 8 small clams, 8 mussels (if you can get them, if not, forget it), 1 cup of crab meat, 1 cup of lobster meat, 1 cup of shelled shrimps, and ½ cup of sliced pimentos, and continue simmering until the fish is done, which should be about 10 minutes. Next, dissolve a bit of saffron in about ¼ cup of very dry American white wine and add to the pot, stirring to distribute the herb. Just before serving, add ½ cup more of the dry white wine. Garlic bread is an indispensable accompaniment to this grand dish, and of course a bottle of dry white wine.

Down in Louisiana they have a variation of bouillabaisse which is called Courtbouillon à la Creole, and it is really something. Only one fish is used, and it is delectable on a cold evening, accompanied with plenty of crusty French bread and a bottle of claret, and perhaps a tossed green salad.

COURTBOUILLON À LA CREOLE

2 *lbs. fish (red snapper, sea trout, or redfish)*	1 *tbsp. chopped parsley*
2 *tbsp. butter*	*Marjoram*
1 *large onion*	*Thyme*
1 *clove garlic*	*Bay leaf*
1 *tbsp. flour*	*Allspice*
4 *large tomatoes*	*Juice ½ lemon*
¼ *cup chopped celery*	*Salt*
1 *green pepper*	*Cayenne pepper*
	1 *cup claret*

Cut 2 pounds of fish (cod, haddock or pompano may be used instead) in slices about 1 inch thick.

Heat 2 tablespoons of butter in a deep skillet or an iron pot, and add to it 1 large onion, peeled and sliced, and 1 minced clove of garlic, and fry until brown. Next, sprinkle in 1 tablespoon of flour, mix well, and let it brown. Now add 4 large tomatoes, peeled and sliced, ¼ cup of chopped celery, 1 green pepper, seeded and chopped, 1 tablespoon of chopped parsley, a generous pinch each of marjoram and thyme, 1 bay leaf, a dash of allspice, juice of ½ lemon, a dash of cayenne pepper, and 1 cup of claret. Mix everything well, and let simmer gently for about 15 or 20 minutes. Dust the fish slices lightly with salt and pepper, and add to the sauce. Simmer for about 20 minutes, or until the fish is tender. Remove the slices of fish to a hot platter, and pour the sauce over them. The sauce should be of about the consistency of cream; if it is too thick, stir in a little more claret, and reheat before pouring over fish.

While crabs, of which there are more than a thousand species, are found all over the world, the residents of Maryland and Virginia will swear that the finest crabs come from the waters of Chesapeake Bay, where the delicious blue, or common crab, is found. Certainly, one of the earliest American soups is Cream of Crab, which culinary historians claim Martha Washington served. If so, she showed rare good judgment, for it is truly a marvelous soup.

CREAM OF CRAB SOUP

2 cups fresh crab meat	3 fresh mushrooms
2 hard-boiled eggs	3 stalks celery
3 tbsp. butter	1 little green onion
Grated rind of 1 lemon	4 cups milk
1 tbsp. flour	1 cup heavy cream
1 tsp. Worcestershire sauce	Salt
1/8 tsp. mace	Pepper

1 cup sherry

Make a paste of 2 hard-boiled eggs, 2 tablespoons of butter, the grated rind of 1 lemon, 1 tablespoon of flour, 1 teaspoon of Worcestershire sauce, 1/8 teaspoon of mace, and mix with 2 cups of fresh crab meat.

In a tablespoon of butter sauté 3 chopped fresh mushrooms, 3 stalks of celery, minced, 1 little green onion, top and bulb minced, for about 5 minutes.

In a double boiler put 4 cups of scalded milk and 1 cup of heavy cream. Add the crab meat and paste and the sautéed mushrooms, onions, and celery. Salt and pepper to taste, and let the mixture thicken. Just before serving, add a cup of sherry, reheat, and serve.

There are many people who claim they cannot abide the various variety meats, such as liver, kidneys, hearts, brains, tripe, and the like, yet they will partake of soups based on these same variety meats and rave over them. I recall one friend who would grow pale at the mention of eating tripe, yet one of his favorite soups was Philadelphia Pepper Pot, which, of course, has tripe as a base. He would have sooner eaten fried angleworms than sampled kidneys, yet one day I made a kidney soup, and after two brimming plate-fuls, he begged me for the recipe for what I told him was *Nieren-suppe*. Having no sadistic tendencies, I refused, saying it was a cherished secret. But here is the recipe, and if he reads about it here, I hope he forgives me my deception.

KIDNEY SOUP
(Nierensuppe)

2 *veal kidneys*	2 *tbsp. flour*
3 *tbsp. butter*	1 *tsp. curry powder*
3 *little green onions*	5 *cups consommé*
½ *cup fresh mushrooms*	*Salt*
Bay leaf	*Pepper*
Marjoram	2 *egg yolks*
Thyme	¼ *cup sour cream*
Mace	3 *tbsp. Madiera*

First, cut 2 veal kidneys into thin slices, removing any useless sections.

In a skillet heat 3 tablespoons of butter and gently sauté 3 little green onions, chopped, and ½ cup of chopped fresh mushrooms until brown. Add a crumpled bay leaf, a pinch each of marjoram, thyme, and mace, and the sliced kidneys, and let cook until light brown. Now sprinkle in 2 tablespoons of flour and 1 teaspoon of curry powder. Stir and cook until flour lightly browns.

Put this mixture into a soup kettle and add 5 cups of consommé, salt and pepper to taste, and let simmer for about 30 minutes.

Beat 2 egg yolks with ¼ cup of sour cream. Remove the soup pot from the fire, and when the contents stop simmering, stir in the egg and cream mixture. Finally, before serving, add 3 tablespoons of Madeira.

Game, both in the uncooked form, or as left-overs and carcasses, lends itself admirably to soups. Some ardent Nimrods may think it a crime to use a succulent wild duck or pheasant in soup; but let me assure them that the aforementioned SWD or SP is far from wasted in a soup. As a matter of fact, a game soup is a really noble end to a noble bird, as witness the following recipe.

GAME BIRD SOUP

1 *duck or pheasant*	*½ cup celery*
Flour	*2 qts. chicken broth with rice*
Salt	*2 cups Burgundy*
Pepper	*2 cans button mushrooms*
¼ lb. butter	*2 tbsp. minced parsley*
2 onions	*Marjoram*
1 clove garlic	*Thyme*
2 diced carrots	*Basil*

Disjoint the duck or pheasant, and roll the pieces in seasoned flour.

In the bottom of a soup kettle melt ¼ pound of butter, and in this sauté the game bird pieces along with 2 peeled and chopped onions, a crushed clove of garlic, 2 diced carrots and ½ cup of diced celery until lightly browned. Then stir in 2 quarts of chicken broth with rice (the canned variety will do very nicely). Next, add 2 cups of Burgundy, 2 cans of button mushrooms, sliced, 2 tablespoons of minced parsley, a pinch each of marjoram, thyme, and basil, and salt and pepper to taste. Bring to a boil slowly, then simmer until the duck or pheasant is tender.

Take out the duck or pheasant and remove all the meat from the bones, and dice. Pour the contents of the kettle through a sieve into another pot, pressing the vegetables through the sieve. Add the diced meat, reheat, and serve.

A well-made chicken soup is a mighty tasty dish. You're most likely to come across it in country homes that have a coal range, with a stockpot simmering on it containing a fat hen, right out of the barnyard, and fresh, home-grown vegetables. If you ever go to Belgium, be sure and try *Le Waterzoie,* which is almost a national dish and chicken soup at its best. The following recipe is an adaptation, and a slight refinement on the Belgium one.

BELGIAN CHICKEN SOUP

5-lb. stewing chicken	Butter
1 lime	¼ cup chopped parsley
Water	1 bay leaf
2 onions	1 tbsp. salt
4 cloves	15 peppercorns
¼ cup cut celery	Marjoram
3 leeks	Thyme
1 carrot	1 bottle dry white wine
1 cup scalded cream	

Rub a 5-pound stewing chicken well with cut-up lime, then cut it up, put in a pot, and pour enough water over it to about half cover it. Bring to a boil, skim, and add 2 peeled onions, each stuck with 2 cloves, ¼ cup of cut celery, 3 leeks, sliced, 1 carrot sliced and previously sautéed lightly in butter, ¼ cup of parsley, 1 bay leaf, 1 tablespoon of salt, 15 peppercorns, a pinch each of marjoram and thyme, and 1 bottle of dry American white wine. Cover the pot and cook gently until chicken is tender—about 3 hours.

At the end of the cooking time remove the chicken from the pot, cut the meat from the bones and dice it. Strain the stock through a sieve into another pot, pressing the vegetables through also. Add the diced chicken to the stock and reheat. Remove from fire and add 1 cup of scalded cream at the last moment before serving, having previously sampled and corrected the seasoning.

There are probably two or three dozen different varieties of canned soup on the market today. Many of them are really excellent and are worthy of a place on any gourmet's menu. And a lot of fun can be had experimenting with different combinations, to the delight of your palate. What sounds like a weird combination is canned onion soup and canned cream of mushroom soup, but it is marvelous. Another combination I am very fond of is Curried Chicken Soup.

CURRIED CHICKEN SOUP

4 *cans condensed chicken soup*	1 *pint heavy cream*
1 *can consommé*	4 *tsp. curry powder*
2 *ounces sherry*	*Diced raw apple*

Heat 4 cans of chicken soup and 1 can of consommé in the top of a double boiler. Add 2 ounces of sherry and 1 pint of heavy cream, stirring in slowly. Then add 4 teaspoons of curry powder, stirring in well. After the soup has been poured into the soup plates, sprinkle the top with chilled, finely diced raw apple.

Of course, there are some soups whose unusual flavor, or combination of flavors, just can't be retained in a can. One of these is mulligatawny. It is of East Indian origin, and the word means "pepper water." Consequently, the soup should be highly seasoned. In old England it was more commonly known as Curry Soup, and, indeed, the original recipe consisted of a rich, thin cream soup flavored with curry powder and plenty of spices, with small pieces of chicken cut up in it, and served with a dish of highly seasoned Indian rice. However, through the years it has changed somewhat, but, with the exception of the sherry, which I think adds a good deal to it, the following is what you might well expect to find in any of the outstanding restaurants or hotels in India.

MULLIGATAWNY SOUP

1 *large chicken*	2 *bay leaves*
¼ *cup butter*	½ *tsp. mace*
2 *medium-sized onions*	1 *tsp. allspice*
1 *clove garlic*	8 *peppercorns*
1 *stalk celery*	3 *cloves*
½ *green pepper*	½ *cup lentils*
1 *tart apple*	¼ *cup grated coconut*
1 *tbsp. flour*	*Coconut milk*
1 *tbsp. curry powder*	4 *cups chicken broth*
1 *tsp. salt*	¼ *cup sherry*
	Boiled rice

Cut up a good-sized chicken as for fricassee, roll in seasoned flour, and brown on all sides in ¼ cup of butter in a heavy pot. Add

2 medium-sized onions, minced, 1 clove of garlic, crushed, 1 stalk of celery, diced, ½ green pepper, minced, 1 tart apple, peeled, cored, and diced. Cook this mixture for about 5 minutes, then sprinkle in 1 tablespoon of flour, 1 tablespoon of curry powder mixed with 1 teaspoon of salt, 2 bay leaves, ½ teaspoon of mace, 1 teaspoon of allspice, 8 peppercorns, 3 cloves, ½ cup of lentils which have been soaked in cold water overnight, and ¼ cup of grated coconut which has been moistened with some of the coconut milk. (If you can't get fresh coconut, or you don't want to bother with it, use the packaged coconut that is grated. But the fresh coconut is more than worth the bother.) Next, add 4 cups of the chicken broth or bouillon. Simmer gently for at least 1 hour, or until the chicken is tender. Then remove the pieces of chicken from the pot, and strain the remainder of the pot into a large saucepan, pressing the vegetables, etc., through the sieve. Remove the meat from the chicken pieces, dice, and add it to the strained soup along with ¼ cup of dry sherry. Simmer once more, and serve very hot in plates or bowls in which 1 teaspoon of boiled rice has been placed.

While today it is possible to obtain excellent turkeys the year round, the Little Woman and I are rather old-fashioned about our national bird. We wait until Thanksgiving for our first turkey, and consequently we enjoy it to the utmost. The phrase, "My God, do we have cold turkey again tonight!" is never heard in La Maison Wood. And when the last meal is eaten from the succulent bird, we drool in anticipation of turkey soup.

TURKEY SOUP

Turkey carcass	*3 tbsp. flour*
Water	*¼ cup uncooked rice*
2 bay leaves	*½ cup celery*
Salt	*Turkey meat*
Pepper	*Turkey gravy*
Generous pinch marjoram	*Turkey dressing*
Generous pinch thyme	*2 cups fresh mushrooms*
Generous pinch basil	*1 lb. chestnuts*
Butter	*3 tbsp. Madeira*
Consommé	*½ cup cooking oil*

After having cut or torn away every particle of meat from your turkey carcass, break it up and put it in a large pot, along with 2 bay leaves, salt and pepper, and a generous pinch each of marjoram, thyme, and basil. Cover the carcass with water, and let it simmer slowly for 3 to 4 hours. Then remove the bones and strain the resulting broth through a sieve. This is your stock.

Melt 2 tablespoons of butter in a saucepan, and into it stir 3 tablespoons of flour until smooth. Gradually stir in the stock (which should amount to about 1½ to 2 quarts) and bring to a boil. Now add ¼ cup thoroughly washed uncooked rice, ½ cup of finely cut celery, additional salt and pepper to taste, and cook gently until the rice is soft—about 25 or 30 minutes.

In the meantime sauté in a couple of tablespoons of butter, 2 cups of fresh mushrooms, halving them if they are medium sized, or quartering them if they are large, for about 5 minutes, and add them to the soup.

While the turkey stock has been simmering, prepare the chestnuts. Pick over enough chestnuts to have a pound of sound nuts. With a sharp, pointed knife cut the skin on the flat side of the chestnuts crisscross fashion. Then in a large skillet heat about ½ cup of cooking oil, add the chestnuts, and let them heat over a fast flame for about 4 or 5 minutes, shaking the pan and stirring the chestnuts all the while. Then drain them and let them stand until they are cool enough to handle (but not cold) and with a sharp knife remove the shell and skin. Put them in a saucepan, cover with canned consommé, and let them cook until they are tender. Then, when you have added the mushrooms to the soup, rub the chestnuts through a sieve and add them to the soup.

Let all this simmer very, very gently until dinner time. Just before serving, add 3 tablespoons of Madeira, stirring it in. After eating this soup, the chances are that you'll go out the next week and buy another turkey, just so you can make the soup again.

The use of almonds in cooking is not nearly so well known in the United States as it is in southern Europe, particularly in Spain. These nuts, whole, chopped, or slivered, are frequently used as a garnish, and their flavor under heat is even more distinctive than when they are eaten as a nut. They go particularly well with fish, as in the case of Fillet of Fish Amandine, the recipe for which you'll find in the chapter on fish. And as the basis for a Spanish soup—well, you'll be nuts about it, if you'll pardon the pun!

ALMOND SOUP

2 cups blanched almonds	2 whole cloves
4 cups chicken broth	Bay leaf
3 stalks celery	Pinch basil
3 tbsp. chopped onion	Pinch thyme
¼ tsp. mace	Salt
¼ tsp. nutmeg	Tabasco

2 ounces sherry

Have 2 cups of blanched almonds to start with. Put 1½ cups through the finest blade of the food grinder, and chop the remaining ½ cup, reserving for later use. Now put the 1½ cups that have gone through the food grinder into a mortar, and with a pestle mash them to a paste, adding a couple of tablespoons of very cold water to keep them from getting oily. (A mortar and pestle—the same sort of thing a druggist uses—are very handy things to have around the kitchen. If, however, you haven't any, or don't want to buy them, use a heavy bowl and the muddler you make Old-Fashioned cocktails with.)

Put 4 cups of chicken broth in a large saucepan and add 3 tablespoons of chopped onions, 3 stalks of celery, finely cut, ¼ teaspoon each of mace and nutmeg, 2 whole cloves, a bay leaf, a generous pinch each of basil and thyme, salt to taste, and a dash of Tabasco. Let the whole simmer for about 30 minutes, then strain through a sieve. Add the almond paste, and let simmer for 20 minutes more. Finally, add the ½ cup of chopped almonds you have reserved, bring to a boil, and just before serving add 2 ounces of sherry.

There are a number of other nut soups, such as walnut soup, black walnut soup, and peanut soup. And then there is the chestnut soup, which is a great favorite in central France, where it is called *Soupe aux Marrons*. If you like chestnuts as well as I do, you'll go for this soup in a big way.

CHESTNUT SOUP

2 *lbs. chestnuts*	1 *stalk celery*
1 *cup cooking oil*	*Salt*
2 *cups consommé*	*Pepper*
4 *tbsp. butter*	3 *cups chicken broth*
1 *onion*	1 *cup scalded cream*
1 *carrot*	*Dry mustard*

1 *cup Madeira*

Prepare the chestnuts for boiling in the same manner as in the recipe for turkey soup.

Put 4 tablespoons of butter in a saucepan and add 1 peeled and sliced onion, 1 sliced carrot, and 1 stalk of celery, cut up, and sauté for about 10 minutes, but do not brown. Now add the peeled and skinned chestnuts, salt and pepper to taste, and 2 cups of consommé, and simmer gently until the chestnuts are soft, about 20 to 25 minutes. Then strain the consommé into a fresh pot, and rub the chestnuts and vegetables through a sieve into the same pot. Add 3 cups of chicken broth and bring to a boil; then stir in 1 cup of scalded cream, seasoned with a tiny pinch of dry mustard and salt. Bring to the boiling point once more, remove from the fire, add 1 cup of Madeira, and serve.

As a drink, rum was in disrepute for many years. Nice people thought of it as a drink for pirates (the ancient kind, not those who unblushingly sock you eight dollars for a two-dollar tie) or rough seafaring men, or as the stock in trade of waterfront dives. Then came the great drouth, when bourbon, Scotch, and gin all but disappeared from the market, and all kinds of rum flooded the country. Then the Demon Rum took on sort of a halo, and everybody used it—or perhaps "misused" would be a better term.

Rum has always been a delightful flavoring agent for many kinds of desserts. Pies, puddings, and ice creams can rise to great gastronomic heights with the addition of rum to the recipe. However, rum as an ingredient in other dishes seems to be known only to a few, so I'm going to let you in on a few secrets here and there throughout this book. The first is Shrimp Bisque with Rum.

A bisque, as you probably know, is a thick, rich, smooth soup, usually made with a shellfish base. However, I have eaten corn, mushroom, and tomato bisques. To make a bisque according to Hoyle (or perhaps I should say, according to Escoffier) the shell-fish is marinated overnight in a white wine court bouillon (I'll tell you about court bouillon in the chapter on fish) and then cooked in the bouillon with fresh tomatoes until it is tender. The shellfish is then strained out and pounded in a mortar until it is smooth, (there comes that mortar again—maybe you'd better get one after all!) and then passed through a sieve and returned to the bouillon. It's all heated again, some sweet cream is added, and sherry, Madeira or brandy donated, and the bisque is served.

In anybody's language, that's a hell of a lot of work to get a soup, or a bisque. So, here's a much easier and simpler way, and if it doesn't taste as good as a thousand-dollar bill looks in your wallet, I'll eat it (the bisque, not the wallet).

SHRIMP BISQUE WITH RUM

1 *can condensed tomato soup*	1 *cup sweet cream*
1 *can condensed pea soup*	1 *lb. boiled shrimps*
1½ *ounces light rum*	

Stir the tomato and pea soup together, (after opening the cans, of course) until thoroughly mixed, in a saucepan or in the top of a double boiler. Then add 1 cup of sweet cream and blend it thoroughly with the soup mixture. Next, add 1 pound of fresh boiled shrimps (if they are jumbo shrimps, break them in half) and bring the whole thing to a boil, stirring slowly. When the mixture comes to a boil, add 1½ ounces of light rum, stir it in well, remove from the fire, and serve.

Of course, if you want to be fancy-pants, and you've bought yourself a mortar and pestle, you can pound the shrimps until smooth before adding them.

No cook book, not even this one, would be complete without a discussion of clam chowder. It's probably one of the best known American dishes, and it is practically a "must" on Friday menus, at least throughout the East and Middle West. I have heard people say that chowder is a native American dish, but I'm going to have to disillusion such folks, because the word "chowder" comes from the French word, *chaudière,* which means cauldron. French peasants and fishermen cook their fish stews in a cauldron. Sometimes it is a community cauldron, and each neighbor contributes something—milk, fish, vegetables, potatoes, herbs, hard biscuits, and so on. These contributions are cooked together in this pot from which the chowder derives its name, and each contributor takes his share of the finished product.

The controversy as to whether clam chowder should or should not be made with tomatoes is probably second only to the argument as to whether mint should or should not be crushed in making a mint julep.

I'll never forget a delightful old Kentucky gentleman I met in the Pendennis Club in Louisville, and his sermon on mint juleps. "You take a large glass," he explained, "and you put a small cube of sugar in the bottom of it. Then you add enough crystal clear spring water to dissolve the sugar. When it is dissolved, you pack the glass with finely shaved ice. Then you pour over the ice three or four ounces of the finest Kentucky bourbon obtainable. You jiggle a spoon up and down in the glass to start the frosting process, then you pack the glass to the brim with more shaved ice. And finally comes the benediction of that beautiful, fragrant, heaven-sent herb that God, in His Infinite Love, saw fit to bless mankind with—tender sprigs of fresh mint. Stick as many sprigs as you can into the glass, being sure that they reach deep into it, to mate with the bourbon. Then drink, son—and, with your nose buried deep in the green foliage, inhale its perfume as the golden liquid caresses your mouth." He took a long pull at his julep, then set his glass down. Suddenly his eyes were filled with fire, and he leaned forward. "Mr. Wood, you may be offered concoctions which are called mint juleps, with mint leaves crushed in the bottom of the glass, with cherries and slices of orange stuck around the rim, and even the blasphemy of rum floated on top. But by God, suh, those are all hellish delusions and snares to cover up the taste of bad whiskey!"

Let's see, where was I? Oh yes, clam chowders. The essential difference between New England clam chowder and Manhattan clam chowder is that the latter has tomatoes in it and no milk.

Personally, I can't see what all the shootin's about, because, for my dough, they are both terrific soups. Try out this Manhattan Clam Chowder, just for size.

MANHATTAN CLAM CHOWDER

24 (*or more*) *clams*	½ *cup celery*
Water	1 *green pepper*
2 *tbsp. olive oil*	*Clam broth*
2 *medium-sized onions*	*Thyme*
2 *leeks*	*Marjoram*
½ *clove garlic*	*Cayenne pepper*
3 *cups diced raw potatoes*	*Salt*
4 *tomatoes*	*Bay leaf*

1 *tbsp. chopped parsley*

Steam 24 clams (or more, depending on how much you like them) in enough water to cover for 15 minutes. Drain off the broth and set aside.

In a heavy pot, sauté, in 2 tablespoons of olive oil, 2 medium-sized onions, peeled and diced, 2 leeks, diced, and ½ clove of garlic, minced, until golden brown. Add 3 cups of diced raw potatoes, 4 tomatoes, peeled and chopped, ½ cup of diced celery, and 1 green pepper, seeded and diced. Next, add the clam broth and enough water to make 2 quarts. Dice the clams (not too fine) and add them, then let the whole thing simmer for 30 to 35 minutes. Add a generous pinch each of thyme and marjoram, a crumpled bay leaf, a dash of cayenne pepper, and 1 tablespoon of chopped parsley. Bring to a boil, then simmer for about 10 minutes. Serve as hot as possible.

The recipe for New England Clam Chowder is a standard one, and can be found in almost any cook book. It follows the recipe for Manhattan Clam Chowder pretty closely, omitting the tomatoes and using cream. However, you can make a very excellent New England Clam Chowder right in your own home with canned clams. For this heresy I shall probably be barred from the Cape in the future, but I'll stick by my guns. Here's how it's done.

NEW ENGLAND CLAM CHOWDER

1 *slice bacon*	4 *ounces milk*
1 *medium-sized onion*	2 *ounces cream*
1 *cup diced raw potatoes*	1 *tbsp. butter*
1 *7-ounce can clams*	*Salt and pepper*
Dry white wine	*Cayenne pepper*

Mince large slice of bacon and peel and dice medium-sized onion, and sauté together (if the bacon happens to be very lean, add a tiny bit more bacon grease). Place this, when it is golden brown, in a saucepan. Add a cup of diced raw potatoes, the juice from the 7-ounce can of clams, and enough dry white wine to cover the potatoes. Cook until the potatoes are tender, then add the clams, either coarsely cut up or minced, and 4 ounces of milk and 2 ounces of cream. Add a tablespoon of butter, salt and pepper to taste, and a dash of cayenne pepper. Let it heat through thoroughly, and serve very hot. This recipe will serve two people, and I think they'll love it. I know I did.

Ernest Byfield, Chicago's well-known gourmet, *bon vivant,* and witty Boniface, wasn't satisfied with creating the Pump Room at the Ambassador East, where almost any and every day movie celebrities are as common as the flaming swords of foods carried by waiters. So he created another unique spot in the Hotel Sherman, which he calls the "Well of the Sea," which is a marine world of make-believe at the "bottom of a sea." The room boasts that you can order almost any seafood dish imaginable, including a number of exclusive items which are not available anywhere else in the city.

One of the specialties is Old Mr. Flood's Black Clam Chowder. It is a most delectable dish named after a character created by Joseph Mitchell in a series of three articles in the *New Yorker* a few years ago. Old Mr. Flood is supposed to be ninety-three years old, and his one and only ambition is to live to be one hundred and fifteen, which he expects to do by eating seafood. Incidentally, Mr. Flood is very fond of black clams, which are supposed to come from the vicinity of Rhode Island and measure about one and three-quarter inches across. Anyhow, I wangled the recipe from Ernie Byfield, and here it is.

OLD MR. FLOOD'S BLACK CLAM CHOWDER

40 *soft-shell clams*

2 *ounces chicken fat*

¼ *ounce curry powder*

4 *ounces flour*

1 *qt. clam stock*

½ *pint stewed tomatoes*

½ *pint tomato purée*

¼ *pint chili sauce*

½ *tsp. salt*

Pepper

3 *ounces diced potatoes*

½ *stalk celery, diced*

1 *large leek, diced*

4 *ounces haddock, diced*

1 *tsp. parsley, chopped*

4 *ounces diced onions*

2 *large green peppers, roughly cut*

1 *clove garlic, finely chopped*

½ *tsp. thyme*

Maggi seasoning

Boil for approximately 15 minutes 40 soft-shell clams in 1 quart of water seasoned with salt and thyme (½ teaspoon each), 1 stalk of celery, and 1 small onion. Strain, and use the stock for the chowder.

Blanch the haddock and potatoes.

Melt the chicken fat and add the curry powder and flour. Cook for approximately five minutes over a slow flame until the mixture takes on body. Add the clam stock, the tomato purée, and the chili sauce. Bring to a boil and add the ½ stalk of celery, diced, and the 4 ounces of diced onions. Cook for 20 minutes and add the leeks, haddock, and potatoes. Cook for 15 minutes more and add the green peppers and the stewed tomatoes. Cook ten minutes more and add the parsley and garlic. Season to taste with salt and pepper and Maggi seasoning and remove from the flame.

The clams used to make the clam stock may be served in the shells with the soup as a side dish. The night I had this chowder, there were three or four clams in their shells in the soup plate. The above recipe makes four quarts of chowder.

There are almost as many varieties of fish chowder as there are varieties of fish. The French, as I have said, excel in the making of a pungent fish chowder, although the fish chowders found along the Atlantic coast from Maine to Florida, and in the Gulf states, are mighty fine eating. Mississippi fish chowder uses red snapper as a base, and the recipe includes a cup of red wine. Down Maine way they use cod, but no wine. However, here's an easy recipe for New England Fish Chowder, and the addition of sherry at the end really does things for it.

NEW ENGLAND FISH CHOWDER

1 *lb. haddock*
1 *lb. cod*
1 *lb. striped bass*
1½ *qt. cold water*
¾ *tsp. salt*
Bay leaf
Sprig green celery leaves
Pinch of thyme
2 *tbsp. chopped parsley*
½ *tsp. whole allspice*
1 *clove garlic*
8 *whole peppercorns*
¼ *lb. salt pork*

1 *carrot*
3 *medium-sized onions*
2 *stalks celery*
2 *cups diced raw potatoes*
1 *cup clam broth*
1 *ounce butter*
1½ *tbsp. flour*
1 *pint milk*
1 *cup scalded cream*
Salt
Pepper
Cayenne
½ *cup sherry*

Put a quart and a half of cold water into a kettle along with ¾ teaspoon salt, bay leaf, sprig of green celery leaves, pinch of thyme, 2 tablespoons chopped parsley, ½ teaspoon of whole allspice, 1 clove of garlic and 8 whole peppercorns. Into the liquid put 1 pound each of cod, haddock, and striped bass, bring to a boil, then lower the flame and let simmer for about 20 minutes. Strain the broth through a fine sieve into a soup kettle. Remove the fish, skin and bone it, and set it aside.

In a heavy skillet fry ¼ pound of salt pork cut into small cubes, together with 3 medium-sized onions, peeled and thinly sliced, 1 carrot, chopped, and 2 stalks of celery cut fine. When the pork and onions are barely golden brown, put the contents of the skillet into the soup kettle. Add 2 cups of diced raw potatoes, and cup of clam broth which has been thickened with an ounce of butter blended with 1½ tablespoons flour. Let everything cook until the potatoes are tender (about 10 minutes), then add the fish, which has been broken into small bits, and stir into the kettle 1 pint of milk. Allow the mixture to cook for 10 minutes, then add 1 cup of scalded cream, salt and pepper to taste, and a pinch of cayenne. Last of all, add ½ cup of sherry just before serving. Crisp or toasted pilot crackers should be served with this chowder.

One thing New Orleans is famous for, among many other things, is Creole Gumbo, or perhaps I should say, Gumbos. They originated in New Orleans, among the very old Creole cooks. It is a unique dish, and must contain the vegetable which we now know as okra, but which was also known as gumbo, or *févi,* as the Creoles called it. Today there are some gumbos which do not contain okra, but to the purist, the name is misapplied.

There is another ingredient that is a must in gumbos, and that is filé powder, or Gumbo Filé. It was first manufactured by the Choctaw Indians who lived in the woods around New Orleans, and is derived from the tender young leaves of the sassafras tree, which are pounded to a powder. Today it is carried by many first-class stores or food specialty shops.

The following recipe for Creole Gumbo is in the best tradition of New Orleans, with an addition I like, dry white wine. I may be damned for it by strict Creole cooks, but my shoulders are broad, theoretically, if not actually.

CREOLE GUMBO

1 3- to 4-lb. chicken	Bay leaf
½ lb. lean ham	Cayenne pepper
12 young okras	Salt
4 tbsp. butter	Pepper
1 clove garlic	2 qts. water
1 large onion	1 pint oyster liquor
½ cup celery	1 pint dry white wine
3 tbsp. chopped parsley	36 fresh oysters
Thyme	2 tbsp. filé powder

Cut up a tender 3- to 4-pound chicken as for fricassee, and dredge with salt and freshly ground pepper to taste. Cut ½ pound of lean ham into dice. Wash and stem 12 young okras and cut into ½ inch slices. In a large kettle melt 2 tablespoons of butter and sauté the okra slices until they are lightly brown. Then remove them and set aside. Add 2 more tablespoons of butter to the kettle and 1 crushed clove of garlic. When the butter is hot, put in the ham and chicken pieces, cover, and let them sauté for about 10 minutes, turning the chicken as necessary to brown it.

Now add to the kettle 1 large onion, peeled and chopped, ½ cup of celery, chopped, 3 tablespoons of chopped parsley, a generous pinch of thyme, a crumpled bay leaf, and a pinch of cayenne pepper. Cook, stirring occasionally, until the onions are nearly browned. Now add 2 quarts of boiling water, 1 pint of boiling oyster liquor, and 1 pint of dry white wine. Simmer for about an hour, or until the chicken and ham are very tender.

Just before you are ready to serve the gumbo, but while it is still boiling, add 3 dozen fresh oysters, and cook until the edges of the oysters begin to curl—about 3 or 4 minutes. Now remove from the fire, and when boiling ceases, gradually add 2 tablespoons of the filé powder to the hot gumbo, stirring slowly to mix thoroughly, and serve.

CAUTION: Never add the filé powder while the gumbo is cooking over heat, and never reheat the gumbo after the filé powder has been added. If either of these things are done, the filé powder will make the gumbo stringy, and unfit for use.

During the hot summer weather, I don't know of anything that is more delicious, more cooling, and more attractive than a cup of jellied consommé (I'm speaking of food, of course, and not of the many wonderful libations that come in tall and/or frosted glasses). I always keep three or four cans of consommé in the ice box at all times. In addition to consommé, and consommé madrilène, there are a number of other canned soups that can be chilled, and you can experiment by combining varieties before chilling them, such as a can of condensed tomato soup, a can of condensed pea soup, an equal amount of light cream, and a touch of basil and sherry.

A favorite soup of Myrna Loy, one of Hollywood's loveliest, most charming, and talented actresses, and, incidentally, now married to my old friend, Gene Markey, is an iced soup variously called Senegalaise Soup, Iced Chicken and Curry Soup, and *Potage Singhalese.* But whatever you call it, it's delicious and invigorating, yet still light enough for a summer diet.

ICED CHICKEN AND CURRY SOUP

2 *apples*	*Pepper*
2 *medium-sized onions*	*Cayenne pepper*
1 *tsp. flour*	1 *pint chicken broth*
2 *tsp. curry powder*	½ *pint dry white wine*
Salt	3 *ounces diced cooked chicken*
	1 *cup cream*

Core, peel, and slice 2 apples, and peel and slice 2 medium-sized onions. Melt 1 tablespoon of butter in a skillet, and cook apples and onions until fairly soft, but do not brown.

Mix 1 teaspoon of flour with 2 teaspoons of curry powder, add to the apple and onion mixture, and cook slowly for about another 5 minutes, stirring frequently. Add salt and pepper to taste, a pinch of cayenne pepper, then 1 pint of chicken broth and ½ pint of dry white wine. Cook over a low fire for about 10 minutes, stirring constantly. Remove from fire and strain, rubbing the solid ingredients through a fine sieve. Allow to cool, then chill thoroughly in the refrigerator.

When ready to serve, add about 3 ounces of diced cooked chicken (white meat) and thicken with about 1 cup of cream that is thoroughly chilled. Serve very cold in cups that are imbedded in crushed ice.

I suppose *Vichyssoise* is the swankiest of all soups. I've never seen *Vichyssoise* on the menus of Main Street lunchrooms, or, for that matter, on the menus of ordinary, good, run-of-the-mill eating places. But it's seldom, if ever, omitted from the *cartes des jours* of the top restaurants and hotels. But the notion that it is difficult to make at home is definitely old hat. If you don't believe me, try this out for kicks and a real taste thrill.

VICHYSSOISE

4 *leeks*	5 *medium-sized potatoes*
1 *medium-sized onion*	3 *cups medium cream*
1 *medium-sized carrot*	*Salt*
½ *cup butter*	*Pepper*
2 *stalks celery*	*Cayenne pepper*
5 *cups chicken broth*	⅛ *tsp. mace*
1 *cup medium dry white wine*	1 *cup heavy cream*
2 *tbsp. chopped parsley*	*Minced chives*

Thinly slice 4 leeks (white part only) and sauté in ½ cup of butter, together with 1 medium-sized onion, thinly sliced, 1 medium-sized carrot, thinly sliced, and 2 stalks of celery, chopped, until lightly browned—about 10 minutes—in a pot. Then add 5 cups of chicken broth and 1 cup of medium dry American white wine to the pot, along with 2 tablespoons of chopped parsley and 5 medium-sized peeled potatoes, sliced thin. Boil for 30 minutes or so.

Strain the mixture into a saucepan, forcing the solids through a sieve. Add 3 cups of medium cream. Season with salt and white pepper to taste, add a pinch of cayenne pepper and ⅛ teaspoon of mace, and bring to a boil. Remove from the fire and allow to cool, then place in the refrigerator and chill thoroughly.

Before serving, add 1 cup of chilled heavy cream, whip with a rotary beater for 1 or 2 minutes, and serve, topping each serving with minced chives.

CAUTION: To prevent discoloration, cool the strained soup in enamel, china, or stainless steel utensil.

((4)) FISH

Two gets you six the vast majority of people who dislike fish have never eaten it properly cooked.

I used to dislike it, too. That is, until I went on a fishing trip in the Adirondacks several years ago. The first afternoon out I didn't hook any trout myself, but the rest of the party returned to camp with a sizable catch, and the guide went to work. First he cleaned the fish, but didn't scale them. Then he covered each fish with a thick layer of mud and buried them in a bed of glowing embers. About a half hour later, when I was wistfully dreaming of corned beef and cabbage at Dinty Moore's, the guide dug several hard, gray masses out of the coals, gently broke them apart, and, minus the skin and scales, laid white and gleaming trout on our tin plates. There, indeed, was a Lucullan banquet under the trees.

You can, by the way, cook fish the same way in your own city apartment.

BAKED FISH WITH CRUST

1 *whole fish apiece*	*Salt*
Dry white wine	*Pepper*
Lime juice	*Flour*
Water	

Clean the fish, wipe them dry, brush with lime juice, season them inside with salt and pepper to taste, dot with butter, and put a tablespoon of dry American white wine inside each fish. Then cover the fish with a very thick flour-and-water paste, place them in the hottest oven you can obtain, and let them bake for about half an hour. A few taps of a knife handle will crack the cover, and all that remains to do is to peel it off gently.

65

Before we go any further into fish, I ought to speak of court-bouillon, which is a French term meaning "short broth." Because plain boiled fish is usually somewhat flat to the taste, some long-forgotten French chef devised a liquid, already well seasoned, in which to cook fish.

The following recipe for courtbouillon is when using white wine.

COURTBOUILLON

4 *cups dry white wine*	1 *tbsp. parsley, chopped*
2 *cups water*	½ *bay leaf*
1½ *tsp. salt*	1 *stalk celery, chopped*
1 *carrot, chopped*	10 *peppercorns*
1 *onion, chopped*	¼ *tsp. thyme*

¼ *tsp. marjoram*

Simmer all the above ingredients together for about 45 minutes, then strain through a fine sieve. If used at once, heat again to the boiling point and immerse the fish in it. If not to be used at once, cool and place in the refrigerator, where it will keep for several days.

To make red wine courtbouillon, substitute a dry American red wine for the white wine, and add about ⅓ more of the carrots and onions.

The French are probably the greatest fish cooks in the world. Certainly no other cuisine has as many delectable methods of preparing and cooking fish. Dione Lucas, in her excellent *Cordon Bleu Cook Book* devotes 90 pages to fish recipes, with 45 recipes for fillet of sole alone.

The deliciousness of many of the French recipes for fish is due to the use of herbs and wine. Thyme, tarragon, parsley, and bay leaf (but used sparingly) lend their piquancy to fish, and for nearly all the great fish dishes wine is a necessity. In fact, in no other phase of cooking is wine so important, because it points up so beautifully the delicate flavor of the fish.

Here is a delicious method of cooking fish—broiled with white wine. You can use mackerel, pike, bass, halibut, or fresh salmon. And you won't miss meat when you eat this!

BROILED FISH WITH WHITE WINE AND OLIVE SAUCE

1 *whole fish*	1 *onion*
Butter	1 *cup dry white wine*
Salt	1 *tbsp. flour*
Pepper	3 *tsp. water*
1 *tbsp. lemon juice*	*Few sliced stuffed olives*

Few drops of onion juice

If a whole fish is used, have it split lengthwise for broiling. Place skin-side down in a buttered shallow pan, sprinkle with salt and pepper and 1 tablespoon of lemon juice, and spread slices of 1 onion, sliced thin, over the whole surface of the fish. Dot with butter and put under the broiler. When butter melts, begin basting with dry American sauterne or Chablis (1 cup). Broil, basting frequently, until fish separates easily into flakes when tested with a fork. Remove fish to hot platter. Thicken liquid in pan with 1 tablespoon of flour mixed with 3 teaspoons of warm water. Add a few sliced stuffed olives and a few drops of onion juice, and pour sauce over the fish.

Erasmus, the great Dutch theologian of the Renaissance, despised fish. "My heart," he said, "is Catholic, but my stomach is Lutheran." Perhaps he lived in boardinghouses (if such things existed during the fifteenth and sixteenth centuries) and couldn't face Fridays, with the lukewarm, greasy, and hard-crusted hunks of fish on the table. But I'll wager he would have written glowingly of Baked Sea Bass with Mushrooms and Mint.

BAKED SEA BASS WITH MUSHROOMS AND MINT

1 *4-lb. black sea bass*	½ *tsp. salt*
Lime juice	⅛ *tsp. pepper*
3 *tbsp. butter*	*Pinch thyme*
1 *medium onion*	*Pinch basil*
2 *stalks celery*	*Pinch tarragon*
1 *cup mushrooms*	1 *tsp. fresh chopped mint*
1 *tsp. chopped parsley*	1 *cup dry white wine*

¼ *cup fine breadcrumbs*

Have 1 black sea bass, about 4 pounds, cleaned, split, and boned. Brush the fillets well with lime juice, and refrigerate 3 to 4 hours before cooking.

Put 2 tablespoons of butter in a saucepan, and when hot put in 1 medium onion, peeled and chopped, 2 stalks of celery, chopped fine, 1 cup of mushrooms, chopped, and 1 teaspoon of chopped parsley. Sauté these until tender.

Melt 1 tablespoon of butter and grease a baking dish with it. Lay the fillets on the bottom of the dish, and sprinkle over them ½ teaspoon salt, ⅛ teaspoon freshly ground black pepper, and a pinch each of thyme, basil, and tarragon.

Now cover the fillets with the onion, celery, and mushroom mixture and sprinkle with 1 teaspoon of fresh mint, chopped. Pour 1 cup of American dry white wine over all, and place the baking dish in a 350-375-degree oven. After about 15 minutes, during which the fish has been basted, sprinkle about ¼ cup of buttered breadcrumbs over the fish, and let become nicely browned, about 15 or 20 minutes more. Serve in the baking dish.

For some reason carp is not a popular fish in the United States, although it is very popular in Europe and other parts of the world. Believe it or not, carp can be domesticated and taught to eat out of one's hand. It seems to me I recall that tame carp abound in the moats surrounding the Japanese Emperor Hirohito's palace in Japan. The carp is reputed to be a very long-lived fish and may live to be over one hundred years old.

Properly prepared and cooked, the carp has a particularly delicious flavor. The Germans frequently cook it with beer. One of Germany's best-known dishes, and one of the most popular, is Carp of the Monks, the recipe for which dates back to the fifteenth century.

CARP OF THE MONKS

2 lb. carp fillets
2 onions
2 carrots
Grated peel of 1 lemon
Juice of 1 lemon
Salt
Pepper
1 bay leaf

¼ tsp. thyme
1 tsp. cinnamon
1 tsp. paprika
Pinch ground cloves
2 tbsp. vinegar
1 tbsp. molasses
½ cup gingersnap crumbs
2 tbsp. butter

Light beer

Cover the bottom of a baking dish with 2 medium onions, peeled and sliced, 2 carrots, sliced, the grated peel of a lemon and its juice. Season the fillets with salt and freshly ground pepper to taste, and lay them on the vegetable bed. Sprinkle over them 1 crumbled bay leaf, ¼ teaspoon of thyme, a pinch of ground cloves, and 1 teaspoon each of cinnamon and paprika. Add 2 tablespoons of vinegar and 1 tablespoon molasses. Spread over the carp ½ cup of gingersnap crumbs, dot with about 2 tablespoons of butter, and pour enough light beer in to just cover. Bake in a 400-degree oven for ½ hour.

To serve, carefully transfer the fillets to a hot platter and strain the sauce over it.

To my mind an even more delicious dish is Fillet of Carp with Mushrooms and Burgundy.

CARP FILLET WITH MUSHROOMS AND BURGUNDY

1 3-lb. carp
2 cups Burgundy
2 tbsp. olive oil
1 medium onion
1 clove garlic
2 tbsp. chopped parsley

½ tsp. ground mace
2 bay leaves
½ lb. fresh mushrooms
Salt
Pepper
1 tbsp. butter

1 tbsp. flour

Have a three-pound carp cleaned, skinned, and 1 large fillet cut from each side. Cut each of these fillets into 3 pieces, and marinate in 2 cups of Burgundy for a couple of hours.

In a saucepan, heat 2 tablespoons of olive oil, and add 1 medium onion, peeled and chopped, 1 clove of garlic, minced, 2 tablespoons of chopped parsley, ½ teaspoon of ground mace, 2 bay leaves, crumbled, ½ pound of fresh mushrooms, chopped, and salt and pepper to taste. Sauté gently for about 10 minutes. Then add the carp and the wine, and let cook slowly for about 1 hour.

Remove the carp fillets to a hot platter, and to the sauce add 1 tablespoon of butter creamed with 1 tablespoon of flour. Bring to a boil, stirring constantly, until sauce thickens. It should not be too thick; if it is, add a little heated Burgundy. Pour sauce over carp and serve.

I don't believe that there is anyone who has fewer food phobias than I have. I'll eat virtually anything that is set before me, provided, of course, it is properly prepared. Naturally, there are comestibles that I have a decided preference for, and there are some that I am not exactly wild about. But during my long eating career, there have been only three things that I wouldn't indulge in—caterpillars fried in deep fat, as served in Mexico; chipped beef in cream; and creamed codfish. The first is repulsive to me, and, in spite of the insistence of friends who have told me how delicious they are, I am quite sure I shall never eat them. I had eaten chipped beef in cream and creamed codfish—each once—and I just happen to despise them.

But a year or so ago I ran across an old French recipe for *Brandade de Morue,* and it was so intriguing that I tried it—and loved it. In case you don't recognize the French name, it's creamed codfish.

A great many people think that the cod is strictly a New England institution. As a matter of fact, a toast at the Twenty-fifth Anniversary dinner of the Harvard class of 1880 went like this:

> Here's to old Massachusetts,
> The home of the sacred cod,
> Where the Adamses vote for Douglas
> And the Cabots walk with God.

Actually, continental Europe holds the cod in high esteem, and *brandade de morue* is one of the most popular dishes throughout France, where it is often referred to as "the glory of Nîmes," the town which it is said the dish hails from.

If you, too, have scorned creamed codfish, let me urge you to try the following method of preparing it, and two gets you six that you'll love it also.

BRANDADE DE MORUE
(Creamed Codfish)

1 *lb. salt codfish*	5 *tbsp. olive oil*
Garlic	1 *tbsp. minced parsley*
1 *tbsp. very dry white wine*	¼ *tsp. white pepper*
5 *tbsp. heavy cream*	*Pinch nutmeg*
	Pinch cayenne pepper

Soak 1 pound of salt codfish in cold water for 8 to 10 hours, changing the water twice. Drain, add enough cold water to cover the fish, and bring to the boiling point. Skim the water and set the fish aside to cool in the covered saucepan.

When the fish is cool, remove all bones and skin, and shred the fish very fine. (If you have a mortar and pestle, pound the shredded fish to a smooth paste. You can accomplish practically the same thing by putting the shredded fish in a crockery bowl, and using a heavy spoon or a cocktail muddler.) This is one of the secrets of a perfect *brandade de morue*.

Rub a split clove of garlic once around the top of a double boiler. You want just a hint of garlic flavor. Put the paste of codfish in the top of the double boiler and keep it hot on the fire. Now beat into it with a wooden spoon 1 tablespoon of very dry American white wine. Next add 3 ounces of slightly warmed olive oil very, very slowly (as in making mayonnaise), stirring constantly until it is perfectly blended. In the same manner add 3 ounces of warmed heavy cream. Then stir into the mixture a tablespoon of finely minced parsley, a small pinch each of cayenne pepper and nutmeg and ¼ teaspoon of white pepper. Serve hot over triangles of not-too-thick toast. Baked potatoes are an ideal accompaniment, and a glass of chilled American Chablis or Riesling is indicated for additional pleasure.

Sometimes particular species of fish are not always obtainable, but I don't believe there is a grocery store or meat market that does not carry some sort of fillets of fish in their frozen food lockers. Sometimes they are labeled fillet of white fish, fillet of bass, fillet of pike, and sometimes just plain fish fillets. While I do not believe that frozen fish retain the delicate deliciousness of fresh fish, nevertheless they can be prepared and cooked with profit for any appetite. Following are two unusual recipes for fish fillets.

FILLETS OF FISH AMANDINE

2 *lb. fish fillets* (*trout, sole, flounder, pompano, or any other firm-fleshed fish*)
Dry white wine
Salted water
3 *little green onions*

6 *large mushrooms*
3 *tbsp. butter*
⅓ *cup slivered almonds*
Salt
Pepper
Lime juice

Poach 2 pounds of fillets of fish in equal parts of dry American white wine and lightly salted water until they are done—when fish flakes easily when tested with a fork.

Sauté 3 chopped little green onions, tops and bulbs, and about 6 large fresh mushrooms, chopped, in 2 tablespoons of butter until tender—about 10 minutes.

Brown ⅓ of a cup of slivered almonds in a little butter until lightly browned.

With a large spatula carefully remove the fillets from the poaching liquid and place in a greased shallow baking dish. Brush them with lime juice and season with salt and freshly ground pepper to taste. Place the sautéed onions and mushrooms in and around the fillets, and spread evenly with all the slivered browned almonds. Brown under a quick broiler flame and serve.

Cooking with red and white wines is becoming better and better known in America, but there is a wine which adds a delicious and unusual flavor to dishes and which is not so well known. I am referring to vermouth. Dry vermouth, more popularly known as French vermouth, is made from delicate white wines selected from the choice vineyards, and, after the finest of wine spirit has been added, a number of different herbs are added.

Sweet vermouth, more commonly known as Italian vermouth, is made chiefly from Marsala with an infusion of herbs. There is also Italian dry vermouth, but it does not rate the popularity of French dry vermouth.

Here is a recipe for Baked Stuffed Fish Fillets with Vermouth.

BAKED STUFFED FISH FILLETS WITH VERMOUTH

8 *small or* 4 *large fish fillets*
3 *tbsp. melted butter*
Salt
Pepper
3 *cups breadcrumbs*
¾ *cup chopped celery*
½ *cup chopped little green onions*

2 *tbsp. chopped parsley*
1 *tsp. thyme*
1 *tsp. marjoram*
1 *tsp. tarragon*
2 *tbsp. dry vermouth*
1 *egg*
½ *cup dry white wine*

Coat 8 small or 4 large fish fillets with melted butter and season with salt and pepper to taste.

Make a stuffing of 3 cups of breadcrumbs, ¾ cup of chopped celery, ½ cup of chopped little green onions, 2 tablespoons of finely chopped parsley, 1 teaspoon each of thyme, marjoram, and tarragon. Moisten with 2 tablespoons of dry vermouth (and a little white wine, if necessary) and bind with a well-beaten egg.

Place half of the fillets (4 small or 2 large) on a greased baking dish. Spread the stuffing over them and top with the remaining fillets. Bake uncovered in a moderate oven (350 degrees) about 25 or 30 minutes, or until done, basting occasionally with ½ cup of dry American white wine.

I suppose that in bringing up the subject of eels your reaction will be similar to that of my secretary, Bette Shields, who helped in the preparation of this book. When I mentioned eels, a shocked look came over her face and she said, "Heavens!"

Europeans, particularly the French and the Scandinavians, have a high regard for the eel as a food item, but few Americans know the possibilities of preparing this delicacy. The meat is sweet and has very little waste. Eels may be prepared in many ways: boiled or grilled, roasted, or baked. Smoked eels are invariably found on all smörgåsbord tables. The most popular method of preparing and cooking eels in France and in Louisiana is *Eels à la Matelote*. If you have an adventuresome spirit and want a new taste thrill, try this.

EELS À LA MATELOTE

3-lb. eel	*Pinch marjoram*
Salt	*Pinch basil*
Pepper	*1 tsp. chopped parsley*
6 ounces butter	*1½ tbsp. flour*
1 onion	*1½ ounces brandy*
1 carrot	*1½ cups of dry red wine*
1 clove garlic	*1 cup red wine court bouillon*
1 bay leaf	*½ lb. fresh mushrooms*
Pinch thyme	*Juice ½ lemon*

Skin the eel, clean thoroughly, and cut into 3-inch sections. Soak in cold salted water for 1 hour, then drain and dry. Roll in blended salt and pepper.

Melt 4 ounces of butter in a pan and put in the eel, together with 1 onion, peeled and diced, plus 1 carrot, diced, a minced clove of garlic, a bay leaf, a pinch each of thyme, marjoram, and basil, and 1 teaspoon of chopped parsley. Sauté until the eels are golden brown. Now add 1½ tablespoons of flour, stirring it into the mixture, then pour in 1½ ounces of brandy and 1½ cups of dry American red wine. Bring to a boil and let the liquid reduce somewhat. Add 1 cup of red wine courtbouillon (page 66). Cover the pan and let it simmer until done—about 25 minutes.

In the meantime, sauté ½ pound of mushrooms in 2 ounces of butter until tender. Remove the eel from the sauce and add to the mushrooms. Strain the sauce through a sieve into another pan, add the juice of half a lemon, and let it boil up until it thickens.

Put the eels and mushrooms on a deep platter, and pour the sauce over them.

The halibut might be mistaken for a gigantic overgrown flounder. It's a cold water fish, firm fleshed yet somewhat fat. Along with the cod and haddock, the halibut supports many a family of New England fishermen.

While the halibut may be pan fried, sautéed or broiled, I think it reaches its height of deliciousness in the following recipe.

BAKED CURRIED HALIBUT

2 *lb. halibut steaks*	1 *small onion*
1 *cup dry white wine*	½ *green pepper*
1 *cup fine breadcrumbs*	1 *stalk celery*
Salt	3 *tbsp. flour*
Pepper	1 *tsp. curry powder*
6 *ounces butter*	*Dash Tabasco*
	1 *tsp. lemon juice*

Place 1 cup of dry American white wine in a dish, or bowl, and dip the halibut steaks in the wine; then dip in fine breadcrumbs and sprinkle with salt and pepper.

Heat ¼ cup of butter in a fireproof baking dish in a hot oven, 500 degrees. Place the breadcrumbed halibut in the baking dish, baste with the hot butter, and bake uncovered for about 10 minutes, or until the crumbs are browned and the fish begins to flake with a fork.

In a saucepan melt 2 ounces of butter and add 1 small onion, peeled and minced, ½ green pepper, minced, and 1 stalk of celery, chopped. Sauté over a low flame for 10 minutes.

Blend 3 tablespoons of flour mixed with 1 teaspoon of curry powder into the mixture, stirring constantly, and add the remaining dry white wine. Stir well, add a dash of Tabasco and 1 teaspoon of lemon juice. Bring to a boil, stirring.

Arrange the halibut on a platter, and pour the hot sauce over it.

One of the best fish cooks, outside of professional chefs, that I have ever known is a friend of mine, Olive Chester, who lives in Kansas City, Missouri. You might wonder how a woman who lives so far from the sea would be an expert in cooking fish, but the explanation lies in the fact that for many years she spent her entire summer on Cape Cod. Olive refutes the pet belief of many professional amateur cooks that only men should cook fish. Under her skillful hands fish becomes an inexhaustible source of gastronomic pleasure. Here is one of her favorite dishes, which I have eaten many times and which she taught me to cook.

FRESH MACKEREL IN WINE SAUCE

2 *lb. fresh mackerel*
2 *tbsp. butter*
2 *tbsp. flour*
½ *cup dry white wine*

½ *cup milk*
½ *tsp. basil*
Salt
Pepper

3 *tomatoes*

Clean, bone, and split 2 pounds of fresh mackerel.

Make a wine sauce out of 2 tablespoons of butter, 2 tablespoons of flour, ½ cup of dry American white wine, and ½ cup of milk, adding ½ teaspoon of basil.

Season fish with salt and pepper to taste, place in buttered casserole, and pour the wine sauce over it. Top with 3 tomatoes, sliced, and bake in a moderate oven (350 degrees), for 50 minutes.

The town of Dijon, France, is probably one of the gastronomic capitals of the world, particularly during the food fair which is held there every year. I shall have more to say about this in a later chapter. However, one of the celebrated dishes is fillet of pike.

Pike is a very delicious fish, with lean, white, firm, and flaky meat. Belonging to the pike family are pickerel, which is found in rivers, and muskellunge, which inhabits lakes as well. I've been told that in the Amazon River a giant species of pike exists whose flesh is said to be the most delicate of any fish there is. If any readers are contemplating a fishing trip to South America, I wish they'd check on this and let me know. Meantime, the best I can do is to offer the recipe for Fillet of Pike, Dijon.

FILLET OF PIKE, DIJON

1 *3- to 4-lb. pike or pickerel*
3 *ounces brandy*
3 *ounces Madeira*
3 *little green onions*
Crumbled bay leaf
Generous pinch thyme
Generous pinch marjoram

1 *tbsp. chopped parsley*
Salt
Pepper
Dry white wine
½ *pound fresh mushrooms*
3 *tbsp. heavy cream*
2 *tbsp. butter*

Have your butcher fillet a 3- to 4-pound pike.

Make a marinade of 3 ounces of brandy, 3 ounces of Madeira,

3 little green onions chopped, bulbs and tops, a crumbled bay leaf, a generous pinch each of thyme and marjoram, a tablespoon of chopped parsley, salt and freshly ground pepper to taste. Lay the fillets in this mixture, pour in enough dry white American wine to cover, and let the fillets remain in the marinade for at least 24 hours.

To cook, take the fillets out of the marinade and place in a well-buttered baking dish. Slice ½ pound of fresh mushrooms and add them to the fillets. Pour the marinade over the whole, and bake in a hot oven (400 degrees) for about 20 minutes, basting the fish frequently. When the fillets are nicely browned, add 3 tablespoons of thick cream and 2 tablespoons of butter. Reheat for a moment, then serve.

If you've ever been in Florida or Louisiana, you've probably eaten pompano, although it is often found in the better class of restaurants throughout the country in general. I was first introduced to pompano at the famous Bradley's Casino in Palm Beach. Two of us went there for luncheon one day during Prohibition. We had a couple of perfect Martinis, *pompano en papillotte, pommes soufflé,* a bottle of Piesporter Goldtröpfchen, a water cress salad, and strawberries Romanoff. I should have been suspicious when I noted there were no prices on the menu, but I wasn't quite prepared for the jolt of a $35.00 check. Later that afternoon I went up to the Baccarat Room and watched Florenz Ziegfeld lose $60,000 in five minutes. After that I didn't feel so bad about the $35.00 check!

Pompano en papillotte is fancy pants for pompano cooked in a paper sack and served with a very delicate shrimp sauce; but it's a very intricate recipe, and I don't advise any but the most accomplished amateur chef to try it. But I don't think anyone would have any trouble with Baked Stuffed Pompano which is pretty delicious, too.

BAKED STUFFED POMPANO

1 3-*lb. pompano*	1 *cup cream*
1½ *cups cooked shrimps*	¼ *cup dry white wine*
1 *cup chopped mushrooms*	*Salt*
1 *egg*	*Pepper*
	Butter

Get a pompano weighing about 3 pounds, and have your butcher bone it for you.

Put 1½ cups of cooked shrimps through a meat grinder, using the finest blade. Putting them through twice won't do any harm. Then add to the ground shrimps 1 cup of fresh mushrooms, chopped, and 1 beaten egg mixed with ½ cup of cream. Season with salt and freshly ground pepper to taste, and mix in ¼ cup of dry American white wine. Stir the whole mixture until smooth, and stuff the pompano with it. Sew the fish up, or fasten it with skewers, and lay it in a buttered baking dish. Pour over it ½ cup of cream, bake in a moderate oven (350 degrees) for 45 minutes, and serve.

If you've ever been anywhere along the Gulf coast or southern Atlantic coast, you've probably eaten red snapper. It seems to me they use red snapper in the deep South in everything except pie, and I don't doubt but that some adventuresome chef, in the privacy of his own kitchen, has tried out red snapper pie. It is a delicious fish—a very delicate morsel. Of all the red snapper recipes, I've never found one that tops that for Baked Red Snapper in White Wine with a Cashew Nut Stuffing.

BAKED RED SNAPPER WITH NUT STUFFING

1 *4-lb. red snapper*	*Pinch thyme*
Lime juice	*½ tsp. nutmeg*
1 *medium-sized onion*	1 *bay leaf*
3 *tbsp. butter*	1 *tbsp. parsley*
½ *cup celery*	*Salt*
1 *clove garlic*	*Pepper*
1 *cup breadcrumbs*	¼ *cup Madeira*
1½ *cups cashew nuts*	2 *cups dry white wine*

Get a 4-pound red snapper, cleaned and beheaded. Rub inside and out with lime juice, lightly salted, and place in refrigerator for 2 or 3 hours.

Sauté in 3 tablespoons of butter 1 medium-sized onion, chopped, ½ cup of celery, chopped, and 1 clove of garlic, crushed, until onion browns very lightly.

In a large bowl mix 1 cup of fine breadcrumbs, 1½ cups of

chopped cashew nuts, a generous pinch of thyme, ½ teaspoon of grated nutmeg, a crumbled bay leaf, a tablespoon of parsley, and salt and pepper to taste. Add the sautéed onion and celery, mix well together, and moisten with about ¼ cup of Madeira.

Stuff the red snapper with this, sew up or skewer the fish, and place it in a well-greased baking dish. Pour over it about 2 cups of dry American white wine and bake in a moderate oven (350 degrees) for about 30 to 40 minutes, basting frequently. Garnish with parsley and serve.

As a rule I don't care much for boiled fish, but I think salmon lends itself particularly to boiling, and, with a shrimp or lobster sauce, it is really a gourmet dish. Here's a recipe for Boiled Salmon with Shrimp Sauce, but if you wish, you can substitute lobster for the shrimp.

BOILED SALMON WITH SHRIMP SAUCE

2 *lb. of salmon*	½ *lb. cooked shrimps*
2 *qt. white wine*	*Salt*
courtbouillon	*Pepper*
1 *tbsp. butter*	1 *egg yolk*
1 *tbsp. flour*	1 *cup cream*
	2 *tbsp. Madeira*

Prepare a white wine courtbouillon (page 66) and bring it to the boiling point.

Wrap about 2 pounds of salmon in cheesecloth, and lower it into the boiling broth. Cover, and simmer for about 20 to 30 minutes, then remove the pot from the fire.

In the top of a double boiler melt 1 tablespoon of butter. Blend in 1 tablespoon of flour. Add ½ pound of cooked shrimps, cut in pieces, and ½ cup of the courtbouillon the salmon has been boiled in, and salt and pepper to taste. Let cook for 3 minutes. Beat 1 egg yolk and pour over it a cup of scalded cream, then add this to the broth and shrimps.

Place the salmon on a hot platter. Add 2 tablespoons of Madeira to the shrimp sauce, blend, and pour over salmon.

As everybody probably knows, roe is the name for fish eggs enclosed in a thin, natural membrane. Shad roe is perhaps the most popular and best known, although today the roe of cod, herring, mackerel, salmon, and whitefish is marketed fresh, frozen, and canned. However, the most famous roe is that which comes from sturgeon. And that brings to mind a little ditty that an old pal of mine used to sing when he became mellow, to the tune of "Reuben, Reuben, I've Been Thinking." As I recall, it goes like this:

> Caviar comes from virgin sturgeon,
> The sturgeon is a very fine fish.
> Virgin sturgeon needs no urgin',
> That's why caviar is my dish.

I don't know whether the virgin shad needs any urgin', but I know I never need any urging to eat shad roe, which is one of the most highly prized of spring sea foods. It may be broiled, baked, or sautéed. While broiled shad roe, with a little lemon juice squeezed over it is pretty hard to beat, shad roe baked in sherry crowds it for top place. By the way, don't ever let anyone talk you into parboiling roe first before other cooking—that is a gastronomic crime.

SHAD ROE BAKED IN SHERRY

2 *pair shad roe*	*Pinch dry mustard*
Butter	*Salt*
1 *medium-sized onion*	*Pepper.*
2 *tbsp. chopped parsley*	1 *cup fresh mushrooms*
Pinch thyme	1 *cup sherry*
Pinch cayenne pepper	½ *tbsp. flour*

Place 2 pair of roe side by each in a well-buttered baking dish. Sprinkle over the roe 1 medium-sized onion, peeled and chopped, 2 tablespoons of chopped parsley, a pinch each of thyme, cayenne pepper, and dry mustard. Salt and pepper to taste.

In a small skillet sauté 1 cup of fresh mushrooms, sliced, in 3 tablespoons of butter until tender. Then add these to the roe, with their butter. Pour in 1 cup of sherry, and bake in a moderate oven (350-375 degrees) for about 25 minutes, basting frequently.

Drain the liquid from the baking dish. In the same skillet that the mushrooms were sautéed in melt 1 tablespoon of butter and blend in ½ tablespoon of flour. Add the liquid from the baking pan and cook until slightly thickened—about 3 minutes. Then pour the sauce over the roe, dot with butter, and place the baking pan under a moderate broiler flame until the tops of the roe are slightly browned—about 5 minutes.

Serve the roe garnished with chopped parsley and wedges of lemon.

The chances are that when you go into any but the high-priced and exclusive eating places and order *filet de sole,* you will get flounder. Actually, the flounder is a family name that includes gray sole and lemon sole. The true English sole, however, is very scarce in this country; but with oversea air express it is becoming available in American markets. If you can get the English sole, use them in the recipes which follow. If not, you can't go too wrong with fillets of flounder. The first is Fillet of Sole *au Vin Blanc* which, of course, means with white wine.

FILLET OF SOLE AU VIN BLANC

4 *large or 8 small fillets of sole*	1 *bay leaf*
1 *tbsp. butter*	1 *cup dry white wine*
1 *tsp. chopped onion*	½ *cup consommé*
1 *tsp. chopped parsley*	*Salt*
3 *mushrooms, chopped fine*	*Pepper*
1 *stalk celery*	2 *tbsp. cream*
Grated Parmesan cheese	

Salt and pepper 4 large or 8 small fillets of sole or flounder. In a large skillet melt 1 tablespoon butter and add 1 teaspoon chopped onion, 1 teaspoon chopped parsley, 3 mushrooms, chopped fine, 1 stalk of celery, chopped, 1 bay leaf, 1 cup American sauterne or Chablis, ½ cup consommé.

Lay fillets in the hot liquid and let simmer 5 to 10 minutes, until barely tender. Remove carefully to shallow baking dish. Boil down the liquid in which fish was cooked until about ¾ cup remains. Add 2 teaspoons cream, and more seasonings if needed.

Strain the liquid over fish in baking dish, sprinkle grated Parmesan cheese over all, and bake on upper shelf of hot oven (450 degrees) for about 10 minutes, or until top is lightly browned. (Serves 4.)

This recipe is prepared with fresh tomatoes—and I do mean fresh tomatoes.

FILLET OF SOLE WITH FRESH TOMATOES

4 *fillets of sole*	1 *cup dry white wine*
Salt	½ *cup cream*
Pepper	4 *tomatoes*
3 *tbsp. butter*	1 *tsp. chopped parsley*
1 *medium-sized onion*	Pinch *tarragon*
2 *little green onions*	Pinch *thyme*
1 *clove garlic*	Pinch *basil*
1½ *tbsp. flour*	¼ *cup fine breadcrumbs*

2 *tbsp. grated Parmesan cheese*

Place 4 fillets of sole in a well-buttered baking dish, and season to taste with salt and freshly ground pepper.

Melt 3 tablespoons of butter in a saucepan. Add 1 medium-sized onion, peeled and chopped, 2 little green onions, chopped, and 1 clove of garlic, minced, and sauté for about 5 minutes without browning. Then stir in 1½ tablespoons of flour, and add 1 cup of dry American white wine. Bring to a boil, then slowly add ½ cup of cream. Simmer for about 5 minutes, season with salt and pepper to taste, add 4 tomatoes, peeled, seeded, and coarsely chopped, and finally 1 teaspoon chopped parsley and a pinch each of tarragon, thyme and basil.

Pour this sauce over the sole. Sprinkle over all about ¼ cup of fine breadcrumbs and a couple of tablespoons of grated Parmesan cheese. Put in a moderate oven (350 degrees) for about 15 to 20 minutes. Remove and serve.

Olive Chester came up with this one at a dinner party in her Cape Cod cottage, and all the guests, including myself, raved about it, even though fillets of flounder were used instead of sole. She called it Fillet of Sole East Indian.

FILLET OF SOLE EAST INDIAN

6 *fillets of sole*	¾ *cup dry white wine*
5 *tbsp. butter*	¼ *cup milk*
Salt	¼ *cup cream*
Pepper	2 *tbsp. flour*
1 *tsp. curry powder*	¼ *lb. fresh mushrooms*
	1 *little green onion*

Place 6 fillets of sole in a buttered skillet; season with salt and pepper to taste and 1 teaspoon of curry powder. Add ¾ cup of dry American white wine and cook slowly for about 5 minutes, or until the fillets are white. Then transfer them carefully to a casserole.

Now make a cream sauce, using the wine the fish was poached in (about ½ cup), ¼ cup of milk, ¼ cup of cream, 2 tablespoons of flour, and 2 tablespoons of butter. When cooked and well blended, pour over the fillets. Garnish with ¼ pound of fresh mushrooms and 1 chopped spring onion, bulb and top. Bake 20 minutes in a 350-degree oven. No more than four people should share this wonderful dish.

I recently ran across three proverbs having to do with fish cookery. One is an old Latin saying, *"Maledictus piscis in tertia aqua."* One scarcely has even to fall back on high school Latin to figure that one out—"Fish is cursed in the third water." The first water is that in which the fish lived; the second is that in which he is cooked, and the third water is that which the unitiated drink with fish.

But I find a glaring fault with that saying, because fish should never be cooked in water. So an old Italian proverb suits me much better. *"Il pesce vive nell' acqua, e deve affogare nel vino,"* which, my Italian department tells me, means, "Since fish thrive in water, it should be drowned in wine." But I like Jonathan Swift's remark about fish best of all. In his *Polite Conversation, Dialogue II,* he writes, "They say fish should swim thrice . . . first it should swim in the sea (do you mind me?), then it should swim in butter, and at last, sirrah, it should swim in good claret."

However, in Normandy they might amend Swift's remarks by saying it should swim in good Calvados, which is apple brandy.

Fillets of Sole Normande is a very delectable creation, but as Calvados is difficult to obtain in America, I have substituted good old New Jersey applejack.

FILLET OF SOLE NORMANDE
(With Applejack)

6 *fillets of sole*	6 *little green onions*
1 *clove garlic*	2 *tbsp. flour*
1 *bay leaf*	1 *cup white wine courtbouillon*
1 *tbsp. olive oil*	1 *cup applejack*
Pinch thyme	1 *cup sliced mushrooms*
Salt	½ *cup cooked shrimps*
Pepper	2 *egg yolks*
5 *tbsp. butter*	2 *tbsp. chopped parsley*

1 *cup buttered breadcrumbs*

Mince 1 clove of garlic and 1 bay leaf very fine, add 1 tablespoon olive oil and a pinch of thyme, and mix. Now rub 6 fillets of sole with this seasoning, and season further with salt and pepper to taste.

Melt 2 tablespoons of butter in a skillet, and add 6 little green onions, tops and bulbs, chopped. Place the fillets on the onions and cook very slowly over a slow fire for about 10 minutes. Then carefully turn the fillets over and cook for another 10 minutes. Remove the fillets to a well-buttered baking dish, and cover to keep hot.

In another pan melt 1 tablespoon of butter, stir in 2 tablespoons of flour, and when well blended, add 1 cup of white wine courtbouillon and 1 cup of applejack. Stir constantly with a wooden spoon until the sauce is smooth and thickened. Add to the sauce the little green onions and the butter in which the fillets were cooked, 1 cup of sliced mushrooms, which have been previously sautéed in 2 tablespoons of butter for about 5 minutes, and ½ cup of cooked shrimps, which have been broken up into smallish pieces. Add more salt and pepper, if necessary, and cook for a minute or two. Remove from the fire, and stir in 2 lightly-beaten egg yolks and 2 tablespoons of chopped parsley.

Pour this sauce over the fillets in the baking dish, cover with buttered breadcrumbs, and bake in a moderate oven (350 degrees) for 15 minutes. Serve hot in the dish in which they were baked.

One of the Italian dishes I am most fond of is *calamaii* (Italian spelling) or *calamari* (Neapolitan spelling), and I'll never forget my introduction to this succulent bit of sea food.

In the early 1920's there was an Italian restaurant called "The Vesuvio," which was located right back of the Capitol Theater in New York. It was an Italian restaurant frequented almost entirely by Italians. Whenever the Italian Ambassador was in New York he always ate there, and another well-known and frequent visitor was Marconi.

I was first taken there by an Italian colonel who was a member of the Italian High Commission in this country. The restaurant was located in an old, brownstone-front house. We entered on the ground floor, walked through the kitchen and out onto a charming garden, which was the back yard of the house. Lanterns swung from the trees and one seemed to be in a world apart, far removed from the clanging traffic of Broadway. The menus were printed in Italian, and as I did not read Italian, Colonel Mario ordered the dinner. He started off with an eye-appealing and taste-teasing plate of Italian *antipasto*. Next we had spaghetti *marinara,* which is "sailor style," and this was followed by the entrée which Mario said was *calamari*. With what might be called true Italian exuberance, I raved about the dish and when I had licked my plate clean I asked him what the hell it was. He said, "I didn't want to tell you what it was before you ate it, because you might have thrown up your hands in horror; but now that you've eaten it and loved it, I'll tell you. *Calamari* is the tentacles of octopus fried in olive oil."

In the early days of my gastronomic experiences, I might have refused the octopus had I known beforehand what I was eating, but I shall always be eternally grateful to Mario for introducing me to octopus, or squid.

I think most Americans would shudder at the thought of eating squid, although the meat is twice as sweet as lobster and as delicate as frogs' legs. Let me urge you to unshudder and take a chance on squids à l'Amoricaine.

SQUIDS À L'AMORICAINE

3 *lb. squids*	½ *bay leaf*
4 *tbsp. olive oil*	*Pinch thyme*
3 *ounces brandy*	*Pinch oregano*
2 *cloves garlic*	1 *cup solid-pack tomatoes*
1 *onion*	*Salt*
3 *carrots*	*Pepper*

1 *cup dry white wine*

Get 3 pounds of squids from an Italian butcher shop, and have the butcher clean them and remove any bones. Then they should be cut into small cubes or strips.

In a large skillet or Dutch oven heat 4 tablespoons of olive oil and add 2 cloves of chopped garlic. When it begins to brown, add the squids, cover, and sauté for about 10 minutes. Uncover and pour over the squids 3 ounces of brandy. Light the brandy and let it burn out, then simmer for about 3 minutes. Next add 1 onion, peeled and chopped, 3 carrots, chopped, ½ bay leaf, crumbled, 1 pinch each of thyme and oregano, 1 cup of solid-pack tomatoes, and salt and pepper to taste. Stir in 1 cup of dry American white wine, cover, and simmer until the squids are done, or tender to the tines of a silver fork. If the liquor is too thin, thicken a very little with flour and water. Heat, and serve the squids in their sauce over boiled rice.

One of Cape Cod's greatest delicacies is swordfish. You'll find it on the menu of nearly every eating place, from small cafés, like Brogan's at the Hyannis airport, to the swanky and beautiful Coonamessett Inn at Hatchville. Swordfish has been called the roast beef and steak of the finny world, and I am in complete accord with that statement.

Swordfish steaks are pretty terrific just plain broiled—with a thin veil of flour over them and sautéed in plenty of butter to keep the delicate meat from drying out.

It was on the Cape that a native Cape Codder told me about a recipe for swordfish in white wine that she said had come down from her forebears. Here is the recipe that I finally wangled from her.

SWORDFISH IN WHITE WINE

1½ *lb. swordfish*	*Salt*
2 *cups dry white wine*	*Pepper*
½ *cup water*	6 *bulbs little green onions*
1 *tbsp. chopped parsley*	¼ *lb. fresh mushrooms*
1 *tsp. chopped chives*	1 *tbsp. flour*
1 *stalk celery*	2 *egg yolks*
Butter	½ *cup cream*

6 *clams, chopped*

Put 1½ pounds of swordfish in a deep skillet and pour over it 2 cups of dry American white wine diluted with a half a cup of water. Add a tablespoon of chopped parsley, a teaspoon of chopped chives, a single stalk of celery, chopped, a tablespoon of butter, and salt and pepper to taste, and let the whole thing simmer until the fish is done.

While the fish is simmering, fry 6 bulbs of little green onions and ¼ pound of fresh mushrooms in butter. Sift into this a tablespoon of flour. When this *roux* is well blended, strain into it the wine in which the fish has boiled (after the fish is done, of course). Let this cook a minute or two, and then thicken with the yolks of 2 eggs, beaten up with ½ cup of cream. Let this heat and then add a few clams to the sauce. When it is thoroughly hot, pour the sauce over the fish, which has been arranged on a platter.

Trout has been called the queen of lakes, rivers, and sea. There is probably no fish that can touch a brook, rainbow, or mountain trout freshly caught and immediately cooked. Then, of course, there are the salmon trout and the sea trout, but they are not as delicate a fish as their gamey fresh-water brothers.

As I have said before, I am not a great fisherman. I never have had any luck, to speak of at all, with a rod and reel except on one occasion. Don't be alarmed, this is not going to be a fish story of the speckled beauty that got away.

There used to be a very delightful and picturesque eating place near Utica, New York, called Troutbrook Inn. Rambling through the front yard was a small stream, and this stream was kept stocked with brook trout. Guests were supplied with a rod and reel and told to go out and catch their own dinner. And for the first time in my life, I really caught myself a fish. And the chef really fixed it up. He called it Brook Trout, Burgundy.

BROOK TROUT, BURGUNDY

6 *brook trout*
Lemon juice
Salt
Pepper
1 *clove garlic*
2 *tbsp. little green onions,*
    chopped

2 *tbsp. chopped parsley*
1 *tbsp. chopped celery*
    leaves
Pinch thyme
2 *cups Burgundy*
Butter
1 *tsp. flour*

Clean 6 brook trout and wash quickly in cold water to which a little lemon juice has been added. Season trout on both sides with salt and freshly ground pepper.

Lightly crush 1 clove of garlic and rub the bottom of a shallow baking dish with it. Lay the trout in the dish and sprinkle over them 2 tablespoons of little green onions, chopped, 2 tablespoons of chopped parsley, 1 tablespoon of chopped celery leaves, and a generous pinch of thyme. Pour over the fish 2 cups of Burgundy, dot the fish liberally with butter, and bake in a moderate oven (350 degrees) for 15 to 20 minutes, basting frequently.

Remove the trout from the baking dish and place on a hot platter. Strain the liquid from the baking dish to a saucepan. Let it reduce over a hot flame to about 1½ cups. Cream 1 tablespoon of butter with 1 teaspoon of flour, and blend in with the sauce. When thickened, pour the sauce over the trout, after having first sprinkled them with lemon juice. Serve, garnished with parsley.

I suppose there is hardly a person alive who doesn't remember those difficult days of rationing. However, I will say one thing for rationing—it taught a lot of people to use ingenuity and devise tasty dishes out of cans and paper bags. But while rationing is no longer with us, I still whip up a tuna fish casserole now and then. It is a swell luncheon dish and even does very well for a light dinner dish.

TUNA FISH CASSEROLE

1 *can chicken tuna fish*   1 *can condensed cream*
1 *pkg. potato chips*   *mushroom soup*
                                         2 *tbsp. sherry*

Put a layer of potato chips in the bottom of a glass baking dish. Then cover the chips with a layer of tuna fish (broken up, of course). Next, top the tuna fish with another layer of potato chips. Now, open the can of cream of mushroom soup and pour a little of it over the contents of the dish. Next, stir 2 tablespoons of sherry into the remainder of the soup and pour the whole thing over the potato chips and tuna. Place the dish in a moderate oven and bake 20 to 30 minutes.

As a rule, chowder recipes are placed in the soup category, but there is one that definitely belongs here, because it is a dry fish chowder. It is a concoction of a rather fabulous friend of mine by the name of Robert W. Jefferson. Bob's vocation is accounting, and I have heard it said that he is one of the cleverest corporation tax men in the country. But his avocation is hunting, fishing, and cooking. He is a much sought-after member of any hunting or fishing party, not only because he can cook, but because he can make a lemon meringue pie out in the woods without an oven! And that, boys and girls, I call a real accomplishment.

Bob's dry fish chowder is one of the most delicious I have ever eaten, and its preparation, over a camp fire or a kitchen stove, is simplicity itself.

DRY FISH CHOWDER, BOB JEFFERSON

2 *lb. firm-fleshed fish*   1 *#2 can tomatoes*
¼ *lb. bacon*   *Salt*
2 *medium-sized onions*   *Pepper*
1 *#2 can of whole-kernel*
   corn

Boil 2 pounds of any firm-fleshed fish (halibut and haddock are both excellent) for about 10 minutes in salted water. In the meantime, in a heavy skillet chop up ¼ pound of bacon and 2 medium-sized peeled onions. Let this cook until the onions are golden brown, then add 1 #2 can of whole kernel corn (drained), 1 #2 can of tomatoes, and the boned and broken-up fish. Mix the whole thing well, and cook for about 10 minutes. Serve over toast, or even better, over good-sized baking powder biscuits. Don't count on this recipe's serving more than four people. The first time I ate it, I had three helpings, and could have surrounded a fourth!

One of the favorite breakfast dishes with Britain's Indian Army, that was, was Kedgeree, originally a Hindu dish of rice, lentils, onions, eggs, and spices, called *khichri;* but believe me, it makes a most unusual dinner dish, particularly when smoked fish or lobster are used.

KEDGEREE

2 *lb. fish (haddock, salmon,*	4 *bay leaves*
red snapper, or whiting)	2 *tbsp. butter*
Water	1 *onion*
5 *ounces sherry*	3 *cups of cooked rice*
Salt	2 *hard-boiled eggs*
Pepper	2 *tbsp. chopped parsley*
4 *cloves*	4 *tsp. curry powder*

1 *tsp. Worcestershire sauce*

Cut 2 pounds of fish into pieces, cover with boiling water, add 3 ounces of sherry, salt and pepper to taste, 4 cloves, and 4 bay leaves, and simmer until tender—about 20 minutes. In another saucepan, melt 2 tablespoons of butter and sauté 1 onion, peeled and chopped fine, until tender. Then add 3 cups of cooked rice, 2 chopped hard-boiled eggs, 2 tablespoons of chopped parsley, 4 teaspoons of curry powder (sprinkle in), and 1 teaspoon Worcestershire sauce. Now remove bones from fish, flake, and put into the rice mixture. Moisten the result with ¼ cup of sherry, mix well, place in a covered casserole, and bake 10 minutes in a 400-degree oven. Serve, garnished with slices of hard-boiled eggs.

One June evening in 1949, I had the most interesting and fascinating gastronomic experience I have ever had—learning (to a very limited degree, of course) the art of Cantonese cookery. I watched, and was instructed in every detail of, the preparation of four intriguing dishes—May May Pike, Tahitian Shrimp Feast, Cantonese Beef with Noodles, and Bali Bali Chicken.

For many months Fred Bethke and Jimmy Moy, the genial and gracious hosts of the Shangri-La Restaurant on North State Street in Chicago, had importuned me to come down and learn about Cantonese cookery. I have always enjoyed Cantonese food, the cooking of which is more refined than ordinary Chinese cooking and more authentic. Actually, it is the type of cooking found only in the area surrounding Canton, China.

I went down to the Shangri-La Restaurant, which is one of the most beautiful of its kind in America, and Jimmy Moy took me out to the kitchen and introduced me to Jimmy Chang, who is the head chef. And although it was right in the midst of a busy dinner hour, Chang divorced himself from his supervising duties in the kitchen and went to work for my special benefit. Inasmuch as Chang's knowledge of English is somewhat limited, Jimmy Moy, a charming Boston-born Chinese, acted as interpreter. Moy, by the way, has always been a student of food and has just concluded a course in a Veterinary Meat and Dairy Hygiene School conducted by the U. S. Army.

In less than half an hour, believe it or not, Chang and Moy had instructed me in Cantonese cooking, and Chang had prepared and cooked the above-mentioned four dishes, explaining the how and why of every step.

Three things impressed me about Cantonese cooking. In the first place, it is very quick; not one of the four dishes mentioned above took more than four minutes to prepare.

The second thing was the simplicity of the preparation and cooking of the food. Vegetables were already prepared, and certain basic sauces had been made up. There wasn't a step in the cooking that involved anything intricate. Most of the cooking was done in four huge bowls resembling salad bowls in appearance. They are made of metal and are 2 feet in diameter and 10 inches deep. They are placed over holes on the top of a long range and heated by gas flames. Peanut oil, which is the best cooking agent for Cantonese food, is put in the bowl, then the main ingredients are put in, perhaps some chicken broth, sauces are added and then everything is mixed and gently tossed, and, presto! the dish is ready to serve.

The third thing that impressed me was the cleanliness observed about the kitchen. Every dish at Shangri-La, and undoubtedly at all other first-class Cantonese restaurants, is cooked to an individual order. Perhaps you can get some idea of the activity in the kitchen when I tell you that over 800 individual dishes are cooked on a single busy Saturday night.

Two faucets with water running from them stand between each of two bowls. When an individual order is finished, the spigot is swung to the empty bowl and it is half filled with water. The cook whisks the water around in the hot bowl with a large fiber whisk, and after the bowl is thoroughly cleansed, he whisks out the water into a trough behind the range and, presto! the bowl is immaculately clean and ready for another dish.

Before giving you the recipe for May May Pike, I should like to say a word about the Chinese vegetables. Pea pods are a separate plant, different from ordinary peas, and are raised extensively in California. The pod is very tender, and is slightly sweet to the taste. It should only be partially cooked at any time, so that there is always a little crispness to it when bitten into. Before using, always remove the string from the pea pod as you would from string beans. Pea pods are available only in Chinese grocery stores.

Water chestnuts, when fresh, are difficult to prepare for cooking. So I would advise using the canned water chestnuts which are available in almost any grocery store. Soy sauce is also available in most stores, and Chinese bead molasses is now put up in jars and is not difficult to obtain.

For centuries the Orientals have used a seasoning to give life and taste to their simple and often monotonous diets. But only recently has Mono Sodium glutamate been processed, refined, and purified, and is now marketed under the name of "Ac'cent." It can be purchased in most food specialty shops.

And now here is the first of four delectable Cantonese dishes, May May Pike. The other three dishes mentioned above will be found respectively at the end of the chapters on shellfish (page 124), meat (page 193), and chicken (page 274).

MAY MAY PIKE

2 *fillets of pike* (1 *lb. each*)
1 *egg*
Chicken broth
2 *tbsp. sifted bread flour*
1 *tsp. salt*
4 *ounces peanut oil*
4 *water chestnuts*
12 *whole pea pods*

1 *cup sliced fresh mushrooms*
1 *tbsp. cornstarch*
1 *tbsp. water*
½ *tsp. Ac'cent*
Dash pepper
¼ *tsp. sugar*
1 *tsp. soy sauce*
Slivered little green onions
Slivered sautéed almonds

Take 2 single fillets of pike, weighing about 1 pound each, being sure that all the bones are removed. Slice each fillet into 3 equal pieces.

Make an egg batter as follows: 1 egg, 1 tablespoon of chicken broth, 2 tablespoons of sifted bread flour, ½ teaspoon of salt. Combine these ingredients and beat until smooth. This should have almost the consistency of whipping cream.

Thoroughly coat all surfaces of the slices of fillets with the egg batter.

Into an iron skillet put about 4 ounces of peanut oil, and place the fillets in this when it is hot—about 400 degrees. The oil should just cover the ½-inch-thick fillets. Cook until the batter is slightly browned—about 3 minutes. Drain off most of the oil, leaving only a film of oil in the skillet. Move the pieces of fish to one side of the skillet.

Place in the skillet 4 water chestnuts, thinly sliced, about 12 whole pea pods, 1 cup of sliced fresh mushrooms, and 1 cup of chicken broth. Let this simmer for about 2 minutes, then add the following mixed seasonings: 1 tablespoon of cornstarch mixed with 1 tablespoon of water, ½ teaspoon of salt, ½ teaspoon of Ac'cent, a dash of pepper, ¼ teaspoon of sugar, and 1 teaspoon of soy sauce. Mix this gently, but thoroughly, with the vegetables, cover, and simmer over a moderate flame for about 1 minute.

Remove fillets to a hot platter and then pour the vegetable sauce over them. Garnish with shredded little green onions and slivers of roasted almonds sautéed in a little butter.

(5) SHELLFISH

"For the female of the species is more deadly than the male." Thus wrote Rudyard Kipling.

To deny or affirm the truth of that statement I should have to be an anthropologist, which I am not. Furthermore, as a married man, I'll have no part in any such argument. But I will stand up on my feet and state that the female of the species—as far as crabs are concerned—is more tender and tasty than the male, and I am sure that most of the citizens of Charleston, South Carolina, will wholeheartedly agree.

If you have ever been in that charming and beautiful southern city, you undoubtedly have heard peddlers hawking crabs through the streets. Their "he-crabs she-crabs she-crabs he-crabs" is practically unintelligible to the uninitiated, but their wares are quickly disposed of; and the she-crabs go first. And one of the most delicious dishes concocted from she-crabs is to be found in the dining room of the Fort Sumter Hotel out on the battery. John Cator, the genial director of the hotel, has named it She-Crab Stew in Cup.

SHE-CRAB STEW IN CUP

2 *cups she-crab meat*	1 *cup cooked fresh corn*
2 *small onions*	1 *cup cooked small lima beans*
2 *tbsp. butter*	1 *tsp. Worcestershire sauce*
2 *tbsp. flour*	*Salt*
4 *cups milk*	*Pepper*
1 *cup cream*	4 *tbsp. sherry*

Simmer 2 small peeled onions, chopped fine, in 2 tablespoons of butter until tender. Then add 2 cups of she-crab meat, with their eggs, and let this heat thoroughly. Then add 2 tablespoons of flour, 4 cups of milk and 1 cup of cream, stirring slowly while

94

adding the liquid, and let the mixture boil gently for about 10 minutes. Now add 1 cup of cooked fresh corn shaved off the cob, 1 cup of cooked small lima beans, 1 teaspoon of Worcestershire sauce, and salt and pepper to taste. Let all this simmer for another 10 minutes, then, just before serving, add 4 tablespoons of sherry.

Another dish for which the Fort Sumter Hotel is famous is its Native Crab Meat Deep-Dish Pie. By the way, the Fort Sumter Hotel has a rather unusual public-relations stunt. On small folders they have had printed a series of recipes for which the hotel is famous. All you have to do is ask the waiter for one or all of the series, and he will present them to you so that you can take them home or send them to your friends.

Now here is the Crab Meat Deep-Dish Pie.

NATIVE CRAB MEAT DEEP-DISH PIE

2 *cups cooked crab meat*	1 *tbsp. butter*
1 *cup thin cream sauce*	1 *dash Worcestershire sauce*
3 *little green onions*	*Salt*
½ *cup white wine*	*Pepper*
½ *lb. pastry dough*	

Simmer 3 little green onions, chopped fine, in 1 tablespoon of butter. Add 2 cups of cooked crab meat and let slowly simmer until heated through. Add 1 cup of thin cream sauce and salt and pepper to taste, letting the mixture boil slowly a few minutes before emptying into deep-dish casseroles. Add ½ cup American white wine, cover with your favorite pastry dough, and bake in a moderate oven until the crust is done.

Cooks in Maryland know more tricks with oysters and crabs than a kitten does with a string. So let's cross the Mason-Dixon line and have a try at this epicurean dish. Crab Meat Maryland Yacht Club. When you serve this with flaky, boiled rice, your guests will want to rise at the conclusion of the meal and sing "Dixie."

CRAB MEAT MARYLAND YACHT CLUB

1 *lb. crab meat*	1 *clove garlic*
1 *large green pepper*	3 *ounces dry white wine*
1 *medium-sized onion*	1 *cup consommé*
4 *tbsp. butter*	*Salt*
1 *medium can tomatoes*	*Pepper*
1 *thin slice ham*	*Paprika*
¼ *lb. fresh mushrooms*	*Cayenne pepper*

Cook in butter 1 pound of crab meat (the fresh is better, of course, but you won't go wrong on canned), 1 large green pepper, 1 medium-sized onion, sliced, and 1 thin slice of ham cut in strips, until the onions and pepper are tender. Then add 1 medium can of tomatoes, ¼ pound of fresh mushrooms, 1 clove of garlic, crushed, 3 ounces of dry American white wine, and 1 cup of stock (or canned consommé or bouillon). Cook this mixture over a low flame for 10 minutes, and season to taste with salt, paprika, and cayenne pepper. Serve with dry boiled rice.

I was rather amazed to learn that there are over one thousand species of crabs, and that they're found all over the world. Of all the varieties, my two favorites are the Dungeness and the Alaskan King Crab. The former is very popular in the Pacific Northwest where it is a highly-esteemed delicacy.

The Japanese or Alaskan King Crab is not known so well in the United States. This species of crab is very large, often weighing up to 75 pounds. Before the last war, the Japanese had a fishing monopoly over the king crab, even those caught in Alaskan waters. Only the legs are sold commercially, and because they are very expensive, even wholesale, only the top restaurants in the United States serve them. The meat is white, speckled with a deep crimson. The meat picked from the body is canned.

In nearly all eating places where they serve crabs, deviled crabs are the most popular. The following recipe is rather unusual in that it utilizes rum as a flavoring agent.

STUFFED DEVILED CRABS

1 *lb. fresh crab flakes*	1 *small tomato*
4 *tbsp. lime juice*	½ *clove garlic*
2 *tsp. onion pulp*	1 *tbsp. chopped parsley*
1 *tsp. black pepper*	*Pinch dry mustard*
2 *dashes Tabasco*	*Pinch mace*
Salt	*Pinch basil*
2 *tbsp. butter*	2 *tbsp. light rum*
2 *tbsp. chopped onion*	2 *tbsp. fine breadcrumbs*
2 *tbsp. chopped green pepper*	*Cracker crumbs*

Grated Parmesan cheese

In a bowl mix 1 pound of fresh crab flakes, 4 tablespoons of lime juice, 2 teaspoons of onion pulp, 1 teaspoon of freshly ground black pepper, 2 dashes of Tabasco, and salt to taste. Let this stand in the refrigerator for a couple of hours before using.

In a skillet melt 2 tablespoons of butter and add 2 tablespoons of chopped onions, 2 tablespoons chopped green pepper, 1 small tomato, chopped, ½ clove of crushed garlic, minced, and 1 tablespoon of chopped parsley. Sauté until vegetables are tender. Then add a generous pinch of dry mustard, a pinch each of mace and basil, 2 tablespoons of light rum, and 2 tablespoons of fine breadcrumbs. Stir over a low flame for about 2 minutes.

Now mix the marinated crab flakes with this stuffing, and heat, stirring well, for about 5 minutes. Remove from heat and pack into cleaned crab shells or individual ramekins. Sprinkle with an equal amount of cracker crumbs mixed with grated Parmesan cheese, dot with butter, and bake in a medium oven (350 degrees), until top is browned—about 5 minutes.

The most epicurean of the crab family are the soft-shell crabs. These crabs are not a species; rather, the term is applied to any crab which has shed its old shell and whose new shell has not yet hardened. To my mind, it is a crime to dip this tender crustacean into a batter and fry it. They should always be sautéed in butter and served with lemon juice over them. However, when they are gently sautéed in butter and covered with a champagne and almond sauce, they are out of this world—and the next.

SOFT-SHELL CRABS AMANDINE
WITH CHAMPAGNE SAUCE

12 *soft-shell crabs*	1 *tbsp. chopped chives*
Flour	1 *tbsp. chopped chervil, or*
Salt	*parsley*
Pepper	2 *cups champagne*
½ *cup blanched almonds*	3 *egg yolks*
6 *ounces butter*	½ *cup cream*
	Cayenne pepper

Get 12 soft-shell crabs and have your butcher prepare them for the stove for you, first telling him you are going to sauté them. When you get them home, wash them in cold water, then pat dry with paper toweling and toss very lightly in seasoned flour.

Blanch and shred ½ cup of almonds, and sauté them in about 2 tablespoons of hot butter until they are lightly browned.

In a heavy iron skillet melt 4 ounces of butter, and when it is bubbling hot put in the crabs, shell side down. Reduce the heat and sauté the crabs until browned. After about 5 minutes, turn the crabs, and brown the under side. Watch carefully during the browning process that the crabs don't stick to the pan or burn. When the crabs are nicely browned, remove from the skillet onto a hot platter and keep warm.

To the butter in the skillet add 1 tablespoon of finely-chopped chives and a tablespoon of chopped chervil or parsley. Then add 2 cups of American champagne and simmer for about 5 minutes. Have ready the yolks of 3 eggs beaten together with ½ cup of cream. Add this to the wine broth, being careful not to let the broth boil after the egg mixture is added. Add a pinch of cayenne pepper, salt to taste, and when the broth is thickened, pour it over the crabs. Sprinkle over all the slivered almonds, and serve.

Although I have eaten many times all the clams I can hold, I have never been able to eat all I wanted. Cherrystone clams, with a little lemon juice squeezed over them, are the ideal first course to a dinner. I very often make an entire meal of steamed soft-shell clams with lots of butter and rich clam juice and a chilled bottle of Chablis. I believe that clams are indigenous to the United

States. They are of two kinds, hard shell and soft shell. The hard-shell clams are often called by their Indian name, quahaugs; eaten raw on the half shell they are known either as Cherrystones or, if the smallest, as Littlenecks. The soft-shell clams are found north of Cape Code all the way to the Arctic Ocean. They have a less pungent flavor than the hard clams.

A real Cape Cod specialty is a Clam Pie. This you can duplicate in your own home in the following manner.

NEW ENGLAND CLAM PIE

1 *pint shucked clams*	*Cayenne pepper*
6 *slices bacon*	*Thyme*
1 *large onion*	*½ cup light cream*
4 *small potatoes, sliced thin*	*¼ cup clam liquor*
Salt	*2 tbsp. dry white wine*
Pepper	*Flaky pastry dough*

Drain 1 pint of shucked clams, or canned clams, and cut the clams in half crosswise.

Chop 6 slices of bacon, and fry in a skillet until crisp. Then add the halved clams and simmer for 3 minutes.

In a casserole, arrange a layer of the clams and chopped bacon, then a layer of thin onion slices, then a layer of thin raw potato slices. Season this last layer with salt and pepper to taste, and sprinkle with a pinch of thyme and a scant pinch of cayenne pepper. Repeat these layers until the clams, and onion and potato slices are used up. Pour over all ½ cup of light cream, ¼ cup of clam liquor, and 2 tablespoons of dry American white wine.

Cover with a flaky pastry dough (your own or a prepared mix), pressing its edges to the rim of the casserole, and cutting two gashes in the top to allow the steam to escape. Bake in a moderate oven (350 degrees) for about 30 minutes. Serve very hot from the casserole.

The following might be called a Cape Cod success story.

The tiny steamed clams, dripping with rich broth, were so succulent that fifty of them seemed a very small order to a hungry me, so, as I got down to the last six or so, I began calling for more. But when the demure young lady in a white starched uniform assured me that even better things were coming, I subsided. And how right she was! In a few minutes she was back, her tray loaded.

First she transferred an ample dish of pickled beets and tiny gherkins to my table. Then followed two ears of steaming, golden corn, a heaping plate of French fried potatoes still sizzling and crackling from the deep fat, a sauce dish brimming with melted butter, and finally the crowning glory of New England's gustatory delights, a two-pound baked lobster, its huge claws, legs, and sides a brilliant red, the tail meat snowy white, and the body cavity filled with an aromatic stuffing topped by golden breadcrumbs. I ate until I was sure I could hold no more, but somehow I managed to find room for a piece of native blueberry pie topped with ice cream!

After finishing this unforgettable meal, I miraculously got up from the table without the aid of a derrick, and went in search of the restaurant's boss man, determined to pry the lobster recipe out of him. And so I met Bill Cox . . . in his large, immaculate kitchen.

Bill Cox is a big, affable man (no lean and hungry chef, he) with blue eyes that are always smiling behind his spectacles. For nearly half of his 64 years he has been feeding people on Cape Cod. A native New Englander, he came to Hyannis, the metropolis of the Cape, in 1911 and started a hotel and restaurant. Fifteen years later he sold it for an amount of money most people only dream of acquiring by the time they are too old to enjoy it, and vowed he would never serve another meal again. For five years he lived the pleasant life of a Cape Codder—sailing and fishing in the summer, hunting ducks and geese in the autumn, and in the winter sitting around a pine-log fire listening to old salts spin their yarns of the sea. But by 1931 he found himself waking up every morning wondering what in hell he was going to do during the day, and when he could stand it no longer, he built a restaurant overlooking Nantucket Sound. Today Bill Cox's Sea Grill serves from 250 to 400 people a day.

"So you want to know about the baked stuffed lobster," he said when we were seated in his tiny office. "Well, seeing as how you aren't figuring on opening an eating place in competition with me, I'll tell you." So, here it is.

BAKED STUFFED LOBSTER, BILL COX

4 *live 2-lb. lobsters*	½ *tbsp. thyme*
1 *large yellow onion*	2 *ounces butter*
1 *clove garlic*	*Salt*
4 *cups fine breadcrumbs*	*Pepper*
2 *tbsp. capers*	2 *ounces sherry*

"After you've split open your live lobsters," Bill continued, "run your finger from their heads to their tails, scraping out all the dark green stuff and the coral in the cavities, and set it aside for the stuffing. Be sure to remove and discard the small sac, which is the stomach.

"Grind up 1 large yellow onion and 1 clove of garlic, and mix with 4 cups of fine breadcrumbs. Add salt and pepper to taste, ½ tablespoon of thyme, 2 ounces of butter, melted, and all the green stuff and coral from the lobster. Mix everything thoroughly, moistening the mixture with about 2 ounces of sherry.

"Place the 4 whole lobsters, each one split, under the broiler for a few minutes, then take them out and stuff their cavities with the breadcrumb mixture. Also stuff the tips with capers (about 2 tablespoons). Place the stuffed lobsters in a moderate oven, with the tails tucked under the grilling to prevent curling, and bake for about 30 to 40 minutes. That's all there is to it."

Not quite all. You eat them, and offer up a prayer of thanks to Bill Cox!

The lobster is rightly called the aristocrat of the sea. In the market or in restaurants they are not inexpensive, but they're worth every penny you pay. They can be cooked in almost any manner: baked, broiled, boiled, fried, made up into stew, made into a soup, or made into a salad. And no matter how you cook them, they are succulent morsels.

One thing I like about lobsters is that you can wade into them with both hands going. The hell with the fork except to extract the body meat. When all the meat possible has been extracted, toss your Emily Post out the window, tie a napkin around your chin and tear the body apart with your bare hands. And with tooth and claw extract what is edible from your lobster. Break off each little leg and suck out all the juices and little tidbits of meat. Take a piece of bread and sop up everything that remains in the body shell until it seems as clean as a whistle. When I finish with a lobster, there's not even enough left to keep a gnat alive. You'll particularly want to use this method of devouring a lobster when you are served Lobster Thermidor.

This recipe was reputedly created for Napoleon Bonaparte. It was apparently first served to the Emperor sometime between July 19 and August 17, because that period was the eleventh month in the calendar of the First Republic and was called Thermidor.

LOBSTER THERMIDOR

2 1½-lb. lobsters	¾ cup milk
4 tbsp. olive oil	¼ cup cream
1 medium-sized onion	2 tbsp. dry mustard
1 cup sliced fresh mushrooms	Pinch paprika
2 tbsp. butter	2 tbsp. grated Parmesan cheese
2 tbsp. flour	⅔ cup sherry
¼ tsp. salt	Breadcrumbs
Pinch cayenne pepper	Additional butter

Split 2 1½-pound lobsters, removing the sac at the back of the head.

Put 4 tablespoons of olive oil in a large pan, heat it, and then put the lobsters in, split side down. Cover and cook slowly for about 10 to 12 minutes. Remove the lobsters from the pan, remove the meat from the bodies and claws, reserving the shells, which should be kept warm.

To the oil the lobsters were sautéed in (adding a little more, if necessary), add one medium-sized onion, peeled and chopped, and 1 cup of sliced fresh mushrooms. Let this cook until tender.

In another pan melt 2 tablespoons of butter over a medium flame. Stir in 2 tablespoons of flour, ¼ teaspoon salt, and a pinch of cayenne pepper, and when smooth, add ¾ cup of milk. Stir over the fire until mixture comes to a boil. Then add this mixture to the mushroom and onion mixture, together with ¼ cup of cream, 2 tablespoons of dry mustard, a pinch of paprika, and 2 tablespoons of grated Parmesan cheese. Reduce this whole mixture to a thick creamy consistency with about ⅔ cup of sherry. Stir the cut-up lobster meat into the sauce and stuff the lobster shells with the mixture. Sprinkle the tops of the lobsters with breadcrumbs, dot with butter, and put under the broiler to brown. Then serve.

Prunier's Restaurant in Paris was the most celebrated seafood restaurant in Europe for many years. Prunier's daughter, or maybe the late Emil himself, devised an unusual way to serve broiled or roast lobster. Butter was poured over it and then a small glass of whiskey was added and set alight, and I can assure you that was not wasting good whiskey! However, here is an even tastier way— Lobster Roasted with Cognac.

LOBSTER ROASTED WITH COGNAC

1 2-*lb. lobster*	4 *tbsp. butter*
Salt	*Pinch dry mustard*
Pepper	*Pinch thyme*
	3 *ounces cognac*

Split a lobster in half, remove the small sac, break the claws, and place in a baking pan, shell side down. Salt and pepper to taste, and on each half put 2 tablespoons of butter mixed with just a pinch of dry mustard and a pinch of thyme. Place lobster in a hot oven (450 degrees) and bake for 15 minutes, or perhaps a little longer, basting well.

To serve, place the lobster halves on a silver platter and pour the basting liquid over them. Pour on 3 ounces of good cognac and set the cognac alight. Baste again with the liquid, and serve red hot.

Another taste-teasing way of baking lobster is to cover it with a deviled sauce. The Italians call this Lobster Fra Diabolo.

DEVILED LOBSTER

2 1½-lb. lobsters
¼ cup olive oil
1 clove garlic
1 medium-sized onion
½ green pepper

4 tomatoes
2 tbsp. chopped parsley
1 tsp. oregano
Dash Tabasco
Pinch cayenne pepper

¾ cup Chianti-type wine

Get 2 lobsters weighing about 1½ pounds apiece. Insert a sharp knife between the body and tail and sever the spinal cord. Put the lobsters on their back and split them open. Remove the small sac just back of the head, but not the green and coral parts. Crack the large claws.

In a skillet heat ¼ cup of olive oil, and brown 1 clove of chopped garlic in it. Add 1 medium-sized onion, chopped, and ½ green pepper, seeded and chopped, and cook until tender. Then add 4 tomatoes, cut up, 2 tablespoons of chopped parsley, 1 teaspoon of oregano, a dash of Tabasco, a generous pinch of cayenne pepper, and ¾ cup of Chianti-type dry red wine. Simmer for about 10 or 15 minutes.

Put the lobsters, cut side up, in a greased baking dish and pour the sauce over them. Bake in a 375-degree oven for about 20 minutes, or until the lobster meat is tender.

Homard à l'Americaine is a very great preparation. Literally translated, it means "lobster American style," and yet there is nothing American about it. It originated in Europe. For a long time this puzzled me, and I don't like to be puzzled. I made inquiries around and about, but no one could solve the mystery for me. One of the readers of my column wrote me that Homard à l'Americaine was a creation of Peter's Café Americaine in Paris, and his authority for that statement was J. Gancel in Gancel's Encyclopedia of Modern Cooking. Finally, one day when I was having lunch with Vincent de Mesemy, Chicago's bon vivant who was educated in the Jesuit College in Dole, France, and Arnold Shircliffe, one of Chicago's best restaurateurs, I told them of my confusion and they really set me back on my heels by stating emphatically that Homard à l'Americaine is an American creation. They pointed out that in Europe they do not have lobsters such as we have in America (with large front claws), but Crustacea called *langoustes,* which are small lobsters without claws. Inasmuch as the recipe for *Homard à l'Americaine* calls for the tail and the claws of the lobster to be cut up in large pieces and cooked at first in their segments of shell, Messrs. de Mesemy and Shircliffe seemed to have an incontrovertible point.

It was Charles Collins, the erudite conductor of the "Line o' Type or Two" column in the *Chicago Daily Tribune,* who came up with another solution. He pointed out that *Amorica* (also spelled *Aremoria*) was an old Latin name for the northwest coast of France and that *à l'Americaine* was probably a corruption of *à l'Amoricaine,* which means "Brittany style" or "in the Breton way."

Well, there you have it, boys and girls; you pays your money and you takes your choice, but for my dough *à l'Americaine* or *l'Amoricaine* means delicious, delectable, and terrific.

To prepare the dish properly you've got to be a murderer of sorts. Your lobster has got to come into your kitchen alive and must be cut up alive to make the perfect recipe. I hope there is no society for the prevention of cruelty to lobsters; for if there is, it will be on my neck as well as on the necks of a number of cooking authorities.

HOMARD À L'AMERICAINE

1 *live lobster*	½ *clove garlic*
4 *tbsp. olive oil*	2 *little green onions*
2 *tbsp. butter*	1 *chopped carrot*
½ *cup cognac*	1 *tsp. parsley*
Salt	1 *tsp. chervil*
Pepper, freshly ground	1 *tsp. tarragon*
Paprika	2 *tomatoes*
1 *cup dry white wine*	1 *tbsp. beef extract*
2 *tbsp. tomato paste*	*Pinch cayenne pepper*

Boiled rice

Split the lobster and remove the coral to a separate plate and retain. Separate the tail and claws from the body and cut them in large pieces with a chopper or a heavy knife, leaving the pieces in their segments of shell. Discard the sac.

Heat 4 tablespoons of olive oil in a large heavy iron skillet. When it is smoking hot, put in the pieces of lobster and heat them until they turn bright red. This should take approximately 10 minutes. When the lobster is the desired color, take it out and remove to a separate platter, throwing away the oil it has cooked in. Now put in the skillet a generous tablespoon of butter, let it melt, and return the lobster to the pan. Pour over it ½ cup of cognac, or any good brandy that will burn, set it alight and let it burn for a moment. Before it burns off, cover the skillet for a moment to extinguish the flame. Next add a little salt, a little paprika, a little pepper, and a cup of American dry white wine.

Let the lobster boil in this for a few minutes, then reduce the flame and add one tablespoon of tomato paste, ½ clove of garlic, minced, 2 green onions, finely chopped, 1 chopped carrot, a teaspoon of finely-chopped parsley, a teaspoon of chervil, a teaspoon of finely-chopped tarragon, and the pulp of 2 fresh tomatoes, with the seeds and any juice removed. Let this whole thing simmer for about a half hour.

At the end of the cooking time remove the lobster to the dish it is to be served in, leaving the sauce in the skillet and reduce it a little over a very low flame. Rub one tablespoon of butter into the coral of the lobster; add one tablespoon of the best beef extract and 1 tablespoon of tomato paste. Put this mixture into the sauce and let it thicken. Taste for seasoning and, if necessary, add additional salt, pepper, and perhaps a pinch of cayenne pepper. Let the sauce simmer for a moment or two, then pass through a sieve directly over the lobster. Serve with boiled rice.

I don't suppose, among the elite, there is a better known dish than Lobster à la Newburg. In the gay 90's this dish was practically a "must" at gay after-theater parties. I remember chuckling over a remark of a perky old *boulevardier* in New York when he was recounting some of his past escapades. "In private dining rooms and bachelor apartments Lobster à la Newburg served in a chafing dish and an iced bottle of champagne were considered to be the perfect prelude to a seduction." (Webster: "to seduce" . . . "to lead or draw (one) astray, as into an evil, foolish, or disastrous course; to tempt or entice.") I have heard a very interesting story about the origin of lobster à la Newburg. I don't know whether it's true or not, but it is still interesting.

During the Civil War one of the well-known men-about-town in New York was a chap by the name of Ben Wenburg, whose favorite eating place was Delmonico's. He was very fond of gathering a group of friends together and preparing his own special lobster dish, which was boiled lobster served in a creamy, aromatic sauce. In honor of his wealthy patron Delmonico named this dish Lobster à la Wenburg, and it became a specialty of that famous restaurant. Sometime later, however, Delmonico and Wenburg quarreled, and in retaliation Delmonico reversed the first three letters of his former patron's now odious name and called it Lobster à la Newburg.

Lobster à la Newburg, of course, calls for precooked lobster. If you don't want to boil your own lobster or use canned lobster meat, you can buy boiled lobster at the market. But here's a tip on buying cooked lobsters. Be sure the lobster was alive when it was put into boiling water. If it was, the tail curls up underneath and, if pulled out straight, springs back into place. However, if the tail hangs limp and lifeless, Mr. Lobster had passed on to his ancestors before he was cooked.

LOBSTER À LA NEWBURG

3 *cups boiled fresh lobster meat*	¼ *tsp. dry mustard*
	1 *cup rich cream*
6 *ounces butter*	¼ *lb. fresh mushrooms*
3 *tsp. flour*	2 *egg yolks*
Salt	2 *ounces brandy*
Pepper	2 *ounces Madeira*
Dash paprika	*Buttered toast*

Melt 2 ounces of butter in the top section of a double boiler, placed over the lower section which has been half filled with boiling water. Gradually add 3 teaspoons of flour, blending well. Add salt and pepper to taste, a dash of paprika, and ¼ teaspoon of dry mustard. Mix thoroughly and cook for about 2 minutes. Then gradually pour in 1 cup of rich cream, stirring constantly. When well blended, remove from the flame to cool.

In a saucepan melt 2 ounces of butter, and sauté ¼ pound of fresh sliced mushrooms for about 10 minutes, or until tender. Keep them hot.

Break 2 egg yolks into a bowl, and beat thoroughly. When they are foamy, pour on them part of the cream mixture from the top of the double boiler, stirring constantly. When they are well blended, return the mixture to the double boiler and add the sautéed mushrooms, mixing gently.

In a skillet melt 2 ounces of butter over a medium flame, and put in 3 cups of lobster meat, cut up into pieces. Pour 2 ounces of brandy over the meat, and light it. When it burns out, let the lobster meat heat, and then add it and the juice to the cream and mushroom sauce. Mix in gently 2 ounces of Madeira, heat for a minute or so, and then serve very hot over slices of buttered toast.

While I invariably prefer fresh comestibles to the canned varieties, there are times when the latter come in mighty handy, particularly lobster and crabmeat. Some night when friends have dropped in, and you've had a session of bridge or gin rummy, and along about midnight when everybody has a yen for a snack, try Lobster au Rhum. It's one of those things you can prepare in a jiffy, and at the same time garner a lot of credit to yourself as an amateur chef. All you need is some good sharp American Cheddar cheese (which is now available again) and a can or two of lobster meat (which any self-respecting host or hostess ought to have stocked in the pantry).

LOBSTER AU RHUM

1 *large can lobster meat*   ⅓ *lb. sharp Cheddar cheese*
2 *ounces butter*   3 *ounces light rum*

Melt the 2 ounces of butter and ⅓ pound of sharp Cheddar cheese in a saucepan. Then stir in 3 ounces of rum. Just as it all begins to boil, add 1 large can of lobster meat which has been shredded. Stir this for a couple of minutes or so, until the lobster is thoroughly heated, and then serve on toast.

I have often wondered who the first man was who ever ate an oyster. I think most people feel that he was a pretty brave fellow, but my guess is that he was a very discerning chap. The farthest back I have been able to trace the oyster has been to the first century of the Christian era. Apicius, the great Roman epicure, was reported to have sent oysters from Britain to the Emperor Trajan who reigned between the years A.D. 53 and 117. Certainly oysters were served at Roman banquets and were greatly enjoyed.

The oyster is a succulent morsel, cooked or raw. Our most famous American oysters are Blue Points, from the south side of Long Island and the Chesapeake Bay; Lynnhavens from Virginia; and Cotuits from Massachusetts. Oysters were apparently highly prized by the American Indians, who ate them in prodigious quantities. There are today mounds of oyster shells extant along the Atlantic coast from Maine to Florida.

There are many tall tales about oyster feasts. It has been said that a man fond of oysters can eat upwards to a half a bushel—unshucked. Probably the best known oyster feast is that of the Walrus and the Carpenter in Lewis Carroll's *Through the Looking Glass:*

> "O Oysters, come and walk with us,"
> The Walrus did beseech.
> "A pleasant walk, a pleasant talk,
> Along the briny beach:"
>
> .   .   .
>
> . . . four young Oysters hurried up,
> All eager for the treat:
>
> .   .   .
>
> Four other Oysters followed them
> And yet another four;
> And thick and fast they came at last,
> And more, and more, and more—
> All hopping through the frothy waves,
> And scrambling to the shore.
>
> The Walrus and the Carpenter
> Walked on a mile or so,
> And then they rested on a rock
> Conveniently low:
> And all the little Oysters stood
> And waited in a row.
>
> .   .   .
>
> "A loaf of bread," the Walrus said,
> "Is what we chiefly need:
> "Pepper and vinegar besides

"Are very good indeed—
"Now if you're ready, Oysters dear,
"We can begin to feed."

.   .   .

"O Oysters," said the Carpenter,
"You've had a pleasant run!
"Shall we be trotting home again?"
But answer came there none—
And this was scarcely odd, because
They'd eaten every one.

One of the most celebrated oyster dishes is Oysters Rockefeller, which is said to have originated many years ago in Antoine's, the famous New Orleans restaurant. According to the legend, the guests to whom it was served exclaimed, "This is as rich as Rockefeller." And so it was appropriately named Oysters Rockefeller. The recipe is supposed to be a deep, dark secret which utilizes eighteen ingredients. This one only contains twelve, but for my money it can't be improved upon.

OYSTERS ROCKEFELLER

3 *dozen large oysters on half shell*
1 *cup minced raw spinach*
6 *little green onions*
¼ *cup minced parsley*
¼ *cup minced celery leaves*
¼ *tsp. tarragon*
¼ *tsp. chervil*
Dash Tabasco
Salt
Pepper
½ *cup buttered breadcrumbs*
1 *tbsp. Herbsaint or Pernod*
½ *cup sweet butter*

Put through a food chopper, using the finest blade, washed spinach leaves separated from their stems, 6 little green onions, celery leaves and parsley, so that you come out with the amounts indicated above. It wouldn't do any harm to put the above ingredients through the food chopper a second time. Sprinkle into the chopped ingredients ¼ teaspoon each of tarragon and chervil, a dash of Tabasco, salt and freshly ground black pepper to taste. Then mix in ½ cup of fine breadcrumbs, which have been browned in a little butter, and add 1 tablespoon of Herbsaint or Pernod, which are absinthe substitutes. If, by any chance, you are the fortunate possessor of some real absinthe (which is no longer permitted to be manufactured), use it, of course. Next, work in ½ cup of sweet (unsalted) butter into the mixture, and knead thoroughly. This is the paste that makes the sauce.

Place 3 dozen large raw oysters on the half shell in a baking pan, or pie tins, filled almost to the brim with rock salt (that's the kind you used in an ice-cream freezer, remember?). Place in a preheated 400-degree oven for about 5 minutes, or until the edges of the oysters begin to curl. Then place a full tablespoon of the sauce over each oyster, return them to the hot oven for about another 5 minutes, and serve immediately. But don't blame me when you suddenly realize that you haven't got the million dollars they taste like!

Creamed oysters on freshly made hot waffles are wonderful for a Sunday breakfast. Nor is there hardly anything better on a cold day than a big bowl of oyster stew made with half milk and half cream. Oysters à la Poulette is a grand late-supper specialty and is fun to make in a chafing dish.

OYSTERS À LA POULETTE

24 *freshly opened oysters*
2 *tbsp. butter*
1 *pint rich cream*
1 *small white onion*
Celery salt
1 *tbsp. Worcestershire sauce*
¼ *tsp. paprika*
1 *tsp. minced parsley*
Dash mace
½ *cup sliced mushrooms*
3 *ounces dry white wine*
2 *egg yolks*

Hot buttered toast

Drain 2 dozen freshly opened oysters.

In a chafing dish melt a tablespoon of butter. Add to it 1 pint of rich cream, lightly beaten, the juice of 1 small peeled white onion, celery salt to taste, 1 tablespoon of Worcestershire sauce, ¼ teaspoon of paprika, 1 teaspoon of minced parsley, a dash of mace, ½ cup of sliced fresh mushrooms which have been sautéed in 1 tablespoon of butter until tender, and 3 ounces of dry American white wine. Allow this mixture to come just to the boiling point, add the whole oysters and poach gently until the edges begin to curl. Then stir in 2 lightly beaten egg yolks, and cook over a low heat until the mixture thickens. Check for additional seasoning, and pour over slices of hot buttered toast, serving immediately.

The swankiest oyster dish I know of is Oysters in Champagne and its creation can immeasurably enhance one's reputation as an amateur chef.

OYSTERS IN CHAMPAGNE

12 *large or 24 small oysters*	*Oyster juice*
1 *cup American champagne*	1 *tbsp. butter*
1 *cup beef bouillon*	*Salt*
(*or consommé*)	*Freshly ground pepper*

Into your chafing dish pour 1 cup of American champagne and 1 cup of beef bouillon or consommé. Bring this mixture to a boil. The minute it boils add the juice from 12 large, or 24 small, oysters. When the mixture reboils, add the oysters, and extinguish the flame under the chafing dish. After a moment or two add 1 tablespoon of butter, season to taste with salt and freshly ground pepper, and serve.

If you are one of those souls who considers his Lenten sacrifice to be fulfilled by giving up truffles, roast wild boar, Napoleon brandy or dollar cigars, you may not be interested in Lenten dishes. But let me assure you there are recipes for many Lenten dishes that are most delectable, and once you've tried them, you'll want to repeat them even after Lent is over. The following, Oyster Scallop, is in this category.

OYSTER SCALLOP

3 *cups cracker crumbs*	*Pepper*
2 *cups canned whole-kernel*	1 *pint bulk oysters*
corn	*Nutmeg*
1 *tbsp. minced onion*	*Thin cream*
Salt	¾ *cup dry white wine*
Pinch mace	*Butter*

Drain 1 pint of bulk oysters, reserving their liquor.

Mix together in a large bowl 2 cups of canned whole-kernel corn, drained, and 1 tablespoon of minced onion. Season to taste with salt and pepper, and add a pinch of mace.

In a buttered baking dish spread 1 cup of coarse cracker crumbs. Top them with the onion and corn mixture, and cover that with another cup of coarse cracker crumbs. Then add a layer of the oysters, and sprinkle them lightly with freshly ground black pepper to taste and a pinch of nutmeg. Then cover the oyster layer with a third cup of cracker crumbs.

Add enough thin cream to the oyster liquor to make ½ cup, and add to this liquid ¾ cup of dry American white wine. Stir it well, and pour over the contents of the baking dish. Dot liberally with butter, and bake in a moderate over (350 degrees) for about 20 to 25 minutes, or until golden brown.

The following recipe I picked up in Cape Cod after having the dish for luncheon. Since then I have served it not only as a luncheon dish, but also as an hors d'oeuvre before dinner when the *apéritif* was chilled dry sherry. Don't serve hard liquor with Oyster-Capped Mushrooms.

OYSTER-CAPPED MUSHROOMS

Mushrooms	*Salt*
Butter	*Freshly ground pepper*
Dry white wine	*Buttered toast*
Oysters	*Water cress*

Cut the stems off as many large mushrooms as you desire to serve, and sauté the caps in butter until tender. Then place them, cup side up, in a buttered baking dish. Into each mushroom cap pour about ½ teaspoon (more or less, according to what the cap will hold) of very dry American white wine. Then top each mushroom cap with an oyster, season with salt and freshly ground pepper to taste, and top with about a teaspoon of butter for each oyster. Bake in a moderate oven (350 degrees) until the edges of the oysters begin to curl, and serve hot on pieces of buttered toast. Garnish each serving with water cress.

There is one more recipe for oysters that I must include in this book, not only because it is so very delicious, but because there is a cute connotation to the dish. Some people call it Oyster Loaf, but I much prefer the Creole designation, *La Mediatrice,* which translated means "the peacemaker." It really is a gastronomic masterpiece—fried oysters served in a hollowed-out loaf of bread.

As far as I can determine, it received its name from one of two sources. When Louisiana parents came home from a party in the small hours and found their children worried and fretful, they'd present them with this loaf of bread filled with oysters. However, a version that I much prefer is the one where the lord and master of the household, coming home in the wee small hours of the morning with a load which he was having difficulty carrying, would present his irate wife with *La Mediatrice*. I have never tried this pacifier, but is sounds like a good gag.

LA MEDIATRICE

1 *unsliced loaf of French bread*	*Salt*
2 *dozen oysters*	*Pepper*
Flour	*Yellow corn meal*
Beaten yolk of one egg	*Fat*
1 *tsp. sherry*	*Slivers of dill pickle*

Cut off the top of an entire loaf of French bread and scoop out the inside to make a basket, leaving about ½ inch of crust all around. Toast the basket and the lid, butter them generously, and keep them warm.

Dip the oysters first in flour, then in the beaten egg yolk, which has been seasoned with salt and pepper and a teaspoon of sherry, and finally dip them in the yellow corn meal. Then fry the oysters in hot fat until brown. Remove them from the fat and drain, and then place them in the toasted loaf. Lay thin slivers of dill pickles over the oysters, place the lid on top and pop the loaf into the oven to get thoroughly warm.

I suppose every American visitor to Paris has, at one time or another, eaten *Coquille Sainte Jacques,* one of the glories of French cuisine. However, there is no reason why you can't duplicate this dish, made with scallops, right in your own home in the authentic French manner. But here's a word of advice. Try to get small, or bay, scallops—the large sea scallops are far less delicate and they have to be cut into halves or quarters.

If you want to impress your friends and if you have a French accent, say, "We'd like to have you over to dinner Tuesday night. We're having Coquille Sainte Jacques." Otherwise, say, "Come on over and try some damn good scallops."

COQUILLE SAINTE JACQUES
(Scallops)

2 *lb. fresh scallops*	*Freshly ground pepper*
1 *pint dry white wine*	*Pinch thyme*
Salt	*Pinch marjoram*
4 *tbsp. butter*	1½ *tbsp. flour*
1 *cup sliced mushrooms*	*Rich cream*
4 *little green onions*	*Fine breadcrumbs*
1 *tbsp. minced parsley*	*Paprika*

Heat 1 pint of dry American white wine, and add 2 pounds of washed fresh scallops along with a pinch of salt. Simmer for about 10 minutes. When the scallops become very white, drain them, reserving the liquid. Keep the scallops warm.

In a saucepan melt 4 tablespoons of butter, then add 1 cup of sliced fresh mushrooms, 4 little green onions, chopped, 1 tablespoon of minced parsley, salt and freshly ground pepper to taste, and a pinch each of marjoram and thyme. When the mushrooms and onions are tender, add about 1½ tablespoons of flour and stir until smooth. Then slowly pour in the warm scallop broth (wine). Add enough rich cream—about 2 tablespoons—to thicken the sauce (it must not be thin). Now add a pinch of paprika and the scallops, each cut into 2 or 4 pieces, depending on the size. After blending the whole over a low flame, cool slightly, and then fill buttered scallop shells with the mixture, which should be heavy enough to form a neat mold. Sprinkle a few fine breadcrumbs over each mound, dot with butter, and place under the broiler flame. Cook until the crust is golden brown.

Why the name of one of the most delectable of crustaceans should be used as a term of opprobrium has always puzzled me. I am referring, of course, to the shrimp. True, he is small; but his goodness is mighty, and he is greatly appreciated in many parts of the world. If Mr. Webster were alive, I think I would write him a letter and strenuously object to one of his definitions of shrimp, namely, a "diminutive or contemptible person or thing."

In the Far East, in France, and in the Gulf States of this country, shrimps are an important item of food. Shrimps cooked in deep fat with garlic are sold by street vendors in Portuguese cities and are eaten on the spot like popcorn. And are they good! While I deplore overemphasis on vitamins and such things in food, shrimps contain those natural protectives against winter health trials, vitamins A, B, and D, and they have a high iodine content.

One of the most delightful shrimp dishes I ever ate was served in the home of Walt Newton, a well-known announcer on the Mutual Broadcasting System. Walt, a Texan, is an excellent host, and instead of lounging in the living room while his better half slaved over a hot stove, he donned an apron and invited us into the kitchen, where he set about preparing what he calls Shrimps Jubalai.

SHRIMPS JUBALAI

2 lb. fresh shrimps	4 bay leaves
2 tbsp. peanut oil	1 tsp. thyme
3 medium-sized onions	2 tsp. chili powder
3 small cloves garlic	Salt
8 stalks Pascal celery	Pepper
1 green pepper	1 4-ounce can mushrooms
1 #2½ can tomatoes	1 small can pimentos

Boiled rice

Into a fairly large skillet with a close-fitting cover put 2 table-spoons of peanut oil (a salad oil may be used, but it's not as good). When the oil is hot, add 3 medium-sized onions, chopped, and 3 small cloves of garlic, peeled and sliced. When the onions are yellow and tender, add ¾ of the chopped celery (including all the leaves). Next, put into the mixture 1 chopped green pepper, and cook over a medium flame for 5 minutes. Now put into the mixture a #2½ can of tomatoes, along with 4 bay leaves, 1 teaspoon thyme, 2 teaspoons of chili powder, and salt and pepper to taste. Put the lid on the skillet, and let everything cook for 10 minutes.

Next add to the mixture 2 pounds of washed and shelled shrimp, and the contents of both a 4-ounce can of mushrooms and a small can of pimentos. Cook for about 7 minutes. Then add the remainder of the chopped celery and cook for about 3 minutes longer. This adds the final "Chinese touch," in that the bits of celery, cooking for only 3 minutes, remain crunchy and tasty.

Serve Shrimps Jubalai over flaky boiled rice (1½ cups uncooked).

One of my favorite friends while I was out in Hollywood was Smiley Burnette. If you're a horse opera fan, you've seen him as the comedy character in Gene Autry's films. He weighs some 225 pounds, and, as his name implies, he is always smiling. He loves music (when I last was in his home, he had three pianos, guitars, banjos, etc.); his hobby is collecting hotel letterheads, his passion is a big, sleek, shiny automobile, and his avocation is eating. Out in the San Fernando valley, where he lives, he has a crony who is an Italian and who cooks up fabulous meals for Smiley and his friends. One dish I shall never forget—*Shrimp à la Italia.* Smiley snagged the recipe for me, and here it is.

SHRIMPS À LA ITALIA

2 *lb. fresh shrimps*	*Salt*
¼ *lb. butter*	*Pepper*
½ *cup olive oil*	1 *tsp. cayenne pepper*
2 *large onions*	1 *small can tomatoes*
3 *leeks*	1 *small can Italian tomato*
1 *clove garlic*	*paste*
¼ *cup chives, chopped*	2 *cups consommé*
1 *pint dry white wine*	1 *tbsp. chopped parsley*

Place about a ¼ pound of butter and ½ cup of olive oil in a heavy skillet. When it is hot, put in 2 large onions, 3 leeks, 1 clove of garlic, and ¼ cup of chives, all chopped fine. (If you haven't any chives, the tops of young green onions will do nicely.) When the ingredients are golden brown, add 2 pounds of fresh shrimps in their shells.

When the shrimps start to turn pink, add one pint of American dry white wine, salt and pepper to taste, and 1 level teaspoon of cayenne pepper. Then mix everything thoroughly. Cook for about

10 minutes over a moderate flame. Now remove the shrimp. To the mixture in the skillet add 1 small can of tomatoes and 1 small can of tomato paste (Italian, if you can get it) and cook for about 5 minutes over a slow flame. Then strain the mixture through a sieve. To the strained mixture add 2 cups of soup stock, or consommé.

While the sauce is cooking, shell and clean the shrimps. Just before serving, return the shrimps to the sauce, add 1 tablespoon of chopped parsley, and heat for 5 minutes.

With this dish serve crusty French bread, or better still, garlic bread, and have plenty of good American Chianti to wash everything down.

It's no longer news when men take up cooking as a hobby and become excellent amateur chefs. But when a man not only attains a high degree of perfection in the art of preparing and cooking scores of gourmet dishes, but mimeographs his recipes, binds them, and sends them to his friends—that's something to write about!

Colonel Frank Dorn, Assistant Commandant of the Armed Forces Information School at Carlisle Barracks, near Harrisburg, Pennsylvania, sometime ago put out his own recipe book, which he called "Recipes à la Dorn," bound between two Manila covers. It comprised 80 mimeographed pages containing 100 recipes for delicious dishes running from Chinese Watermelon Soup to *Gateau à l'Orange* (orange cake). So successful was this book among his friends that he recently enlarged it and has renamed it "Eat and Enjoy It." This time there are over 200 pages, and the book includes suggested menus for breakfasts, luncheons, dinners, cocktail parties, and, believe it or not, a suggested diet for reducing, not only the waistline, but household bills as well.

Colonel Dorn is a handsome, distinguished-looking bachelor in his early forties. He has seen considerable service in the Orient, and he served with the late General "Vinegar Joe" Stilwell in Burma. Invitations to his dinner parties on the post are much sought after, and I am told that his table settings and service are like his food—impeccable! One of his most unusual dishes is Shrimps à la William Washington.

SHRIMPS À LA WILLIAM WASHINGTON

3 *lb. fresh shrimps*	*Salt*
8 *eggs*	*Pepper*
1 *tsp. sugar*	12 *small bay leaves*
2 *cups sour cream*	½ *cup brandy*
Dash Tabasco	½ *cup chopped bacon*

1 cup grated Parmesan cheese

Boil 3 pounds of fresh shrimps in their shells, with seasoning added to the water, for 30 minutes. Then shell the shrimps, cut in half lengthwise, and set aside. Next, beat up the whites of 8 eggs, adding 1 teaspoon of sugar, until stiff. Beat the yolks of *4* eggs *only,* and fold in 2 cups of sour cream. Then fold the yolk and cream mixture into the whites.

And now for the cooking. On the bottom of a well-buttered casserole spread a ½-inch layer of the egg and cream mixture. Then cover the surface with a layer of shrimps. Sprinkle with salt and pepper to taste, a dash of Tabasco, and distribute over the shrimps 6 small bay leaves, ¼ cup each of chopped bacon and grated Parmesan cheese. Then pour over all ¼ cup of brandy. Now spread a second ½-inch layer of the egg and cream mixture, and top this with the remaining shrimps, and the same amount of bay leaves, chopped bacon, grated cheese and brandy as on the previous layer of shrimps. Spread on top of this the remaining egg and cream mixture, and top that with another ½ cup of grated cheese. Place the whole in a 350-degree oven for 25 minutes, then take out and serve from the casserole. Eat, and render a snappy salute to Colonel Dorn!

Another very delicious luncheon or Lenten dinner dish is Shrimp-Mushroom *Suprème.* A slight Italian touch has been added here in that Marsala is used instead of sherry.

SHRIMP-MUSHROOM SUPRÈME

2 *lb. freshly boiled shrimps*	2 *cups cream*
1 *lb. fresh mushrooms*	¼ *tsp. grated lemon rind*
3 *tbsp. butter*	1 *tsp. onion juice*
1 *tbsp. flour*	1 *tbsp. chopped parsley*
3 *ounces dry Marsala*	*Fine buttered breadcrumbs*

Grated Parmesan cheese

In a saucepan, sauté 1 pound of sliced fresh mushrooms in 3 tablespoons of butter until they are tender—about 8 to 10 minutes. Then sprinkle in 1 tablespoon of flour, blending it with the butter in the pan. Then blend in 3 ounces of dry Marsala. Next add 2 cups of cream, ¼ teaspoon of grated lemon rind, 1 teaspoon of onion juice, and 1 tablespoon of chopped parsley. Stir all this over a low flame until smooth and thickened.

To the sauce add 2 pounds of freshly boiled shrimps, which have been shelled and cleaned, and transfer to a buttered casserole or a shallow baking dish. Sprinkle the top with fine buttered breadcrumbs and grated Parmesan cheese, place in a 400-degree oven, and bake for about 15 minutes, or until thoroughly hot and lightly browned.

One of my favorite types of food is curry. Almost every type of shellfish can be made into a curry. I think the finest shellfish curries I have ever eaten were made the way curry is prepared and cooked in Penang, the town and island which, after Singapore, forms the most important part of the British Crown Colony of Straits Settlements.

EAST INDIAN SHRIMP CURRY

2 *lb. fresh boiled shrimps*	*Pinch dried mint*
4 *ounces butter*	2 *cloves*
1 *clove garlic*	¼ *tsp. basil*
1 *large onion*	2 *tbsp. flour*
3 *stalks celery*	2 *tbsp. curry powder*
1 *green pepper*	½ *tsp. salt*
1 *apple*	½ *tsp. pepper*
1 *carrot*	¼ *tsp. cayenne pepper*
2 *tomatoes*	¼ *tsp. nutmeg*
1 *tbsp. chopped parsley*	2 *cups consommé*
1 *bay leaf*	1 *cup dry white wine*
Pinch thyme	*Boiled rice*
Pinch marjoram	*Chutney*

Melt 4 ounces of butter in a large saucepan, and add 1 clove of garlic, crushed, 1 large onion, peeled and chopped fine, 3 stalks of celery, chopped, 1 green pepper, seeded and chopped, 1 apple.

peeled, cored, and chopped, 1 carrot, chopped, 2 tomatoes, peeled, seeded, and chopped, 1 tablespoon chopped parsley, 1 crumbled bay leaf, a pinch each of thyme, marjoram, and dried mint, 2 whole cloves and ¼ teaspoon basil. When the vegetables are soft, sprinkle in 2 tablespoons of flour mixed with 2 tablespoons curry powder, ½ teaspoon salt, ½ teaspoon freshly ground pepper, ¼ teaspoon cayenne pepper, and ¼ teaspoon nutmeg. Mix well with the contents of the pan, stirring well, and cook for about 5 minutes. Then slowly add 2 cups of consommé, and when the mixture begins to thicken, add 1 cup of dry American white wine. Cook over a slow fire for about ½ hour.

Now you can do one of two things. If you like a thin curry sauce, you can strain the above mixture into another saucepan, add 2 pounds of freshly boiled shrimps, shelled and cleaned. Simmer for about 10 minutes. On a platter have a ring of 1 cup of raw rice which has been boiled, and pour the shrimp curry into the center of the ring. Sprinkle with finely chopped parsley, and serve with chutney.

Your second choice is to add the shrimps to the sauce without straining it, let heat, and serve on individual plates over a mound of fluffy rice. Of course, chutney is also indicated in both methods. Personally, I prefer this latter method.

If you've come home some night and found you've forgotten to order meat and you have some canned shrimp on the pantry shelf, try Shrimps de Jonghe. It's easy to make if you follow this original recipe from the once famous Chicago restaurant of the same name. The difficulty you will have in serving this wonderful dish will be proving that you aren't old enough to have obtained the recipe from Papa de Jonghe. Of course, this dish is even better if fresh shrimps are used.

SHRIMP DE JONGHE

3 lb. cooked shrimps	Pinch tarragon
1 large clove garlic	Pinch marjoram
¾ cup butter	1 cup fine breadcrumbs
1 tsp. salt	½ cup dry sherry
Chopped parsley	

Mash 1 large clove of garlic until it is almost a paste, then add to it ¾ cup of butter, softened to room temperature, 1 teaspoon salt, and 1 pinch each of tarragon and marjoram. Cream these together until well blended, then add 1 cup of fine breadcrumbs and ½ cup of dry sherry. Blend the whole well.

For six people have 3 pounds of cooked shrimps. In a fairly large buttered baking dish place alternate layers of the shrimps and the breadcrumb mixture, sprinkling chopped parsley over the top of each layer. Bake in a 400-degree oven for 20 to 25 minutes, and serve immediately.

The following recipe, I suppose, should have been included in the chapter on hors d'oeuvres because it is really a first course appetizer. It is called Shrimp Arnaud and was devised, I believe, by the famous restaurateur in New Orleans. I've also heard it called Shrimp Remoulade.

This recipe calls for Creole-style mustard, which is apparently rather difficult to obtain. So I'm including a free advertisement for the maker of this mustard. It is manufactured by Zatarain's Pure Food Products Company of New Orleans, Louisiana.

SHRIMP ARNAUD

2 *tbsp. red wine vinegar*	½ *tsp. salt*
6 *tbsp. olive oil*	½ *heart of celery*
1 *tbsp. paprika*	½ *white onion*
4 *tsp. Creole mustard*	1 *tbsp. chopped parsley*

Mix 2 tablespoons of red wine vinegar, 6 tablespoons of olive oil (imported, please), 1 tablespoon of paprika, 4 tablespoons of Creole mustard, ½ teaspoon of salt, half a heart of celery, chopped, ½ white onion, chopped fine, and a small amount of chopped parsley. Serve over cold boiled shrimps bedded down on crisp lettuce, or over shrimps placed on a large shell all by their delicious selves.

There are a number of wonderful recipes for snails—snails *abbaye,* with cream; snails *chablisienne,* with white wine; snails *à la Provençale,* cooked with garlic and white wine; or snails *Bourguignon.* The latter is the most popular and best known, and here is the recipe.

SNAILS BOURGUIGNON

4 *dozen snails and shells*	1 *tsp. thyme*
5 *cups dry red wine*	7½ *ounces butter*
5 *little green onions*	1 *ounce flour*
5 *sprigs parsley*	1 *clove garlic*
1 *bay leaf*	*Salt*
1 *ounce chopped mushrooms*	*Freshly ground pepper*
Pinch cayenne pepper	

Boil together 5 cups of excellent American dry red wine, 5 little green onions, minced, several sprigs of parsley, 1 bay leaf, 1 ounce of chopped mushrooms, and 1 teaspoon of thyme, until the wine is reduced by one-half. Strain it through a fine sieve and thicken with *buerre manie* (that is, 1½ ounces of butter kneaded with 1 ounce of flour until perfectly blended). Allow to cool, then cream into this wine mixture 6 ounces of butter, 1 clove of garlic crushed to a paste, salt and freshly ground pepper to taste, and a little cayenne pepper. This is the *Bourguignon* butter, and it will keep in the refrigerator for weeks. It is delicious served over grilled fish, meat, or eggs.

Now have ready 4 dozen snails and their shells. Place a nugget of the prepared butter into each shell. Then put the snails back in their shells, and seal the opening with more of the butter mixture, pressing it down well. Place the snails, in their shells, on a flat baking tin and set them in a hot oven (400 degrees) for 7 or 8 minutes, or until they are heated through and the butter is melted. Serve immediately.

This is the second of the Cantonese recipes.

TAHITIAN SHRIMP FEAST

1 *lb. fresh shrimps*	1 *cup sliced mushrooms*
1 *egg*	2 *cups chopped Cantonese*
Consommé	*greens (or celery cabbage)*
2 *tbsp. sifted bread flour*	2 *tbsp. cornstarch*
1 *tsp. salt*	2 *tbsp. water*
Deep fat	1 *teaspoon Ac'cent*
3 *tbsp. peanut oil*	*Dash pepper*
4 *water chestnuts*	½ *tsp. sugar*
12 *whole pea pods*	1 *tsp. soy sauce*

Clean and shell 1 pound of fresh jumbo shrimp and split each one down the center, but do not cut through.

Make an egg batter as follows: Combine 1 egg, 1 tablespoon of consommé, 2 tablespoons of sifted bread flour and ½ teaspoon of salt. Beat until smooth and the consistency of very thick cream.

Dip the shrimps into the egg batter, thoroughly coating them. Then put them into deep boiling fat (peanut oil is best, although ordinary cooking fat will do). When the shrimps are lightly browned, remove them from the deep fat, and place immediately in a skillet containing 3 tablespoons of hot peanut oil. Add 4 water chestnuts, thinly sliced, 12 whole pea pods, 1 cup of sliced fresh mushrooms, and 2 cups of very coarsely chopped Cantonese greens (these are similar to celery cabbage, and can be obtained in almost any Chinese grocery store; if you can't get the Cantonese greens, you can use the same amount of celery cabbage), and 1 cup of consommé. Let this simmer for about 2 minutes, then add the following mixed seasonings: 2 tablespoons of cornstarch diluted with 2 tablespoons of water, ½ teaspoon of salt, 1 teaspoon of Ac'cent, a dash of pepper, ½ teaspoon of sugar, and 1 teaspoon of soy sauce. Mix this gently, but thoroughly, with the vegetables, cover, and simmer over a moderate flame for about 1 minute.

Remove to a hot platter and serve.

((6)) MEAT

It is an old saying that "a bottle of Burgundy, a ragout, and a beautiful and intelligent woman are the three best table companions possible to find."

Of course, there are bound to be differences of opinions as to the beautiful and intelligent woman. One person might prefer an intellectual brunette, another a witty blonde, and still another a philosophical redhead. But there can be no difference of opinion on the Burgundy and the ragout; the Burgundy, *Romanée Conti,* and the ragout, *Boeuf Bourguignon.*

Before the recent war, along about November, the celebrated *Foire Gastronomique* was held each year in Dijon, France, in connection with the grape harvest. During the week of the food fair the leading hotels and restaurants planned a series of menus that were gastronomic masterpieces, and each proprietor followed the designated *carte de jour.* And one of the most popular dishes was *Boeuf Bourguignon.*

I have had *Boeuf Bourguignon* served to me in some of the top restaurants across this country, from New York to California. Usually the dish includes various vegetables such as carrots, turnips, tomatoes, and whatnot. I've even had it prepared with prunes stuffed with almonds. But none of these dishes is a true *Boeuf Bourguignon.* The real *Boeuf Bourguignon* is simply Burgundy Beef, or beef stewed in Burgundy. The only extraneous flavors which mingle with it are onions, which have already been cooked, set aside, and added later, and the delicate flavor of mushrooms.

This delectable dish is really a very simple one to cook. Get yourself a couple of bottles of good Burgundy (Romanée Conti is practically impossible to get in America, so, depending on the state of your pocketbook, try either Chambertin or Vougeot from France, or Pinot Noir from California), your favorite feminine or masculine companion, and two pounds of lean beef (chuck is the

125

best), and I'll guarantee you an evening that you'll not forget very soon. It's really as easy as that . . . and this.

BOEUF BOURGUIGNON
(Burgundy Beef)

2 *lb. lean beef*	*Thyme*
2 *tbsp. bacon drippings*	*Salt*
10 *small or 5 medium-sized*	*Pepper*
onions	½ *cup beef bouillon*
1½ *tbsp. flour*	1 *cup dry red wine*
Marjoram	½ *pound fresh mushrooms*

Peel and slice the onions and fry them in the bacon drippings until brown, using a heavy skillet. Then remove to a separate dish. Cut the lean beef into about 1-inch cubes, and sauté them in the same drippings, adding a little more fat if necessary. When the cubes of beef are browned on all sides, sprinkle over them 1½ tablespoons of flour, and a generous pinch each of salt, pepper, marjoram, and thyme. Then add ½ cup of beef bouillon to the contents of the skillet, and 1 cup of the red wine (don't use your imported wine for this, rather, a good American Burgundy). Stir the mixture well for a moment, then let it simmer as slowly as possible for 3¼ hours. The mixture, during this cooking, should just barely bubble occasionally. If necessary, put a mat under the skillet. The liquid may cook away some, so add a little more bouillon and wine (in the proportion of 1 part of stock to two parts of wine) as necessary to keep the beef barely covered.

After the mixture has cooked the 3¼ hours, return the brown onions to the skillet, add ½ pound of sliced fresh mushrooms (you can add ¾ of a pound or a pound if you like mushrooms). Stir everything together well, and then let it cook for ¾ of an hour or even an hour longer. Again, it may be necessary to add a little more stock and wine. The sauce should be thick and dark brown. With this main dish serve crusty French bread, a tossed green salad, and your imported Burgundy, and follow it with a light dessert.

There is scarcely any Russian restaurant of repute that doesn't feature Beef Stroganoff on its menu, and you'll often find it on the

menu of other very fine restaurants. It was named, I am told, for a
Russian gay blade and gourmet, Count Paul Stroganoff, but
whether it was a concoction of his own or of his chef I have never
known. But it is one of the most taste-teasing beef dishes ever
devised, and it never fails to bring exclamations of delight from
guests. There are many variations of Beef Stroganoff, but I think
this one is tops.

BEEF STROGANOFF

1½ lb. lean beef	2 cups beef bouillon or con-
3 tbsp. butter	sommé
1 cup sliced fresh mushrooms	2 tbsp. tomato paste
1 large onion	1 tsp. dry mustard
2 tbsp. flour	3 tbsp. sherry

⅔ cup sour cream

Get 1½ pounds lean beef, remove all the fat and gristle from it,
and cut it into narrow strips about 2½ inches long, ¾ inch wide,
and between ¼ and ½ inch thick. Dust the strips with salt and
pepper and set them aside for about 2 hours, but not in the refrigerator or other cold place. When you are ready to prepare the
dish, melt 2 tablespoons of butter in a heavy skillet, and sauté 1
cup of sliced fresh mushrooms until tender (about 15 minutes),
then remove them and set them aside. In the same butter sauté the
peeled and sliced onion until brown, then remove and set aside.
Add at least one tablespoon of butter to the skillet, and when it is
bubbling hot put in the strips of beef and sear them on both sides,
but leave them rare. Remove them and set them aside, and to the
remaining butter in the skillet sprinkle in 2 tablespoons of flour
and blend it with the butter, browning it well. Then slowly add 2
cups of beef bouillon (or consommé), stirring well to form a
smooth gravy. Next add 3 tablespoons of sherry, 2 tablespoons of
tomato paste, and 1 teaspoon of dry mustard, blending them well.
Now put into the sauce the meat, onions, and mushrooms, and let
the whole thing simmer very slowly over the lowest possible flame
for about 20 minutes. About 5 minutes before serving add ⅔ cup
of sour cream and blend it in thoroughly. Whipped or riced potatoes make an ideal accompaniment to the dish.

Mushrooms and tomato paste and the sherry are not a part of the original Russian recipe for Beef Stroganoff, but to my way of thinking they make for a more interesting dish.

The chances are ten to one that, when the Christmas holidays are over, you go into a conference with the Little Woman and say firmly: "Look here, darling, I got up enough courage to look at the bank balance today and I find that we're just two jumps ahead of the sheriff, and the sheriff is taking jumping lessons. So we've got to cut down on the food budget." Then the Little Woman, who's painfully aware of what things cost in the markets and grocery stores, gives you the cold and fishy eye: "Oh, yeah! How?"

Well, there are a number of ways. Take boiled beef, for instance. For boiled beef (or mutton) the brisket should be used. Inasmuch as boiled beef has little or no flavor, it requires a pungent sauce, and I think a horseradish sauce is the ideal accompaniment.

BOILED BEEF AND HORSERADISH SAUCE

3 *lb. brisket of beef*	1 *clove garlic*
3 *carrots*	1 *tsp. thyme*
6 *medium-sized onions*	1½ *tsp. salt*
2 *turnips*	10 *peppercorns*
1 *cup chopped celery*	*Boiling water*

Horseradish Sauce

¼ *cup dry white wine*	3 *tbsp. fine breadcrumbs*
¾ *cup consommé*	*Salt*
1 *cup sour cream*	*Pepper*
½ *cup grated horseradish*	1 *tsp. dry mustard*

Place 3 pounds of brisket of beef in a kettle and add 3 sliced carrots, 6 medium-sized onions, cut in half, 2 turnips, cut in quarters, 1 cup of chopped celery, including the leaves, 1 clove of garlic, minced, 1 teaspoon of thyme, 1½ teaspoons of salt, and about 10 slightly bruised peppercorns. Then add enough boiling water to just cover, put the lid on the kettle, and let simmer until the meat is tender—3 to 4 hours. If necessary, add a little more boiling water occasionally.

When the meat is done, remove it to a hot platter. Strain the bouillon and bottle it for future use, for this is the real McCoy as far as beef bouillon goes. Slice the beef across the grain, and serve with horseradish sauce, made as follows:

In a saucepan mix together ¼ cup of dry American white wine, ¾ cup of consommé, 1 cup of sour cream, and ½ cup of grated horseradish and simmer for about 15 minutes. Then add 3 tablespoons of fine breadcrumbs, salt and freshly ground pepper to taste, and 1 teaspoon of dry mustard. Blend thoroughly. If you prefer the sauce thicker, complete the cooking by adding a beaten egg yolk mixed with a little cream, stirring constantly while the egg thickens the sauce.

Another inexpensive dish is the *Cassoulet,* the greatest and richest of French stews. Its full name is *Cassoulet de Midi* and it is a favorite from Montpellier to Toulouse. It is simply a combination of meats, beans, and wine, and when served with rye bread, a green salad, and a flagon of dry American white wine, it makes one of the most delectable meals imaginable. I am inclined to think the *Cassoulet* was the great-granddaddy of Boston baked beans and pork.

One special advantage of the dish is that it can be reheated two or three times without losing one whit of its original deliciousness.

When you eat this *Cassoulet,* close your eyes and imagine you are in the dim interior of the Inn of the Queen in Castelnaudary, France, with its smoke-blackened rafters and an immense *Cassoulet* bubbling in its earthenware container. There, the *Cassoulet* rises to a gastronomic pinnacle of pure delight.

CASSOULET

1 *pint beans*	½ *lb. lean pork*
Water	4 *ounces olive oil*
½ *bay leaf*	1 *clove garlic*
¼ *tsp. thyme*	*Dry white wine*
8 *peppercorns*	2 *tbsp. mushroom catsup*
4 *good-sized onions*	6 *little link sausages*
½ *lb. veal*	2 *slices bacon*

The first requisite for a *Cassoulet* is beans. If you're from New England, you'll probably prefer the dry pea beans. If from the deep South, you may insist on the "black-eyed Susans." Red kidney beans also are excellent, to say nothing of the Texas variety called pintos. So you can take your choice.

Soak a pint of beans in water overnight. In the morning, drain them and put them into an earthenware casserole along with ½ bay leaf, ¼ teaspoon of thyme, 8 black peppercorns, and 4 good-sized onions quartered, and cover the whole with boiling water. Put the lid on and bake all day very slowly in a 225-degree oven, adding just enough water from time to time to keep the beans covered.

A couple of hours before dinner, cut up ½ pound of veal and ½ pound of lean pork and sauté the meat in plenty of butter or olive oil, to which a minced clove of garlic has been added, until tender. Then cover the meat in the pan with dry American white wine. If you wish (and I should advise it), add a couple of tablespoons of mushroom catsup. Cover the mixture and simmer for half an hour, adding white wine as necessary to keep the meat covered. At the end of the simmering time, pour the meat and wine mixture into the beans in the casserole. Also add about 6 little link sausages cut into thirds, which have been fried in a pan (but do not add any of the sausage renderings). Then a couple of slices of diced raw bacon go into the casserole and enough water and white wine, in equal parts, to cover the whole mixture. Put the cover on the casserole, put it back into the oven, and forget about it until time to serve.

Another way of serving *Cassoulet* is to put a layer of the cooked beans into a very large casserole, cover this with a layer of half the meat, add another layer of beans, another of the remaining meat, and top the whole with a layer of the remaining beans, to which the pieces of link sausage have been added. Then add the wine mixture (and additional wine if needed), cover, and bake until dinner time.

From the inexpensive dishes of boiled beef and *Cassoulet,* it's quite a jump to one of the most expensive cuts of beef, *tournedos* of beef. This is the heart of a *filet mignon.* When properly cut it is so tender that you can cut it with a fork and so delicious that you can't describe it, especially when it is made with *pâté de foie gras* and truffles. It is a specialty of the Imperial House, one of Chicago's finest restaurants and one which, to my way of thinking, has no peer in this country. Max Guggiari, one of the owners, has as fine a feeling for food as any man I have ever known, and is one of the most delightful hosts. One of the most memorable dinners I have ever had consisted of melon wrapped in wafer-thin slices of Prosciutto ham, accompanied by chilled sherry; fillet of sole *à la Bonne Femme,* accompanied by a fine Chablis; *Tournedos* of Beef Rossini, served with a Chambertin, 1929; and fresh pineapple with a kirsch sauce, accompanied by that golden nectar of the gods, Chateau Yquem, 1929.

TOURNEDOS OF BEEF ROSSINI

10 *ounces beef tenderloin*	½ *cup Madeira*
Salt	½ *cup thick beef gravy*
Pepper	1 *ounce chopped truffles*
3 *ounces melted butter*	2 *mushroom caps*

2 ounces purée of *foie gras*

Place two 5-ounce *tournedos* of beef (the heart of a *filet mignon*) in a shallow pan in which 3 ounces of butter have been melted. Sauté them on both sides for about 4 minutes, or a little longer if you don't like them too rare. Remove the *tournedos* and keep warm. Add to the pan ½ cup of Madeira and ½ cup of thick beef gravy, 1 ounce of chopped truffles, and 2 mushroom caps. Cook for 5 minutes.

Spread the *foie gras* on a round piece of hot toast. Place each *tournedos* on the toast and top with a slice of *foie gras* and the cooked mushroom cap. Finish by pouring the sauce over the *tournedos.* (Serves **2.**)

I can't imagine anyone who likes to eat not putting a broiled steak near the top of the food hit parade. Broiled over charcoal or in the oven, or pan broiled, and dotted with butter, steak is a dish fit for any king or queen. But sometimes you may feel you'd like to have a change, so here are two recipes for broiled steak with a sauce. The first is with a Burgundy sauce.

STEAK BURGUNDY

1 *steak*	1 *tbsp. chopped parsley*
6 *little green onions*	*Salt*
6 *tbsp. butter*	*Freshly ground pepper*

1 *cup dry red wine*

Chop fine 6 little green onions, and sauté in a small saucepan with
3 tablespoons butter for about 3 or 4 minutes. Add 1 tablespoon
of chopped parsley and 1 cup of dry American red wine, and let
it simmer very slowly while the steak is being pan broiled in a
heavy skillet. When steak is done as you prefer it, remove it to
a hot platter, and to the juices of the steak add 3 tablespoons of
butter. When it has melted, add the chopped onions and wine to
the skillet, stirring slowly. Add salt and freshly ground pepper
to taste, let it boil up, and then pour over the steak.

The second broiled steak recipe with a sauce is a Piquante
Paste which, incidentally, is a favorite of Joan Crawford's.

BROILED STEAK WITH PIQUANTE PASTE

1 *steak*	2 *tbsp. Madeira*
4 *tbsp. Roquefort or blue*	*Dash Tabasco*
cheese	*Juice ½ lemon*
1 *tbsp. butter*	*Salt*
1 *tbsp. scraped onion pulp*	*Freshly ground pepper*

Make the piquante paste as follows: Mix together 4 tablespoons
of Roquefort (or blue) cheese, 1 tablespoon of butter, 1 tablespoon of scraped onion pulp, 2 tablespoons of Madeira, a dash of
Tabasco, the juice of ½ lemon, and salt and freshly ground
pepper to taste.

Broil 1½- or 2-inch steak in whatever way you prefer—I like
to pan broil my steaks; it saves a lot of stooping over, unless one
has a waist-high broiler. Cook your steak as you like it, rare or
medium rare. When it is done, spread the paste over it (on top
side only) and put it under the broiler for about 10 seconds, then
serve immediately.

One evening I was dining with a group of friends who live to
eat, instead of eating to live. We were an oddly assorted group,
of varied nationalities, vocations, and interests—an Englishman

who is an art appraiser, a Greek whose business and hobby is photography, an Italian who is a top-notch mechanic and who can sing any aria from any opera, and a Russian who is a certified public accountant. There were a couple of other Americans besides myself, and our host was a retired automobile dealer who is more at home with a rod and line in his hand than behind the wheel of an automobile. But there was one bond of brotherhood among us all—cooking and eating.

As we were finishing our dinner, I had told an amusing story about national flowers, and that led to a discussion of national dishes—of steak and kidney pie as it was made at the old Cheshire Cheese in London, of *moussak à la Grecque* at the Grande Bretagne Hotel in Athens, of Beef Stroganoff in the restaurant at the Tsarkoe Selo railway station near the czar's palace in Russia, of *pasta faggioli* at the Falcone in Naples, and of Louisiana Jambalaya.

Let's take a little gastronomical tour, starting in London with beef steak and kidney pie.

I believe that the famous old Cheshire Cheese in London was demolished by German bombs, a fact that should bring tears to the eyes of anyone who has ever been there. What roast beef and Yorkshire pudding they served! The Yorkshire pudding was served from a huge copper bowl the size of a timpani and, of course, the steak and kidney pie was out of this world. It's not a difficult dish to make and, naturally, should be washed down with Bass's ale or Guinness's stout, or your favorite American ale or beer.

BEEFSTEAK AND KIDNEY PIE

1 *lb. veal kidneys*	1 *bay leaf*
Salt	1 *tbsp. Worcestershire sauce*
Vinegar	*Freshly ground pepper*
2 *lb. rump steak*	1 *cup beef bouillon*
Flour	1 *cup dry red wine*
1 *clove garlic*	3 *tbsp. butter*
3 *tbsp. bacon fat*	1 *cup sliced mushrooms*
1 *medium-sized onion*	3 *ounces brandy*
2 *pinches thyme*	*Pastry crust*
2 *pinches marjoram*	*Cream*

Soak 1 pound of veal kidneys for a hour in cold salted water to which 2 tablespoons of vinegar have been added. Then drain the kidneys, clean, trim away any gristle and tubes, and slice them thin.

Cut 2 pounds of ½-inch-thick rump steak into 1- by 1½-inch pieces.

In a Dutch oven sauté 1 clove of sliced garlic until brown in 3 tablespoons of bacon drippings. Remove the garlic and add the cubed beef which has been dredged with flour. Brown the meat on all sides, then add 1 medium-sized onion, peeled and chopped fine, 2 pinches each of thyme and marjoram, a crumbled bay leaf, 1 tablespoon of Worcestershire sauce, and salt and freshly ground pepper to taste. Cook for about 5 minutes, then add 1 cup of beef bouillon and 1 cup of dry American red wine. Cover closely and simmer over a low flame for about 1½ hours, or until the meat is nearly tender. Stir occasionally, and, if necessary, add a little more bouillon and wine in equal parts.

In a saucepan put 1 tablespoon of butter, and when it is bubbling, add the sliced kidneys and cook for about 5 minutes, then add them to the simmering meat. Add about 2 more tablespoons of butter to the same pan, and put in 1 cup of sliced mushrooms. Sauté these gently for about 7 or 8 minutes, then add them to the simmering meat.

Now add 2 tablespoons of flour to the butter the kidneys and mushrooms have cooked in, and when well blended, add this *roux* to the simmering meat, kidneys, and mushrooms, and stir until well blended. Stir in 3 ounces of brandy, remove from the flame, pour all into a buttered casserole or a round baking dish, and set aside to cool.

Prepare a crust, to cover the top, by your favorite recipe, or from prepared pie crust mix, and chill the dough in the refrigerator. Then roll out the rich pastry so that it is about an inch larger in diameter than the dish you are to cover. Press it down in a fluted edge around the rim of the dish. Cut a few little slits on the top to allow the steam to escape. Brush the top of the pastry crust with a little cream, and bake in a 450-degree oven for 15 minutes; then reduce the heat to about 300 degrees, and cook for 15 or 20 minutes longer, or until the pastry is a rich brown.

Well, next stop is Germany and the famous sweet-sour pot roast which is called *Sauerbraten*. This dish is a specialty in nearly all good German restaurants. It is not too difficult to prepare, but it does take time.

SAUERBRATEN

4 *lb. rump or round of beef*
   (*1 piece*)
2½ *cups dry red wine*
1½ *cups tarragon vinegar*
1 *tsp. salt*
1 *tsp. black peppercorns*
½ *tsp. thyme*
½ *tsp. mace*
⅛ *tsp. sage*
¼ *tsp. allspice*

1 *tsp. dry mustard*
3 *bay leaves*
12 *whole cloves*
2 *large onions*
1 *carrot*
6 *sprigs celery tops*
3 *tbsp. bacon fat*
2 *tbsp. flour*
5 *gingersnaps*
1 *cup sour cream*

2 *tbsp. Madeira*

Put a 4-pound rump or round of beef (in one piece) in a large enamel, earthenware, or stainless steel kettle. Mix together 2½ cups of dry American red wine, 1½ cups of tarragon vinegar, 1 teaspoon of salt, 1 teaspoon of black peppercorns, ½ teaspoon each of thyme and mace, ⅛ teaspoon of sage, ¼ teaspoon of allspice, 1 teaspoon of dry mustard, 3 bay leaves, 12 whole cloves, 2 large onions, peeled and sliced, 1 large carrot, sliced, and 6 sprigs celery tops. Pour this mixture over the meat. Cover with doubled cheesecloth, and let marinate for 4 days at room temperature, turning the meat twice each day in the marinade.

Melt 3 tablespoons of bacon drippings in a heavy frying pan or skillet, put in the meat, taken from the marinade, and brown it on all sides. Then put the meat into a heavy kettle or large Dutch oven.

Blend about 2 tablespoons of flour with the bacon drippings and gradually pour in the marinade, then add 5 crushed gingersnaps and cook until thickened. Add this sauce to the meat, cover, and simmer slowly over a low flame until the meat is tender— about 3 hours. If necessary, add a little more red wine.

When the meat is cooked, remove it to a hot platter and slice.

Into the gravy stir 1 cup of sour cream and 2 tablespoons of Madeira. Heat, then pour the gravy over the meat, and serve.

Hungarian Goulash, what crimes are committed in thy name! In thousands of restaurants, both good and bad, across America, one will find goulash on the menu. I have seen on the menu of a cheap hash house the item Hungarian Goulash, and it was about as close to Hungarian goulash as is chop suey.

There are a number of authorities on food who differ on what constitutes a true Hungarian goulash. Some say it is founded on pork, others on veal, and still others, on beef. Truth to tell, this famous dish is rarely prepared in the correct way outside of Hungary. If you can't go out on the plains of Hungary and get it made by a Hungarian cowboy, you could get it in many cafés on Budapest's St. Joseph Quai. One day I was talking about food with a friend of mine who's on the staff of WGN in Chicago, and on discovering that he was a Hungarian, I asked him for a real recipe for goulash. Before he gave it to me, he told me of its origin.

In the old days, Hungary had its great plains on which vast herds of cattle grazed. The Hungarian cowboy was known as a *gulyas*. He always carried with him some potatoes, onions, and, of course, paprika. Occasionally a young calf would be cut out of the herd, butchered, and used for food. And at night, the cowboys would make their favorite stew, which was called **Magyar** (Hungarian) gulyas. And here's the way they made it.

HUNGARIAN GOULASH PETEKO

2 *lb. lean beef*	½ *tsp. caraway seeds*
2 *ounces lard*	½ *cup dry red wine*
2 *large red onions*	*Beef bouillon*
Salt	5 *medium-sized boiled potatoes*
Rosen paprika	½ *ounce butter*
3 *ounces tomato paste*	*Warm water*

Have 2 pounds very lean beef cut into about 1½-inch cubes. Melt 2 ounces of lard in a stewpan, and then fry in this 2 large red onions, peeled and sliced thin. Do not allow them to brown, but when tender add the cubed meat, and shake the pan and stir until the meat and the onions become golden brown. Season with salt to taste, and add a generous tablespoon of paprika (if it is at all possible, use the genuine Hungarian Rosen paprika), about 3 ounces of tomato paste, ½ teaspoon of caraway seeds, ½ cup of dry American red wine, and enough beef bouillon to cover. Put the lid on the pan and allow to simmer very slowly for 2 to 3 hours, adding more stock and a little red wine if the liquid boils away too much.

When the meat is quite soft, add 5 medium-sized boiled potatoes, cut into pieces about the size of walnuts, and mix the potatoes and meat thoroughly. Cook for another ten minutes.

Just before serving, melt ½ ounce of butter in a small saucepan, stir in quickly ½ teaspoon of Rosen paprika, and add immediately a little warm water—a tablespoon or so. Pour this liquid into the stew. It gives it the coveted red color and the peculiar Hungarian flavor.

Leaves stuffed with meat are a great favorite among the peoples of Asia Minor, the Armenians and the Turks. They call them *dolmas* and utilize grape leaves The Russians call it *golubtsi* and cabbage leaves provide the wrapping.

I learned from George Mardikian, the celebrated Armenian owner of one of San Francisco's best-known restaurants, Omar Khayyam's, that according to the legend of the Armenians, grape leaves date back to the time of Noah's Ark. Inasmuch as all vegetation was destroyed by the Flood, the first plant to sprout leaves after the water subsided were the grape vines—so Noah and his family ate grape leaves.

Russians would probably challenge this statement, but who's to say who is right? The Russian name for meat wrapped in cabbage leaves means "pigeons," and the derivation of the name of the dish comes from the fact that the rolls of meat-stuffed cabbage leaves somewhat resemble a pigeon in shape. Well, so much for origin. Here's the recipe for stuffed cabbage leaves. If you can get grape leaves, use them, by all means, as I think they are far more flavorsome than cabbage.

Golubtsi, by the way, was one of the favorite dishes of the late Feodor Chaliapin.

STUFFED CABBAGE LEAVES

1 *large head of cabbage*	*Pepper*
1 *lb. ground round steak*	½ *tsp. paprika*
½ *lb. ground lean pork*	1 *tbsp. chopped water cress*
1 *tbsp. bacon fat*	*Juice ½ lemon*
1 *medium-sized onion*	2 *egg yolks*
1 *green pepper*	4 *tbsp. butter*
3 *stalks celery*	1 *tbsp. flour*
1 *clove garlic*	1 *cup tomatoes*
1 *cup cooked rice*	½ *cup dry red wine*
2 *tbsp. chopped parsley*	1 *bay leaf*
Salt	¾ *cup sour cream*

Get a large head of cabbage, separate the leaves, and pick out 12 perfect ones. Cut away the hard part at the bottom of each leaf, and scald the leaves in salted water for 10 minutes. This makes them pliable. Spread the scalded leaves out on a towel and let dry.

In a skillet put 1 tablespoon of bacon drippings, and gently sauté until tender 1 medium onion, peeled and chopped, 1 green pepper, seeded and chopped, 3 stalks of celery, chopped, and 1 clove of garlic, chopped.

In a large bowl mix 1 pound of ground round steak and ½ pound of ground lean pork. Add to the meat 1 cup of cooked rice, 2 tablespoons of chopped parsley, the sautéed vegetables, salt and pepper to taste, ½ teaspoon of paprika, a tablespoon of chopped water cress, the juice of ½ lemon, and 2 beaten egg yolks. Stir the mixture well until thoroughly blended, then divide into 12 portions. Roll each portion, and wrap in a cabbage leaf, folding the leaf all around to make a neat package. Then tie them with thread, or fasten with toothpicks.

Heat 4 tablespoons of butter in a heavy pan, lay the 12 rolls in the pan and brown them, then remove them and keep them warm.

Stir 1 tablespoon of flour into the butter in the pan, and blend smoothly. Then add 1 cup of tomatoes (breaking up any large pieces) and ½ cup of dry American red wine. Let this boil up, then add 1 crumbled bay leaf and ¾ cup of sour cream and mix well. Then, after carefully removing the binding threads, or toothpicks, from the stuffed cabbage rolls, put them back in the pan. Cover, and cook in a moderate oven (350 degrees) for about 1 hour.

And now let's journey down to Mexico, or rather to Texas, for a Mexican dish—Chili Con Carne. In World War I days, when I was a young lieutenant of infantry stationed at San Antonio, Texas, one of the company cooks in my regiment was a Mexican named Jesus Mendoza. He was a gay *caballero* among his pots and pans, particularly when he was whipping up one of his native concoctions. I don't think I'll ever forget the day when one of them practically saved my life.

On the afternoon of a very warm day in early December I had driven out into the country, wearing a white linen uniform. Then, on the way back to the post, a Texas norther struck. If you've ever been in Texas when one of "them thar things" sweeps across the plains, you'll get the point. But if you haven't, let me state without fear of contradiction that subzero blasts in the windy city of Chicago never reach the very marrow of your bones the way a Texas norther can.

Well, when I got back to my quarters, I thought I was permanently frozen and, as I was wondering how my obituary would read, someone knocked on my door, and there stood Mendoza with a steaming bowl of chili con carne. Man, O man, I never tasted anything better, or hotter! I thought the first mouthful had burned away the roof of my mouth, but I didn't care. And before I had finished the chili, I was perspiring!

CHILI CON CARNE

2 *lb. round steak*	1 *large can tomatoes*
1 *lb. fresh pork*	3 *bay leaves*
3 *tbsp. bacon fat*	1 *tbsp. salt*
3 *medium-sized onions*	1 *tbsp. oregano*
4 *cloves garlic*	1 *tbsp. red wine vinegar*
6 *tbsp. chili powder*	1 *tbsp. brown sugar*
1 *tbsp. flour*	1 *pint ripe olives*

1 *large can beans (if desired)*

140   WITH A JUG OF WINE

Cut 2 pounds of round steak and 1 pound of fresh pork into small cubes. In 3 tablespoons of lard or bacon drippings brown 3 medium-sized onions, chopped, and 4 cloves of garlic, chopped. Remove the onions, and to the remaining fat add 6 tablespoons of real chili powder mixed with 1 tablespoon of flour. Stir until smooth, then add the cubed meat. When it is brown, stir in 1 large can of tomatoes and cook gently for 20 minutes. Next add 3 bay leaves, 1 tablespoon each of salt and oregano, 1 tablespoon of red wine vinegar, and 1 tablespoon of brown sugar. Cover and cook slowly for about 2 hours.

Last of all, cut 1 pint of ripe olives from the pits, add to the mixture, and cook for another half hour. If you want beans with the chili, heat a large can of frijoles, pintos, or red kidney beans, put them in a deep dish, and pour the chili con carne over them.

Occasionally some of the officers would get together and present Mendoza with a bottle of dry sherry, and he would reciprocate by making up a batch of *Chili Rellenos*. They're easy to prepare and are delicious, especially when accompanied by cold beer.

CHILI RELLENOS

1 *lb. ground round steak*	½ *tsp. salt*
2 *tbsp. lard*	½ *cup seedless raisins*
½ *cup sugar*	6 *green chilies*
¼ *tsp. cloves*	½ *cup dry sherry*
¼ *tsp. cinnamon*	3 *eggs*

Grind 1 pound of round steak and brown it in 2 tablespoons of hot lard. Then add ½ cup of sugar, ¼ teaspoon each of cloves and cinnamon, powered, ½ teaspoon of salt, ½ cup of seedless raisins, 6 green chilies, chopped, and ½ cup of dry sherry. Mix well, then mold into slightly oblong balls about the size of an egg. Next beat the whites of 3 eggs until very stiff, then add the yolks and beat thoroughly. Roll each ball in flour, then in the beaten eggs, and fry in deep fat. Eat them with tortillas.

The number of ways to ruin spaghetti and meat balls, if laid end to end, would be very depressing to anyone except a vegetarian. I have seen this delectable dish listed on the menus at lowly lunch counters, tea rooms, alleged "Italian" restaurants, commercial hotels, de luxe hostelries, and top-bracket restaurants and night clubs. The price may be anywhere from thirty-five cents to three dollars and a half. But in the majority of places the concoction is pretty dreadful.

If you have ever been fortunate enough to dine on spaghetti and meat balls in an Italian home, or have it cooked expressly for you in a real Italian restaurant, you know what a superlatively delicious dish it is. In your own home it is not difficult to prepare, nor does its preparation consume a great deal of time. It is made in three easy stages; the tomato sauce is made first, then the meatballs are cooked, and, as the first two stages are nearing completion, the spaghetti is cooked.

ITALIAN MEATBALLS AND SPAGHETTI, WITH TOMATO SAUCE

Meatballs

1 *lb. chopped beef*
3 *tbsp. grated Parmesan cheese*
2 *tbsp. chopped parsley*
1 *clove garlic*
¼ *tsp. dry mustard*
1 *tsp. salt*
1 *tsp. pepper*
1 *tsp. Worcestershire sauce*

1 *cup fine breadcrumbs*
Pinch mace
¼ *cup chopped onions*
¼ *cup chopped green pepper*
2 *eggs*
3 *ounces dry red wine*
Flour
3 *ounces olive oil*

Sauce

3 *tbsp. olive oil*
2 *onions*
1 *clove garlic*
½ *tsp. basil*

½ *tsp. oregano*
1 *large can tomatoes*
Salt
Pepper
½ *tsp. sugar*

Spaghetti

8 *ounces thin spaghetti*
Boiling water

Salt
Parmesan cheese

For the tomato sauce, fry 2 onions, sliced, and a minced clove of garlic in 3 tablespoons of olive oil for about 5 minutes. Add ½ teaspoon each of basil and oregano. Then strain 1 large can of tomatoes through a sieve, add to the onions, and let the whole thing simmer for about 45 minutes. Stir this frequently, and at the end of the cooking time, or when the tomatoes are cooked to a thick sauce, add salt and pepper to taste and ½ teaspoon of sugar. Again stir thoroughly, and simmer 15 minutes longer.

While the tomato sauce is cooking, put 1 pound of chopped beef in a mixing bowl or saucepan. To it add 3 tablespoons of grated Parmesan cheese, 2 tablespoons of chopped parsley, 1 clove of garlic, minced, ¼ teaspoon of dry mustard, 1 teaspoon each of salt and freshly ground pepper, 1 teaspoon of Worcestershire sauce, 1 cup of fine breadcrumbs, a pinch of mace, ¼ cup each of chopped onion and chopped green pepper, 2 beaten eggs, and 3 ounces dry American red wine (of the Italian type). Mix this all very thoroughly with your hands, and shape into balls about the size of an egg, and roll in flour.

In a skillet heat 3 ounces of olive oil, and when it is hot fry the meatballs for about 10 minutes, or until golden brown.

About 10 minutes before the meatballs and the tomato sauce are ready, put your spaghetti (about 8 ounces of the thin type) into a large pot of boiling water, slightly salted. Don't—oh, please don't—break the spaghetti in order to get it into the pot. Immerse the ends, and when they soften, the bunch will gradually curl down into the water. Cook for about 10 or 12 minutes if you like it *al dente* (when there is a slight resistance to biting) or up to 15 minutes if you like it softer. Drain the spaghetti, pour the tomato sauce over it, and sprinkle it with some freshly grated Parmesan or Romano cheese, mix thoroughly, and put on a hot platter. Then nest the meatballs over the spaghetti and serve.

One of my favorite dishes is *Boeuf Bourguignon* which has the place of honor in this chapter. But an interesting and tasty variation of it is made by the Breton peasants and is called Brittany Beef *en Casserole*.

BRITTANY BEEF EN CASSEROLE

1½ lb. beef round, cut in inch cubes	½ tsp. salt
3 strips bacon	1½ cups diced carrots
1 clove garlic, peeled	6 small onions, peeled
½ cup consommé	4 peppercorns
½ cup claret	2 whole cloves
	2 bay leaves

Dredge with flour ½ pound of beef round, cut in 1-inch cubes. Cook three strips of bacon in a heavy frying pan until brown, but not crisp, and remove from pan. To the hot bacon fat add a crushed clove of garlic and then brown the beef cubes on all sides. Add ½ cup of consommé, ½ cup of American dry red wine, and ½ teaspoon of salt, and heat to boiling. Now turn this mixture into a casserole or a baking dish, add 1½ cups of diced carrots, 6 peeled small onions, 4 black peppercorns, 2 whole cloves, 2 bay leaves, and the bacon cut into 1-inch pieces. Cover and bake in a slow oven (300 degrees) for 2 to 2½ hours.

If you wish (and it's more often done this way in French provincial homes), simmer the whole thing in a heavy kettle on top of the stove, adding more consommé or wine as needed.

I don't believe there are cooks anywhere else on earth who can do as many tricks with beef as the cooks of France. As a rule they utilize the cheaper cuts, and the concoctions are always out of this world. One of my favorites is *Boeuf en daube,* which is translated either as braised beef or beef stew. *Daube* is a name applied to braised poultry or meats. The *daube* was originally cooked in a closed earthenware pot, buried in hot cinders with charcoal added to keep it hot, and left alone for a long time.

Boeuf en daube came originally from the Provence section of France, I believe, and has been known for many centuries. It also is a great favorite in the Pyrenees, but it is made almost everywhere in France and is a great household stand-by in that country. It has a rather odd characteristic, in that it is equally delicious hot or cold. The cold version is said to have been perfected by Jean-Jacques Rousseau—the meat when cooked is put in a bowl and the gravy, which is strained over it, will set in a firm jelly when kept in a cold place.

In some localities, and especially among the Creoles of Louisiana, a whole piece of beef, such as you would use for a pot roast, is cooked as is. This method should be used if you are going to serve it cold. If you've never tried *boeuf en daube,* you'll find a new taste thrill from it.

BOEUF EN DAUBE

3 *lb. round of beef*	1½ *cups dry red wine*
Salt	12 *small white onions*
Pepper	12 *small carrots*
Flour	6 *whole peppercorns*
6 *strips bacon*	4 *whole cloves*
2 *cloves garlic*	1 *bay leaf*
1 *ounce brandy*	2 *tbsp. chopped parsley*
12 *small mushrooms*	*Pinch marjoram*
1 *cup beef bouillon*	*Pinch thyme*

Cut 3 pounds of round of beef into about 1½-inch pieces and roll in seasoned flour. Fry about 6 strips of bacon in a heavy skillet. When they begin to brown, but are not crisp, remove them and cut into 1-inch pieces, and place in an earthenware casserole. In the fat in the skillet, crush and chop finely 2 cloves of garlic, then put in the floured pieces of beef and brown quickly on all sides, turning frequently. When the pieces are browned, pour 1 ounce of warm brandy into the skillet, and in a few moments remove the meat to the casserole.

Now put about 12 small mushrooms into the skillet, and when they are browned, transfer them to the casserole. Next add to the fat and the brandy in the skillet 1 cup of beef bouillon and 1 cup of American dry red wine, preferably a claret type. Bring this to a boil, stirring from the bottom of the pan to loosen all meat particles that may adhere. Then pour the liquid in the skillet into the casserole, over the beef, and add to the casserole 12 very small peeled white onions, 12 small carrots, sliced; 6 peppercorns, slightly bruised; 4 whole cloves, a crumbled bay leaf, 2 tablespoons of chopped parsley, and a generous pinch each of marjoram and thyme. Pour over the contents of the casserole another

½ cup of the dry red wine, and then cover the casserole tightly and bake in a 300-degree oven for 3 hours. Serve from the casserole.

Probably the most popular dish in America among all classes of people is the hamburger, which has a very close relation to the meatball. You'll find hamburgers on the menus of the most expensive restaurants and in the lowliest of eating places. There are chains of eating places, stretching across the country, in which the only meat served is the hamburger. The hamburger is an integral part of one of the popular comic strips, "Popeye, the Sailor." I think one of the reasons for the popularity of Wimpy, who has a deep and abiding passion for hamburgers, is that he typifies so many Americans. I believe the hamburger originated in Hamburg, Germany. I don't know how this original hamburger was made, but I am told that it is quite different from that which we know today.

I have two rather unusual hamburger recipes, and the first is for Broiled Deviled Hamburgers.

BROILED DEVILED HAMBURGERS

1 *lb. boneless chuck beef,* *ground*	½ *cup fine breadcrumbs* *Salt*
3 *tbsp. chili sauce*	*Freshly ground pepper*
1 *tsp. Worcestershire sauce*	1 *clove garlic, minced*
1 *tbsp. minced onion*	¼ *tsp. mace*
1 *tsp. prepared mustard*	¼ *cup dry red wine*
1 *tsp. fresh-grated or bottled* *horseradish*	

Combine 1 pound of boneless chuck beef, ground, 3 tablespoons of chili sauce, 1 teaspoon of Worcestershire sauce, 1 tablespoon of minced onion, 1 teaspoon of prepared mustard, 1 teaspoon of horseradish, ½ cup of fine dried breadcrumbs, salt and freshly ground pepper to taste, ¼ cup of dry red wine, a clove of garlic, finely minced, and ¼ teaspoon of mace. Shape into 6 patties, and broil about 3 minutes on each side, or 4 minutes on each side if you like them better done.

The last time I was in Washington I was a dinner guest of Walter Trohan, chief of the Washington Bureau of the *Chicago Tribune* and one of the Capitol's best-known correspondents as well as gourmets. He can whip up a delectable dish of his own devising almost as quickly as he can pound out a brilliant story on his typewriter, which is practically in nothing flat.

After dinner, which was perfect, Walter and I naturally got on the subject of food, and we spent some time swapping favorite recipes. One of Walter's I must pass on here, for it is one of the most intriguing hamburger recipes I have ever come across. In all honor due its creator, I shall call it "Hamburger Walter Trohan."

An interesting footnote on this recipe is that Otto Eitel, the managing director of the Bismarck Hotel in Chicago, thought so highly of this dish that he put it on the menu of the hotel, and he tells me it is one of the most popular dishes served.

HAMBURGERS WALTER TROHAN

1 *lb. ground round steak*	*Pepper*
1 *small can of Smithfield ham*	*Roquefort or blue cheese*
spread, or deviled ham	*Dry red wine*
Salt	*Butter*

Blend 1 small can of Smithfield ham spread or deviled ham with 1 pound of fresh ground round steak. Add very little salt, and freshly ground pepper to taste.

Cut pieces of Roquefort or blue cheese into 1¼-inch squares, about ½ inch thick. Mold hamburgers around these squares, and put them in a crock. Cover the hamburgers with dry American red wine, and let them stand, covered, in the refrigerator for about 3 hours. At the end of the marinating time, put a little butter into a skillet, with a little of the marinade, and pan broil the hamburgers to taste (rare, medium, or well done). Remove them to a hot plate, add a little more butter and marinade to the pan, let boil up, and pour the sauce over the hamburgers.

When anyone is faced by a difficulty, problem, or dilemma and grapples with it boldly, we say he "takes the bull by the horns." Back in the troublesome days of 1946 there were plenty of difficulties, problems, and dilemmas, what with New Dealers (if you were a Republican), Republicans (if you were a New Dealer) and shortages (no matter who or what you were). In common with 129,999,999 other Americans, I had difficulties, problems, and dilemmas. So I said to myself, "I will grapple with them boldly."

Taking the bull by the horns, I walked in on my tailor and said firmly, "I want two good suits of clothes, each with two pairs of trousers!" Well, I later convinced myself that the patches on my prewar suits were hardly noticeable.

Not daunted, however, I walked in on my butcher and said stoutly, "Ed, I want a thick porterhouse steak, a three-rib roast, and a couple of pounds of bacon." (Taking the bull by the horns, you see.) But I ended up taking the bull by the tail! And . . . here's what I did with it (the tail, not the bull).

BRAISED OXTAILS

2 lb. oxtails	2 tbsp. chopped parsley
Flour	1 bay leaf
Salt	½ tsp. thyme
Pepper	1 large can tomatoes
4 tbsp. bacon fat	12 small white onions
½ cup chopped onions	¼ tsp. ground cloves
½ cup chopped carrots	Beef bouillon
½ cup chopped celery stalks	Dry red wine
1 clove garlic, crushed	1 cup sliced mushrooms

3 tbsp. brandy

Have 2 oxtails (approximately 2 pounds) disjointed. Wash them thoroughly and dry them on a towel, then dredge with seasoned flour. In a heavy iron skillet heat 4 tablespoons of bacon fat, then add the oxtails, ½ cup each of chopped onions, chopped carrots, and chopped celery stalks, and 1 clove of garlic, crushed. Brown these over a fast flame for about 10 minutes, stirring constantly with a wooden spoon. Next, transfer the mixture to an iron stew pot, and add a large bay leaf crumbled, ½ teaspoon of thyme, 2 tablespoons chopped parsley, 1 large can of tomatoes, 12 small peeled white onions, salt and pepper to taste, ¼ teaspoon of ground cloves, and enough beef bouillon and dry American red wine (in equal parts) to cover the mixture. Bring the whole slowly to a boil, then cover, and transfer to a moderate oven (350 degrees) and let it cook for 2 hours.

One half hour before serving add 1 cup of sliced mushrooms, and continue cooking gently. To serve, place the contents of the pot on a deep hot platter. Heat about 3 tablespoons of brandy in a large ladle, then set the liquor alight, and sprinkle the flaming brandy over the contents of the platter. There you have a dish to sniff, as well as to eat, with great gusto.

In those depressing days when meat was rationed, or was exceedingly scarce, people were glad to buy cheaper cuts of meat, and they quickly learned to prepare and cook them so they were not only tender and flavorsome, but even mighty succulent.

Therefore I'd like to suggest that people who find the choice cuts too high-priced get acquainted again with such things as short ribs, pot roasts, chuck roasts or steaks, oxtails, end cuts of ham, shoulder lamb chops, neck of lamb, beef, and veal, lamb shanks, and those old stand-bys, which are cheap and yet delicious, variety meats. Most of these cuts need some marinating and long, slow cooking to tenderize them, and some imagination in preparing them, but believe me, you can make dishes out of them that will make your mouth water. For instance, try using chuck or flank steak. You may call the following recipe pepper steak or Swiss steak or Spanish steak, but the name doesn't matter—the result is the same . . . delicious.

PEPPERED CHUCK STEAK BURGUNDY

3 lb. chuck beef	1 #2 can tomatoes
Flour	1 small can tomato paste
Salt	¾ cup dry red wine
Pepper	Bay leaf
¼ cup bacon drippings	6 sprigs parsley
2 green peppers	2 green celery tops
3 medium-sized onions	Sprig thyme

Get a medium-thick cut of beef chuck weighing about 3 pounds. Dredge it with seasoned flour, and pound it with a meat pounder or the edge of a saucer. Now brown it on both sides in ¼ cup of cooking fat or bacon drippings. Place the steak in a baking pan having a cover, and spread the steak with 2 green peppers, halved, seeded, and cut into strips about ½ inch wide, and 3 medium-sized onions, thinly sliced. Combine 1 large can of tomatoes and 1 small can of tomato paste, pour this over the steak, and season the whole with salt and pepper to taste. Now add to the pan ¾ cup of dry American red wine, and a *bouquet garni* of a bay leaf tied with 6 sprigs of parsley, 2 green celery tops, and a sprig of thyme. Bring everything to a boil, then cover, and bake in a moderate oven (350 degrees) for at least 2 hours.

A much more refined version of the pepper steak is the dish that Mike Fritzel serves in his beautiful restaurant on the edge of the Loop in Chicago. Instead of chuck, prime beef tenderloin is used and I must say the result justifies the more expensive cut of meat.

PEPPERED STEAK À LA MIKE FRITZEL

1¾ *lb. prime beef tenderloin*
2 *ounces butter*
4 *ounces diced Bermuda onion*
4 *ounces diced green bell pepper*
4 *ounces diced fresh mushrooms*

2 *cloves garlic*
1 *tsp. salt*
1 *tbsp. crushed peppercorns*
1 *ounce Maggi seasoning*
2 *ounces dry sherry*
3 *dozen small parisienne potatoes, rissole*

Place 1 ounce of butter in a skillet. When melted, put into the skillet 4 ounces of diced Bermuda onion, 4 ounces of diced green bell pepper, 4 ounces of diced fresh mushrooms, and 2 crushed cloves of garlic, and sauté until well done. In the meantime, have 1¾-pound beef tenderloin sliced into squares approximately ¼ inch thick, and then sauté them in 1 ounce of butter until they are nicely browned. Then add the meat to the vegetables in the skillet, together with 1 teaspoon of salt, 1 tablespoon of crushed peppercorns, 1 ounce of Maggi's seasoning, and 2 ounces of dry sherry. Blend everything thoroughly, and simmer for about 5 minutes. Then empty the contents of the skillet into a chafing dish, and top with 3 dozen small *parisienne* potatoes, *rissole* (which merely means well browned). In serving use a ladle and give a small quantity to each person as a first helping. Keep the chafing dish lit so that the remaining meat will stay hot.

Another inexpensive cut which comes from the plate of beef is short ribs. Sometimes when we have standing rib roast at the Maison Wood, we have the butcher cut off the ribs close to the main meat and we later have Short Ribs of Beef Burgundy. Believe me, it's pretty delicious.

SHORT RIBS OF BEEF BURGUNDY

2 lb. short ribs beef	1 cup dry red wine
2 tbsp. bacon fat	½ cup beef bouillon
1½ tsp. salt	4 medium-sized potatoes
¼ cup chopped onion	4 carrots
Dash Worcestershire sauce	4 turnips
Pinch marjoram	4 small onions
Pinch thyme	Salt

Pepper

Roll two pounds of short ribs of beef (cut in serving size pieces) in flour, and brown slowly on all sides in 2 tablespoons of bacon drippings in a heavy kettle. Add 1½ teaspoons of salt, ¼ cup of chopped onion, a dash of Worcestershire sauce, a pinch each of marjoram and thyme, and 1 cup of California Burgundy or claret. Cover and simmer slowly for 2 hours, or until tender. Skim the excess fat from the liquid and add ½ cup of beef bouillon. Then add 4 or 5 whole peeled potatoes (medium size) and the same number of carrots, small turnips, and small onions. Sprinkle with salt and pepper, cover, and cook for about another hour, or until the vegetables are tender. If you want to cut the time of cooking, add the vegetables after cooking the short ribs an hour and a half and cook for another hour. But I am a great believer in slow cooking of such dishes, so don't skimp on the cooking time unless necessary. Serve this dish piping hot, with the same type of wine used in the cooking.

To many people "hash" is a word to shudder over. I know scores of people who would never think of eating hash in a restaurant, and, by and large, I agree with their phobia because almost anything can go into a hash, including scraps and leftovers of meats. But hash in your own kitchen is something else again, and I always look forward to the end of a roast beef because that means roast beef hash either for breakfast or dinner. Roast beef hash can be made dry or moist. I personally prefer the following type, which is moist.

ROAST BEEF HASH

4 *cups cooked roast beef*	2 *ounces butter*
2 *cups raw potatoes*	1 *clove garlic*
1 *onion*	1 *cup dry red wine, or more*
1 *green pepper*	*Roast beef gravy (if any)*
1 *tomato*	*Salt*
	Pepper

In a large chopping bowl put 4 cups of cold roast beef, 2 cups of raw potatoes, cubed, 1 onion, peeled, 1 green pepper, seeded, 1 peeled tomato, and chop all together.

In a large skillet melt 2 ounces of butter, then add 1 clove of garlic, minced. When the garlic browns, add the meat and vegetable mixture, 1 cup of dry American red wine, and any roast beef gravy that may be left over. Salt and pepper to taste, and let simmer over a low flame until the potatoes are tender. This is a moist hash, and if more liquid is needed, add more wine. Stir frequently, and when done, serve as is, or over buttered toast.

One of my favorite lusty breakfast dishes is corned beef hash with a poached egg on top, and I recently discovered that canned corned beef hash works just as well as freshly made hash and is a lot easier and quicker.

One Sunday morning not long ago, the Little Woman decided just at breakfast time that she had an uncontrollable yen for corned beef hash. Always aiming to please (a highly sensible attribute for any husband), I looked on the pantry shelf and, sure enough, there was a can of corned beef hash. Being in an experimental mood, I went to work; and here's what I came up with, much to the delight of all concerned.

CORNED BEEF HASH

1 *can corned beef hash*   1 *tsp. Worcestershire sauce*
3 *little green onions*   2 *ounces dry red wine*
1 *small tomato*   1 *tbsp. bacon fat*
                    1 *small clove garlic*

In a mixing bowl empty the contents of a can of corned beef hash. Add 3 little green onions, bulbs and tops, chopped fine, a small tomato, chopped, 1 teaspoon of Worcestershire sauce, and 2 ounces of dry American red wine. Mix all this thoroughly.

In a large skillet melt a scant tablespoon of bacon drippings, and when hot, add 1 small clove of garlic, minced. When the garlic begins to brown, add the corned beef hash. Cook until the hash is thoroughly heated through. If you like a crisp crust, don't stir it, but turn it out on a platter with the crisp side up. If you don't like a crisp crust, stir the hash a couple of times while it is heating.

Of course, poached eggs are a "must" with this dish.

Curry, or, as the Dutch call it, *rijstafel* (which means "rice table"), is the world's heavyweight champion food. It is a gastronomic miracle that rises to the pinnacle of perfection in the Dutch East Indies.

Let's say you are in Batavia, seated at the table in the Hotel Nederlanden, with a huge Dutch napkin tucked under your chin, and you order rice "toffel." Then things begin to happen!

Out of the kitchen comes a line of barefooted, gaily dressed waiters, each bearing a huge platter. The Number 1 boy offers a big bowl of snowy white rice, and you heap your plate with it. Then Number 2 boy offers another huge bowl, containing curry, usually made of chicken. You make a crater in your plateful of rice, and heap it to overflowing with the succulent, aromatic curry, spreading it evenly over the rice. And then the parade continues with Numbers 3, 4, 5, 6, and so on, boys.

Each boy carries a different delicacy. There are various kinds of chutney, vegetables, eggs, shrimps, fish, pickles, bananas, chopped nuts, raisins, coconut, pineapple, hors d'oeuvres, and what not. You help yourself to a portion of each, spreading it over the rice and curry, then you mix the entire outlay with your knife and fork. And then you proceed to eat, and I do mean eat!

Of course, in these days when Huldas, Dinahs, or Berthas are demanding television sets, two or three days off, perhaps the use of the family car, a helper to do the cleaning and another to do the laundry, to say nothing of thirty to forty dollars a week, it is questionable whether you have even one servant, or Number 1 boy, let along anywhere from 11 to 22. But don't despair, because I'll tell you how to make a succulent curry and serve it, buffet style, all by yourself. It may look a touch difficult, but, believe me, it's not.

LAMB CURRY

2 *cooking apples*	1 *cup consommé*
1 *green pepper*	½ *cup dry red wine*
2 *onions*	1 *lemon, juice and grated*
1 *clove garlic (crushed)*	*rind*
2 *tbsp. olive oil*	½ *cup seedless raisins*
2 *tbsp. flour*	2 *whole cloves*
1 *tbsp. curry powder*	2 *cups diced cold lamb*
½ *tsp. salt*	*(cooked)*
½ *tsp. marjoram*	¼ *cup shredded coconut*
½ *tsp. thyme*	1 *tbsp. sour cream*

Core, pare, and slice 2 cooking apples, chop up a green pepper, and slice two peeled onions. Sauté these, together with a crushed clove of garlic, in 2 tablespoons olive (or cooking) oil, until onions are limp. Then sprinkle over the contents of the skillet 2 level tablespoons of flour, 1 level tablespoon of curry powder (the best), and ½ teaspoon each of salt, marjoram, and thyme. Mix the contents of the skillet well, stirring constantly, and cook for 5 minutes. Then add 1 cup of consommé, ½ cup of dry red wine, the juice of a lemon and its grated rind, ½ cup of seedless raisins, and 2 whole cloves. Let all this simmer for 20 to 30 minutes.

Now add 2 cups of diced cold cooked lamb (leave some of the fat on the lamb) and ¼ cup of shredded coconut. Let this heat for 15 minutes, and just before serving add a tablespoon of sour cream, mixing it well into the whole concoction.

On your buffet table have a large wooden bowl of hot, flaky rice. Next to it place your bowl of curry. And that's all there is to it. Of course, if you want to be swanky (and who doesn't?), you should have small dishes of condiments, with a small spoon in each, containing chutney, chopped sweet pickles, chopped hard-boiled eggs, chopped mild (or little green) onions, chopped nuts, shredded canned pineapple, and finely chopped orange peel. Turn the guests loose, telling them first to make a mound of rice on their plates, then cover it with curry, and finally to sprinkle a little of each condiment over the whole. Next day they'll probably start a movement to make you . . . well, at least vice-president.

Californians, with their love of outdoor living, are probably the foremost proponents of the backyard barbecue.

Of course, barbecuing is not the invention of Californians, as some of them would have you believe. The term "barbecue" really means a whole animal roasted or broiled, in its entirety, for a feast. It probably comes from the French *barbe à queue,* which, translated, is "from beard to tail." Yet centuries ago, the Chinese had barbecue ovens, the natives of the South Pacific islands have cooked that may for hundreds of years, and the people of the Caucasus have long practiced a form of barbecuing, roasting meats on the point of their swords.

Shashlik is the Caucasian way of broiling lamb, and is ideally suited to either the outdoor barbecue pit or the home oven. All you need in the way of extra equipment are some skewers, 7 or 8 inches long, with a loop at the end as a handle. Their price is quite moderate.

RUSSIAN LAMB SHASHLIK

4-lb. *leg of lamb*
1½ tsp. *salt*
½ tsp. *freshly ground pepper*
2 *medium-sized onions*
Crumbled bay leaf
1 *clove garlic*

1 tbsp. *chopped parsley*
1 tbsp. *Worcestershire sauce*
3 *ounces olive oil*
Dry red wine
Small ripe tomatoes
Mushroom caps

Slices bacon

Sauce

1 tsp. *caraway seeds*
½ *cup butter*
1 *cup sour cream*
Salt

Freshly ground pepper
Cayenne pepper
½ *cup brandy*
2 tbsp. *chopped parsley*

2 tbsp. *chopped onions*

Get a 4-pound leg of lamb, remove the skin, and cut into pieces about 2 inches square and ¾ inch thick.

Mix together 1½ teaspoons of salt, ½ teaspoon freshly ground black pepper, 2 medium-sized onions, peeled and grated, a crumbled bay leaf, 1 minced clove of garlic, 1 tablespoon of chopped parsley, 1 tablespoon of Worcestershire sauce, and 3 ounces of olive oil. Rub this mixture well into the cubes of lamb. Then put the cubes into an enamel, earthenware, or stainless steel bowl, and cover with dry American red wine. Cover, and allow the meat to marinate for 24 hours.

Make a sauce as follows: In a saucepan mix 1 teaspoon of caraway seeds, ½ cup of butter, 1 cup of sour cream, salt, freshly ground pepper and cayenne to taste, ½ cup brandy, 2 tablespoons finely chopped parsley, and 2 tablespoons finely chopped onion, and boil slowly for about 5 minutes.

When ready to cook the *shashlik,* have ready thick slices of small ripe tomatoes, bacon slices cut in thirds, and large mushroom caps. Thread individual spits or skewers in the following order: bacon slice, lamb slice, tomato slice, bacon slice, mushroom cap, bacon, lamb, tomato, bacon, mushroom, bacon, lamb, tomato, bacon, mushroom.

Roll the filled skewers thoroughly in the sauce and set to cook.

In the home, with a gas stove broiler, place the wire rack so that the filled skewers will be as close to the flame as possible, putting a pan under the rack to catch the bastings. Put the skewers on the rack, removing every few minutes to roll again in the sauce, and slightly turning them when placing them on the rack. The *shashlik* is ready to eat when the meat is well cooked and starts to blacken on the edges—about 10 minutes.

Outdoors, broil the *shashlik* over a charcoal fire, removing it every few minutes to roll it in the sauce, and, returning it to the fire, turn it slightly.

I can't conceive of finding lamb shanks on the tables of Fifth Avenue or Park Avenue mansions (or at least what is left of them). Nor would I expect to see them on the menus of the Drake or Pump Room in Chicago, or the Savoy or the Colony Club in New York. But we prepare them at the Maison Wood, and if you prepare them the same way at your house, you'll agree that they rate orchids, raves, or four bells! I call them "Lamb Shanks Beatrice," with a deep bow to my wife, who concocted them.

LAMB SHANKS BEATRICE

4 *lamb shanks*
3 *slices of bacon*
Flour
Salt
Pepper
1 *medium-sized can tomatoes*
1 *cup chopped celery*

½ *cup chopped parsley*
2 *medium-sized onions*
1 *clove garlic, chopped*
1 *tsp. Worcestershire sauce*
1 *tbsp. grated horseradish*
1 *cup dry red wine*
½ *lb. fresh mushrooms*

Render 3 slices of bacon, finely cut, then take out the bacon bits. Coat 4 lamb shanks thickly with seasoned flour, then brown them slowly in the bacon fat, turning on all sides until nicely browned. This should be done in a deep iron kettle, a Dutch oven, or a drip-drop roaster, without the top. When the shanks are browned, add a medium-sized can of tomatoes, the bacon bits, 1 cup of chopped celery, ½ cup of chopped parsley, 2 medium-sized onions, peeled and finely chopped, 1 finely chopped clove of garlic, 1 teaspoon of Worcestershire sauce, 1 tablespoon of grated horseradish, and 1 cup of dry American red wine (Burgundy type preferred). Cover this mixture and let it simmer for 2 hours. Then add ½ pound of fresh mushrooms, separating the stems from the tops and, if the mushrooms are very large, halving or quartering them. Now let the whole thing cook for about ½ to ¾ of an hour longer. If the gravy has not thickened to the desired stage, just before serving make a flour paste (flour and a little water) and thicken the gravy slightly. The gravy should not be watery, neither should it be very thick— just a nice consistency that allows you to get it all up with the crusty French bread that you should serve with this epicurean delight.

New potatoes, served with parsley butter, and new lima beans make a delicious accompaniment, and if you're really hungry, serve a tossed green salad, too. And, of course, serve dry red wine. If you're going to have a dessert, be sure it's light, because when dessert time comes, you'll find you've packed away a lot of food. The foregoing recipe serves four, but it can be reheated again with additional profit if only two are served.

Walter Drennan is one of the leading real estate operators on the South Side in Chicago. He is a very astute businessman, a devotee of hunting and fishing, an accomplished skeet shooter, and he plays a wicked game of gin rummy. But with all these interests, I think his favorite avocation is cooking. He really goes in for cooking in a serious way, and has done considerable experimenting in roasting meats and fowls at a low temperature. He is one of the most enthusiastic members of the Wine and Food Society in Chicago and the Streeterville and Sanitary Canal Gourmet and Study Society. At one of the meetings where he was host and designated chef, he came up with another version of lamb shanks which ranks right along with the preceding recipe. This recipe calls for white wine.

LAMB SHANKS DRENNAN

4 *lamb shanks*	1 *tsp. paprika*
¼ *lb. butter*	1 *tsp. powdered ginger*
2 *onions*	1 *tsp. salt*
½ *cup dry white wine*	½ *tsp. pepper*
½ *cup tomato juice*	1 *cup chicken broth*

Remove all the fat from 4 lamb shanks. Melt ¼ pound of butter in a large skillet, brown the shanks well, and place in a casserole. In the same butter, sauté 2 sliced onions, then stir into the onions and butter ½ cup each of dry American white wine and tomato juice, 1 teaspoon of paprika, 1 teaspoon of powdered ginger, 1 teaspoon of salt, ½ teaspoon of pepper, and 1 cup of chicken broth. Cook and stir the mixture for a few minutes, then pour it over the shanks in the casserole. Cover, and bake in a 250-degree oven for 3 hours, or until tender, when the meat will come free of the bone easily.

Roast lamb, to my mind, is a great delicacy, whether plain roasted or roasted with wine. But roast lamb with mint gravy is something superlative. Notice that I said mint *gravy,* not mint sauce.

I've always been very fond of mint in drinks and as a flavoring agent. But mint sauce has always been too thin to suit my taste. On the other hand, I like rich brown lamb gravy. So I said to myself, why can't they be combined? So, after a bit of experimentation, a mint gravy resulted. And for my money it is tops in the category of roast meat gravies.

ROAST LAMB PROVENÇAL WITH MINT GRAVY

1 6- *to* 7-*lb. leg of lamb*	*Rosemary*
Garlic	*Water*
Flour	*Dry white wine*
Salt	*Bunch fresh mint*
Pepper	*5 tablespoons sugar*
	Cider vinegar

In a 6- or 7-pound leg of lamb insert a number of slivers of garlic so that they are distributed throughout the meat. Then sprinkle the top of the leg of lamb with flour, salt and pepper, and rosemary. Put the lamb in a roaster, pour in 1 cup of dry American white wine and 1 cup of water, cover, and put in a 500-degree oven. Let it remain for ½ hour, or until it begins to brown and a crust begins to form on top. Baste, turn the oven to 350 degrees, and let the lamb cook for 2 hours, basting it every half hour, and after each basting, squeezing a little lemon juice over it. At the end of 2 hours lift the leg of lamb out of the roaster, skim off the grease, and put the lamb back in and let cook for another half hour. If necessary during the cooking, add more white wine and water, in equal proportions.

The mint sauce should be made about 3 or 4 hours before the lamb has started cooking. Remove all the leaves and the tender tips of the stems from a bunch of fresh mint and chop them very fine. Put in a deep bowl, and add 5 rounded tablespoons of sugar. Cover this completely with cider vinegar. Stir well and cover. Let stand for about 6 hours, stirring every hour.

At the end of the 3-hour-cooking time, remove the leg of lamb to a hot platter, and if the juices have concentrated too much, add a little more white wine. In the meantime make a flour and water paste. Put in a separate saucepan 3 tablespoons of flour and a couple of pinches of salt. Start mixing this well with dripping cold water. Keep whipping constantly as the water is added, until it has a creamy consistency.

159

Into the juices of the roasting pan stir the flour paste slowly, until the juices are thickened. The gravy should be thicker than the average gravy, as the mint sauce to be added will thin it out. When the gravy is perfectly smooth, add the mint sauce and again stir thoroughly. Serve this mint gravy in a separate gravy boat.

Lamb and mutton are staples in Australia and many meat recipes are built around them. Two of the most interesting Australian recipes are those for curried kangaroo tail and curried lamb or mutton chops. I have never tasted the first, although I've been told that kangaroo tail is quite similar to oxtail. But I have prepared the curried chops, and I'm very fond of them.

CURRIED LAMB OR MUTTON CHOPS AUSTRALIAN

6 *lamb or mutton chops*	1 *tsp. salt*
2 *tbsp. bacon fat*	1 *tsp. sugar*
1 *small onion*	¼ *tsp. dry mustard*
1 *small apple*	½ *cup water*
1 *tbsp. flour*	1 *cup dry red wine*
1 *tbsp. curry powder*	*Cooked rice*

Lemon slices

Trim 6 lamb or mutton chops, removing the fat and gristle. Then heat 2 tablespoons of bacon drippings in a skillet and brown the chops. Next, remove the chops from the skillet, and fry in the same fat 1 small onion, sliced, and 1 small apple, cored and sliced, until they are slightly browned. Now add 1 tablespoon of flour, 1 tablespoon of curry powder, 1 teaspoon of salt, 1 teaspoon of sugar, ¼ teaspoon of dry mustard, ½ cup of water, and 1 cup of dry red wine. Mix well, then return the chops to the pan and simmer in the sauce until they are tender. In serving, make a border of cooked rice on the platter, put the chops in the center, and garnish with slices of lemon.

In many European countries, Easter, from a gastronomic standpoint, is one of the most important festivals of the year. In Italy, even breakfast on Easter day has its traditional menu, consisting of eggs prepared with vegetables and varied herbs, crusty Italian bread, and *caffe espresso,* which is served in 4-ounce glasses with a twist of lemon peel. Dinner is perhaps the most festive one of all the year, with a *pasta* of some sort, *agnellino al forno* (roasted whole baby lamb), roasted artichokes, a mixed salad, and for dessert the traditional *cassatelli* (cream tartlets), along with spumoni ice cream, cookies, and a basket of piping hot roasted chestnuts.

In old Russia, the greatest day of all the year used to be Easter. After midnight a special supper was served. There would be a table of *zakooskas* (assorted hot and cold hors d'oeuvres) with carafes of vodka. On another table would be a great ham, which had been wrapped in a paste of flour and water and slowly baked, fat ducks with *kasha* stuffing (*kasha* is buckwheat groats), and the *paskha* and a tall *baba,* which were a part of every Easter table in Russia. The *paskha* is a confection of cottage cheese, sugar, butter, seedless raisins, chopped almonds, and chopped or grated orange peel molded in a triangular wooden mold. *Baba,* or *kulitch,* as it also is called, is a tall cylindrical cake made with rum, chopped almonds, white raisins, grated orange peel, and, of course, flour, eggs, butter, milk, sugar, and yeast. It always is sliced in rounds, across the cake, with the top taken off first to be saved and put back, like a lid, on the part which remains.

Of the Easter season in eighteenth-century France, Brillat-Savarin wrote: "The strict observance of the Lenten fast gave rise to a pleasure unknown today—namely, that of breaking our fast by breakfasting on Easter day. I have seen two of my great-uncles, intelligent, serious men, almost faint with pleasure when on Easter day a ham was carved."

If it can be said that there is a traditional Easter dish in America, probably baked ham would be named. There are many ways of baking ham, all the way from using champagne down to ginger ale or cider. In rural Russia, fresh ham is even cooked with hay and beer. But I don't imagine that many people have ever had ham baked in crust with brandy. For most it will be a new gastronomic experience.

HAM BAKED IN CRUST WITH BRANDY

1 *10-lb. tenderized ham*   ½ *cup chopped herbs* (*chives,*
1 *cup brown sugar*   *parsley, tarragon, chervil,*
1 *cup honey*   *minced garlic, little green*
2 *tbsp. dry mustard*   *onion, oregano, pinch nut-*
Whole cloves   *meg*)
4 *lb. rye flour*   1 *tsp. caraway seeds*
Beef bouillon   *Brandy*

Remove the skin and rind from a 10-pound tenderized ham. Score the surface of the remaining fat.

Make a thick paste of 1 cup of brown sugar, solidly packed, 1 cup of honey, and 2 tablespoons of dry mustard, thoroughly mixed. Smear this over the ham (the paste should be thick enough not to run down the side of the ham, but not too thick to spread evenly. If too thick, thin with a little brandy). Stick a number of cloves over the top of the ham, being generous with them.

Next make a pastry crust by mixing 4 pounds of rye flour with enough canned beef bouillon to make a thick dough. On a slightly floured bread board, roll this dough out to about ½-inch thickness. Brush the dough with brandy, then sprinkle it with ½ cup of chopped mixed herbs, such as parsley, chervil, chives, tarragon, minced garlic, little green onion, oregano, and a pinch of nutmeg, all thoroughly mixed. Then scatter over the dough 1 teaspoon of caraway seeds. Now wrap the dough around the ham, forming a bottle-like opening on the top. Fashion a stopper of dough, roll it in flour, and set it lightly in the opening. Then put the encrusted ham in a 325-degree oven until the dough has set hard. Take the ham out, remove the stopper, and very slowly pour in all the brandy that the honey-sugar-mustard jacket will absorb. Then cork up the opening again, and bake in the same moderate oven for about 50 minutes more, or until the crust is thoroughly baked and brown. Break the crust and serve.

A year or so ago, while I was in Washington, I was invited for dinner to the home of a Virginian who has a colored cook noted for the way he prepares the famous Virginia ham. My host and I were in the kitchen fixing a libation, and I thought I would have some fun with the cook. I said I had a recipe for ham that would make it taste even better than Virginia ham. Sam, the cook, pricked up his ears, and asked how it could be done.

"Well," I told him, "I place the ham in a deep pan and the first day I soak it in a bottle of rye whiskey, and let it cook for a while. The second day I add a bottle of Jamaica rum, let it cook a little, and set it aside. The third day I add a bottle of port wine, and the fourth day a bottle of bourbon."

My host turned to his cook and asked, "What do you think of that, Sam?" "Well, suh, Mistuh Robert," Sam replied, "Ah don't know 'bout de ham, but it sho' sounds like mighty fine gravy!"

Although my recipe was strictly a gag, I think I'll have to try it sometime. I might be surprised. But I have tried and am very fond of ham baked in beer, which I learned from two old-maid sisters who had one of the finest eating places in San Antonio, Texas, during World War I. No one seemed to be able to put their finger on the wonderful flavor of their ham. It took me months to wangle the secret from them. But, as the copy book says, perseverance always wins.

BAKED HAM IN BEER

1 *boiled or tenderized ham*	1 *cup brown sugar*
Cloves	*Water*
½ *cup dry mustard*	12 *bay leaves*
	1 *quart beer*

Remove most of the fat from a previously tenderized or boiled ham, then score the entire surface of the remaining fat. Stick cloves over the entire surface of the ham, using the cloves generously. Next, mix a paste of ½ cup of dry mustard, 1 cup of brown sugar, and enough water to bring the paste to the consistency of the ordinary prepared mustard. Smear the mustard paste over the outside surface of the ham, and fasten a dozen small bay leaves to the ham with toothpicks. Place ham in a roaster, pour in 1 quart of beer, cover, and cook in a 450-degree oven for about 20 minutes per pound of ham.

One-dish or one-pot meals are an excellent idea, particularly when one has limited facilities or space. Many of them, after they are started, require little attention. And they're usually pretty succulent, too, because the various flavors blend together into one appetizing whole. This dish is a little different in that the ham butt is simmered in red wine.

WINE-SIMMERED HAM BUTT AND SAUERKRAUT

1 *lean smoked pork butt*
2 *medium-sized onions*
2 *medium-sized carrots*
Generous pinch thyme
2 *tbsp. chopped parsley*
10-12 *peppercorns*

4 *cups dry red wine*
4 *cups water*
1 *large can sauerkraut*
2 *tart apples*
2 *whole cloves*
½ *tsp. caraway seeds*

Put ham butt in a pot with 2 medium-sized onions, peeled and sliced, 2 medium-sized carrots, sliced, a generous pinch of thyme, 2 tablespoons chopped parsley, 10 or 12 peppercorns, 4 cups of dry red wine, and 4 cups of water. Bring to a boil slowly and boil for about 5 minutes, then reduce the heat and simmer until tender —about an hour and a half. Remove from the fire, and keep warm in the covered pot.

In another kettle put 3 cups of the stock the ham butt was boiled in, and add a large can of sauerkraut, 2 tart apples, peeled, cored, and sliced thin, 2 whole cloves, and ½ teaspoon of caraway seeds. Cook over a moderate flame until the stock is nearly absorbed and cooked away—about ¾ hour. Drain the sauerkraut, and arrange it around the ham butt on a hot platter. Slice the ham butt crossways with a very sharp knife, and serve with a helping of sauerkraut. Boiled white potatoes, mustard, and pickles contribute to make up a very delicious meal.

Have you ever tried fresh ham? It's not so easy to get as smoked ham, but it is delicious, especially when cooked according to this recipe which came from a Belgian convent.

BELGIAN HAM

1 *thick slice of fresh ham*
Lemon juice
1½ *tbsp. bacon fat*

2½ *cups dry white wine*
1 *cup mushroom stalks*
1 *lb. mushroom caps*

Cooked macaroni

Soak a thick slice of fresh ham in a little lemon juice for 4 hours. Dry well, then brown lightly on both sides in 1½ tablespoons of bacon drippings. Add 2 cups of American dry white wine and 1 cup of mushroom stalks, then close the pan tightly and cook for 2½ hours over a very low flame. Skim fat off sauce, strain, and add ½ cup of dry white wine. Fry one pound of mushroom caps, chop them, stir them into the sauce, and pour sauce over the macaroni, which has been cooked and placed on a platter around the ham.

The usual method of cooking a ham steak is to broil, to pan broil it, or to bake it in milk, all of which methods are mighty good. But they can't hold a candle to a ham steak baked with port.

HAM STEAK BAKED WITH PORT

1 *slice of ham*	4 *tbsp. prepared mustard*
½ *cup brown sugar*	¾ *cup port wine*

Water cress

Rub into both sides of a fairly thick slice of ham ½ cup of brown sugar. Then coat both sides with prepared mustard. About 4 tablespoons should be sufficient.

Place the prepared ham in a baking dish, and add ¾ cup of port wine. Bake in a moderate oven (350 degrees) for about 1 hour, basting occasionally with the port wine.

Remove the ham to a hot platter, skim off the fat, pour a little more port into the pan if necessary, stir well, and pour the sauce over the ham. Garnish with water cress.

In the Louisiana bayou country there is a famous dish called Jambalaya. It perhaps reaches its perfection among the Afro-American parish plantation cooks on the Delta. But the Louisiana Jambalaya is usually made of, or with, chicken, and therein it belies its name. But don't get me wrong—Louisiana Jambalaya is something to dream about, even though you are only mildly hungry.

Jambalaya probably started out as being "jambon à la ya," which is a mixture of French and African. *Jambon* is French for ham, and *ya* is sort of African for rice. Hence, to the purist, Jambalaya is a ham and rice stew. But there are shrimp Jambalayas, lobster Jambalayas, Jambalayas made with veal, and Jambalayas made with chicken. Trader Vic recalls his early days when his mother made Jambalaya which included both ham and shrimp. And I've eaten Jambalaya made with crab meat, but that would go at the bottom of my list. I've also eaten it made with ham, chicken, and pork sausages, which goes well to the top of my list. But best of all I like this recipe I got from an old mammy down in Louisiana who said that Jambalaya should have ham in it, or it should be called something else.

JAMBALAYA

1½ cups diced ham
½ lb. large, shelled shrimps
2 tbsp. olive oil
1½ tbsp. butter
2 onions
½ clove garlic
1 bay leaf
Salt
Pepper
1 cup uncooked brown rice
1 qt. consommé
½ green pepper
4 small tomatoes
Cayenne pepper
½ cup sherry
¼ cup dry red wine

In 2 tablespoons of olive oil sauté lightly 1½ cups of diced ham and ½ pound of large, peeled shrimps. Next add 1½ tablespoons of butter, 2 onions, finely chopped, ½ clove of garlic, minced, 1 bay leaf, and salt and pepper to taste. Then add 1 cup of washed, uncooked brown rice (not wild rice) or long-grain white rice. Sauté this until the rice is golden brown. At this point add 1 quart of consommé, which has been brought to the boiling point in a separate pan. Add ½ green pepper, finely chopped, and 4 small finely chopped tomatoes (or 1 cup of canned tomatoes). Also sprinkle in some cayenne pepper to taste.

Now cover the mixture, after carefully stirring, and let it simmer until the rice is done—about 25 to 30 minutes. Then comes the final touch, omitted in so many Jambalaya recipes. Add ½ cup of sherry and ¼ cup of California dry red wine. Do not stir again, but let it cook through, simmering until ready to serve. The best way to serve it is in an earthenware casserole; and if you want to be very swanky, you can garnish the casserole with broiled mushrooms.

I doubt whether there is any city in America that has as wide a variety of cooking as Hollywood. The one exception may be New York; yet I have never found a New York restaurant that served real English food in the English manner as perfectly and as tastefully as the Cock n' Bull on Hollywood's Sunset Boulevard. Perhaps because Hollywood has a flair for the unusual, there are a large number of unusual restaurants there, restaurants which serve foreign dishes cooked the way people in foreign countries cook them. In downtown Los Angeles there is a French restaurant which one would swear had been transplanted from the Left Bank in Paris; there is a Russian restaurant on Sunset Boulevard which seems to be a part of old Russia, and out in the valley is a Spanish restaurant that serves hot chocolate such as you never tasted outside of Spain. No matter what country one may come from, it is possible to find a restaurant which serves native food, properly cooked, and not an American version of it.

I used to live in the San Fernando valley, and at least once a week my wife and I had dinner at the Spanish restaurant mentioned above. And what meals they were, always topped off with a cup of hot chocolate. One dish I remember particularly was Spanish roast pork, and it so intrigued me that I coaxed the recipe from the señora who did the cooking.

SPANISH ROAST PORK

3-lb. *loin of pork*	2 *cans tomato soup*
¼ *cup olive oil*	1 *cup consommé*
⅓ *cup minced green pepper*	¼ *cup sherry*
1 *onion*	1 *tbsp. chili powder*
Salt	1 *cup ripe olives*
Pepper	½ *cup seedless raisins*
1 *clove garlic*	2 *cups cooked rice*

Buy a 3-pound loin of pork and have the butcher make a pocket in the roast by opening from the rib end to the chine. Then make the sauce. Heat ¼ cup of olive oil in a saucepan. Add ⅓ cup of green pepper, minced fine, 1 onion, minced fine, 1 minced clove of garlic, and salt and pepper to taste. Sauté these until they are wilted. Now add 2 cans of tomato soup (or tomato sauce) and 1 cup of consommé, and bring the mixture to a boil. Next combine

¼ cup of sherry with 1 tablespoon of chili powder and a pinch of salt, mix into a paste, and stir slowly into the boiling sauce. Add 1 cup of ripe olives, sliced (and pitted, of course) and ½ cup of seedless raisins, and cook about 4 or 5 minutes longer.

In the meantime cook the rice. Now to 2 cups of cooked rice add ¼ cup of the sauce, mix well, and stuff into the pocket of the roast. Place the roast in a baking pan or roaster, fat side up, and bake in a moderate oven (350 degrees) about 1 hour. Remove the roast from the oven, drain off most of the fat, and pour the remaining sauce over the meat. Return to the oven and bake for another hour. Then take out and serve. Sweet potatoes go well with this, although I am very fond of riced white potatoes with the pork. Avocado, either cut in half with French dressing poured in the pit cavity, or peeled and sliced on lettuce, should also accompany the roast. And there, amigos, is a very fine dish, a dish that will even bring amity to warring factions of Spanish politics—at least during meal time.

Cooking plain dishes is very simple, and not beyond the ability of almost any man, woman, or child above the age of twelve. Yet with a little imagination, or by following recipes whose directions are given in simple, orderly fashion, many gourmet dishes can be made from plain fare. For instance, let's take some plain fare—say pork chops—and make a gourmet dish.

PORK CHOPS IN SOUR CREAM AND MADEIRA

4 *loin pork chops*   ⅓ *cup sour cream*
3 *tbsp. Madeira*   *Salt*
                 Pepper

Pan broil 4 pork chops in the usual way. When tender, and a nice brown, remove them from the pan for a moment. If there is an excess of fat in the pan, pour it off. Then add 3 tablespoons of Madeira and ⅓ cup of sour cream, stirring well into the gravy, and scraping the pan to loosen any particles of meat that may adhere. Now return the pork chops to the pan, and cook for another five or ten minutes, frequently basting the chops. That's eating, brothers and sisters, and there's certainly nothing mysterious about the recipe or its preparation.

No matter how weak and puny an appetite may be, a broiled steak, a broiled lamb chop or two, or pan fried pork chops will put a hungry edge on an appetite, especially when you can sniff their savory odors while cooking. But as it would be impossible to judge a symphony by one or two passages, so it would be impossible to run the gamut of gastronomic delights that chops offer if you stick to broiling or frying.

Almost every country has its special ways of cooking chops—lamb, pork, or veal. The Hungarians cook pork chops submerged for the better part of an hour in water, to which a handful of caraway seeds and a spoonful of paprika have been added. The water simmers away, and the chops emerge ruddy brown on both sides, tender as the flesh of a peach, and with an incomparable flavor.

Norwegians prepare mutton chops in aspic, and in Normandy veal chops are prepared the same way. The Russians bread pork chops and serve them with a cherry or prune sauce. The Germans sandwich cooked apples and prunes between two pork chops, bread them, then fry them in butter. This dish is called *Kasseler Rippespeer* and is served with sauerkraut.

The Portuguese marinate pork chops in wine, garlic, and herbs for three or four days, then fry them and make a gravy out of the marinade and flour, which is then poured over them. And what a flavor!

Pork chops *charcutière* gets its name from the fact that it is the way Parisian pork butchers (*charcutiers*) cook their own pork chops.

PORK CHOPS CHARCUTIÈRE

6 *thick pork chops*	½ *cup dry white wine*
1 *large onion*	*Salt*
5 *tbsp. lard*	*Pepper*
1 *tsp. flour*	2 *tbsp. gherkins*
1 *cup consommé*	1 *tsp. prepared mustard*

Simmer 1 large or 2 small chopped onions in a small saucepan with 2 tablespoons of lard until tender, but don't brown. Then sprinkle in 1 teaspoon of flour, blending thoroughly with a wooden spoon, over a gentle fire, until mixture is golden. Now pour in gradually 1 cup of consommé and ½ cup of dry American white wine, stirring constantly. When the mixture begins to thicken, season to taste with salt and freshly ground black pepper. Bring to a boil, then skim well. Lower the flame and let the mixture simmer for about 30 minutes.

Meantime, cook 6 thick pork chops (2 pounds) in 2 or 3 tablespoons of lard. Brown on both sides over a hot flame, then lower heat and cook until chops are tender—about 20 to 25 minutes. Season to taste with salt and freshly ground pepper, and arrange chops on a hot dish. Now skim the sauce again, add 2 tablespoons of thinly sliced small gherkins and 1 teaspoon of prepared mustard. Let sauce heat for a moment, then pour it over the chops, dust the whole with chopped parsley, and serve at once.

Early in 1949 an article appeared in the *Saturday Evening Post* under the title, "What's Wrong with Southern Cooking?" It was written by Ralph McGill. In the article Mr. McGill deplored the corrupted corn bread, chicken fried in old crankcase oil, salad dressing of oily fat fit for drowning witches, and similar culinary crimes which have spread a blight across Dixie.

At this point a damyankee would like to disagree with Mr. McGill. In my perigrinations about the South, I have encountered some of the finest cooking to be found any place in this, or any other, country. I've lived in Texas, eaten my way through Louisiana, and exercised my dentures in Alabama, Georgia, Virginia, and Maryland. Perhaps, according to Mr. McGill, I've eaten in the wrong places, but I don't remember ever having an unpalatable dish. I think one reason why so many casual tourists do not get down to real eating in the South is because they dash madly through, gulping a hurried meal at a wayside restaurant or at a hotel. I travel leisurely, taking real time out to eat, and I have had a number of noteworthy dishes in the South. One of them was Maryland pork chops.

MARYLAND PORK CHOPS

4 *pork chops*
4 *slices tomato*
4 *slices onion*
4 *strips green pepper*
4 *strips red pepper*
4 *tbsp. uncooked rice*
Chopped celery
1 *cup Marsala*

Have pork chops cut 1 inch or more thick. Brown them slightly on both sides in a skillet. Then on each chop place a slice of tomato, a slice of onion, a strip of green pepper, and a strip of red pepper, and top with a tablespoon of uncooked rice. Fill the spaces between the pork chops, thus decorated, with chopped celery, pour in 1 cup of Marsala and bake for 3 hours in a very moderate oven.

With the exception of its use in Welsh rabbit, beer or ale as a cooking agent is almost unknown among Americans. But in Europe beer is frequently used in the preparation of many delectable dishes. Germany, of course, uses it in soup and in cooking fish, veal, pork, and beef. The Danes use beer in cooking roast beef. They prepare a roast of beef in the usual manner, start roasting it, and when it is ready to baste, they add dark beer to the pan, and baste the roast frequently until it is done to a beautiful brown.

The Danes also make a beer bisque, which is called *Ølost,* and the Germans are very fond of *Weissbiersuppe,* which is ale soup. One of Luxemburg's national dishes is a piquant veal stew, made with light beer and gingersnaps. And, of course, ham baked in beer is out of this world

One of the most typical American dishes is barbecued spareribs. There is one restaurant in Chicago—The Pit—which is so famous for its spareribs that people in Hollywood order them flown out there by air express. But have you ever tried stuffed barbecued spareribs cooked with beer? It really is pretty terrific, and productive of a new taste thrill. And it's slick for that outdoor barbecue party.

BARBECUED SPARERIBS WITH BEER

3 *lb. fresh spareribs (in two pieces)*	1½ *cups beer*
	Prepared mustard
1 *large onion*	2 *tbsp. vinegar*
¼ *lb. butter*	1 *tbsp. Worcestershire sauce*
4 *cups soft breadcrumbs*	2 *tbsp. lemon juice*
1 *tsp. poultry seasoning*	2 *tbsp. brown sugar*
½ *tsp. salt*	½ *cup chili sauce*
¼ *tsp. freshly ground pepper*	

Get yourself about 3 pounds of spareribs, in two pieces. First lightly brown a large onion, peeled and minced, in ¼ pound of butter. Then add 4 cups of soft breadcrumbs, 1 teaspoon of poultry seasoning, ½ teaspoon of salt, ¼ teaspoon freshly ground pepper, and ½ cup of beer. Mix this well together, and then spread it between the two pieces of spareribs. Fasten the two pieces together with short metal skewers and brush the ribs with prepared mustard. Then combine 1 cup of beer, 2 tablespoons of vinegar, 1 tablespoon of Worcestershire sauce, 2 tablespoons of lemon or lime juice, 2 tablespoons of brown sugar, and ½ cup of chili sauce. Heat this mixture in a saucepan, stirring until the sugar dissolves. Now broil your spareribs over charcoal, or bake in a moderate oven, for about an hour (45 minutes to 1 hour over charcoal, or 1 to 1½ hours in the oven), until thoroughly cooked, brown and crisp, basting frequently with the sauce.

Another interesting way of preparing spareribs is to cook them with Burgundy.

SPARERIBS BURGUNDY

3 *lb. fresh spareribs*	3 *apples*
Salt	½ *cup chili sauce*
Pepper	1 *cup Burgundy*
½ *cup chopped onion*	3 *tbsp. brown sugar*

Wipe 3 pounds of fresh spareribs with a damp cloth, sprinkle with salt and pepper, and lay in a large roaster. Cover with ½ cup of chopped onion. Pare and core 3 apples, cut in half lengthwise, and place around the meat. Mix ½ cup chili sauce with ½ cup Burgundy, and spread it over the apples and the meat. Dot the apples with 3 tablespoons of brown sugar. Cover, and bake in a hot oven (450 degrees) for 1 hour; then uncover, pour another ½ cup of Burgundy over all, and bake until brown (about 15 minutes), basting occasionally. This might serve six, but don't count on it. Better not stretch it over more than four. There'll be nothing left, I assure you.

The number of people who are unenthusiastic about veal is surprising. Some claim it is indigestible, others think it dry and stringy, and most say that it is too bland and without any particular flavor. Well, my answer to the first statement is that, in France, veal is highly recommended for invalids. And to the other objections, I claim that veal, properly cooked, is one of the most delicate and subtly flavored meats obtainable. Veal roasted with red wine yields one of the most delicious gravies you've ever tasted, and there are dozens of ways of cooking delectable veal chops and veal stews.

I think my favorite veal dish is Veal Scallopini Marsala. I am not an Italian, and yet I have never found veal scallopini Marsala in any Italian restaurant, even the finest, that even approached my recipe. But you, dear reader, can make it just as well as I can if you will heed my warning as to some of the ingredients. First, use only the best olive oil; second, use only imported Parmesan or Romano cheese, and third, use only the imported Florio Marsala, because it is virgin dry while most of the others are too sweet. These three ingredients are back on the market now. The dish is really simple to prepare and cook—here's the recipe.

VEAL SCALLOPINI MARSALA

1 *lb. veal cutlet*	1 *clove garlic*
½ *cup grated Parmesan cheese*	½ *cup consommé*
Salt	2 *tsp. lemon juice*
Pepper	*Marjoram*
2 *tbsp. olive oil*	*Thyme*
	½ *cup Florio Marsala*

Get a veal cutlet weighing about 1 pound, and cut not more than 1 inch thick. Place it on a wooden board, sprinkle it generously with grated Parmesan cheese, and pound it with a wooden mallet or wooden potato masher. Then turn it over, sprinkle again generously with the grated Parmesan cheese, and pound it again. Repeat this process until you have used about ½ cup of the grated cheese and the cutlet has become between ¼ and ½ inch thick. Sprinkle on both sides with salt and pepper, then cut the meat into 3-inch strips, each about 1 inch wide.

Heat 2 tablespoons olive oil with a crushed clove of garlic in it, and then put in the meat and brown it on both sides. Add ½ cup of consommé, ½ cup of Florio Marsala, and 2 teaspoons of lemon juice. As this begins to cook, add a pinch each of marjoram and thyme. Then cover the skillet and simmer slowly for about 30 minutes, or until the veal is tender.

On the Midway, near the University of Chicago, is a small restaurant that is popular with the students, faculty members, and near-by residents. Often I stop there to pick up some ice cream to take home or, if it is late at night, for a hamburger and cup of coffee. One night I got to talking with the daughter of the proprietor about Greek cooking. I asked her whether she was familiar with *Moussak à la Grecque,* and her face lighted up.

"O, yes," she replied, "we frequently have it at home. No one can make it quite like my mother. It is so delicious, you should try it some time."

When I told her I was fond of it myself and had prepared it, she insisted on hearing how I made it so that she could compare my recipe with her mother's. She was thrilled when she found my recipe was almost identical with that of her mother. It should be, for mine came from the chef of the Grande Bretagne Hotel in Athens and is authentic. I can recommend it as being easy to prepare, inexpensive, and delicious beyond words.

MOUSSAK À LA GRECQUE
(Veal and Eggplant)

1½ lb. ground veal	4 tbsp. olive oil
3 large eggplants	Fine breadcrumbs
2 medium-sized onions	1 whole egg
2 tbsp. butter	Parmesan cheese
1 tbsp. tomato paste	1¾ cups milk
Salt	¼ cup sherry
Pepper	3 tbsp. melted butter
3 tbsp. chopped parsley	2 tbsp. flour
4 ounces dry white wine	Yolk of 1 egg
Pinch nutmeg	

Peel and chop 2 medium-sized onions, and sauté them in 2 tablespoons of butter in a skillet. Then add the ground veal, and sauté until both the onions and the meat are nicely browned. Then add 1 tablespoon of tomato paste, 3 tablespoons of chopped parsley, salt and pepper to taste, and 4 ounces of dry American white wine. Cover the skillet, and let simmer slowly until the meat is well cooked and the juices have almost been absorbed.

Meanwhile, cut 3 large eggplants into ⅜-inch slices, and fry them in 4 tablespoons of olive oil in another skillet until golden brown.

Add 3 tablespoons of fine breadcrumbs to the meat-and-onion mixture, and 1 lightly beaten egg. Mix together well.

Now butter a casserole and sprinkle the bottom with fine bread-crumbs. First, put in a layer of the eggplant over the crumbs. Then put a layer of meat on top of the eggplant, and liberally sprinkle the meat mixture with grated Parmesan cheese. Then add another layer of the eggplant, the remaining half of the meat mix-ture, sprinkled with the cheese, and a final layer of eggplant.

In the meantime, prepare the sauce. Bring 1¾ cups of milk to the boiling point, then add to it 3 tablespoons of melted butter and ¼ cup of sherry. Thicken this with 2 tablespoons of flour and season with salt and pepper to taste and a pinch of nutmeg, stirring all the while to keep the mixture smooth and free from any lumps. Remove from the fire and add 1 beaten egg yolk.

Pour this sauce over the eggplant and meat in the casserole, sprinkle with grated Parmesan cheese and fine breadcrumbs, dot with butter, and bake uncovered in a moderate oven (350 degrees) for about ¾ hour. When finished, the top should be a golden brown.

Excellent companions with this delectable Greek dish are whipped potatoes, baby lima beans, and, of course, a dry Amer-ican white wine. After such a dinner, you perhaps will be moved to write a poem on Greece even as Lord Byron did.

The little duchy of Luxemburg—"Luxembish," as the dough-boys of World War I called it—is noted for its excellent but low-cost food. A majority of the population are said to be gourmets, and I can well believe it after tasting one of their national dishes, a delicious, piquante veal stew. Strange to say, it is a favorite dish among the hairdressers of France, where it is known as *Veau des Coiffeuses*. But then, French hairdressers are usually gourmets, so perhaps it isn't so strange after all.

A couple of the ingredients may bother you, but don't let them stop you from preparing it. You'll be well paid for this adventure in cooking.

LUXEMBURG VEAL STEW

2 *lb. shoulder of veal*	*Pinch thyme*
Flour	*Pinch marjoram*
3 *tbsp. butter*	*Dash cayenne pepper*
1 *large onion*	*Salt*
3 *tomatoes*	*Pepper*
1 *bay leaf*	2½ *cups light beer*
5 *whole cloves*	5 *gingersnaps*

Juice 1 *lemon*

Cut 2 pounds of shoulder of veal into about 1-inch square cubes, roll them in flour, and fry them lightly in 3 tablespoons of butter. Take them out of the pan and set aside for a moment, then fry one large onion, sliced, in the same butter. Now, put the meat and the onion together in a stewpan, add 3 tomatoes, peeled, seeded, and cut in quarters; one bay leaf, 5 cloves, a pinch of thyme, a pinch of marjoram, a dash of cayenne pepper, and salt and pepper to taste. If you have a dried red pepper bean, put half of it in place of the red pepper.

Next add 2½ cups of light beer. Cover your pan tightly, and cook very slowly for 2 hours. Then moisten 5 gingersnaps with water, crush, and add to the contents of the pan. Put the lid back on and continue cooking slowly for 30 minutes more. Just before taking up, add the juice of one lemon. With this stew, serve riced potatoes.

Olives are most often served as a relish. But they have great value in cooking, and the secret of many a delicious French or Spanish recipe lies in the use of olives, green or ripe. If you have never used olives in cooking, try this dish of veal rolls with olive sauce that is a favorite of gourmets along the Riviera.

VEAL ROLLS WITH OLIVES

2 *lb. veal steak*	*Onion juice*
Sausage meat	1 *clove garlic*
Breadcrumbs	*Flour*
Sherry	2 *tbsp. butter*
Pinch nutmeg	½ *cup condensed tomato soup*
Pinch marjoram	½ *cup consommé*

2 *tbsp. chopped green olives*

Flatten a 2-pound veal steak to about a ½-inch thickness. This can be done if you have a meat cleaver; if not, use a wooden mallet or the handle of a large heavy knife. After the steak is flattened, cut it in strips about 3 inches wide and 4 inches long. On the strips spread sausage meat mixed with a small amount of breadcrumbs which have been slightly moistened with sherry. Flavor the strips with a speck of nutmeg, a pinch of marjoram, and a few drops of onion juice. If you are fond of garlic, rub the strips of veal lightly with a peeled clove of garlic before covering with the sausage meat and breadcrumbs and omit the onion juice. Now roll up the pieces of veal, fasten with wooden toothpicks, sprinkle well with flour, and brown them in 2 tablespoons of butter in a heavy skillet.

When browned, remove the rolls, and add about ½ cup of tomato sauce (canned soup will do very well) and ½ cup of consommé to the skillet. Let it boil up, then replace the veal rolls, cover the pan, and cook slowly for 30 minutes. Now add 2 tablespoons of chopped green olives, and cook 10 minutes more. Serve very hot, and accompany the veal rolls with buttered noodles sprinkled generously with Parmesan cheese. A tossed green salad goes best with this dinner, and a dry American white wine marries with the whole beautifully.

Leafing through a magazine one evening, I ran across a paragraph with the caption, "Meals Mere Men Can Make." And underneath was this statement: "With so many fine foods in cans to choose from, plus the agreeable fact that canned foods are so simple to prepare and serve—you can turn even a husband loose in the kitchen and expect a feast! He just can't go wrong in preparing a meal to be proud of—a most economical and nutritious meal—around canned foods."

Now I will admit that delicious meals can be prepared from food in cans. But I must take exception to the words "mere man" and "you can turn even a husband loose in the kitchen and expect a feast" (out of cans).

Gentlemen, are we men or mice? Are we to be mere (only this and nothing else) men, or a positive force? Let us then be up and doing, and prove our worth. Let us assert ourselves! Let us show the Little Women in our households that we are not slaves to food in cans but really are ingenious, resourceful, and capable. For instance, send the wife to a good movie this afternoon, make a quick trip to the grocery and meat market, and then in her absence whip up the following for dinner.

SPANISH STEAK

1 *lb. veal steak*	1 *tbsp. lemon juice*
2 *tbsp. bacon fat*	1 *tbsp. minced onion*
2 *tbsp. flour*	½ *cup Madeira*
½ *tsp. salt*	½ *cup consommé*
½ *tsp. paprika*	½ *cup sliced pimentos*
2 *tbsp. brown sugar*	*Stuffed olives*
	Parsley

Brown 1 pound of veal steak well in 2 tablespoons of bacon drippings in a heavy skillet, then remove meat from pan. Add 2 tablespoons of flour to the fat and stir until smooth. Add ½ teaspoon of salt, ½ teaspoon of paprika, 2 tablespoons of brown sugar, 1 tablespoon of lemon juice, 1 tablespoon of minced onion, ½ cup of Madeira, and ½ cup of consommé. When all this is blended, return the meat to the skillet and simmer over a low heat until tender (about 30 minutes). Now add ½ cup of sliced pimentos and the stuffed olives and cook 5 minutes longer. Garnish with hot whole pimentos, olives, and parsley, and serve. Whipped or riced potatoes and an avocado salad go well with this.

Taste, according to that great gastronomer, Brillat-Savarin, has two principal functions. It invites us, by pleasure, to repair the continual losses which we suffer by the activities of life, and it aids us to select, among the various substances which nature presents to us, those which are nutritious. "Taste," he writes, "is yet one of our senses that, all things considered, procures to us the greatest number of enjoyments, because (a) the pleasure of eating is the only one that, taken in moderation, is never followed by fatigue; (b) it belongs to all times and all ages; (c) it occurs necessarily at least once a day, and may be repeated without inconvenience two or three times in this space of time; (d) it may be combined with other pleasures, and even console us for their absence; (e) in eating we receive a certain indefinable and special comfort, which arises from the intuitive consciousness that we repair our losses and prolong our existence by the food we eat."

Brillat-Savarin also believes that without the participation of smell there is no perfect taste, and I thoroughly agree with him. Practically all foods having flavor are odorous, a fact which places them in the empire of smell as well as in the empire of taste. Take veal chops with Madeira and mushrooms, for instance.

VEAL CHOPS WITH MADEIRA AND MUSHROOMS

6 *veal chops with kidneys*	1 *tbsp. chopped parsley*
4 *small onions*	1 *cup consommé*
½ *lb. fresh mushrooms*	1 *cup sour cream*
2 *stalks celery*	1 *tbsp. tomato paste*
5 *tbsp. butter*	*Salt*
Flour	*Cayenne pepper*
Pinch thyme	½ *cup Madeira*
Pinch marjoram	2 *tbsp. brandy*

Slice 4 peeled small onions and ½ pound of fresh mushrooms, and chop 2 stalks of celery. Sauté these in 4 tablespoons of butter until they are tender. Then add a generous tablespoon of flour, a pinch each of thyme and marjoram, and 1 tablespoon of chopped parsley, and, after mixing well with the sautéed vegetables, cook for about 5 minutes. Then add 1 cup of consommé, 1 cup of sour cream, 1 tablespoon of tomato paste, salt to taste, and a little cayenne pepper. Boil this up and add ½ cup of Madeira. Now turn the flame low, and allow to simmer while the chops are prepared.

Dust 6 veal chops, with the kidneys attached (however, you can omit the kidneys if you don't care for them), on both sides with flour, and sauté in 1 tablespoon of hot butter until they are nicely browned (this should be done in a fairly deep skillet that can be covered). When the chops are browned, pour 2 tablespoons of brandy over them, set it alight and let burn for a few minutes. Then extinguish the flames by pouring the onion-mushroom-wine sauce over them. Cover the skillet and cook for at least 30 minutes over a very low heat. Fast cooking will ruin this dish.

Here's another dish that will sharpen the most dulled appetite and start the nostrils quivering.

VEAL CHOPS PARMESAN IN WHITE WINE

4 veal chops   Flour
Lime juice   Grated Parmesan cheese
Salt   1 beaten egg
Freshly ground pepper   2 tbsp. butter
                  ¾ cup dry white wine

Trim 4 veal crops, brush with lime juice, sprinkle with salt and freshly ground pepper, then dip them first in hot butter, then in flour, and then in grated Parmesan cheese. Let them remain thus until they are well soaked. Then dip them in the beaten egg, once more in flour, and then in the grated cheese, and let the seasoning soak in for about 2 hours.

When ready to cook, sauté the chops quickly in 2 tablespoons of hot butter until they are browned on both sides. Then pour into the skillet around the chops ¾ cup of dry American white wine. Cover, and summer slowly for 30 to 40 minutes, or until very tender.

Boiled macaroni, well buttered and sprinkled with grated Parmesan cheese, is practically a "must" with this delectable dish.

I have never been able to figure out why the so-called "variety meats" are looked upon with contempt and so heartily disliked among Americans. One of the easiest ways to gain gastronomic distinction, and at the same time keep a very sensitive food budget from falling apart at the seams, is to use these variety meats. European cooks have long recognized their excellence, and some of the most celebrated gourmet dishes are prepared from kidneys, tripe, brains, tongue, sweetbreads, and liver. The last two have moved up into the higher-price brackets, but the others will not strain even the most fragile budget. They are not only excellent eating—when properly prepared—but there is little or no waste to them. They're also excellent for our well-being.

I am going to start with an assertion that will be difficult to contradict: Either you like kidneys or you don't. Now, I am going to make a suggestion: If you don't like them, forget your inhibitions and try the following recipe for ragout of kidney. There was a time when I didn't like kidneys, but my wife made this dish for me, and I was converted after the first mouthful. I almost might say, after the first delightful aroma was wafted to my nostrils.

A word about preparing kidneys: Wash them first in cold water and remove the outer skin. Then soak them in salted water for 2 or 3 hours. When preparing them, remove the white centers and tubes with a sharp, pointed knife, or better still, with a pair of manicure scissors.

And now for a leader on the gourmet's hit parade, Lamb Kidney Stew with Wines and Brandy.

LAMB KIDNEY STEW WITH WINES AND BRANDY

12 *lamb kidneys*	*Salt*
1 *lb. mushrooms*	*Pepper*
6 *little green onions*	*½ cup dry white wine*
¼ *green pepper*	*2 ounces Madeira*
4 *tbsp. butter*	*2 ounces brandy*
1 *tbsp. chopped parsley*	*½ cup sour cream*

Wash 12 lamb kidneys in cold water, remove the outer skin, and soak them in salted water for 2 or 3 hours. Then cut them in half, remove the white centers and tubes with a sharp pointed knife, and slice them thin.

Slice 1 pound of fresh mushrooms. Chop 6 little green onions very fine and chop ¼ green pepper, after removing the seeds. That's your preliminary work.

Sauté the chopped onions and the chopped green peppers in 4 tablespoons of butter slowly until they are slightly browned. Then add the sliced kidneys, the pound of sliced mushrooms, 1 tablespoon of chopped parsley, salt and freshly ground pepper to taste, ½ cup of dry American white wine, 2 ounces of Madeira, and 2 ounces of brandy. Cover and simmer gently for about 1½ hours, stirring every once in a while.

Shortly before serving add ½ cup of sour cream. Cook a few minutes longer, check for seasoning, and serve.

Broiled kidneys are almost indigenous to the English breakfast, and I have known Britons who had kidneys shipped to them when they traveled beyond the source of supply. In the days of the czars some Russian gourmets made special trips to the station restaurant at Tsarkoe Selo just to enjoy some of its famous kidney specialties.

You don't have to go out onto the highways and byways to find delectable kidney dishes. Just a trip to your favorite butcher and wine merchant is all you need to do to prepare either or both of the following kidney recipes.

LAMB KIDNEYS SAUTÉED IN WHITE WINE

8 *lamb kidneys*	1 *little green onion*
5 *tbsp. butter*	1 *tbsp. flour*
1 *cup sliced mushrooms*	*Salt*
1 *clove garlic*	*Pepper*
1 *tbsp. chopped parsley*	½ *cup dry white wine*
Buttered toast	

Get 8 lamb kidneys, cut them in half, skin them, and remove the white core. Then slice them very thin.

In a saucepan melt 1 tablespoon of butter, and sauté 1 cup of sliced mushrooms until they are tender—about 7 or 8 minutes. Remove the mushrooms, and keep them warm. Then add 4 tablespoons of butter and 1 minced clove of garlic to the saucepan the mushrooms were cooked in, and when the butter is bubbling add the sliced kidneys, 1 tablespoon of chopped parsley, and 1 little green onion, finely chopped. Stir over a brisk flame while the kidneys brown—about 5 minutes. Then add 1 tablespoon of flour, and when it is blended in, add the sautéed mushrooms, salt and pepper to taste, and ½ cup of dry American white wine. Reduce the flame, and cook for about 5 minutes more. Serve over slices of buttered toast.

Beef kidneys are usually better when sliced. The following dish is not so fancy as kidney stew, but is equally delicious.

KIDNEYS IN RED WINE

1 *beef kidney*	1 *tbsp. flour*
3 *tbsp. butter*	1¼ *cups canned tomatoes*
1 *onion*	*Pinch marjoram*
½ *clove garlic*	*Pinch thyme*
Salt	2 *cups dry red wine*
Pepper	1½ *ounces brandy*

Remove the skin, fibers, and fat from a beef kidney, and cut it in thin slices.

Melt 2 tablespoons of butter, and sauté in it 1 thinly sliced peeled onion and ½ clove of garlic until butter is brown. Then add the kidney slices, with salt and pepper to taste, and let them cook through—about 5 minutes. Then remove the kidneys and set them aside.

Add 1 tablespoon of flour to the butter and onions, and blend thoroughly. Then add 1¼ cups of canned tomatoes, a pinch each of marjoram and thyme, salt and pepper to taste, and 2 cups of dry American red wine. Let this simmer for about 10 minutes.

In the meantime melt 1 tablespoon of butter in another saucepan, and when it is well browned, add the slices of kidneys. Then pour over the kidneys 1½ ounces of brandy, and set it alight. When it has burned out, add the kidneys and juices to the onions and tomatoes, and cook without a cover until the gravy is thick enough to serve.

There was a time when the butcher gave away liver, or, at worst, charged only a few cents for it. But that quaint old custom is gone forever. Ever since the medical profession discovered the tremendous value of liver in malnutrition cases of almost every kind, it jumped into the luxury class. But properly prepared, liver is worth what you pay for it, not only in taste but in its healthful properties. There is no waste to liver, and it shrinks very little, unless overcooked. In order of quality come calf's liver, beef liver (from young cattle), lamb's liver, pig's liver, and sheep's liver. Good fresh liver should be clear, bright, and of a yellowish red color.

Liver and bacon and liver and onions are probably the two best-known liver dishes, but on too many cook stoves they are horribly mistreated. When liver has been cooked too slowly and too long, especially when fried, it is frequently tough and flavorless. When perfectly cooked, its juices are pinkish, its flavor is superb, and it is as tender as a woman's heart. . . . Well, anyway, tender.

The Italians have a marvelous way of cooking liver and onions, as follows:

LIVER AND ONIONS, ITALIAN STYLE

8 *thin liver slices*	*Flour*
½ *cup dry red wine*	*Salt*
4 *medium-sized onions*	*Pepper*
6 *tbsp. olive oil*	1 *pinch oregano*

Add about ½ cup of American dry red wine to 8 thin liver slices, and let stand in the refrigerator for an hour or so, turning the liver occasionally. About ½ hour before serving time sauté 4 sliced medium-sized onions in about 4 tablespoons of olive oil until lightly browned. Then remove them and keep them hot. Add about 2 more tablespoons of olive oil to the skillet, drain the liver slices, keeping the marinade, roll in seasoned flour, and brown them, adding a little more butter or oil if needed. The cooking time should be about 3 or 4 minutes to each side. Take out the liver and keep it hot. To the fat in the skillet add 1 tablespoon of flour and a pinch of oregano, blend well, and then stir in the wine in which the liver was marinated. Cook, stirring, until the gravy is smooth and slightly thickened. Season to taste. Arrange the liver and onions on a hot platter, and pour the wine gravy over all.

Down South the Creoles have a pretty terrific way of cooking liver and bacon.

LIVER AND BACON, CREOLE STYLE

6 *thin slices liver*
Flour
Salt
Pepper
2 *tbsp. bacon fat*
1 *cup onion rings*
1 *cup sliced green pepper*
1 *cup sliced mushrooms*
1 *cup canned tomatoes*

1 *clove garlic*
1 *bay leaf*
Pinch thyme
Pinch marjoram
1 *tbsp. chopped parsley*
10 *peppercorns*
½ *tsp. dry mustard*
Dash paprika
½ *cup dry white wine*

3 *tbsp. Madeira*

Dust 6 thin slices of liver with seasoned flour. Brown on both sides in 2 tablespoons of bacon drippings; then add to the skillet 1 cup of thinly sliced onion (rings separated), 1 cup of thinly sliced green pepper (seeds and white ribs removed), 1 cup of thinly sliced fresh mushrooms, 1 cup of canned tomatoes, 1 crushed clove of garlic, 1 bay leaf, a pinch each of marjoram and thyme, 1 tablespoon of chopped parsley, 10 peppercorns, slightly bruised, ½ teaspoon of dry mustard, salt to taste, and a dash of paprika. Then pour over all ½ cup of American dry white wine. Now cover the skillet tightly, and bake in a moderate oven (350 degrees) for 1 hour. When ready to serve, stir in 3 tablespoons of Madeira.

Perhaps one reason more Americans aren't fond of liver is because, all too often, it is cooked too long. The delightful nutty flavor is vitiated by long-drawn-out sautéing or frying. Try sautéing liver in bacon fat for about 3 or 4 minutes on each side. Or try sautéing it in claret.

LIVER SAUTÉED WITH CLARET

1½ *lb. calves liver*
Flour
Salt
Pepper

Oregano
6 *tbsp. olive oil*
2 *onions*
½ *cup claret*

Have 1½ pounds of calf's liver sliced about ¾ inch thick. Toss in seasoned flour, then sprinkle with oregano.

Put 6 tablespoons of olive oil in a heavy skillet, and when hot, brown 2 peeled and sliced onions in it until soft, which should be about 3 or 4 minutes. Remove the onions, and fry the liver in the same olive oil for about 3 minutes on each side over a high flame. Put the sautéed onions back in the pan with the liver, add ½ cup of American claret. Let everything cook over the high flame for a couple of minutes, then remove from the fire and serve immediately.

Sweetbreads seem to be thought of as a delicacy peculiar to the rich and to exclusive restaurants where expensive chefs prepare only costly dishes. But they can be prepared in the ordinary home and made into the most delightful and palatable dishes.

There is one important point to remember about sweetbreads. When they come from the butcher, do not put them in the refrigerator but immediately plunge them into lukewarm water to draw out the blood. Let them remain in soak for at least an hour, changing the water several times. Then put them in a pan of cold water, add a pinch of salt and the juice of half a lemon for each pair of sweetbreads, bring the water slowly to the boiling point, and then simmer gently for 15 minutes. This is a culinary process called "blanching." Next put them again into cold water and let them stand for 15 minutes or so; then remove the tubes and membranes, being careful not to tear or break the tissues. Only then should the sweetbreads be placed in the refrigerator. They should be prepared as soon thereafter as possible, for they easily absorb the flavor of other foods with which they come in contact.

One of the most delightful ways I know for cooking sweetbreads is the following:

SWEETBREADS SMOTHERED IN WINE

1 *pair sweetbreads*	*Pinch thyme*
Water	*Salt*
4 *tbsp. butter*	*Pepper*
1 *small onion*	¼ *lb. fresh mushrooms*
1 *small carrot*	½ *cup consommé*
1 *stalk celery*	½ *cup Madeira*
1 *bay leaf*	1 *tsp. flour*

Soak 1 pair of fine sweetbreads in cold water for 1 hour. Then parboil them slowly in a good quantity of water for about 20 minutes, and plunge them again into cold water. When cool, remove any undesirable bits, and press out the water.

Melt 2 tablespoons of butter in a saucepan, put the sweetbreads into the pan, and brown slightly. Then add 1 small onion, peeled and chopped, 1 small carrot, finely chopped, and 1 stalk of celery, finely chopped, 1 minced bay leaf, and a pinch of thyme. Season with salt and freshly ground pepper to taste, cover the saucepan tightly, and continue cooking until the sweetbreads are a golden brown. During the cooking, occasionally uncover the pan and turn the sweetbreads, so that they will brown evenly.

While the sweetbreads are cooking, melt 2 tablespoons of butter in another pan, and sauté ¼ pound of fresh mushrooms until they are tender—about 7 or 8 minutes.

When the sweetbreads have attained their proper color, add the sautéed mushrooms to the sweetbreads and vegetables, and pour in ½ cup of consommé and ½ cup of Madeira. Cover the pan and let the whole thing simmer for about 20 minutes. Then remove the sweetbreads to a hot platter, thicken the gravy with a scant teaspoon of flour, heat up, and pour the sauce over the sweetbreads and serve.

I venture to say that there will be some readers who will wrinkle their noses or arch their eyebrows at the mere mention of tripe. But then, once upon a time, I was that way too—that is, until I was induced to partake of *Tripe à la Mode de Caen.*

Since the days of ancient Babylon (and possibly even before that) tripe has been a great delicacy among the aristocrats and a relished staple among the peasantry. In the *Taming of the Shrew,* Katherina admits to Grumio that she likes well a fat tripe, finely broiled; so Shakespeare evidently had a fondness for tripe. Tripe is a favorite dish in most of the countries of Europe, but in France it can be listed as almost indispensable. In many French cities there are special shops, called triperies, which deal only in tripe. It is sold already cooked, in a dozen or more different ways, and one has only to take it home and heat it.

One of the great restaurants in Paris, Pharamond's, was made famous by a dish that originated in the medieval city of Caen, better known for its stone quarries. At Pharamond's, *Tripe à la Mode de Caen* is served in individual pewter plates, with small ovens built into them in which glowing charcoal is placed to keep the heavenly dish bubbling hot as one eats it.

Tripe à la Mode de Caen is not a dish to whip up on arriving home from the office, or one to be decided upon when friend husband 'phones he is bringing the boss home for dinner and demands (or begs) something unusual. After the preliminary preparation, it should remain in the oven for at least 12 hours (in Normandy it is cooked 16 hours!). But if Uncle Thwacker (the bachelor with cardiac trouble and a safety deposit box stuffed full of tax-exempt bonds) writes and tells you he is planning to drop in for dinner come Whitsuntide, by all means, plan on *Tripe à la Mode de Caen*. Such a dish, served to Uncle Thwacker, will put you in the Number 1 spot after his words, "I give and devise and bequeath . . ."

TRIPE À LA MODE DE CAEN

3 *lb. fresh honeycomb tripe*	*Thyme*
4 *slices fat salt pork*	*Marjoram*
2 *sliced carrots*	*Mace*
2 *sliced onions*	2 *large bay leaves*
2 *chopped tomatoes*	8 *small peppercorns*
2 *leeks*	2 *whole cloves*
2 *stalks celery*	1 *teaspoon salt*
1 *large green pepper*	*Cayenne pepper*
1 *clove garlic*	1 *cup bouillon*
2 *calf's feet (meat and bones)*	1 *cup dry white wine*
1 *tbsp. minced parsley*	6 *little green onions*
	1 *cup brandy*

Wash 3 pounds of fresh honeycomb tripe in two or three changes of cold water, drain, and cut in strips about ¾ inch wide and 2½ to 3 inches long. Line the bottom of an earthenware casserole (or a metal Dutch oven) with 4 slices of fat salt pork. Add 2 sliced carrots, 2 sliced onions, 2 chopped tomatoes, 2 leeks, 2 stalks of celery, 1 large green pepper rather finely minced, and a clove of garlic, also minced. Over this vegetable layer arrange the strips of tripe, and add 2 calf's feet (meat and bones) cut up.

Season with 1 tablespoon of minced parsley, a generous pinch each of thyme, marjoram, and mace, 2 large bay leaves, 8 small peppercorns, slightly bruised, 2 whole cloves, 1 teaspoon salt, and a slight sprinkling of cayenne pepper. Cover the whole with equal parts of beef bouillon and dry American white wine—probably a cup of each will be sufficient. Now, put the cover on the pot, seal with flour and water paste, and bake in the slowest possible oven overnight, or for at least 12 hours.

When you break the seal and remove the cover, your nostrils will be assailed by the most heavenly odor you have ever experienced. But a final step remains. Add 6 finely minced little green onions and a cup of brandy. Heat again, and serve bubbling hot.

The Italians are very fond of tripe and have a number of excellent ways of preparing it. *Tripe à la Mode de Caen* is still my favorite, but this Italian recipe runs it a close second.

TRIPE WITH WHITE WINE, ITALIAN

2½ lb. honeycomb tripe	6 dry salted capers
1 lb. Italian sausage	1¼ cups canned tomatoes
Water	5 crushed peppercorns
½ cup olive oil	Salt
¼ cup chopped onion	Dash allspice
1 clove garlic	Tiny pinch cayenne pepper
½ stalk celery	½ cup beef bouillon
¼ medium-sized carrot	1 cup dry white wine
1 tbsp. chopped parsley	½ cup grated Parmesan cheese
Generous pinch oregano	½ cup fine breadcrumbs
	Boiled rice

Wash 2½ pounds of fresh honeycomb tripe in cold water, slice it in strips about ½ inch wide and 3 inches long. Boil it for about 15 minutes in enough water to cover. Wash it again in cold water and drain thoroughly.

In a medium-sized frying pan put 1 cup of cold water and 1 pound of Italian sausage (*salsiccia*). Boil briskly for 3 minutes, then lower the flame and prick the sausage with a fork, allowing the fat to escape. Cook about 20 minutes, or until the water evaporates and the sausage is brown. Turn off the heat, and let the sausage stand until ready to use.

In a large deep skillet or Dutch oven put ½ cup of olive oil, ¼ cup of chopped onion, 1 minced clove of garlic, ½ stalk of celery, chopped fine, ¼ medium-sized carrot, chopped fine, 1 tablespoon of chopped parsley, a generous pinch of oregano, and 6 capers (the dry, salted variety), minced. Fry these ingredients lightly, then add 1¼ cups of canned tomatoes, 5 crushed peppercorns, salt to taste, a dash of allspice, a tiny pinch of cayenne pepper, ½ cup of beef bouillon, and ½ cup of dry American white wine. Simmer for about 10 minutes, then add the tripe and the Italian sausage, which has been cut in pieces. Cover tightly, and cook slowly for 2 hours. Then uncover, and add ½ cup of grated Parmesan cheese, ½ cup of fine breadcrumbs, and ½ cup of dry white wine. Stir thoroughly, and simmer slowly for another half hour. Serve very hot, with boiled rice.

In a small town near Chicago I have a Polish friend who is the president of a bank and also the owner of an excellent grocery and meat market. During our late, but not lamented, meat shortage, I stopped in to see him, hoping against hope that I might be able to wangle a bit of Polish ham from him. In a half hour's chat I agreed enthusiastically with him on politics, on a number of international questions, on the state of the Union, and even told him a few things he didn't know about Kosciusko, the great Polish patriot. But—no dice! If he had any Polish ham, he wasn't giving it away or even selling it. But he did send me down to his market with a note, and I came away with four pounds of Polish sausage.

Our first dish at home was a very simple one—the sausage cut into 3 inch pieces and mixed in with a large can of sauerkraut. For a few weeks the rest of the sausage remained in the refrigerator, as we had had a windfall of meat from—well, never mind whom. Then one day I met a well-known Chicago artist who is a Pole. I was singing the praises of Polish sausage to him when he asked me whether I had ever tasted *bigos*. Instantly my gastronomical ears pricked up. *Bigos,* it seems, is a hunter's stew which was a favorite of the landed gentry in prewar Poland. I obtained the recipe and could hardly wait to get home to try it. But my wife was skeptical. Looking over the list of ingredients, she noted sauerkraut, Polish sausage, and mushrooms, three of her favorite items. She shook her head. "Don't worry," I told her, "this is terrific!" "It had better be," she warned.

My artist friend had told me to let the dish stand in a cold place overnight after it had been cooked, and then to reheat it and serve it the next night. But I couldn't wait. It was really terrific when it came from the fire. And after dinner my Lady of the House surrendered, capitualted, and almost went down on her knees to praise it. (Well, I can dream a little, can't I?) We had it the next night, reheated as suggested, and it was even better, the flavor really improved.

BIGOS
(Polish Hunter's Stew)

1 *lb. Polish sausage*	*½ lb. fresh mushrooms*
1 *large can sauerkraut*	*Butter*
1 *can consommé*	*2 tbsp. flour*
1 *tomato*	*¼ cup dry red wine*
1 *apple*	*½ tsp. salt*
1 *onion*	*Pepper*

2 *cups cold cooked veal*

Empty a large can of sauerkraut into a heavy saucepan, add a can of consommé, cover tightly, and let simmer. Now chop together 1 tomato, 1 apple (peeled and cored), 1 onion, and ½ pound of fresh mushrooms. Put a little butter in another saucepan, and simmer the chopped items with about 1 pound of Polish sausage (cut into pieces about an inch long) over a low flame for 10 minutes. Next add 2 tablespoons of flour and ¼ cup of dry American red wine and stir the whole well. When blended, add this mixture to the sauerkraut, and mix well. Next add 2 cups of left-over meat (I used diced cooked veal, but lamb can be used), ½ teaspoon of salt, and pepper to taste, and again mix well. Then cover and simmer 1 to 1½ hours, adding more consommé and red wine, if necessary, to prevent sticking. Serve with this boiled potatoes, sliced cucumbers with a sour cream dressing, and a good dry red wine.

In France the art of eating has reached the peak of perfection. As Paris is the capital of France, so it is the capital of epicurean delights, peopled with chefs who titillate the palates of emperors, kings, and millionaires. But in the provinces there are hundreds of little roadside *auberges,* or inns, where ordinary folk may obtain undreamed-of gustatory pleasures for a few francs. I recall one dish in particular, that I'd like to pass on to the more adventuresome of amateur chefs. It is a sausage specialty called *Saucisses Soubise,* or sausages with onion sauce.

SAUCISSES SOUBISE
(Sausage cooked in onions and white wine)

1 *lb. link sausages*	*Pinch thyme*
1 *lb. onions*	*Salt*
1 *cup dry white wine*	*Pepper*

In a skillet fry 1 pound of little link sausages golden brown. Then remove them and pour off about ¾ of the fat. Next fry 1 pound of thinly sliced onions in the remaining fat for about 10 minutes, but do not brown them. Cover the skillet, and cook the onions until they are quite tender, stirring occasionally. Now add 1 cup of American dry sauterne, a pinch of thyme, and salt and pepper to taste. Cover again, and let simmer for about 45 minutes. Then add the sausages and let the whole thing simmer very slowly until the onions become a creamy sauce. Remember, the secret of a perfect *soubise* is slow cooking.

Pineapple marries beautifully with a number of other ingredients, but one of the most unusual late snack or luncheon dishes I've ever tasted is a dish called Pineapple Rabbit with Sausage Cakes.

PINEAPPLE RABBIT WITH SAUSAGE CAKES

1 *lb. sausage meat*	*Prepared horseradish*
6 *slices canned pineapple*	1 *cup sherry*
	Cheddar cheese

Take 6 slices of canned pineapple and spread a light coating of prepared horseradish over each slice. Divide 1 pound of sausage meat into six portions and fashion 6 patties, slightly smaller in diameter than the pineapple slices. Put the sausage patties on top of the pineapple slices, put them in a shallow baking dish, and pour in a cup of sherry wine. Bake in a moderate oven (350 degrees) for about ½ hour, basting frequently.

A few minutes before serving, top each sausage patty with a slice of sharp American Cheddar cheese. As the cheese begins to melt, remove the pineapple-sausage cakes from the oven, sprinkle with paprika, and serve immediately.

One evening the Little Woman and I had a session of bridge with some friends who live in the country. The game ended along about midnight, after we had lost a very tricky hand. While my partner (and much-better half) launched into an extended dissertation on the desirability of getting out trumps while the getting was good, our host slipped away from the table. Twenty minutes or so later he returned bearing a tray whose odor made us all drool. "Creole Hot Dogs!" he announced, setting the tray down on the bridge table. To say that they were wonderful is putting it mildly. The speed with which we reached for them and the eagerness with which we devoured the second helping were ample testimony as to their goodness. Of course I asked for the recipe, and here it is.

CREOLE HOT DOGS

2 *tbsp. bacon fat*	½ *cup chili sauce*
¼ *cup chopped onion*	1 *tbsp. brown sugar*
¼ *cup chopped celery*	*Dash cayenne pepper*
⅓ *cup Madeira*	*Dash Tabasco*
2 *tsp. prepared mustard*	8 *frankfurters*
1 *tbsp. Worcestershire sauce*	8 *long buns*

In a large skillet melt 2 tablespoons of bacon drippings. Add ¼ cup of finely chopped onion and ¼ cup of finely chopped celery and sauté until lightly browned. Then add ⅓ cup of Madeira, 2 teaspoons of prepared mustard (the hot type if you prefer it, and I do), 1 tablespoon of Worcestershire sauce, ½ cup of chili sauce, and a dash of cayenne pepper and Tabasco. Let the mixture simmer slowly for about 5 minutes.

Now prick the skins of 8 frankfurters and place them in the sauce. Cover, and cook slowly for about 15 minutes, or until the franks are thoroughly heated through. When they are ready, split 8 long buns, spread them with butter, and heat them a moment in the oven. Then take them out, place a frank inside each bun, and top with Creole sauce. Place cold cucumber slices, radishes, and little green onions on the plates around the franks and buns. Either cold beer or hot coffee is a grand accompaniment.

And now here is the third Cantonese dish:

CANTONESE BEEF AND NOODLES

1 *lb. trimmed beef tenderloin*	*½ tsp. salt*
5 *tbsp. peanut oil*	2 *dashes pepper*
24 *whole pea pods*	*½ tsp. sugar*
1½ *cups sliced fresh mush-*	1 *tsp. Ac'cent*
rooms	*¾ tbsp. Cantonese bead*
6 *water chestnuts*	*molasses*
1½ *cups chicken broth*	*Slivered little green onions*
½ lb. raw noodles	2 *tbsp. cornstarch*
2 *tbsp. water*	

Have 1 pound of beef tenderloin cut into slices about ¼ inch thickness.

Place ½ pound of raw noodles in a strainer or collander, and immerse in boiling water for 30 seconds. Remove, drain thoroughly, and place immediately into a hot skillet containing 3 tablespoons of hot peanut oil, distributing the noodles evenly on the bottom of the skillet. Lightly brown on one side, then turn with a spatula and lightly brown on the other side. Then place on a hot platter in the form of a mound, and keep warm.

In another skillet put 2 tablespoons of peanut oil, and when hot, add the tenderloin slices, stirring them about the pan for approximately 15 seconds, so that they become coated with the hot oil. Then add 24 whole pea pods, 1½ cups of sliced fresh mushrooms, 6 water chestnuts, sliced, and 1½ cups of chicken broth. Mix thoroughly, and let this simmer for about 1 minute, covered.

Next, add the mixed seasonings: 2 dashes of pepper, ½ teaspoon of sugar, 1 teaspoon of Ac'cent, ¾ tablespoon of Cantonese bead molasses, 2 tablespoons of cornstarch, and 2 table-spoons of water. Stir thoroughly, cover again, and simmer for 15 seconds over a moderate flame.

Remove the beef and vegetables and place them over the mound of the Cantonese fried noodles. Garnish with shredded little green onions.

 **(7)** GAME

It frequently has been said that the cooking of game belongs entirely in male hands; that the Little Woman who normally presides in the kitchen hasn't (a) culinary imagination, (b) learned the art of cooking improvisation, or (c) had any experience to speak of with game cookery.

Although it may be *lèse majesté,* I am going to disagree for two reasons. The first is that I am thoroughly in accord with the Duc de Talleyrand, who said, "There are two things essential to life: to give good dinners and to keep on fair terms with women." The second reason is that a recipe for one of the most delicious duck dishes I ever ate came from a woman.

However, I should like to say a few words in behalf of the harassed housewife who is expected to whip up a gourmet dish with the game her husband brings home. She may be an excellent cook, and probably is, but unless she is the wife of an enthusiastic and regular hunter, she isn't used to game cookery, and she'll hunt in vain through her favorite cookbooks for proper ways and means of bringing a delectable dish to the table of her husband and friends. So at this point I'd like to recommend three additions to a cooking library: *Fish and Game Cookbook* by Harry Botsford, published by the Cornell Maritime Press, New York; *The Derrydale Cookbook of Fish and Game* by Louis De Gouy, published in two volumes by the Derrydale Press (this may be difficult to obtain, but it's worth searching for); and *Cooking Wild Game,* by Ashbrook and Slater, published by the Orange Judd Publishing Company of New York.

Ducks were highly prized as a delicacy by the Greeks and Romans in the days of antiquity. In the Middle Ages ducks were hunted with a bow and arrow (a feat I'd give a pretty penny to see some of my duck-hunting friends perform today). But I venture to say that even in the dim past, arguments went on as to the proper length of time to cook a duck. On this question I am a middle-of-the-roader. Let those who like wild ducks cooked 6 minutes cook them 6 minutes, but don't tender me an invitation to partake of them. And let those who like them overcooked (and tough) overcook them. I'll duck that invitation, too.

Probably the most conventional way to cook wild duck is to roast it, either with or without stuffing. Young mallards and canvasbacks are said to be at the peak of succulence broiled. But my favorite recipe is Duck à la Frederic, as prepared by my old friend, Ric Riccardo.

Ric is the owner of Riccardo's Studio Restaurant and Palette Bar at 437 Rush Street, in Chicago. This unusual place is the rendezvous for artists, opera singers, stage and motion picture celebrities, and Bohemians in general, whether they live in Chicago, are playing there, or merely passing through. Ric bears a striking resemblance to one of his most famous patrons, the late John Barrymore, and he is just as unpredictable. A painter, linguist, sculptor, writer, musician, hunter, amateur photographer, and magician, he also excels in the culinary art. A great showman, his preparation of Duck à la Frederic takes on the air of a major production, as they would say in Hollywood. Watching him, surrounded by a gleaming duck press, a large chafing dish, several bottles and containers, and a pan of roasted duck in front of him, you begin to drool before he has hardly started.

DUCK À LA FREDERIC RICCARDO

4 *mallards*
2 *large carrots*
2 *large onions*
¼ *lb. butter*
1 *clove garlic*
Rind 1 *orange*
1 *tbsp. chopped parsley*

4 *tbsp. currant jelly*
1 *tbsp. Worcestershire sauce*
Juice from 2 *pressed duck*
    carcasses
Salt
Pepper
4 *ounces Marsala*

Stuff each of 4 mallards (or canvasbacks) with ½ of a large carrot and ½ of a large peeled onion. Place in a roasting pan and bake in a 400-degree oven for exactly 12 minutes. Then carve out the breasts from the ducks, remove the skin, and set them aside. Take the remaining carcasses of two of the ducks, place them in a duck press and extract the essences, and reserve for a moment. In a large skillet melt ¼ pound of butter, to which a mashed clove of garlic has been added. When the butter is bubbling, put the duck breasts in, and sauté them for one minute on each side. Remove the breasts to a warm platter, remove the clove of garlic from the butter, and add to the butter in the skillet the juices from the pressed ducks, the finely chopped rind of an orange, 1 tablespoon of chopped parsley, 4 tablespoons of currant jelly, 1 tablespoon of Worcestershire sauce, salt and pepper to taste, and 4 ounces of Marsala. Blend this well, then return the breasts to the sauce, and sauté the breasts for 30 seconds more on each side.Then place the breasts on a hot platter, pour the sauces over them, and serve with wild rice, bananas fried in breadcrumbs, a tossed green salad, and a good Burgundy.

One day last fall a letter came to me from a reader of my column on cookery, "For Men Only!" It was signed "Della B. Benedict," and in part she said, "After forty years of experience in cooking game I am sending you the recipe—simplest and best-liked by my husband and his friends—for mallard duck." In her portscript she added, "I am the wife of a hunter." Her recipe was for mallard fricassee, and, after trying it myself, I could easily understand her husband's enthusiasm. Here's how Mrs. Benedict does it.

MALLARD FRICASSEE

1 *mallard*	1 *tbsp. salt*
1 *cup flour*	½ *tsp. allspice*
1 *tbsp. powdered marjoram*	1 *tbsp. bacon drippings*
½ *tsp. black pepper, freshly ground*	1 *tbsp. butter*
	¾ *cup sherry*

Clean the duck well, then dry-pick by pouring melted paraffin over the duck, letting it cool, and then removing it. All the down will adhere to the paraffin. Cut the duck into four pieces by cutting across and lengthwise. No marinating or soaking, Mrs. Benedict cautions. Next, prepare an herb flour by using 1 cup of flour, 1 tablespoon of powdered marjoram, ½ teaspoon of freshly ground black pepper, 1 tablespoon of salt, and ½ teaspoon of allspice. Put this herb flour in a clean paper bag, and shake each piece of duck in it until it is thoroughly coated with the flour.

Heat about 1 tablespoon of bacon drippings and 1 tablespoon of butter in a heavy iron frying pan or Dutch oven. Put the pieces of duck in, and when they are browned all over, pour off some of the fat and replace with ¾ cup of sherry. Cover, and let simmer for about an hour. Make a sauce with what is left of the liquid in the pan, thickening with a little of the herb flour, if necessary.

"Candied linganberries, rice, a green vegetable such as broccoli, a tossed salad, and mince pie make a meal fit and suitable for a Nimrod and his friends," Mrs. Benedict's letter concluded. Well, I'll go all the way with this hunter's wife on her recipe and her menu. And I might add—lucky Mr. Benedict!

The canvasback is probably the most famous of America's migratory water fowls. It is supposed to acquire its very delectable flavor from the wild celery on which it feeds.

There is a story about how the canvasback got its name. I don't put much credence in it, but it's a good story whether true or not. In the early 1900's one of the arbiters of New York society was Ward McAllister. His parties and dinners were fabulous affairs and one of the favorite items on his menu was ducks which he had shipped to him from North Carolina. The ducks were shipped in especially made canvas bags which were supposed to be returned to the shipper. His bills were always made out, "50¢ a pair. Canvas back." So, the story goes, these North Carolina ducks became known as canvasbacks. Well, if you know of a better story, go to it. But you can't find a better recipe for canvasbacks in casserole.

CANVASBACKS EN CASSEROLE

2 *canvasbacks*	1 *little green onion*
Flour	1 *tbsp. chopped parsley*
Salt	¼ *tsp. thyme*
Pepper	¼ *tsp. marjoram*
2 *tsp. powdered ginger*	¼ *tsp. basil*
2 *ounces butter*	4 *ounces dry white wine*
½ *clove garlic*	1 *tbsp. brandy*
½ *lb. fresh mushrooms*	½ *cup cream*

Cut 2 canvasbacks into serving pieces, dredge them well with seasoned flour, and sprinkle with 1 teaspoon of powdered ginger for each duck.

In a heavy skillet melt 2 ounces of butter, and add ½ clove of minced garlic. When the butter is hot add ½ pound of fresh mushrooms, sliced, and the duck pieces, and when the latter are nicely browned on all sides, put the contents of the skillet into a casserole. Add 1 little green onion (tops and bulb), chopped, 1 tablespoon of chopped parsley, ¼ teaspoon each of thyme, marjoram, and basil, 4 ounces of dry American white wine, and 1 tablespoon of brandy. Cover the casserole, and bake in a moderate oven (350 degrees) for 1 hour. Then add ½ cup of cream and cook for about 25 to 30 minutes longer, or until the ducks are tender.

For some reason oranges seem to go with ducks just as ham goes with eggs. One of the outstanding recipes for duck goes back, I am told, to a fifteenth-century Italian cook book. It is called *Duck à la Jus Orange,* and to me there is no duck recipe that tops it.

DUCK À LA JUS ORANGE

Pair of wild ducks
Orange juice
Brandy
1 cup uncooked wild rice
Boiling water
1 cup boiling chicken broth
4 tbsp. sweet butter
1½ tbsp. minced chives
1½ tbsp. minced parsley
1½ tbsp. minced little green
* onions*
1½ tbsp. minced celery tops
1½ tbsp. minced sweet basil
1 tsp. gin
Salt
Freshly ground pepper
Duck giblets
1 tsp. grated orange rind
2 tsp. lemon juice
2 cups dry red wine
3 tbsp. curaçao
Tiny pinch nutmeg

Rub a pair of wild ducks, which have been drawn and cleaned, with an equal portion of orange juice and brandy, inside and out.

Wash 1 cup of wild rice. Put 4 cups of boiling water, to which
1 teaspoon of salt has been added, in the top of a double boiler
directly over the fire, and add the rice slowly without checking the
boiling, and cook for 5 minutes. Then place it over boiling water
in the under part of the double boiler, add 1 cup of boiling
chicken broth, cover tightly, and steam from 30 to 45 minutes,
or until the rice is tender.

While the rice is steaming, cream 4 tablespoons of sweet butter,
brought to room temperature, with 1½ tablespoons each of finely
minced chives, parsley, little green onions, green celery tops, and
sweet basil. Then season this butter with 1 teaspoon of gin, salt
and freshly ground pepper to taste, and a tiny pinch of freshly
grated nutmeg.

Put the prepared butter in a saucepan, melt, and add the wild
rice and the chopped giblets of the ducks. Cook briefly, tossing
the rice until it is thoroughly impregnated with the prepared
butter. Then stuff the ducks with the rice and giblets.

Put the ducks in an open roasting pan, and pour into the pan
1 cup of orange juice, 1 teaspoon of grated orange rind, 2 teaspoons of lemon juice, and 1 cup of dry American red wine. Place
the roaster in a 400-degree oven, and roast from 15 to 25 minutes,
depending on the size and age of birds, basting frequently.
Remove the ducks to a very hot platter.

Add another ¾ to 1 cup of red wine to the juices in the roaster,
scraping the pan well to dislodge any particles of duck, and also
add 3 tablespoons of curaçao. Bring to a boil on top of the stove;
pour the sauce over the ducks, and serve.

The Bohemians combine duck with sauerkraut, with great profit
to the appetite. Apparently the favorite method of preparing duck
among the ancient Greeks and Romans was to roast it and concoct a sauce to pour over it. But the aucients missed a trick in
not combining wild duck and brandy. Who knows, perhaps Cleo-
patra would not have sought her asp if her Roman lover had
plied her with Brandied Wild Duck.

BRANDIED WILD DUCK

Pair of wild ducks	*½ tsp. thyme*
Salt	*½ tsp. marjoram*
Pepper	*¼ tsp. allspice*
4 ounces brandy	*1 bay leaf*
1 cup dry red wine	*1 tbsp. butter*
2 large onions	*3 ounces olive oil*
1 tbsp. chopped parsley	*1 clove garlic*
	½ lb. fresh mushrooms

Disjoint a pair of wild ducks, and place the pieces in an earthenware or enamel crock or in a large bowl. Sprinkle them with salt and pepper and add 4 ounces of brandy, 1 cup of dry American red wine, 2 large onions, peeled and chopped, 1 tablespoon of chopped parsley, ½ teaspoon each of thyme and marjoram, ¼ teaspoon of allspice, and 1 bay leaf. Allow this to stand about 5 hours at room temperature, turning the pieces of duck occasionally.

In a heavy skillet or Dutch oven put 1 tablespoon of butter, 3 ounces of pure olive oil, and 1 crushed clove of garlic. When hot, add the pieces of duck, and brown well on all sides, about 15 or 20 minutes. Then add ½ pound of fresh mushrooms, sliced, and the strained marinade. Cover, and simmer until the duck is tender—about 1½ hours.

Serve from the casserole; or remove the duck to a hot platter, thicken the sauce slightly by vigorous boiling, and pour the sauce over the duck.

If you have brought home some ducks or have had some given to you, and have been persuaded to overcook them, and then don't like them; or if you have some legs and breasts left over from other methods of preparation, here are a couple of recipes for utilizing cooked duck. The first is Duck Pilau (pilau being Turkish for rice).

DUCK PILAU

2 cups cooked duck meat
Duck carcass
4 cups water
1 chopped onion
1 bay leaf
Chopped celery leaves
1 cup uncooked long-grain
    rice

Duck stock
Salt
2 tbsp. butter
¾ cup chopped celery
1 tbsp. grated onion
½ cup chopped pimentos
    and their oil
¼ cup dry white wine

Dash paprika

Remove all meat from a cold roast duck, and add to it any other duck meat you may have on hand. In any event, there should be about 2 cups of cooked duck meat.

Break the carcass or carcasses apart, put them in a pot, and add 4 cups of water, 1 chopped onion, a bay leaf, and a few chopped celery leaves. Simmer this for about 1 hour, and strain off the stock.

Thoroughly wash and rinse 1 cup of long-grain rice. Bring the duck broth to the boiling point, then slowly stir in the rice. The stock should be about knuckle-deep above the rice. Add a pinch of salt, bring the liquid to a boil, then lower the flame and cook for about 30 minutes. If you don't have enough stock, add consommé to make up the difference.

In a saucepan melt 2 tablespoons of butter. When hot, add ¾ cup of chopped celery, 1 tablespoon of grated onion, and ½ cup of chopped pimentos with the oil they come in. Sauté for about 5 minutes, then add the 2 cups of chopped duck meat, the cooked rice, ¼ cup of dry American white wine, and ¼ cup of duck stock (if there isn't any left, add ½ cup white wine). Mix ingredients well with a fork, add a dash of paprika, salt to taste. Serve hot.

Another delightful way to fix left-over duck is a recipe that comes from the Riviera and utilizes olives.

WILD DUCK WITH OLIVES

2 cups cooked duck meat	1 bay leaf
1 tbsp. butter	1 tbsp. flour
½ clove garlic	1 cup consommé
1 medium-sized onion	½ cup Madeira
1 tsp. thyme	1 cup pitted green olives
1 tbsp. chopped parsley	Salt
	Pepper

Cut the duck meat into small cubes, ending up with 2 cupfuls.

Put 1 tablespoon of butter in a saucepan with ½ clove of minced garlic. As the butter browns, add 1 medium-sized onion, peeled and chopped. Brown the onion lightly, then add the 2 cups of duck meat, 1 teaspoon of thyme, 1 tablespoon of chopped parsley, and 1 bay leaf, crumbled. Cover the pan and cook gently for about 10 minutes, stirring frequently. Sprinkle in 1 tablespoon of flour, blend thoroughly, and then add 1 cup of consommé, ½ cup of Madeira, and 1 cup of pitted green olives. Add salt and pepper to taste, and simmer, covered, for about 20 minutes. Serve over triangles of buttered toast.

I'm always rather confused when the subject of partridge comes up. When I was living in the South and cooked some partridges for some guests from the North, one chap spoke up and said, "Hell, those aren't partridges, they're quail." Go into New England and they'll tell you a grouse is a partridge. Once I served quail on toast, and pointed with pride to it with southern guests, one only remarked "Isn't that just like a damyankee? He doesn't know a partridge when he sees one." At that point, I gave up.

One of the tastiest breakfast dishes I know of is to take a partridge, salt and pepper it, and broil it, basting with plenty of butter. But for a regal dinner dish, I would like to recommend Partridges à la Chasseur.

204 WITH A JUG OF WINE

PARTRIDGES À LA CHASSEUR

3 *partridges*	1 *tbsp. chopped parsley*
Salt	*Generous pinch thyme*
Pepper	*Generous pinch marjoram*
2 *tbsp. butter*	2 *tbsp. flour*
2 *ounces brandy*	1 *cup consommé*
4 *little green onions*	½ *cup dry white wine*
1 *carrot*	2 *cups fresh mushrooms*

Disjoint 3 partridges as you would young chickens, and rub the pieces well with salt and pepper.

In a skillet melt 2 tablespoons of butter. When hot, put the pieces of partridges in and brown them on both sides—about 15 minutes. Then pour over the partridges 2 ounces of brandy, and set alight. When the flame dies out, add to the pan 4 little green onions, chopped fine, 1 carrot, chopped fine, 1 tablespoon chopped parsley, and a generous pinch each of thyme and marjoram. Let these ingredients brown for about 2 or 3 minutes, and then sprinkle in 2 tablespoons of flour. Blend well, and then stir in 1 cup of consommé, ½ cup of dry American white wine, and 2 cups of sliced fresh mushrooms. Salt and pepper to taste. Simmer, covered, for about 25 to 30 minutes, or until the partridges are tender.

Serve partridges and sauce, using croutons as a garnish.

With a bow to the North, I want to include a wonderful quail dish. The quail is also known as the bobwhite. They are exciting to hunt and a succulent morsel to eat. I think they originally came from the Eastern Hemisphere and were a favorite dish of the ancient Egyptians. The following recipe is a favorite of mine.

QUAIL AND MUSHROOMS IN CLARET

2 *quail*	½ *cup consommé*
Brandy	½ *cup claret*
4 *tbsp. butter*	*Celery salt*
1 *cup sliced fresh mushrooms*	*Freshly ground pepper*
Juice of 1 *orange*	

Split 2 quail lengthwise, rub with a cloth soaked in brandy, and then dust with flour.

Melt 2 tablespoons of butter in a saucepan and let it begin to brown. Then put in the quail, cover, and allow to cook 5 minutes. Then turn, and cook 5 minutes more.

In another saucepan melt 2 tablespoons of butter and, when hot, add 1 cup of sliced mushrooms. Sauté gently until tender— about 7 or 8 minutes.

Add sautéed mushrooms to the quail, along with ½ cup of consommé, ½ cup of American claret, or similar wine, a sprinkling of celery salt, and freshly ground pepper to taste. Simmer gently until the quail is tender—about 10 minutes. A minute or so before serving, add the strained juice of 1 orange. Let become hot, and serve.

Of all game birds, pheasant is my favorite. To me it has a succulency and perfume that no other bird possesses. Properly cooked, its flesh is tender, sublime, and tastes of chicken and venison. As a matter of fact, pheasant can be cooked in nearly all the ways that chicken can be cooked—broiled, roasted, baked, stewed, or sautéed. One of the easiest and most delicious ways of cooking pheasant is what I call smothering.

SMOTHERED PHEASANT

1 *pheasant*	*Thyme*
4 *small onions*	*Marjoram*
5 *stalks celery*	*½ cup consommé*
Butter	*½ cup dry red wine*
Flour	*Chopped parsley*

Salt and pepper

Disjoint the cleaned and plucked pheasant, shake the pieces in a bag containing seasoned flour until they are thoroughly coated, then lay them in a roaster or a Dutch oven. Around them place four peeled onions (as many as six can be used, depending on size). Sprinkle the pieces with a generous pinch each of thyme, marjoram, and chopped parsley. Liberally dot the pieces of pheasant with pieces of butter the size of grapes. Lay 5 single stalks of celery, leaves and all, across the pheasant pieces and the onions.

Next, pour into the roaster ½ cup each of consommé and dry American red wine. Cover, and place in a hot oven (450-500 degrees) for about ½ hour, basting once. Then turn down the oven to 300 degrees, and cook for about 1½ hours, adding more wine, as necessary, and basting at least every half hour. Next, uncover, turn up the oven for a quick browning, and then remove the pheasant, onions, and celery to a hot platter. Put the roaster on top of the stove over a medium flame, add a little more red wine, scraping the pan well to loosen any particles of the dish that adhere, and when the gravy is heated, pour over the pheasant, onions, and celery.

George Washington is known to every school child as the Father of our Country; but it has also been said that he was the "father" of the first pheasants in the United States, having imported several pair from England. From another source I learned that the pheasant was first introduced to the United States in the Pacific Northwest from its native China around 1880. Being a prolific bird, it has settled in nearly all parts of the United States, a fact for which I, for one, give thanks to *le bon Dieu*.

Some gourmets prefer their pheasant roasted without any stuffing, or with just an onion and a bit of celery inside the bird. But I don't think any epicure would turn up his nose at a roast pheasant with brandied orange stuffing.

ROAST PHEASANT WITH BRANDIED ORANGE STUFFING

2 *cock pheasants*	*Salt*
3 *cups breadcrumbs*	*Pepper*
3 *ounces butter*	2 *cups diced celery*
3 *ounces brandy*	*Pinch chervil*
2 *tbsp. grated orange rind*	*Pinch marjoram*
⅔ *cup orange pulp*	*Pinch rosemary*
1 *egg*	1 *cup dry red wine*

This recipe calls for 2 fat cock pheasants, ready for cooking.

For the stuffing, sauté 3 cups of breadcrumbs in 1 ounce of butter. Mix with these 3 ounces of brandy, 2 tablespoons of grated orange peel, ⅔ cup of orange pulp, 2 cups of diced celery, 2

ounces of melted butter, 1 beaten egg, salt and pepper to taste, and
a pinch each of chervil, marjoram, and rosemary. When all is thoroughly mixed, stuff the pheasants with the mixture, truss them, and
place in an uncovered roaster. Add 1 cup of dry American red
wine, and place the roaster in a moderate oven (350 degrees).
Roast for 30 minutes per pound per bird, basting frequently with
the red wine. If necessary, add more red wine during the roasting
period.

When the birds are tender, remove to a hot platter, pour the
pan juices over them, and serve.

This next recipe shows the Italian influence, being somewhat
similar to Chicken *Cacciatora*. But, of course, no chicken was
ever raised that had the flavor of pheasant.

PHEASANT CACCIATORA

2 *young pheasants*	4 *small onions*
Flour	1 *clove garlic*
Salt	1½ *cups canned tomatoes*
Pepper	*Pinch oregano*
5 *tbsp. olive oil*	½ *cup consommé*
1 *green pepper*	½ *cup Marsala*
	1 *cup sliced mushrooms*

Cut 2 young pheasants into serving pieces and roll the pieces in
seasoned flour.

Into a deep heavy skillet pour 5 tablespoons of olive oil, and
when it is hot, put in the pieces of pheasant and brown them on all
sides.

Seed and slice 1 green pepper lengthwise, and mix with it 4
small onions, peeled and chopped, 1 clove of garlic, chopped, 1½
cups of canned tomatoes, a pinch of oregano, and add this mixture to the pheasant pieces. Also add ½ cup of consommé and
½ cup of Marsala. Cover, and simmer for about 1 hour. Then add
1 cup of sliced fresh mushrooms and simmer for about 30 minutes longer.

Serve with an endive salad and plenty of crusty Italian bread.

Although a golden browned turkey is a delight to the eye and
delectable to the palate, many people get their fill of it on Thanks-

giving and for many days after. Then, less than a month later, on Christmas, American tradition decrees turkey again, and in some instances families are eating the remains of the holiday bird up to the end of the year.

Far be it for me to decry our noble gobbler, but for those who would welcome a change in the Christmas menu, I'll make a suggestion or two. Why not try roast goose? It is a traditional holiday comestible in many places on the globe and was so long before America and the turkey were discovered.

The goose is excellent eating. The Vikings considered it an outstanding Christmas delicacy. On many occasions of gayety and feasting, the Germans serve goose. In England, when Good Queen Bess received the news of the Spanish Armada's defeat on Michaelmas, she decreed that, in celebration of the victory, roast goose be eaten on that day as long as England endured. Two French holiday goose dishes are *Oie à la Dijonnaise* and *Oie Tour d'Argent*.

Assuming I've sold some customers a bill of goods, suppose we get down to the business of stuffing and roasting Sir, or Herr, or Monsieur Goose. To my mind, a stuffing of chestnuts flavored with Madeira is tops.

ROAST GOOSE WITH CHESTNUT AND MADEIRA STUFFING

1 10- *to* 12-*lb. goose*	½ *cup cooking oil*
Madeira	1 *cup consommé*
Salt	½ *lb. sausage meat*
Pepper	¼ *tsp. mace*
Pinch nutmeg	¼ *tsp. basil*
Goose liver	¼ *tsp. rosemary*
3 *chicken livers*	¼ *clove garlic, minced*
3 *large mushrooms*	*Fine white breadcrumbs (if*
3 *tbsp. seedless raisins*	*necessary)*
1 *lb. chestnuts*	1 *cup sour cream*

Clean, singe, and wash a 10- to 12-pound goose, wipe dry, and rub inside and out with Madeira which has been seasoned with a little salt and pepper and a pinch of nutmeg.

Carefully remove the gall sac from the goose liver (unless it has already been done by your butcher), and put the goose liver, 3 chicken livers, 3 tablespoons of seedless raisins, and 3 large mushrooms, chopped, in a bowl and add 1 cup of Madeira. Let these delicacies remain in the marinade overnight.

On the day of the goose dinner heat 1 pound of chestnuts (after scoring the flat side with a sharp knife) in about ½ cup of cooking oil for about 3 or 4 minutes, shaking the pan constantly. Then, when the chestnuts are cool enough to handle, remove the shells and skin, and simmer in about 1 cup of consommé until tender.

At the same time cook ½ pound of sausage meat slowly to fry out most of the fat, breaking up the meat with a fork.

While the above two operations are going on, transfer the livers, raisins, mushrooms, and Madeira to a saucepan and bring to a boil. Remove the livers and chop them. Then combine the sausage meat, the chopped livers, the mushrooms and raisins, and the chestnuts, which have been coarsely chopped. Add salt and pepper to taste, ¼ teaspoon each of mace, basil, and rosemary, ¼ clove of minced garlic, and the Madeira. If the dressing should be too moist, add a few fine breadcrumbs, but not enough to make it dry.

Stuff the goose with this mixture. Truss and skewer the bird and place it on a trivet low in the roaster, after having pricked the goose all over with a fork. Roast in a very hot oven (475 degrees) for about 8 minutes. Remove the goose, and drain off the fat which has run out, then return the goose to the pan, put in the oven for another 8 to 10 minutes. Again drain off the fat, and place the bird on the trivet in the roasting pan (never let goose rest in the grease). Pour a cup of Madeira over the goose, and continue cooking in a moderate oven (about 325 degrees), basting frequently with the wine in the pan. Allow 25 minutes to the pound.

Remove the goose to a hot platter. Add another cup of Madeira and a cup of sour cream to the juices in the pan. Blend thoroughly, bring to a boil, and pour it into a gravy boat.

The goose is a very useful bird in many respects. His liver goes to make up one of the greatest of epicurean delights, *pâté de foie gras*. In the time of our grandmothers, goose grease was a very handy household item. As I recall, goose grease played quite a part in the motion picture *Grandma's Boy,* which, I think, starred Harold Lloyd. (I wish I hadn't brought that up because it sort of dates me.) Goose feathers are about the softest feathers there are, although maybe ducks would object to that statement. And, of course, geese, according to legend, saved ancient Rome from its enemies.

Enough of goose lore. Let's get back to the baking and stuffing of the goose. The following recipe is somewhat similar to the one used in the famous La Tour d'Argent restaurant on the Quai de la Tournelle in Paris, but it is not so difficult to prepare as that.

ROAST GOOSE WITH PRUNE STUFFING

1 12-*lb. goose*	*Pepper*
Clove garlic, cut	1 *tbsp. chopped parsley*
½ *lb. prunes*	1 *cup soft breadcrumbs*
Dry white wine	*Melted butter*
½ *lb. sausage meat*	*Pinch powdered ginger*
6 *cooking apples*	*Water*
6 *medium-sized onions*	*Pinch crushed juniper berries*
1 *bay leaf*	(*or* 1 *tsp. gin*)
½ *tsp. leaf thyme*	1 *tsp. brandy*
½ *tsp. leaf marjoram*	1 *tbsp. currant jelly*
Salt	*Flour*

Singe, clean, and dry a 12-pound goose, and rub it all over with a cut clove of garlic.

Soak ½ pound of prunes in water overnight, then cook until tender in enough dry American white wine to cover. When prunes are cold, pit them and reserve, also reserving the wine they were cooked in.

In a large skillet cook ½ pound of sausage meat until it begins to brown, breaking it up with a fork while cooking. Take out the sausage meat, and reserve. In the sausage fat sauté for about 5 minutes 6 cored, peeled, and chopped cooking apples (about 2 pounds) and 6 medium-sized onions, peeled and chopped. Then add 1 bay leaf, ½ teaspoon each of thyme and marjoram, salt and pepper to taste, 1 tablespoon of chopped parsley, and enough dry American white wine to just cover. Cook until the apples are tender, stirring occasionally, then rub the mixture through a fine sieve into a bowl. Add the sausage meat, and the prunes, and about 1 cup of soft breadcrumbs, or enough to make a rather dry stuffing. Cool the mixture thoroughly, then stuff the goose with it.

Sew up or skewer the vent, truss the bird and rub it all over with melted butter seasoned with salt and freshly ground pepper and a pinch of powdered ginger. Prick the skin in several places to allow the fat to run out. Place the goose in a covered roasting pan, breast side down, and roast in a 400-degree oven for about 1 hour. Then drain the fat from the roaster, add the wine the prunes were cooked in, and enough more, if necessary, to make 1 cup, and 1 cup of water. Place the goose breast side up, and cook until done—about 2 hours (allow 25 minutes per pound total roasting time), basting frequently.

When the goose is done, remove to a hot platter. Skim any fat from the roaster, and measure the remaining liquid. If necessary, add enough dry white wine to make 3 cups. Add a pinch of crushed juniper berries (or 1 teaspoon of gin), 1 teaspoon of brandy, and 1 tablespoon of currant jelly. Blend in enough flour to make a gravy of good consistency and let get hot. Serve in a gravy boat.

Guinea hen is another species of wild fowl that is encountered in only the finest restaurants in America. For sheer goodness it is hard to beat. In many places in Italy, no Sunday dinner is complete without roast guinea hen. The following recipe for Breast of Guinea Hen, with Sauce Colbert is by Crosby Gaige, about whom I want to speak shortly.

BREAST OF GUINEA HEN COLBERT

6 *breasts guinea hen*	*Chopped chervil*
Salt	*Chopped tarragon*
Freshly ground pepper	*Chopped parsley*
Dry mustard	*Chopped chives*
Melted butter	3 *tbsp. hot water*
Fine breadcrumbs	2 *bouillon cubes*
4 *ounces sweet butter*	*Dash cayenne pepper*
Juice ½ lemon	1 *tbsp. Madeira*
Buttered toast	

Fillet out the breasts of 3 guinea hens, leaving the wing bone on (if you think that may be too tough a job, take your guinea hens to your butcher, and he'll do it for you). Season the breasts with salt, freshly ground black pepper, and a little dry mustard. Then dip each breast into a little melted butter, roll in fine breadcrumbs, and broil for 10 minutes.

Meanwhile, make your Sauce Colbert. Melt together 4 ounces of sweet butter, the juice of ½ lemon, freshly ground black pepper to taste, a dash of cayenne pepper, enough chopped chervil, parsley, tarragon, and chives to make up 1 tablespoon combined, 3 tablespoons of hot water, in which 2 bouillon cubes have been dissolved, 1 tablespoon Madeira, and ½ teaspoon of dry mustard. Blend well and simmer for 5 minutes.

Place the breasts of guinea hen on pieces of hot buttered toast, cut to the same shape as the breasts, and pour the sauce over them.

It was with deep regret and a keen sense of personal loss that I learned in March, 1949, of the passing of one of the most passionate disciples of the art of gracious living I have ever known— Crosby Gaige.

Crosby Gaige was a fabulous personage. He became a world-famous theatrical producer, with such smash hits as *Within the Law, Twin Beds, Smilin' Through,* and *The Circle.* He was a scholar, *bon vivant,* connoisseur of fine wines, food, and books, and the owner of the famous Watch Hill Press. His unusual avocations included limited-edition publishing and the intensive study of food and wines.

When he left the theatrical world at the age of 55, broke and owing nearly half a million dollars, he turned to the business of food and feeding, and in a short time became an authority in that field. At his charming Watch Hill farm in Westchester County, New York, he had a completely equipped kitchen and laboratory, set apart from the main house, and there, up to the time of his death, he experimented in the art of cookery. He wrote a syndicated newspaper column, "Meals for Males"; he had a five-day-a-week radio program called "Kitchen Cavalcade"; he was a consultant to several food companies; he wrote for a number of magazines; and in between he found time to write cook books and one of the most fascinating biographies I have ever read, *Footlight and Highlights.*

His holiday greetings in 1948 took the form of a beautifully executed little brochure entitled "A Christmas Tribute to the Cook," and I think parts of it are worth sharing with all who cook:

As the Dinner Table is the most loved and gracious symbol of the Christmas festival, it seems fitting at this time to offer grateful salutations to those who browned the turkey and who baked the pies—to mothers, sisters, aunts and wives; to all home cooks in general.

We are much too casual about our food. In the brief winking of the eye or smacking of the lips the work of patient kitchen hours speeds unsung to swift oblivion. So in our praise of cooks let's pause before we eat, and shape the form and attributes of the sapient chef. He must have component within himself and available for instant use more sorts of skills and knowledge than are requisite for the practice of almost any other craft or art or profession. His road to learning is long and exacting and arduous.

As the foundation of his education he first must learn of vegetables and of the other fruits of the earth, their varieties, their values and their preparation, and thus finally he knows as much or more of these matters than do the husbandmen who grow them.

He has to learn of fire as from Prometheus himself; and how to tame its fury and to use it as an obedient and accurate servant.

Undoubtedly he must learn of soups—of a thousand soups and of the stocks that are their foundation.

It is necessary that he study the beasts of the field and of the forest, that he may learn those most fitting for his purposes. Like a skilled anatomist he must come to know about all their organs and of the best uses to which he may put them.

He must inform himself about the birds of the farmyard—of chickens and turkeys, and of geese and ducks and guinea fowl, and of their eggs. Likewise he must know of the wild birds of the air and of the thicket.

The sea and the lakes and the rivers that run into the sea hold myriads of fish that must claim his attention. The sea is also the home of mollusks and crustaceans—oysters and clams, mussels and scallops; crabs and lobsters and shrimp—all rare and admirable delicacies when submitted to the varied artistry of his presentation.

A competent chef must well understand the chemical mysteries by which yeast inspires dull and sodden dough to brown and fragrant loaf and to light and tender cake.

He must study the grasses of Ceres and their seeds, their composition and their treatment for the betterment of mankind.

Assuredly he must have profound knowledge of the alchemies that can be wrought with spices and herbs, with condiments and seasonings—by which the cook creates the subtle overtones and undertones that constitute the great symphony of flavor.

An open book to him must be the just composition of sweet and sour and the gentle unction of oil, of many oils.

So this chef of ours must be a man of a hundred sauces and of one religion, and I do not much care what his formal religion may be so long as he knows his sauces and that he also gives daily thanks to the good God for the many blessings that He has conferred upon us.

In concluding, let us quote what Ben Jonson in his play, "The Staple of News," produced in London over three centuries ago, had to say about chefs:

> Why, he's the man of men
> For a professor! He designs, he drawes,
> He paints, he carves, he builds, he fortifies,
> Makes citadels of curious fowls and fish.
> Some he dry ditches, some moats round with broths,
> Mounts marrow bones, cuts fifty-angled custards,
> Rears bulwark pies, and for his outer works
> He raiseth ramparts of immortal crust,
> And teacheth all the tactics at one dinner—
> What ranks, what files, to put his dishes in—
> The whole art military! Then he knows
> The influence of the stars upon his meats,
> And all their seasons, tempers, qualities,
> And so to fit his relishes and sauces
> He has Nature in a pot, 'bove all the chymists
> Or airy breathren of the rosy-cross!
> He is an architect, an engineer,
> A soldier, a physician, a philosopher,
> A general mathematician!

In the past, Crosby Gaige and I exchanged recipes. He had in preparation at the time of his death a cook book to which I contributed three menus. One of his favorite recipes which he sent to me was for squab as he prepared it at his lovely estate overlooking the Hudson in the Westchester hills, Watch Hill Farm.

SQUAB CROSBY GAIGE

6 *jumbo squabs*	*Toasted breadcrumbs*
3 *to* 4 *dozen muscat grapes*	*Brandy*
Salt	*Port*
Freshly ground pepper	*Water*
	Arrowroot

Start with 6 jumbo squabs, already dressed, and 3 or 4 dozen peeled and seeded muscat grapes.

In each bird put 4 grapes, mixed with enough breadcrumbs, toasted and seasoned with salt and freshly ground pepper to taste, and flavored with a few drops of brandy and port wine to fill. Then place the birds in a row in a well-buttered baking dish or pan, sprinkle them liberally with, first, some brandy, and then with port, and let them stand for at least 2 hours.

When they are ready for the oven, put 2 ounces each of port and water in the baking dish, and put them in a hot oven (400 degrees) for about 30 minutes, basting frequently.

When the squabs are cooked, take them out of the baking dish and place them on a hot platter. Add a little more port to the juices in the dish, and the rest of the peeled grapes. Thicken the sauce with a little arrowroot, season to taste, and serve in a gravy boat.

I think some people are apt to confuse squabs and chickens. There are squab chickens, but squabs are really young pigeons. A squab should never be more than four weeks old. After that they are technically pigeons, and their meat becomes lean and dark. An interesting squab combination is squab roasted in vermouth.

SQUAB ROASTED IN VERMOUTH

4 *jumbo squabs*	¾ *cup breadcrumbs*
3 *tbsp. butter*	*Salt*
3 *little green onions*	*Pepper*
½ *cup chopped mushrooms*	*Vermouth*
¼ *cup chopped pecans*	4 *slices bacon*
¼ *cup chopped apple*	*Buttered toast*

Melt 3 tablespoons of butter in a saucepan and, when hot, add to it 3 little green onions, finely chopped, and ½ cup of finely chopped canned button mushrooms. Sauté lightly until mushrooms and onions are tender, then add ¼ cup each of finely chopped pecans and finely chopped apple, and ¾ cup of breadcrumbs. Sprinkle in salt and freshly ground pepper to taste, and enough dry vermouth to bind all together after thoroughly mixing. Stuff the squabs with this mixture and place them in a roasting pan, with 2 half-slices of bacon over each breast. Pour into the pan 1 cup of dry vermouth.

Roast in a very hot oven (450 degrees), basting frequently, for about 20 minutes, or until birds are tender. Then place the squabs on individual slices of hot buttered toast, and pour the sauce from the pan over them.

Recipes for frogs' legs are found in most cook books under the classification of fish. But inasmuch as frogs are amphibious and as one goes out to hunt them, I am being different and including them as game. As a matter of fact, there are species of frogs which live in trees.

Regardless of whether they are fish, fowl, or game, in my opinion, frogs' legs—*Jambes des Grenouille,* as the French call them —make one of the most delicious and delicate morsels in the world. Mention *Jambes des Grenouille à la Provençale* to a true Frenchman, and he will rhapsodize over the dish, with gestures. You will be able to get frogs' legs à la Provençale cooked to the queen's taste throughout France, even in the humblest inn, and you can prepare them in your own home with a minimum of fuss and effort so that they will be just as delicious as in France.

FROGS' LEGS PROVENÇALE

12 *medium-sized frogs' legs*	*Pepper*
5 *tbsp. butter*	2 *tbsp. tarragon*
2 *cloves garlic, crushed*	2 *tbsp. chopped chives*
Juice ½ lemon	2 *tbsp. chopped parsley*
Salt	1 *ounce brandy*

2 *ounces dry white wine*

Wash the frogs' legs well in lemon juice and water, dry, and dust with flour. (The number you need depends on their size. I avoid very small ones or very large ones. There is not enough meat on the former, and the latter are likely to be a little tough. The recipe here calls for about a dozen medium-sized legs.) Put about 5 tablespoons of butter in a pan or skillet, heat to a point where it foams, and add 2 cloves of garlic, crushed, and the juice of ½ lemon.

Cook this for 1 minute, and then put in the frogs' legs. Shake them in the pan until they are golden brown on each side, then add salt and pepper to taste and 2 tablespoons each of finely chopped tarragon, chives, and parsley (the latter two should be fresh, the tarragon can be dried). Cook for another minute, and then add 1 ounce of lighted brandy and 2 ounces of good American white wine. Let cook for another minute, then rush the result to the table in a very hot dish and prepare to go into ecstasies.

For a long time I never ordered or cooked frogs' legs any other way than *à la Provençale*. Then one day a friend of mine gave me a recipe he had picked up along the Riviera. I tried it, and it rates a close second to the Provençale.

FROGS' LEGS IN WHITE WINE

2 *dozen frogs' legs*	6 *little green onions*
Milk	1 *cup canned mushrooms*
Flour	1 *small green pepper*
Salt	4 *ounces dry white wine*
Cayenne pepper	1½ *cups cream*
9 *tbsp. butter*	1 *fresh tomato*
¼ *clove garlic*	2 *tbsp. sherry*
1 *bay leaf*	*Pinch sugar*
Pinch thyme	*Chopped chives*
Chopped parsley	

Dip 2 dozen frogs' legs in milk, then dust with flour seasoned with salt and cayenne pepper.

In a large saucepan melt 4 ounces of butter, and add ¼ clove of garlic, crushed, 1 crumbled bay leaf, 1 pinch of thyme, 6 little green onions, chopped fine, 1 cup of canned mushrooms, chopped, 1 small green pepper, seeded and chopped, and the frogs' legs. When the legs are a delicate brown, add 4 ounces of dry American white wine, along with 1½ cups of cream and a fresh tomato chopped in medium-sized pieces. Cook slowly for about 15 minutes, covered. Then add 1 tablespoon of flour mixed with 1 tablespoon of soft butter, and cook over a high flame, stirring constantly until it thickens. Then lower the flame, and stir in 2 tablespoons of sherry and a pinch of sugar. Mix well and serve, garnishing the dish with a sprinkling of chopped chives and chopped parsley.

I am a push-over for magic and sleight-of-hand. In any gathering, I am always the eager beaver who selects a card, looks at it, slips it back into the deck, and stands with mouth agape while the performer manipulates the deck and finally retrieves my selected card from my buttoned rear pants pocket. Sometimes the magician shows me how the trick is done. Thereafter, I practice it for days, only to muff it at the big moment when I attempt to display my newly acquired feat.

So, I should never attempt to try to tell anyone how to pull a rabbit out of a hat. But I can tell you how to fix a rabbit and pull it out of the oven, to the gastronomic delight of your guests and your own amazement.

This recipe comes from the proprietor of a little inn at St. Jean d'Angely, in the heart of the cognac country in France.

JELLIED RABBIT WITH COGNAC

	Sliced carrots
2 rabbits, disjointed	*Sliced onion*
Bacon slices	*Salt*
Bay leaves	*Pepper*
Thyme	*½ cup brandy*

Flour-and-water paste

Cut 2 rabbits into small joints, leaving in the bones. At the bottom of a fireproof casserole lay thin slices of bacon, half a bay leaf, a pinch of thyme, and a few slices each of onion and carrot. Then put in a layer of rabbit, packing the pieces in closely, and add salt and pepper. Now repeat the layer of onion and carrot (omitting the bacon), the layer of rabbit, and continue this until the dish is full, with the top layer consisting of onion and carrot.

Pour ½ cup of brandy over the dish, cover with bacon slices, and put the cover on the casserole. Seal the edges with flour-and-water paste and bake slowly for 3 hours. Then let the dish cool, and after it is cool, chill it thoroughly.

In the Mother Goose nursery rhyme, daddy went a-hunting for a rabbit so he could keep Baby Bunting nice and warm with its skin. But today it is much more sensible for daddy or mother to go a-hunting for a rabbit to eat, what with the current price of beef, lamb, pork, or chicken.

For hundreds of years rabbit, or hare, has been regarded as a real delicacy in Europe, and most countries have their special recipes. The Savoy Hotel in London is famous for its jugged hare; France has its *Lapin au Vin Blanc* and Rabbit à la Dijon; Hungarians delight in *Paprikasnyul* (which is hare with paprika); *Hasenpfeffer* is practically a national dish in Germany; and at the Stork Club in New York, Rabbit à la Cacciattore is something really to drool over.

The flesh of young, plump rabbits, or hares—wild or domestic —makes mighty fine eating. Those who enjoy a delicate, gamey flavor will prefer the dark meat of the wild rabbit; others will find more enjoyment in the mild, white flesh of the domesticated animal. The latter is so similar to chicken that it can be prepared in exactly the same way and requires about the same cooking time. There is almost no limit to the number of ways a rabbit, or hare, can be cooked. You can bake, boil, broil, or fry your rabbit; combine it with vegetables in a potpie, mix it with celery and mayonnaise and stuff it in a tomato, stew it, roast it, make a soup out of it, or serve it à la king. But no matter how you fix it, it is bound to be wonderful eating.

During the hunting season in the Netherlands, *Jachtschoter,* or Hunter's Stew, is served in almost every restaurant, hotel, or inn throughout the country. It takes a little time to prepare, but the result is well worth it and the labor is not difficult.

JACHTSCHOTER

(Rabbit Hunter's Stew)

1 3- *to* 4-*lb. rabbit*	¼ *lb. sliced onions*
2 *qt. water*	½ *lb. green sour apples*
2 *sprigs parsley*	2½ *lb. cooked potatoes*
1 *tbsp. salt*	*Salt*
3 *stalks celery with leaves*	*Pepper*
2 *carrots, scraped*	*Nutmeg*
1 *medium-sized onion*	¾ *cup dry red wine*
¼ *tsp. black pepper*	1¾ *cups rabbit broth*
6 *tbsp. butter*	½ *cup breadcrumbs*

A 3- to 4-pound dressed rabbit is put into a kettle with 2 quarts of cold water, 2 sprigs of parsley, 1 scant tablespoon of salt, 3 stalks of celery with their leaves left on, 2 carrots, scraped, 1 medium-sized onion, peeled and quartered, and ¼ teaspoon of black pepper. The lid is put on the kettle, and when the water boils the flame is lowered to allow the rabbit to simmer very slowly until it is tender. This will take pretty close to 3 hours. Then the rabbit meat is taken from the bones, and the broth is strained. This is the basic recipe for boiled rabbit.

To make *Jachtschoter,* melt 3 tablespoons of butter in a heavy skillet, and add ¼ pound of peeled and sliced onions. Sauté them until golden brown, keeping the rings intact, then remove from the skillet. Next, sauté ½ pound of peeled sliced green apples in another 3 tablespoons of butter. Now, take a heat-proof cas-serole and, using care not to break them, put in a layer of ⅓ of 2½ pounds of sliced cooked potatoes. On the potatoes put a layer of the cooked rabbit meat, sliced, and ⅓ of the onion rings and apple slices. Season with salt and pepper to taste and a pinch of nutmeg. Now repeat the layers, until all the ingredients are used. Pour over the contents of the casserole 1¾ cups of the strained rabbit broth and ¾ cup of good dry American red wine. Top with ½ cup of buttered breadcrumbs and bake in a moderate (350 degrees) oven for 1 hour.

One of the best known German dishes is *Hasenpfeffer*. There is a German restaurant in Chicago, the Red Star Inn on North Clark Street, which serves delicious food the year round. But imme-diately after the first frost, I start calling up to know when they are going to serve *Hasenpfeffer,* and for many years I have been among the first customers to partake of this specialty.

Hasenpfeffer is, of course, a spicy dish, and after you have eaten it, you'll understand the old Pennsylvania Dutch saying, *"Do is 's wo d'r haws im pef'r sitst"* (here is where the rabbit sits in the pepper).

HASENPFEFFER

1 *large (or 2 small) rabbit*	1 *tsp. mustard seed*
2 *cups dry red wine*	½ *tsp. thyme*
2 *cups tarragon vinegar*	5 *whole cloves*
2 *onions*	4 *tbsp. olive oil*
1 *carrot*	*Juice 2 lemons*
2 *whole allspice*	2 *tbsp. chopped parsley*
3 *bay leaves*	*Bacon drippings*
1 *tbsp. salt*	¼ *lb. diced raw ham*
1 *tsp. black pepper*	5 *little green onions*

Consommé (if necessary)

Disjoint a large dressed rabbit (or 2 small ones) and put the pieces in an earthenware crock or enamel bowl. Cover with the following marinade: 2 cups of dry American red wine, 2 cups of tarragon vinegar, 2 large onions, peeled and sliced, 1 carrot, sliced, 2 whole allspice, crushed, 3 bay leaves, 1 tablespoon of salt, 1 teaspoon of black pepper, 1 teaspoon of mustard seed, ½ teaspoon of thyme, 5 whole cloves, 4 tablespoons of olive oil, the juice of 2 lemons, and 2 tablespoons of chopped parsley.

Meantime, melt 2 tablespoons of bacon drippings in a skillet and add ¼ pound of diced raw ham. Brown it lightly, then remove the ham to a Dutch oven or a pot with a heavy lid. In the same fat, brown 5 little green onions, chopped, and then put them in the pot with the ham. Next, brown the rabbit pieces (which have been drained and rolled in flour) in the same fat, adding more, if necessary. Then add the browned rabbit to the ham and the browned onions, and pour the marinade over them. It should just cover the rabbit. If it doesn't, add more red wine, and consommé, in equal parts. Cover the pot, and simmer until the rabbit is very tender—about 2 hours.

To serve, remove the rabbit to a platter, strain the gravy, skimming off any excess fat, and serve separately. Or you can serve the whole thing as is, which is the way I prefer it.

To many people the knowledge of rabbit is limited to the pages of *Uncle Remus*. I don't recall whether Brer Rabbit was a cotton-tail or a jack rabbit, but perhaps I have come up with a new species of rabbit. In any event I call this Applejack Rabbit.

APPLEJACK RABBIT

2 *young rabbits, disjointed*	2 *tsp. baking powder*
1 *tbsp. flour*	1 *medium-sized onion*
1 *cup fine white corn meal*	1 *egg*
¾ *tsp. salt*	6 *tbsp. milk*

Applejack

Cut 2 young rabbits into serving pieces.

Mix together 1 tablespoon of flour, 1 cup of fine white corn meal, ¾ teaspoon of salt, and 2 teaspoons of baking powder. Add 1 medium-sized onion, grated, and 1 egg, and stir well. Add 6 tablespoons of rich milk, and beat until smooth.

Roll the pieces of rabbit in this batter, and fry them in bacon drippings until brown. Then cover the rabbit with applejack, put a lid on the skillet, and simmer until the meat is tender and the liquid is absorbed.

Many people are very finicky about eating rabbit. Let's face it now and get it over with. They are afraid they may be eating cat instead of rabbit. But inasmuch as there are millions more rabbits than cats, the chances of getting cat instead of rabbit are one in some astronomical figure. However, in this connection it is inter-esting to note that in many European countries it is against the law to sell wholly skinned rabbits—the front paws must be left on, and are chopped off by the butcher only after he has made the sale.

Another reason for the phobia against rabbits is the fact that wild rabbits may transmit to human beings a usually fatal illness called tularemia, but this disease can only be contracted through skinning a wild rabbit and not by eating it.

Today, rabbits are found in almost every first-class market and are dressed with the same care afforded chickens.

Here is a recipe for rabbit in the Hungarian manner.

RABBIT PAPRIKA

1 *tender young rabbit, dis-jointed*	3 *medium-sized onions*
Salt	1½ *tbsp. Rosen paprika*
Pepper	1 *clove garlic, minced*
Flour	2 *fresh tomatoes*
4 *tbsp. butter*	½ *cup dry sherry*
	1 *cup sour cream*

Cut a tender young rabbit into serving pieces, and rub them well with salt and pepper, then roll them in flour.

In a heavy iron skillet or a Dutch oven melt 4 tablespoons of butter, and add 3 medium-sized onions, peeled and chopped. Let these cook very slowly for about 30 minutes, watching carefully to see that they don't burn. Then add 1½ tablespoons of Rosen paprika, and cook for another 15 minutes, stirring constantly.

Now add the rabbit pieces, 1 clove of garlic, minced, 2 fresh tomatoes, cut up, and ½ cup of dry sherry. Cover the skillet and let all this simmer for about an hour, or until the rabbit is tender.

Just a few minutes before serving, add 1 cup of sour cream to the rabbit. Mix it in well, correct for seasoning, and let everything simmer just long enough to heat the sour cream. Serve hot.

Venison is one of the oldest and best of foods. In Europe it has always been a favorite of royalty. In the early days of America venison was a staple meat, and as the pioneers pushed westward, it often was the only meat they had. But now that the telephone, or a short walk to the corner market, has replaced the gun as a means of obtaining the week's meat supply, venison has almost disappeared from the American table, unless the head of the house is a mighty Nimrod or has friends who are.

Ladies, if the Big Shot of your household writes, wires, or 'phones that he's bringing home some venison, don't fly into a tizzy. First, write, wire, or 'phone back and caution husband, son, or brother to be sure that the venison has been hung a sufficient time before he expects you to cook it. (A few weeks in a refrigerator improves the flavor and greatly enhances the natural virtues of venison.) Then be sure there are a few bottles of good dry American red wine in the cellar and herbs and seasonings on the pantry shelf, and sit back and await the great day.

The three most common ways of cooking venison are broiling, making a ragout, and roasting. The following recipe was given me by an old friend who never misses going after deer during the hunting season. He is not only an excellent shot, but a damn good game cook, and is much sought after as a companion on any hunting trip.

ROAST HAUNCH OF VENISON

6- to 7-lb. haunch venison
5 tbsp. butter
1 large onion, chopped
2 tbsp. chopped little green
  onions
2 large carrots, chopped
4 whole cloves
½ tsp. thyme
½ tsp. marjoram
½ tsp. tarragon
½ tsp. basil
½ tsp. rosemary

2 cups dry red wine
Olive oil
Salt
Freshly ground pepper
½ lb. salt pork
2 cloves garlic
1 cup red currant jelly
Pinch powdered ginger
Pinch powdered cloves
1 tsp. lemon juice
¼ cup sour cream
Flour (if necessary)

1 tbsp. brandy

First, marinate the meat. The standard marinade at many hunt clubs is ⅔ red wine and ⅓ water, to which generous seasonings of pepper, bay leaves, thyme, tarragon, and mustard seed have been added. But here's a better one that dates back to the seventeenth century. Fry out 1 large mild onion, chopped, 2 tablespoons of chopped little green onions, and 2 large carrots, chopped, in 5 tablespoons of butter. Add 4 whole cloves, ½ teaspoon each of thyme, marjoram, tarragon, basil, and rosemary. Add 1 cup of red wine. Then put everything through a coarse sieve. Now brush the vension with olive oil, dust with plenty of freshly ground pepper and salt, and pour the marinade over the venison and let it soak in it for about 8 hours.

To cook, lard the venison generously with salt pork and insert slivers of garlic into the meat. Roast in a 450-degree oven, 20 to 30 minutes to the pound, basting frequently with the drippings and the marinade, which has been added. When the meat is tender, remove from the roasting pan but keep in a warm oven while making the gravy.

And now the gravy! In the roasting pan slowly melt 1 cup of red currant jelly with the drippings and the marinade, to which 1 cup of red wine has been added. While this is simmering, add a pinch of powdered ginger, a pinch of powdered clove, and 1 teaspoon of lemon juice. When the gravy has thickened and reduced a little, slowly add ¼ cup of sour cream and blend everything thoroughly. If you prefer the gravy a little thicker, sprinkle in a little flour, being sure no lumps form. Just before serving, add 1 tablespoon of good brandy, and pour into the gravy boat.

Mashed potatoes, baked Hubbard squash, and old-fashioned cole slaw are perfect accompaniments to the roast venison, and don't stint on that gravy! Of course, a good red dry wine is a "must"— preferably an American Burgundy.

For the last two or three years the *Chicago Tribune* has handled a great outdoor show at Navy Pier in Chicago. There are many exhibits of boats, all the way from 45-foot cruisers down to rowboats, and hundreds of exhibits of all sorts of hunting and fishing equipment. This year a novel experiment was tried—a demonstration of game cookery. A completely equipped, ultra-modern electric kitchen was installed on the stage of a theatre seating about 1000 people. Each afternoon Jane Foster and her staff from the Commonwealth Edison Company in Chicago demonstrated how women cook game, and each evening men showed their talents and skill in game cookery. I was the master of ceremonies at the afternoon shows (this gave me a fine chance to spy on the talents of the fair sex), and I officiated also at the evening shows. On four of the five evenings of the week I had guest chefs, and one evening I was the chef. One evening Ric Riccardo demonstrated how to cook duck à la Frederic. Another evening Bob Jefferson (he of the dry fish chowder) and Walter Drennan, both strictly amateur chefs, demonstrated fish and partridge cooking. On another evening Arnold Shircliffe, manager of the Wrigley Building Restaurant in Chicago and one of the foremost chefs in the country, put on a brilliant demonstration of fish cookery. He also showed how to prepare and serve *blinis* with caviar and sour cream, a Valentine salad, and *café Diablo*.

On a Tuesday night Max Guggiari, of the Imperial House in Chicago, was the guest chef, and he and his two marvelous assistants, Emile Foyaly and Felix Monego, prepared a dinner truly fit for a king. The menu: tenderloin of venison *Smitane, pommes soufflés,* endive salad with a special French dressing, and *zobaglione* for dessert.

Here is the way Max prepared the tenderloin of venison.

TENDERLOIN OF VENISON, SMITANE

6 *tenderloin of venison*	*Pinch caraway seeds*
6 *strips of bacon*	½ *cup dry white wine*
¼ *lb. butter*	1½ *cups cream*
1 *medium-sized onion*	½ *pint sour cream*
4 *large mushrooms*	*Salt*
2 *bay leaves*	*Freshly ground pepper*
Pinch thyme	*Dash Worcestershire sauce*

Juice ½ lemon

Wrap 6 tenderloin of venison in 6 strips of bacon, and pan broil over a medium flame for about 6 minutes on each side. Then put them in a warm oven while the sauce is being prepared.

Place ¼ pound of butter in a saucepan with 1 medium-sized onion cut *julienne,* 4 large mushrooms, also cut *julienne,* 2 bay leaves, and a pinch each of thyme and caraway seeds. Let this simmer for a little while—say three or four minutes—then add ½ cup of dry American white wine. Continue to simmer until the onions and mushrooms are tender; then add 1½ cups of cream, and let it simmer for about 20 minutes more. Remove from fire and add 1 cup of sour cream, salt and freshly ground pepper to taste, a dash of Worcestershire sauce, and the juice of ½ lemon. Reheat.

Serve the tenderloin of venison with this sauce poured over them.

Last year Curly Bradley, who plays the part of Tom Mix on the coast-to-coast radio program of that name, and Lee Bennett, Jan Garber's former crooner turned radio announcer, joined Hal Lansing, another popular announcer over the Mutual Broadcasting System, at his camp in the North woods. Knowing my predilec-

tion for venison, they brought me back a very nice supply of meat.
And did I go to town with it! If you're lucky enough to bag a
deer yourself, or have some venison given to you, try this recipe
out and you'll feel that the gods have smiled on you.

VENISON RAGOUT

5 *lb. venison*	6 *green celery tops*
Vinegar	6 *sprigs parsley*
1 *clove garlic*	*Generous pinch thyme*
½ *cup bacon drippings*	12 *peppercorns*
1½ *cups diced carrots*	2 *tsp. salt*
1½ *cups diced celery*	½ *lb. fresh mushrooms*
1 *cup chopped onions*	2 *ounces butter*
2 *cups dry red wine*	¼ *cup flour*
3 *cups consommé*	1½ *cups sour cream*
2 *bay leaves*	2 *tsp. Rosen paprika*

Cut 5 pounds of venison into 2-inch pieces. Then melt ½ cup of
bacon drippings in a heavy frying pan. After wiping the meat
with vinegar, put it, along with a large clove of garlic, crushed,
into the pan. Sear the meat until it is browned on all sides. Now
arrange the meat in a large casserole, and add 1½ cups each of
diced carrots and celery, 1 cup of minced onions, 2 cups of good
American dry red wine, 3 cups of consommé, 2 large bay leaves,
about 6 green celery tops, about 6 sprigs of fresh parsley, a very
generous pinch of thyme, 12 black peppercorns, gently crushed,
and 2 teaspoons of salt. Cover the casserole and place in a slow
oven (300 to 325 degrees) for 30 minutes. Then add ½ pound
of fresh mushrooms, sliced, and cook for about 30 minutes longer,
or until the meat is tender. (The cooking time will depend on
how long the meat has hung; generally a week or two of hanging
will bring it to its maximum deliciousness.)

Next, melt ¼ cup of butter in a saucepan and stir in ¼ cup
of flour. When the mixture is well blended, strain the liquid in
which the venison has been cooked and pour it into the pan with
the butter and flour. Stir this constantly, over a low flame, until the
mixture has thickened and has bubbled for about 3 minutes. Then
stir in 1½ cups of sour cream and, if necessary, correct for salt
seasoning. Blend the mixture well, adding 2 teaspoons of paprika

(imported, if you have it or can get it). Pour the sauce over the meat and vegetables in the casserole. Serve immediately, garnished with fresh water cress, and with currant jelly on the side.

Venison steaks can be plain broiled, or grilled, or fried, or fixed up fancy. I wouldn't walk a mile for any brand of cigarette, but I would walk a mile for venison steak the way a friend of mine in Montana prepares it. And I think you would, too.

VENISON STEAK WITH WINE SAUCE

1¼-inch-thick venison steak
Soft butter
Salt
Freshly ground pepper
2 tbsp. butter

1 cup dry red wine
Tiny pinch cayenne pepper
Tiny pinch powdered mace
1 tbsp. chopped parsley
1 tbsp. chopped chives

2 tbsp. quince jelly

Rub a 1¼-inch-thick venison steak all over with softened butter and put into a hot skillet. Broil about 4 minutes on each side. Season with salt and freshly ground pepper to taste, and put steak on a hot platter, and keep it hot while the sauce is made.

Add 2 tablespoons of butter to the skillet in which the steak was cooked, bring it to the bubbling point, and remove the skillet from the fire. Pour in 1 cup of dry American red wine, add a tiny pinch each of cayenne pepper and powdered mace, 1 tablespoon each of chopped parsley and chives, and 2 tablespoons of quince jelly. Put the skillet back over a medium flame, and stir contents until well blended and hot. Then pour sauce over steak, and serve very hot.

Occasionally, throughout this book, I have mentioned the Streeterville and Sanitary Canal Gourmet and Study Society. The membership is limited to ten men, among whom are Jack Thompson, the famous paratroop war correspondent of the *Chicago Tribune;* Ward Walker, another war correspondent for the same paper; a lawyer; a writer; 2 radio executives; a real estate operator; an accountant; a major general of the United States Army; and "Slim Jim" Gavin, commander of the famous 82nd Airborne Division.

All these men, including myself, are fond of good eating and drinking. Once a month we designate one as a chef and he holds the dinner meeting at his home. He also appoints one of the members as a cellarer. The entire meal is planned and prepared by the host-chef, and the wines are selected with great care to complement the food. There are a couple of members who are not expert chefs, but they are fast learning the art of gourmet cookery by acting as observers during the preparation of the meals. And finally two members are designated for scullery duty—washing and wiping the pots, pans, and dishes, and leaving the kitchen immaculate. One of the most unusual dinners the society has had was held in the home of Francis Coughlin, Continuity Editor for Station WGN and the Mutual Broadcasting System in Chicago.

It isn't difficult to fashion a gourmet dinner from the elaborate dishes or menus popular in New York in the gay nineties or in the antibellum period of the South. But to prepare and serve a fabulous meal based on early American food is an achievement which deserves to be recorded.

When the members of the society assembled at Fran Coughlin's home Thursday evening early in 1949, host Coughlin handed each member a mimeographed menu. I think it's worth reproducing.

FORT DEARBORN DINNER

Coughlin's Cross Roads

559 West Surf

Chicago Settlement

Early Sundown

February 17th, 1949

Cocktails "Liberty and Prosperity" ....from New Jersey

Hardtack and Bacon ....from the sutlers' stores

Buffalo Chuck ....à la Michigammi
Baked Squash ....à la Potawatomi
Wild Rice ....à la Winnebago

Salad with onion, Chi-ca-gou ....John Kinzie

Corn Doin's ....Fort Wayne
Conserves ....Fort Machilimackinac

Condiments ....Fort Detroit

Dessert Stockade (with New England rum) ....Fort Dearborn

Coffee

Trade Tobaccos

Ash-kan-ti-neebish, Ish-kat-ti-waboe, Skinny-waboe.

Toasts will include:

"Free Trade and Sailor's Rights," "The American Eagle,"
"The Absent Fair," "General Washington," "Confusion to the Hudson's
Bay Company," "Mr. Jefferson," "The Free Trapper," "Woodland
Frolics," "Winnebago Girls," etc., etc.

NO LIQUOR SERVED TO MINORS OR INDIANS

The Buffalo Chuck came from Ed Butters' buffalo farm in Cold-
water, Michigan. In 1945 Ed Butters bought 175 buffalo in South
Dakota and shipped them to his 600-acre Michigan farm. The
difficulties in carrying out this project were tremendous, but the
experiment paid off handsomely, for buffalo meat is fine eating and,
during wartime rationing, required no ration points. Today, many
exclusive eastern restaurants buy all the buffalo meat that Butters
slaughters, except a small supply that he sells to local gourmets
and visiting firemen.

The cooking of a good cut of buffalo should hold no terrors for
the amateur chef. Like beef, it may be roasted, braised, or cut into
steaks and broiled. Of course, the meat should be marinated from
12 to 48 hours beforehand. And here is how Fran Coughlin prepared his buffalo chuck *en casserole*.

BUFFALO CHUCK EN CASSEROLE

6- to 8-lb. buffalo chuck   Flour
4 tbsp. bacon fat   Water
Dry red wine (Burgundy)   Generous pinch tarragon
2 medium-sized onions   Generous pinch oregano
2 bay leaves   Generous pinch thyme
           Generous pinch basil

First, sear a 6- to 8-pound piece of buffalo chuck in hot fat, then
place it in a large kettle about half full of an American Burgundy,
and add 1 very large onion (or 2 medium ones) and 2 bay leaves
in a cloth sack. Cover and cook slowly on top of the stove until the

meat is tender—about 5 to 6 hours—turning the meat occasionally. Next, remove the meat and the sack of onion and bay leaves. Let the liquor cool, and remove the fat which congeals on the surface. Slice the meat from the bone and arrange the slices in a casserole. Thicken the fat-free liquor with flour-and-water to make a fairly thin gravy. Add salt and black pepper to taste and a generous pinch each of tarragon, oregano, thyme, and sweet basil. Cover the sliced meat with the gravy, and bake in a medium oven until the gravy is rich and brown. Add a ½ cup of Burgundy before serving.

(8) POULTRY

I know of no other animal or bird that is more of a cosmopolitan than our barnyard friend, the chicken. From earliest times, the chicken has been served on the tables of almost every nation under the sun, and certainly no other edible is so universally admired. King Henry IV of France, who raised and cooked his own chickens, and even wrote a small cook book dealing with the preparation of his favorite chicken recipes, once promised his disgruntled peasants a chicken in the pot for every family in his kingdom (the Republicans promised that, too, in 1932, but they went King Henry one better by adding "a car in every backyard to boot!").

Poultry is for the cook what canvas is for the painter. There are as many nuances of flavor as there are of color. Chicken can be boiled, roasted, fried, stewed, grilled; it can be served hot or cold, whole or in part, with or without sauces, boned or stuffed. The Phoenicians simmered it in oil; the American Indians covered it with mud and baked it in hot coals. But it remained for the perfect artistry of the Gallic chef really to glorify it and raise it to un-dreamed-of gustatory heights with such a dish as Chicken Truffled *à la Perigueux*. I believe it was Brillat-Savarin who said, "If Adam and Eve ruined themselves for an apple, what would they have done for a truffled fowl?"

Very few people tire of chicken, because the meat is so delicate and tasty no matter how it is cooked. However, Napoleon apparently did. During his campaigns, it is said, roast chicken was served nearly every night. His chef, uncertain as to when dinner would be served, roasted a fresh chicken every 20 minutes. One night, it is reported, Napoleon complained to a marquis on his staff that chicken always had the same taste. The officer, a gourmet, replied that he would wager his title that he could serve his emperor chicken twice a day for a whole year, and that the taste would always be different. I should be inclined to make the same wager.

In the Bois de Boulogne in Paris there used to be, and probably still are, some of the finest restaurants in the world. In the middle of the Bois, resting against a beautiful natural waterfall, was the Pavillon de la Cascade. It was an enchanting place to lunch before going to the races, which were just around the corner at Auteuil. And one of their most delicious dishes was Chicken *à la Chasseur*. This is the way it was made.

CHICKEN À LA CHASSEUR

1 *young chicken, 2-2½ lb.*	2 *young green onions*
Salt	1 *ounce brandy*
Pepper	1 *cup dry white wine*
Lemon juice	2 *fresh tomatoes*
1 *tbsp. butter*	½ *cup chicken broth*
1 *tbsp. olive oil*	1 *tbsp. minced parsley*
10 *medium-sized mushrooms*	*Pinch tarragon*

Joint a tender young chicken, rub the pieces with lemon juice, and sprinkle them with salt and pepper, freshly ground. In a heavy iron skillet put 1 tablespoon each of butter and good olive oil. When this is hot, put in the chicken pieces and sauté over a medium flame until they are golden brown on all sides. Then add 10 medium-sized mushrooms, and let cook for 5 minutes. Now add 2 finely chopped young green onions (including tops), 1 ounce of brandy, 1 cup of dry American white wine, 2 fresh tomatoes, skinned, peeled and chopped, ½ cup of chicken broth, and 1 tablespoon of minced parsley. Cover the skillet, and let it cook over a gentle fire for about 25 minutes, or until the chicken is tender. Before serving, sprinkle a pinch of tarragon over it.

With this dish, crusty French bread is a "must," as is also a bottle of fine dry American white wine. Wild rice and tiny string beans go along excellently, and a salad of fresh tossed greens with a mild dressing.

Among most people in America today, there are no lukewarm feelings about garlic—they either love it or hate it. Yet I have known people, who said they hated it, to rave over a dish that was *lightly* flavored with garlic. Garlic lovers (notably Italians and Spaniards) want a pronounced flavor of garlic in their food.

The southeastern province of France, bordering on the Mediterranean and lying between the Rhone and the Italian Alps, is called Provence. Like its near neighbor on the east, Italy, and its not-so-near neighbor on the west, Spain, its people have a fondness for garlic. As a matter of fact, any French dish with the appellation, *"à la Provençale,"* has garlic in it. The following dish, Chicken *à la Provençale,* further shows the Italian influence in that it calls for Prosciutto ham.

CHICKEN À LA PROVENÇALE

2 *broilers* (2 *lb. each*)	3 *ripe tomatoes*
Salt	½ *cup diced Italian ham*
Pepper	*Pinch thyme*
3 *ounces olive oil*	*Pinch oregano*
2 *cloves garlic*	6 *ounces very dry white wine*

1 *cup pitted green olives*

Cut 2 broilers (about 2 pounds each) into 8 pieces, and season with salt and pepper.

Put 3 ounces of olive oil into a heavy skillet and add 2 cloves of garlic, crushed and minced. When the oil is hot, put the chicken pieces in, and sauté until golden brown on all sides. Then add 3 ripe tomatoes, peeled, seeded, and chopped, ½ cup of diced Prosciutto ham (lean ham will do if you have trouble getting the Italian), a pinch each of thyme and oregano, and 6 ounces of very dry American white wine (a Riesling or Chablis). Simmer, turning the chicken pieces occasionally, for about 25 minutes. Then add 1 cup of pitted green olives, and cook for about 5 minutes more.

Remove the chicken pieces from the skillet and place on a hot platter. Increase the flame slightly, and let the sauce reduce a little if it is too thin. Then pour it over the chicken, and serve.

An herb not too well known in America is rosemary. It belongs to the mint family. It is an old favorite in English herb gardens. If you're a Shakespearian student, you'll remember the reference to it in Act IV, Scene V, of *Hamlet:* "There's rosemary, that's for remembrance." I believe there's also an old legend about rosemary—when Mary hung the clothes of the Infant Jesus on a rosemary bush, it flowered at once.

The pungent and refreshing scent of rosemary can lend a rare charm to cooling drinks, and, of course, it is wonderful to use in seasoning stuffings, lamb, pork, soups, and especially chicken. The following dish is unusual.

CHICKEN ROSEMARY

1 3- *to* 4-*lb. broiler*	4 *tbsp. olive oil*
Salt	2 *cloves garlic*
Freshly ground pepper	1 *tsp. rosemary*
	⅓ *cup dry Marsala*

Cut a 3- to 4-pound broiler into serving pieces and rub with salt and freshly ground pepper to taste.

Put 4 tablespoons of olive oil into a skillet, and add 2 crushed cloves of garlic. When the oil is hot, add the chicken pieces and brown them on both sides—about 15 minutes. Then sprinkle the chicken pieces with about 1 teaspoon of rosemary, and slowly add about ⅓ cup of Marsala. Cover, and simmer over a low flame for about 30 minutes, or until the chicken is tender. If necessary, add more Marsala to prevent burning. Serve very hot.

Among the American soldiers who participated in the Normandy invasion during the last war, there probably aren't a baker's dozen who didn't at one time or another partake of Calvados, the Normandy apple brandy distilled from cider made from the apples of Normandy, or Calvados, orchards (the ancient province of Normandy is now the province of Calvados).

Calvados is not for mild drinkers, because it is distilled at a high strength. The French have a story about a mild little Norman mouse who quenched his thirst from a little puddle in the cellar which came from a leaking Calvados cask. The first lap of his tongue somewhat stunned Mouse Michel. But he went back, and the second taste pleased him. So he lapped and lapped and lapped. When the puddle was dry, he reared up on his hind feet and squeaked raucously, *"Sacrebleu, ou est cette maudit chat!"*—"By God, where is that damn cat!" (Don't tell me—I know that's an old gag; but I just wanted to show that jokes are international!)

The following is a typical Normandy dish. But if you haven't any Calvados, or can't get any, use good old New Jersey apple-jack, which will do very nicely, thank you!

CHICKEN NORMANDY

2 *young chickens*	2 *hearts of celery*
Salt	2 *apples*
Pepper	1 *tbsp. chopped parsley*
4 *ounces butter*	*Pinch of thyme*
3 *ounces brandy*	3 *ounces Calvados* (*or apple-*
1 *onion*	*jack*)

3 *ounces rich cream*

Quarter 2 tender young chickens, and season them with salt and freshly ground pepper.

In an iron skillet melt 4 ounces of butter, and when the butter is hot, but not brown, add the chicken pieces, and sauté them until they are a light brown. Then pour over them 3 ounces of brandy. Light the brandy, let it burn a moment, then extinguish the flame. Remove the chicken pieces and keep them warm.

In the same skillet put 1 onion, peeled and thinly sliced, 2 hearts of celery, sliced, and 2 apples, peeled, cored, and sliced. Sauté slowly until the vegetables are soft and nearly cooked. Add 1 tablespoon of chopped parsley, a pinch of thyme, and blend in. Then put the chicken pieces back, together with 3 ounces of Calvados, or applejack if you don't have the former. Cover the skillet and finish cooking until the chicken is tender—about 40 minutes. Just before serving, stir in very slowly 3 ounces of rich cream. Add the seasoning if necessary, heat, and serve.

Almonds are most frequently used in desserts, as a garnish, or for just plain eating (when salted) with cocktails. But they can also give a delicious flavor to foods, particularly to fish, certain species of shellfish, and to chicken. In the following recipe, they are not only used as a finishing touch, but, ground, they are incorporated in the cooking of the dish itself.

CHICKEN AMANDINE

2 *young broilers* (1½-2 *lb.*   2 *tbsp. brandy*
    each)   4 *ripe tomatoes*
Salt   1 *tsp. tomato paste*
Pepper   2 *tbsp. flour*
1 *cup shelled almonds*   1 *cup consommé*
2 *ounces butter*   ½ *cup dry white wine*
            ¾ *cup rich cream*

Cut 2 young broilers (about 1½-2 pounds each) into serving pieces and season with salt and pepper.

Blanch 1 cup of shelled almonds. Crush ¼ of them, and shred the rest.

In a skillet melt 2 ounces of butter, and when hot, add the chicken pieces. Sauté slowly until light brown. Then pour over them 2 tablespoons of warm brandy and set it alight. When the flame dies out, remove the chicken pieces from the skillet and keep them warm.

Add to the skillet 4 ripe tomatoes, peeled, seeded, and chopped, and cook briskly for a few moments until the tomatoes are pulpy. Remove the skillet from the fire and add 1 teaspoon of tomato paste, 2 tablespoons of flour, and salt and pepper to taste, stirring these in briskly. Put the skillet back over the fire and add 1 cup of consommé and ½ cup of dry American white wine. Stir until the mixture comes to a boil, then add ¾ cup of rich cream, the crushed almonds, and ¼ cup of the shredded almonds. Mix well, and put the chicken pieces back in the skillet. Cook slowly for about 35 minutes, or until chicken is tender.

Remove the chicken pieces to a heat-proof shallow baking dish or casserole, pour the sauce over them, and sprinkle with the balance of the shredded almonds. Dot with butter, and place under the broiler flame until the almonds are golden brown. Remove and serve.

One hundred and forty-eight years ago, in the vicinity of a little village in Piedmont, in Northern Italy, a famous French dish was invented by a battlefield chef of Napoleon Bonaparte. The latter, then first consul, having failed to conclude a peace with Austria and England, determined to stake all on the chance of a campaign and entered Italy. His first brilliant success was at Marengo; but near the battlefield that evening Napoleon's chef faced disaster. The supply train had not been able to keep pace with the troops, and there was practically nothing with which to make a dinner for the temperamental Napoleon.

Probably quaking in his dusty boots, the poor cook scurried around desperately, seeking ingredients for the proper meal to celebrate the victory. Alas, all he could find was a lone chicken, a bottle of wine, olive oil, some mushrooms, a few onions and tomatoes, and, of course, garlic. But he set to work and finally came up with a masterpiece, which became known as *Le Poulet Marengo.*

There must be dozens of legends about the original creation of Chicken Marengo. The one point upon which all authorities agree is that olive oil was used because there was no butter. But there the agreement ends. Some say there were crayfish in the original dish; others insist that fried eggs accompanied it. In one story I read the statement that onions were absolutely incompatible with the dish; in another it was said that olives were used. In any event, since the days of Napoleon, many famous chefs have experimented with the dish, adding this or that, or fashioning a variety of garnishes.

Actually, chicken Marengo starts out as fried chicken—a delicacy in any man's language—and takes on other culinary delights as it progresses. To be perfectly honest, I wasn't present at the inception of the dish; but here's my version of it, and I think even Napoleon would go for it.

CHICKEN MARENGO

2 2½-lb. broilers	1½ cups sliced fresh mushrooms
Flour	
Salt	2 tsp. minced parsley
Pepper	4 tomatoes
¼ cup olive oil	1 cup dry white wine
4 small white onions	1 tbsp. brandy
1 small clove garlic	1 tbsp. tomato paste

1 tbsp. flour

Wash and clean two 2½-pound broilers, then cut them up as for frying and dust the pieces lightly with seasoned flour. In a large skillet heat ¼ cup olive oil, and sauté the chicken until it is golden brown, turning frequently so that all the pieces are done evenly. Then remove the chicken and keep warm.

In the same skillet put 4 peeled and chopped small white onions, 1 small clove of garlic, crushed, 1½ cups of sliced fresh mushrooms, 2 teaspoons of minced parsley, and, if necessary, a little more olive oil. Cook this mixture until the mushrooms are tender; then add 4 sliced and peeled tomatoes, 1 cup of dry American white wine, 1 tablespoon of brandy, 1 tablespoon of tomato paste, and 1 tablespoon of flour. Mix and blend the ingredients well, and allow to simmer over a medium flame for about 10 minutes. Now put the chicken in the sauce, cover the pan, and cook for about 30 minutes, or until the chicken is completely tender. Serve in the sauce.

The name given this next chicken dish may sound rather formidable, but don't worry. After eating it, you won't stand up on your two feet and yell, "Now, where is that damn mouse!" But I'll bet you will stand up and announce emphatically, "Now, there's a dish!" because the blend of flavors is something entirely different from most.

CHICKEN SAUTÉED IN MIXED LIQUORS

2 2½-lb. young chickens	1 cup sliced fresh mushrooms
Salt	1 cup dry white wine
Pepper	1 cup white port
4 ounces butter	2 ounces Kirsch
1 little green onion	2 ounces brandy
1 clove garlic	2 egg yolks
1 cup rich cream	

Disjoint 2 tender young chickens, 2 to 2½ pounds each, and season with salt and pepper to taste. Melt 4 ounces of butter in a skillet, and add 1 little green onion (bulb and tops), chopped, and 1 minced clove of garlic. When butter is hot (not brown), add the chicken pieces. Cook over a low heat for about 20 minutes, then add 1 cup of sliced mushrooms. Continue to cook until the chicken becomes a light golden brown—about 10 minutes more.

Now add to the chicken and mushrooms 1 cup of dry American white wine, 1 cup of white port, 2 ounces of Kirsch, and 2 ounces of brandy. Bring to a boil, light the liquors, and shake the skillet until the fire dies out. Continue cooking the chicken until tender— about 30 minutes more. When the chicken is done, remove the pieces to a hot plate.

The liquor in the skillet should be reduced to about half by the time the chicken is done. Combine the beaten yolks of 2 eggs with 1 cup of rich cream, and add this to the juices in the skillet. Cook until the sauce thickens (but do not allow it to boil), and stir constantly. When the sauce is thickened, pour it over the chicken and serve.

Along about August, June brides begin to realize there is a lot more to marriage than treading the rosy path of the honeymoon, hand in hand with Dream Boy. All of a sudden they find that a nasty old Fate has presented them with a brand-new set of problems, such as living within a budget, running a home, and cooking at least two meals a day. Some of the more fortunate ones, who have taken courses in home management and cooking, are prepared. Others, less fortunate in that respect, are blessed with courage and ingenuity, and they quickly catch on to most of the tricks. Then there are those poor souls who don't even know how to boil water, and wouldn't even try unless they had specific directions in front of them.

My heart goes out not only to those in that last group, but also to their husbands. And I could weep for them when I think of the sweet young things trying to whip up some of the meals they are advised to try. For example, the following menu recently was recommended to brides for their first dinner: A sweet fruit-juice rickey, a melon and grape salad made with ginger ale and fruit juices, biscuits made with tomato and cheese, and a rather tricky chocolate cake for dessert! Can you imagine Tall, Dark, and Handsome coming home from a hard day at the office, with only enough time off at noon for a sandwich and a glass of milk, and being confronted with a dinner such as that? If it wouldn't drive any self-respecting male to pack his grip and go home to mother, I'm a ring-tailed monkey!

If I might be so bold as to make a suggestion, brides, try this meal on your newly acquired lord and master. Start with cold jellied consommé and, for the main course, serve wine-fried chicken.

SAUTÉED CHICKEN WITH WINE AND BRANDY SAUCE

1 *young frying chicken*	*Pinch thyme*
Salt	2 *fresh tomatoes*
Pepper	½ *cup dry white wine*
3 *tbsp. butter*	½ *cup consommé*
¼ *lb. sliced mushrooms*	1 *tbsp. chopped parsley*
Pinch marjoram	2 *tbsp. minced onion*

1 *ounce brandy*

Disjoint a young fryer, rub the pieces with salt and freshly ground pepper, and put in a heavy skillet with 3 tablespoons of butter. Cook over a quick fire, turning the pieces frequently so that they brown evenly on all sides. When the pieces are golden brown, add ¼ pound of sliced fresh mushrooms, a pinch each of marjoram and thyme, and 2 fresh tomatoes, peeled and cut in quarters. Cook for about 5 minutes, then add ½ cup of dry American white wine and ½ cup of consommé. Season with salt and freshly ground pepper to taste. Cook slowly until chicken is tender, about 30 minutes or more. Then remove the pieces of chicken and keep them hot while making the sauce.

To the liquid in the pan add 1 tablespoon of finely chopped parsley and 2 tablespoons of minced onion. Cook the sauce slowly for about 10 minutes, remove from the fire, and add 1 ounce of brandy. Stir well, then pour the sauce over the chicken.

A long time ago, when America was young, French chefs came to the New World to make their home in the French settlements in Louisiana. Then chefs from Spain journeyed to the New World, and settled down in the same section. From time to time the French chefs would borrow from the Spanish chefs, and vice versa. And thus gradually evolved that wonderful method of preparing food that the whole world now knows as Creole cooking.

Creole cooking particularly lends itself to chicken, and this chicken dish is named for the sauce in which the delightful birds cook.

CHICKEN À LA CREOLE

2 *broilers* (1½-2 *lb. each*)   1 #2 *can tomatoes*
Flour   12 *pitted green olives*
Salt   1 *cup sliced fresh mushrooms*
Pepper   2 *slices canned pimentos*
3 *ounces butter*   2 *tbsp. chopped parsley*
2 *small cloves garlic*   *Generous pinch thyme*
1 *large onion*   *Generous pinch marjoram*
1 *green pepper*   1 *cup dry white wine*
              4 *tbsp. sherry*

Quarter 2 broilers, about 1½ to 2 pounds each, and shake them in a paper bag with seasoned flour.

In a large skillet or Dutch oven melt 3 ounces of butter and add 2 cloves of garlic, crushed and minced. Put the chicken quarters in, and sauté to a golden brown on all sides. Then add 1 large onion, peeled and chopped, and 1 green pepper, seeded and chopped, and let them brown lightly. Next, sprinkle in 2 tablespoons of flour, blend well, and cook until the flour is lightly browned. Then add 1 #2 can of tomatoes, 12 green olives, pitted and sliced, 1 cup of sliced fresh mushrooms, 2 slices of canned pimentos, chopped, 2 tablespoons of chopped parsley, a generous pinch each of thyme and marjoram, and salt and pepper to taste. Cover, and let simmer gently for about 20 minutes. Then add 1 cup of dry American white wine, cover, and simmer gently for about 45 minutes, or until the chicken is tender. Remove the chicken and place on a hot platter. Add 4 tablespoons of sherry to the sauce, blend in well, and pour the sauce over the chicken. Serve this dish with flaky boiled rice.

The Italians have a way with chickens, too. One of the best known Italian chicken dishes is Chicken *Cacciatora,* which is chicken, hunters' style. You'll probably find it on the menu of nearly every Italian restaurant in these United States, but it won't always be a top-notch dish. I've tried it in many places, but I've always been a little disappointed, save in a very few instances. Usually, it's not made with dry red wine, which, so far as I'm concerned, is an absolute necessity. There may be Italians who object to that statement; in fact, in an Italian cook book of mine, there are 2 recipes for Chicken *Cacciatora,* and one of them ignores wine and the other calls for sherry.

Well, that's the way the world goes. But I'll put the following recipe up against any other for Chicken *Cacciatora,* and I'll bet mine will get the most votes! (Ho! Hum! There I go bragging again.)

CHICKEN CACCIATORA

2 *tender chickens* (*about 2 lb. each*)
Flour
Salt
Pepper
1½ *ounces butter*
2½ *ounces pure olive oil*
1 *large clove garlic*
2 *medium-sized onions*

2 *small green peppers*
2 *slices canned pimento*
2 *cups canned tomatoes*
1 *tbsp. tomato paste*
2 *tbsp. chopped parsley*
Generous pinch thyme
Generous pinch oregano
1 *cup dry red wine*
2 *cups sliced mushrooms*

Cut 2 tender chickens (about 2 pounds each) into serving pieces and shake them in a paper bag of seasoned flour.

In a heavy skillet put 1½ ounces of butter, 2½ ounces of pure olive oil, and a large clove of garlic, minced. When the fat is hot, add the chicken pieces along with 2 medium-sized onions, peeled and chopped, and 2 small green peppers, seeded and chopped. Sauté until the chicken pieces are a nice golden brown. Then add to the skillet 2 slices of canned pimento, chopped, 2 cups of canned tomatoes (the Italian variety if you live near an Italian grocery store), 1 tablespoon of tomato paste, salt and pepper to taste, 2 tablespoons chopped parsley, a generous pinch each of thyme and oregano, and 1 cup of dry American red wine (or an American Chianti). Cover and simmer gently for about 1 hour. Then add 2 cups of thinly sliced mushrooms, and continue simmering, covered, for about 30 minutes longer, or until chicken is tender. Serve as hot as possible, with spaghetti *al burro,* which is plain boiled spaghetti well buttered.

Here's another Italian treatment of chicken—with the pungent Prosciutto ham, and this time a white wine. If you'd really like to have this dish completely Italian, you would have to use Orvietto, one of the leading Italian white wines. So far as I know, there isn't any American-Italian type wine quite like it. But you can't go wrong with an American dry white wine—so far as I'm con-- cerned, you'll never go wrong with any honest American wine.

CHICKEN ITALIENNE

2 *broilers (about 2 lb. each)*	6 *little green onions*
Salt	½ *cup diced Italian ham*
Freshly ground pepper	24 *small mushroom caps*
3 *ounces olive oil*	½ *tsp. oregano*
1 *clove garlic*	3 *ounces dry white wine*
1 *ounce brandy*	

Disjoint 2 tender broilers weighing about 2 pounds each, and season with salt and freshly ground pepper.

In a large iron skillet put 3 ounces of pure olive oil, and add 1 crushed and minced clove of garlic. When the oil is hot, put the chicken pieces in, and sauté quickly over a brisk flame. When the pieces are golden brown on all sides, turn down the flame and add 6 little green onions (bulb and tops), chopped, ½ cup of Italian ham (or ordinary lean ham), diced, 24 small mushroom caps, halved, ½ teaspoon of oregano, 3 ounces of dry American white wine, and 1 ounce of brandy. Blend well, then simmer for about 25 minutes, or until the chicken is tender.

Remove the chicken to a hot platter. Turn up the flame under the skillet a little, and let the wine sauce reduce about half. Then pour it over the chicken and serve.

In many foreign grocery stores, and particularly in Italian grocery stores, you'll find dried mushrooms. They're dark, shriv- eled-looking things, and, compared with the pristine beauty of the large luscious-looking white fresh mushrooms, remind one of an old hag. But don't be deceived, boys and girls. The flavor of dried mushrooms is very concentrated, and when they're soaked in liquid, particularly wine, and used in stews or sauces, they're quite the equal of their more aristocratic brothers, or sisters (I'm not acquainted with the love life of mushrooms, so I don't know whether or not they have sex).

This recipe is quite typical of Italian cookery, and, like most Italian dishes, very delicious.

CHICKEN WITH RIPE OLIVES AND MUSHROOMS

2 2- to 2½-lb. *young chickens*	¼ *clove garlic*
Flour	2 *tbsp. brandy*
Salt	18 *ripe olives*
Pepper	*Pinch thyme*
1 *cup dried Italian mush-*	*Pinch nutmeg*
rooms	*Pinch powdered ginger*
Dry American white wine	1 *bay leaf*
3 *ounces olive oil*	1½ *cups cream*

Cut 2 tender young chickens, 2 to 2½ pounds each, into quarters, and shake in a paper bag containing seasoned flour.

Wash and soak 1 cup of dried Italian mushrooms (you can get them in any Italian grocery store) in enough dry American white wine to cover, until they are plump—about ½ to ¾ hour.

Put 3 ounces of olive oil in a heavy skillet and add ¼ clove of minced garlic. When the oil is hot, put in the floured chicken, and brown the quarters well, turning frequently. When the chicken is golden brown, put 2 tablespoons of brandy in a ladle, heat it a little, set it alight, and pour over the browned chicken. Then add the mushrooms (which have been coarsely chopped), 1 cup of the wine they were plumped in, 18 ripe olives, which have been pitted and quartered, a pinch each of thyme, nutmeg, and powdered ginger, a crumbled bay leaf, salt and freshly ground pepper to taste, and 1½ cups of scalded cream. Cover the skillet, and simmer gently for about 1½ hours, or until the chicken is tender, turning the chicken pieces occasionally.

Put the chicken quarters on a hot platter, pour the sauce over them, and serve hot.

As all of my friends know, I am a curry addict. Even after having eaten an excellent dinner, the thought of a lobster, chicken, lamb, or shrimp curry can make my mouth water. If I know in advance that I'm going to have a curry dish of an evening, I'll breakfast very lightly and not eat again until dinner time, so that

I can do full justice to every last morsel of one of the most succulent dishes ever devised.

I have avidly eaten curry dishes devised and cooked by Hindus and Dutchmen. In all immodesty, I think that my lamb curry is tops. But the finest chicken (and lobster) curry that I have ever eaten was prepared for the Little Woman and me by Max Guggiari, of the Imperial House in Chicago. He gave me the recipe, and permission to use it, so I pass it on here. Believe me, the service of this dish will make you a prince among hosts, or a princess among hostesses.

CAPON AND LOBSTER CURRY

1 *lb. cooked lobster meat*	1 *stalk celery*
1 *lb. cooked white meat,*	2 *bay leaves*
chicken or capon	3 *ounces flour*
¼ *lb. butter*	2 *ounces curry powder*
1 *apple*	1 *qt. chicken broth*
1 *large onion*	1 *cup cream*

1 *coconut, milk and meat*

Melt ¼ pound of butter in a very large skillet, and fry 1 apple, cored, peeled and sliced, 1 large onion, peeled and sliced, 1 stalk of celery, cut up, and 2 bay leaves, and smother this mixture for 15 minutes. Then sprinkle 3 ounces of flour and 2 ounces of the best curry powder in the mixture. Stir well, and cook slowly for another 15 minutes. Now add 1 quart of chicken broth, 1 cup of cream, the milk and the shredded meat from the coconut, and again cook slowly for another 15 minutes. Remove from the fire and strain the sauce through a coarse piece of cheesecloth or a fine sieve into a large saucepan, and add 1 pound each of cooked lobster meat and the cooked white meat of a chicken or capon. The pieces of the lobster meat and the white meat of the fowl should be about 1 inch square. Season to taste with salt and pepper, and let the curry heat thoroughly over a very low flame. Serve over rice, and put a generous tablespoon of chutney over each serving. This amount of curry could serve five or six people, but you'd better count on its serving only four.

Whoever conceived the idea of cutting up chickens and selling the various parts of their anatomy separately should be awarded some sort of gastronomic medal or decoration. No greater boon could be brought to small households, or to individuals who have a decided preference for one part of a fowl over another.

The breast has always been my favorite part of a chicken, with the second joint running a close second. Breasts of chicken can be prepared in a number of intriguing ways, and they're always very swanky to serve. I don't know of any breast of chicken dish that is any better than that served at the Fort Sumter Hotel in Charleston, South Carolina . . . Breasts of Chicken with Wild Rice

BREAST OF CHICKEN WITH WILD RICE

1 *breast of chicken*	1 *large mushroom*
1 *small onion*	2 *ounces sherry*
1 *carrot*	2 *ounces cognac*
1 *stalk celery*	1 *cup of cream*
Tiny bit of garlic	½ *cup of wild rice*
Salt	*Pepper*

Bone and skin the breast of a young roasting chicken, season with salt and freshly ground black pepper, place in a buttered heavy frying pan, and add 1 small onion, a sliver of garlic, 1 small carrot, a tender stalk of celery, 1 large mushroom chopped, 2 ounces of sherry, 2 ounces of good brandy or cognac, and 1 cup of cream. Cover the pan, and simmer slowly until the breast is done. In the meantime, take ½ cup of wild rice, which has been soaked and thoroughly washed in cold water, boil about 20 minutes, wash again in cold water, and put in a steamer. When the breast of chicken is done, place it on a mound of rice and pour the sauce over all. Believe me, you-all will just "love that dish!"

In any man's language, just good old plain fried chicken is tops in eating. Fried with or without batter, in butter or olive oil or bacon drippings, it appeals to the most jaded appetite.

The South Americans have a special way of frying chicken that is not only exotic, but delicious. I think you'll find it that way, too.

FRIED CHICKEN SOUTH AMERICAN

2 *young chickens*	2 *ounces olive oil*
Salt	1 *onion, coarsely chopped*
Pepper	1 *clove garlic, sliced*
Powdered thyme	½ *tsp. chili powder*
Powdered mace	1 *cup dry white wine*
Flour	1 *tbsp. Madeira*
	½ *cup beef bouillon*

Disjoint 2 young chickens and dust the pieces with pepper, salt, powdered thyme, and pinch of powdered mace. Dredge the pieces lightly with flour and fry in 2 ounces of hot olive oil until golden brown. Then remove the chicken to a hot platter, and put it in a warm oven where it will keep hot.

Now put 1 coarsely chopped onion in the frying pan, add a small clove of garlic, sliced, and sprinkle in ½ teaspoon of chili powder. (Don't use a cheap chili powder; a brand that comes from Texas is the best of the domestic ones.) Stir this mixture for a few minutes so that the chili powder won't lump. Then pour in a cup of dry American white wine, 1 tablespoon of Madeira, and ½ cup of beef bouillon. Cook this mixture slowly for 20 minutes, and then pour it over the fried chicken, and serve. Plain boiled rice goes best with this, and fried bananas.

Another way of cooking chicken that's hard to beat is broiling it. But leave it to the French to think up a different way of broiling chicken—with a basting agent of chopped chicken giblets and white wine.

BROILED CHICKEN AU VIN BLANC

2 *fryers (about 1½ pounds each)*	1 *cup very dry white wine*
	Clove garlic
1 *small onion, diced*	*Lime juice*
1 *tbsp. chopped parsley*	*Salt*
Pinch of thyme	*Freshly ground pepper*
Pinch of marjoram	2 *tbsp. butter*
1 *cup cold water*	*Flour*

Have 2 fryers (about 1½ pounds each) split for broiling. Cut off the necks.

Put the necks and the giblets in a saucepan with 1 small onion, peeled and sliced, 1 tablespoon of chipped parsley, a generous pinch each of thyme and marjoram, and 1 cup of cold water. Cover, and let simmer until tender, then add 1 cup of very dry American white wine (an American Chablis or Riesling). Strain and reserve the liquid. Chop the giblets fine, and set aside.

Rub the chickens with a cut of clove of garlic, sprinkle with lime juice, salt and freshly ground pepper, and brush with soft butter. Then place the halves, skin side down, in a shallow pan and place low under the broiler. Turn occasionally, and baste frequently with the wine stock. When the chickens are well browned and tender (about 30 minutes), remove from the pan and thicken the remaining wine sauce with a little flour blended with soft butter. Heat, pour sauce over the chicken, and serve.

Of all of America's possessions, Hawaii undoubtedly is the most glamorous. Its climate is practically ideal; its women, especially those in which the races have intermingled, are beautiful; its scenery is breath-taking; and from the islands come some of the world's choicest recipes. To one who has attended a *luau,* or native feast, the experience is Aladdin-like—the soft music, the *lei* of welcome placed about the neck, the table, or ground, covered with green *ti* leaves and sprinkled with yellow and red hibiscus, and the tantalizing aroma of roasting pork scenting the air.

Some of the dishes seem strange to American palates, such as *lomi lomi* (salt salmon massaged with the fingertips with onion and tomato), and the pasty *poi* (boiled taro root mixed with milk or water and set aside to ferment). But *laulau* (salt salmon and pork wrapped in taro leaves and steamed), chicken *luau* (chicken cooked in coconut milk and taro leaves), *haupia* (coconut corn-starch pudding), and banana coconut rolls, are unforgettable.

Of all these exotic dishes, there is one that tops them all— *Niu Moa Ai,* chicken baked in a coconut! To my way of thinking, it is one of the outstanding triumphs of gastronomy, from the standpoint of both flavor and service. Served in your home, it will be a topic of conversation among your guests for a long, long time. It requires no ingredient that is not available in almost any grocery and meat market, and it is not difficult at all to prepare and cook.

NIU MOA AI
(Chicken Baked in Coconut)

1 *spring chicken*	6 *small tomatoes*
4 *fresh coconuts*	1 *tsp. brown sugar*
5 *slices bacon*	1 *clove garlic*
Salt	*Dash of tabasco*
Pepper, freshly ground	2 *ears fresh corn*
1 *large onion*	4 *small bay leaves*
1 *green pepper*	4 *tbsp. dry white wine*

Disjoint a spring chicken, and remove the skin. Dice 5 slices of bacon and fry out in a skillet, then lightly brown the chicken pieces in the bacon fat after sprinkling them with salt and freshly ground pepper. Take the chicken out, remove all the meat from the bones and set it aside. Next, chop a large, peeled onion and a seeded green pepper, and lightly brown them in the bacon fat. Then add 6 small tomatoes, which have been stewed with 1 teaspoon of brown sugar, salt and pepper to taste, a small clove of garlic, minced, and a dash of Tabasco. Cook until the mixture thickens.

In the meantime, you will have taken the tops of 4 fresh coconuts by sawing them through at a point about ¼ of the way down. Remove half the meat from the coconuts by scraping it away in shreds. Shave the corn from 2 ears and mix it with the coconut meat, moistening it with a small amount of the coconut milk. When the onion-pepper-tomato mixture has thickened, remove it from the fire and mix it well into the coconut meat and corn, then add the diced chicken meat, and again mix everything well. Fill the coconuts two thirds full with the mixture and add a small crumbled bay leaf and a tablespoon of white wine to each.

Now replace the tops on the coconuts, and seal the joinings tightly with a thick flour-and-water paste. Set the coconuts in a roasting pan, with about an inch of water on the bottom (or in the depressions of a large muffin tin), and bake in a medium oven (about 375 degrees) for 45 minutes to an hour. If the outer shells of the coconuts should tend to scorch, baste them occasionally with the water in the bottom of the pan. After having removed the tops, serve one coconut to each individual. If the coconuts are small, and there is more of the chicken mixture than will fill them, put the remaining mixture in a greased baking dish, and set in the oven along with the coconuts. This will provide "seconds" for the guests who have emptied their coconuts.

This is a magnificent dish, and, incidentally, an ideal one to serve to guests who have a tendency to be late, for the contents, if coconut is not unsealed, will remain hot for 4 or 5 hours.

Dijon is the capital of the department of Côte-d'Or, whence come the greatest Burgundies in the world. Dijon is also well known for its mustard and for the black currant liquor called *Cassis de Dijon*. It is a gastronomical center as well as a wine center, and its restaurants, particularly Les Trois Faisans, Grande Taverne, Restaurant Pre-aux-Clercs, and Hotel de l'Escargotière, are famous all over Europe.

Along with *Boeuf Bourguignon* and *Suprême de Brochet, Dijonnaise, Coq au Chambertin* is a specialty at all Dijon's fine restaurants. The preparation of this exalted chicken dish runs contrary to the usual rule of white wines with chicken dishes. When you prepare it, use a fine American Burgundy.

COQ AU CHAMBERTIN

2 *young chickens* (2 *to* 2½ *pounds each*)	2 *cloves garlic*
Salt	¼ *tsp. thyme*
Freshly ground pepper	¼ *tsp. marjoram*
Paprika	¼ *tsp. rosemary*
Nutmeg	1 *bay leaf*
Flour	1 *tbsp. chopped parsley*
2 *ounces butter*	*Leaves from* 1 *stalk celery*
⅛ *lb. bacon*	½ *cup sliced mushrooms*
12 *tiny onions*	3 *ounces brandy*
	3 *cups American Burgundy*

Disjoint 2 young chickens (2 to 2½ pounds each) and rub the pieces well with salt, freshly ground pepper, paprika, and a little nutmeg, and then dredge them with flour.

In a skillet melt 2 ounces of butter, then add 2 ounces of lean bacon (⅛ pound), diced. When the bacon has browned lightly remove and set it aside.

Put the chicken pieces into the fat in the skillet, and lightly brown them on all sides. Then add 12 tiny onions, peeled, 2 crushed cloves of garlic, ¼ teaspoon each of thyme, rosemary, and marjoram, 1 minced bay leaf, 1 tablespoon chopped parsley, the green leaves from a stalk of celery, chopped fine, and ½ cup of sliced mushrooms. Let all simmer for about 5 minutes, then pour over the mixture 3 ounces of brandy, and ignite. When the flame has burned out, transfer the contents of the skillet to a casserole, add the diced bacon, and 3 cups of American Burgundy. Cover the casserole and seal with a thick flour-and-water paste, put into a moderate oven (325 degrees), and cook for 2 hours.

Unseal the casserole, and reduce the gravy, as desired, with additional red wine, or thicken with equal parts of flour and soft butter, blended together.

Casserole cookery is always a rather simple and easy way of handling meats and fowl. For ages the French have used casseroles, and the casserole is an essential part of Mexican and Spanish kitchens. This utensil may be large or small, squat or high or shallow, but it must have a tight fitting cover. The best casseroles are earthenware ones, because they are slow to heat, and retain the heat for a long time. However, casseroles are also made of heat-proof glass, or metal. My favorite type is a large earthenware casserole with a long handle. Small individual earthenware casseroles, I have also found, come in mighty handy, and they make for an attractive table setting as well.

The following chicken dish provides for the cook a minimum of labor, and for the food a maximum of flavor.

CHICKEN EN CASSEROLE

1 *roasting chicken* (4 *to* 5 *pounds*)	3 *small carrots*
	½ *cup sliced fresh mushrooms*
Flour	1½ *cups dry white wine*
Salt	2 *tbsp. chopped parsley*
Pepper	*Pinch thyme*
4 *ounces butter*	*Pinch marjoram*
1 *clove garlic*	*Dash Worcestershire sauce*
2 *medium-sized onions*	6 *peppercorns*
6 *celery hearts*	1 *bay leaf*

½ *cup brandy*

Disjoint a 4- to 5-pound roasting chicken and shake pieces in a paper bag containing seasoned flour.

Melt 4 ounces of butter in a skillet, and add 1 clove of garlic, quartered. When the butter is bubbling hot, remove the garlic and discard. Add the floured chicken pieces and sauté them until they are golden brown. Then transfer them to a casserole.

In the same skillet put 2 medium-sized onions, peeled and sliced thin, 6 celery hearts, chopped, 3 small carrots, chopped, and ½ cup sliced fresh mushrooms. When the vegetables are lightly browned, add 1½ cups of dry American white wine, 2 tablespoons chopped parsley, a pinch each of thyme and marjoram, a dash of Worcestershire sauce, 6 slightly bruised peppercorns, salt to taste, and 1 crumbled bay leaf. Simmer gently for a few minutes to blend all the flavors, then pour the contents of the skillet over the chicken in the casserole. Cover, and put into a 350-degree oven for 1¼ hours. Then remove the casserole, and uncover. In a large ladle put ½ cup of warm brandy, and set it alight. When it has reduced ½, pour it over the contents of the casserole, re-cover, and put it back in the oven for another 1¼ hours. Serve hot from the casserole.

In the latter part of 1947 I received a letter one day asking for a recipe for Chicken Country Captain. I searched all my recipe books, and queried my gourmet friends, but to no avail. So I finally appealed to the readers of my syndicated column, "For Men Only!" for help, and they responded nobly. I received letters from several different localities, each giving the recipe for what appeared to be a delectable dish. The recipes were almost identical, varying only in small details. One of the most interesting letters was from Mrs. H. F. Crecelius, of Prairie du Sac, Wisconsin. She wrote:

This is the original recipe for Chicken Country Captain, as prepared by the famous 70-year-old colored cook, Aire Mullen, of Columbus, Georgia.

I am an army wife, and whenever we have been stationed at Fort Benning, Aire has always prepared this famous dish for me, but I have also served it in many faraway places, and it is always a great sensation. It always brings back fond memories of home when we are serving in various remote stations. Needless to say, I am a native of Columbus, Georgia.

Here is Mrs. Crecelius' recipe, and it is slightly terrific!

CHICKEN COUNTRY CAPTAIN

1 3-lb. chicken	½ tsp. pepper
Olive oil	1½ tsp. curry powder
1 onion	6 large tomatoes
1 green pepper	½ tsp. chopped parsley
1 clove garlic	½ tsp. powdered thyme
8 ounces water	½ lb. almonds
1 tsp. salt	3 tbsp. dried currants

Cooked rice

Cut into 12 pieces a 3-pound chicken or 1 large guinea flowl. Skin and fry to a golden brown in olive oil. In the meantime, brown for 10 minutes in more olive oil 1 onion, peeled and finely chopped, 1 green pepper, seeded and chopped, and 1 clove of garlic, minced. Stir them as they cook, and moisten with 8 ounces of water. Then season with 1 teaspoon of salt, ½ teaspoon of pepper, and 1½ teaspoons of curry powder. Again stir well, and add 6 large red tomatoes, peeled and crushed, ½ teaspoon of chopped parsley, and ½ teaspoon of powdered thyme, and stir well.

Now put the fried chicken in a casserole, cover with the foregoing mixture, and add about ½ of the oil in which the chicken was fried. Cover the casserole and bake for 45 minutes. Have blanched and roasted to a light brown ½ pound of almonds, and add these to the chicken along with 3 tablespoons of dried currants. Arrange cooked rice on a platter, place the chicken in the center, and pour the sauce over all. Serve each person a helping of the chicken and the rice and sauce, accompanying each portion with a piece of crisp bacon.

This dish should serve six, Mrs. Crecelius writes; but I'd be tempted to double the recipe if for that number, because I doubled the recipe, and four hungry people cleaned the platter.

This dish, by the way, was a great favorite with the late President Franklin D. Roosevelt.

One can stick one's finger on almost any spot on the globe and discover a delectable chicken recipe from the country indicated.

In Mexico and Spain they have any number of delicious chicken recipes. *Pollo con Arroz, Pollo Relleno* (chicken stewed in sherry), are notable, but Colonel Dorn, who has been introduced previously, comes up with a bell-ringer. He calls it Mexican Chicken, and it really rates several hearty *vivas*.

MEXICAN CHICKEN À LA DORN

1 5-*lb. chicken*	1½ *cup pineapple cubes*
Salt	⅛ *tsp. powdered cinnamon*
Cayenne pepper	⅛ *tsp. powdered cloves*
¼ *cup bacon drippings*	1½ *cups orange juice*
¼ *cup blanched almonds*	2 *tbsp. flour*
⅓ *cup seedless raisins*	¼ *cup water*

Disjoint a 5-pound chicken, season to taste with salt and cayenne pepper, and brown on all sides in ¼ cup of bacon drippings (or olive oil). Then place the chicken and the remaining grease in a saucepan, and add ¼ cup of blanched almonds, ⅓ cup of seedless raisins, ½ cup of pineapple cubes, ⅛ teaspoon each of powdered cinnamon and powdered cloves, and 1½ cups of orange juice. Cover and simmer for at least 1 hour.

When chicken is tender, remove it to a hot serving platter. Make a smooth paste of 2 tablespoons of flour and ¼ cup of water, and add to the contents of the pan. Cook, stirring constantly until the sauce thickens, then pour it over the chicken. Garnish the platter with avocado wedges, orange sections, and water cress. Serve with rice and a green salad.

One of the most exciting dishes in Spanish or Mexican cuisine is the justly famous *Arroz con Pollo*. The English translation of this is rice with chicken, but *"pollo"* means a young and tender chicken, and not an old barnyard habitué, which the Spanish and Mexican chefs call a *"gallina."* Such a one is too ancient even to lay eggs, and beware of her in an *Arroz con Pollo!* Garlic is normally used in this dish, but I think the little green onions give it a more delicate flavor. That's really a concession from me, a passionate devotée of garlic!

ARROZ CON POLLO

2 *young chickens*	1 *green pepper*
Lime juice	1 *sweet red pepper*
Salt	2 *tbsp. chopped parsley*
Pepper	1 *bay leaf*
¼ *cup olive oil*	¼ *tsp. saffron*
¼ *pound lean raw ham*	2 *cups chicken broth*
6 *little green onions*	2 *cups long-grain raw rice*
4 *large tomatoes*	2 *ounces Madeira*

Cut 2 young tender chickens into serving pieces, brush with lime juice, season with salt and freshly ground pepper, and put in the refrigerator for about 2 hours.

Heat ¼ cup of pure olive oil in a heavy skillet or Dutch oven, and when smoking hot, put in the chicken pieces and lightly brown on all sides. Then add ¼ pound of diced lean raw ham, and 6 little green onions (bulb and tops), chopped. When the onion begins to brown, add 4 large tomatoes, peeled and quartered, 1 green and red pepper, each seeded and chopped, 2 tablespoons chopped parsley, salt and pepper to taste, 1 bay leaf, crumbled, and ¼ teaspoon of powdered saffron. Mix all these ingredients well and simmer for about 5 minutes; then add 2 cups of boiling chicken broth, and simmer, closely covered.

When the chicken is nearly tender add 2 cups of long-grain rice which has been washed in several changes of water and well drained. Cover again, and simmer gently for about 30 minutes.

When the chicken is tender and the rice is cooked (it should have absorbed most of the juices), add 2 ounces of Madeira.

If you've cooked this dish in an earthenware casserole, serve it, as is, on the table. If not, make a mound of the rice on a very hot platter, and surround it with the chicken pieces. If you really want to go to town, sauté at least 2 dozen medium-sized mushroom caps in butter and a little sherry, and border the chicken with them, and then lay some pimento strips across the rice.

Pollo Mole is one of the festival dishes in Mexico, playing somewhat the same role as that of turkey in the United States. It utilizes a delightful flavoring agent—one that may seem odd to

Americans—bitter chocolate. Naturally, this is a one-dish meal, and it will delight your guests, and yourself.

POLLO MOLE
(Mexican Chicken)

1 *large chicken*	¼ *cup ground almonds*
Salt	¼ *cup ground peanuts*
2 *bay leaves*	½ *tsp. anise seed*
Water	¼ *cup seeded raisins*
4 *tbsp. olive oil*	*Grated rind* 1 *orange*
2 *cloves garlic*	⅛ *tsp. powdered cinnamon*
1 *medium-sized onion*	2 *pinches nutmeg*
1 *green pepper*	2 *pinches powdered cloves*
2 *large tomatoes*	*Black pepper*
3 *slices canned pimentos*	*Dash tabasco*
2 *tbsp. chili powder*	2 *squares bitter chocolate*
2½ *cups chicken stock*	¼ *cup light rum*

Place 1 large chicken, cut into serving pieces, into a pot with 2 bay leaves, add enough slightly salted water to cover. Cook until almost tender, then remove the chicken pieces and drain through a colander. Reserve the stock

Put 4 tablespoons of olive oil in a deep heavy skillet, add 2 cloves of garlic, crushed and chopped, and when the oil is hot, brown the chicken pieces on all sides, then remove them from the skillet and set aside, keeping them warm.

To the oil in the skillet add 1 medium-sized onion, peeled and chopped, 1 green pepper, seeded and chopped, 2 large tomatoes, seeded and chopped, and 3 slices of canned pimentos, chopped. When the vegetables are tender, add 2 tablespoons of chili powder, and blend in well so that there are no lumps.

Next, add to the skillet 2½ cups of the chicken stock (filling out, if necessary, with canned chicken broth), ¼ cup each of ground almonds and peanuts, ½ teaspoon of anise seed, ¼ cup of seeded raisins, the grated rind of 1 orange, ⅛ teaspoon of powdered cinnamon, 2 pinches each of nutmeg and powdered cloves, black pepper to taste, and a dash of tabasco. Simmer for about 30 minutes, stirring often.

Now put the chicken pieces into the skillet with the sauce,

and shave 2 squares of bitter chocolate over the top. Cover, and let the whole simmer for about 30 minutes more. Five minutes before serving, add ¼ cup of light rum, stir in, reheat, and serve. The *mole* sauce should be rich and thick.

Paella is an ancient Spanish chicken dish. The name comes from the Spanish word in which the dish is cooked, a *paella,* or iron pot. Somerset Maugham was a great admirer of this dish, and mentions it in his *Don Fernando.*

This is not a simple dish to prepare. It really requires work; but the final result will be worth all the time and trouble spent on it.

PAELLA
(Chicken and Shellfish Cooked with Rice)

2 *tender broilers*	12 *thin slices Italian or*
2 *dozen cherrystone clams*	*Spanish sausage*
2 *dozen fresh shrimp*	3 *cloves garlic*
1 *qt. chicken broth*	1 *tsp. saffron*
½ *cup pure olive oil*	2 *ounces dry sherry*
3 *medium-sized onions*	*Salt*
2 *cups long-grain rice*	*Pepper*

Strips canned pimento
Grated Parmesan cheese

Disjoint 2 tender broilers, and have on hand 2 dozen cherrystone clams, in their shells, and 2 dozen fresh shrimp, cleaned. Also, have 1 quart of chicken broth on the fire, just at the boiling point.

In a good-sized casserole, or not too deep iron pot, put ½ cup of pure olive oil, and when it is hot add 3 medium-sized onions, peeled and chopped, and then add the pieces of chicken. Sauté until the chicken pieces are golden brown on all sides. Then add 2 cups of well-washed, long-grained rice. When the rice begins to dry out a little, add 1 cup of chicken broth. When this is absorbed, add another. Continue to simmer until the chicken and rice are nearly tender. (When the rice is thoroughly cooked, each grain should be separate; it should not be a mushy mess.)

When the chicken and rice are tender, add the 2 dozen clams in their shells (which have been well scrubbed), the 2 dozen fresh shrimp (in their jackets) and about a dozen thin slices of Italian or Spanish sausage.

In a mortar (or heavy bowl) put 3 cloves of garlic and a level teaspoon of saffron, and pour into this about 6 ounces of the chicken broth. Go to work with a pestle (or a muddler), and when the broth is thoroughly impregnated with both the color and the flavor of the garlic and saffron, strain it into the casserole, and add 2 ounces of dry sherry and salt and pepper to taste.

Over the top of the contents of the casserole lay a few strips of canned pimento, and sprinkle a film of grated Parmesan cheese. Put the casserole under the broiler for about 5 minutes. Serve from the casserole.

By and large, I'm not overly fond of stewed chicken. Or perhaps I should say that I like stewed chicken least of all ways of fixing chicken dishes—that is, I did, until I first tasted Stewed Chicken Monterey. I'm not at all sure whether it originated in Monterey, Mexico, or Monterey, California, although I should guess the latter. It has all the standard Mexican ingredients— oregano, chili powder, olives, tomatoes; but the inclusion of pea- nuts throws me somewhat. Anyhow, I think it's pretty terrific, and I am sure you will find it so, too.

STEWED CHICKEN MONTEREY

1 5-*lb. chicken*	½ *tbsp. salt*
½ *cup water*	1 *tsp. oregano*
2 *cups sherry*	1 *tsp. lemon juice*
2 *cups canned tomatoes*	¼ *tbsp. chili powder*
1 *onion*	2 *cups ripe olives*
2 *bay leaves*	½ *cup ground peanuts*
3 *cloves garlic*	*Flour*
	Butter

Cut a 5-pound chicken into serving pieces, and put in a large heavy saucepan with ½ cup of water and ½ cup of sherry. Bring liquid to a boil, and then lower flame, and cook for about 15 minutes. Then add 2 cups of canned tomatoes, 1 onion, peeled and chopped, 2 bay leaves, 3 cloves of garlic, chopped, ½ table- spoon of salt, 1 teaspoon oregano, and 1 teaspoon of lemon juice.

Simmer gently for about 45 minutes, then add ¼ tablespoon of chili powder, 2 cups of ripe olives, pitted and chopped, and ½ cup of finely ground roasted peanuts, and 1½ cups of sherry. Simmer until the chicken is tender, about 1 hour. Thicken the gravy with flour blended with butter, and boil up for about 5 minutes. Serve over or with flaky boiled rice.

At the same time my friend Louis Peteko told me about real Hungarian Goulash, he told me how his mother prepared Chicken Paprikas, which, in English, is paprika chicken. It is typically Hungarian, and, like all true Hungarian dishes, is delicious beyond words.

PAPRIKA CHICKEN PETEKO

3 *tender spring chickens*	1 *tsp. tarragon vinegar*
2 *ounces lard*	¾ *cup chicken broth*
4 *ounces chopped red onion*	¼ *cup dry sherry*
1 *tbsp. Rosen paprika*	6 *tbsp. sour cream*

12 *small boiled potatoes*

Quarter and sprinkle with salt 3 spring chickens. In a heavy stewpan melt 2 ounces of lard, mix in 4 ounces of chopped red onions, and cook until tender, but do not brown. Then add 1 tablespoon of Rosen paprika and 1 teaspoon of tarragon vinegar. Add the pieces of chicken to the contents of the stewing pan, shaking it to prevent burning. As soon as the chicken is lightly fried, not brown, add ¾ cup of chicken broth and ¼ cup of dry sherry, cover, and stew for about 45 minutes. Then add 6 tablespoons of thick sour cream and 12 small boiled potatoes. Let this heat up thoroughly, then serve.

Southerners believe that there is no stew more delicious than a Brunswick Stew. Down Georgia way they usually cook it in a big kettle and over hickory logs at a moonlight barbecue. But you don't need to have Georgia hickory logs or moonlight to enjoy this famous southern dish. I've made it in my own home, and it tasted just as good as any I've had down South.

Incidentally, this is a dish that is a favorite of probably the world's greatest golfer—Robert Tyre Jones, Jr., better known as Bobby Jones.

BRUNSWICK STEW

1 3-*lb. chicken*	2 *cups lima beans*
1 *pound lean beef*	3 *ears corn*
2 *onions*	3 *potatoes*
2 *tbsp. bacon fat*	1 *cup okra*
1 *pint consommé*	1 *teaspoon paprika*
Salt	½ *cup breadcrumbs*
Pepper	2 *tsp. Worcestershire sauce*
3 *tomatoes*	½ *cup sherry*

Brown 2 onions, sliced, in 2 tablespoons of bacon fat, then add a 3-pound chicken (cut into pieces as for stewing) and a pound of fresh beef, and brown. Next, transfer the onions, chicken, and beef to an earthenware casserole or a heavy kettle. Add a pint of consommé, and salt and pepper to taste, and let simmer for about 2 hours. Remove the chicken and beef to a separate dish. To the broth that is left add 3 peeled and quartered tomatoes, 2 cups of lima beans, corn cut from 3 ears, 3 sliced potatoes, 1 cup of okra, and a teaspoon of paprika. The equivalent amounts of quick-frozen or canned vegetables may be used. Let these ingredients simmer together for about an hour, meanwhile removing the chicken meat from the bones. Now add ½ cup of breadcrumbs, 2 teaspoons of Worcestershire sauce, ½ cup of sherry, the chicken meat, and the beef.

Let the whole thing heat thoroughly, then serve piping hot with hot corn bread.

A couple of years ago a Chicago matron living on the North Shore wrote to a friend of hers in Kentucky and asked for the recipe for the celebrated Kentucky Burgoo, which she wanted to try out in her new chafing dish. She received the recipe, but to her dismay it called for incredients measured in hundreds of pounds, such as "200 pounds of onions, 200 pounds of fat hens, 180 pounds of corn," and so forth.

Now, burgoo is an old hunter's dish, not confined to Kentucky, but more or less common wherever hunters and guides gather.

Its base may be squirrel, rabbit, venison, bear meat, or muskrat. I've eaten it in the Adirondacks made with venison, and it was delicious.

Accurate recipes for burgoo seem to be, for some reason, very rare. I've run across a couple, but the recipes start off with the statement, "This will serve a small party of twenty-five."

Burgoo is definitely not a chafing dish item. But it's a swell dish, and, to my way of thinking, should be made of squirrel, chicken, and beef. The following will be ample for a chummy little party of six.

KENTUCKY BURGOO

3 *dressed gray squirrels*	1 *green pepper*
1 *4-lb. chicken*	¼ *cup chopped parsley*
2 *lbs. lean beef*	1 *tbsp. Worcestershire*
5 *quarts water*	*sauce*
2 *medium onions*	1 *tbsp. salt*
2 *carrots*	1 *tsp. pepper*
1 *#2 can tomatoes*	½ *tsp. thyme*
2 *stalks celery*	½ *tsp. marjoram*
¼ *head cabbage*	2 *ears fresh corn*
1 *large potato*	2 *cups dry red wine*

Skin, dress, and clean 3 gray squirrels, being sure to remove the small sacs from the forequarters, or get 3 dressed squirrels from your butcher shop. Put the squirrels in a large pot with 1 4-pound chicken and 2 pounds of lean beef which has been cut up into about ¾-inch cubes. Pour over this 5 quarts of water, and boil until the meat is tender, about 1 hour. Then remove the squirrels and the chicken from the pot, remove their meat from the bones, cut into pieces, and return it to the pot.

Next, add to the pot 2 medium onions, peeled and sliced, 1 #2 can of tomatoes, 2 chopped carrots, 2 stalks of celery, chopped, ¼ head of cabbage, chopped, 1 large potato, peeled and diced, 1 green pepper, seeded and chopped, ¼ cup of chopped parsley, 1 tablespoon of Worcestershire sauce, 1 tablespoon of salt, 1 teaspoon of pepper, and ½ teaspoon each of thyme and marjoram. Let this simmer for about an hour. Then cut the kernels from 2 ears of fresh corn and add to the pot, together with 2 cups of dry

American red wine. Let this cook for about 30 minutes more, and serve, very hot, in soup plates with plenty of crusty French or Italian bread close at hand.

Burgoo is a thick stew. However, if it seems to be too thick, add more red wine, and reheat just before serving.

Purveyors of foodstuffs are making things easier every day for the amateur cook. There are pies, complete with crust, which have been frozen. You pop them into the oven, and, after a time, they come out tasting just like the pies that grandmother used to make. Frozen fruits and vegetables come from the deep freeze and when cooked, they are often as delicious as those that have just been picked, or at least, as those that you buy in the markets. And chicken put up in jars is really just as good as you can cook in your own kitchen. One day I bought a case of boned chicken in jars, and for a week I had a field day trying out recipes using cooked chicken.

Nature has harmonized the flavors of chicken and olives and tomatoes, and they combine beautifully in Chicken Monte Carlo.

CHICKEN MONTE CARLO

2 *jars boned chicken*
2 *small onions*
2 *tbsp. butter*
2 *cups canned tomatoes*
1 *bay leaf*
1 *tbsp. chopped celery*
2 *ounces dry white wine*

2 *tbsp. melted butter*
½ *cup consommé*
2 *tbsp flour*
Salt
Freshly ground pepper
¼ *tsp. paprika*
¼ *tsp. sugar*

8 *ripe olives*

Rice Cakes

1 *egg*
2 *cups cooked rice*
2 *ounces sherry*

Salt
Pepper
Dash nutmeg

3 *tbsp. butter*

Slice 2 small onions and brown them lightly in 2 tablespoons of butter. Add 2 cups of canned tomatoes, 1 bay leaf, 1 tablespoon of chopped celery, and 2 ounces of dry American white wine, and simmer for about 20 minutes. In the meantime, make a thickening of 2 tablespoons of melted butter, ½ cup of consommé, and 2 tablespoons of flour.

When the tomatoes and seasonings have simmered the required time, add the thickening, season to taste with salt and pepper, and add ¼ teaspoon of paprika, and ¼ teaspon of sugar. Cook the whole mixture for 10 minutes more. Then add 2 jars of the boned chicken, diced, and 8 olives, pitted and quartered. Let this heat up, then serve.

If you want to go to a little more trouble, serve this dish on hot rice cakes, which are simple to make. Mix 1 beaten egg with 2 cups of cooked rice and 2 ounces of sherry, and add salt and pepper and a dash of nutmeg. Shape the rice into flat cakes and fry golden crisp in 3 tablespoons of butter. Serve crabapple jelly on the side if you use the rice cakes under the chicken.

Probably the best known and most popular cooked chicken dish is Chicken à la King. And I also venture to say that it is dreadfully prepared more often than any other chicken dish, the trouble being usually in the sauce. But it is really quite simple to prepare and it can well take its place alongside of Loster à la Newburg as the perfect late supper dish. King Edward VIII—now the Duke of Windsor—is particularly fond of Chicken à la King, and is reputed to have devised his own recipe. Knowing his love of living and eating, his recipe ought to be something. But I can't imagine that it could be any better than this one, made with Madeira, as the original Chicken à la King was.

CHICKEN À LA KING

2 cups cooked chicken	Pepper
4 ounces butter	1 green pepper
4 tbsp. flour	1½ cups sliced mushrooms
1 cup chicken broth	2 egg yolks
1½ cups medium cream	2 tbsp. chopped pimentos
Salt	3 ounces Madeira

Melba toast

First, make a white sauce as follows: Melt 2 ounces of butter in a saucepan and blend in 4 tablespoons of flour. Add 1 cup of chicken broth and 1½ cups of medium cream, and cook slowly, stirring constantly until the mixture is thick. Add salt and white pepper to taste, and 2 cups of coarsely chopped cooked chicken, preferably the white meat only.

In another saucepan melt 2 ounces of butter, and put in it 1 green pepper, seeded and chopped, and 1½ cups of thinly sliced fresh mushrooms. When these are tender—in about 10 minutes—add them to the cream sauce and chicken. Simmer for about 10 minutes, stirring constantly. Then add 2 lightly beaten egg yolks, turn the flame low, and stir the whole constantly for just about 1 minute. Remove from the heat and add 2 tablespoons of chopped canned pimento and 3 ounces of Madeira. Stir, and serve over Melba toast.

When I lived down in San Antonio, Texas, during my army career, there was a fabulous Mexican restaurant near the Alamo called the Casa del Rio. I am sure that you couldn't get any better Mexican food in Mexico itself than you got there, and maybe not as good. One of the dishes I was very fond of was their *Tamal de Pollo,* or chicken tamale pie. They, of course, made it of freshly cooked chicken and freshly made tamales. But I experimented with boned chicken in jars and jars of tamales, and I believe I came up with something that was as good as the specialty of the Casa del Rio. Well, almost as good, anyway; and if you've never eaten the dish in Mexico, you'll never know the difference.

CHICKEN TAMALE PIE

2 *cups cooked chicken*	¼ *cup seedless raisins*
1 *jar tamales*	2 *tsp. chili powder*
1 *cup tomato paste*	1 *cup consommé*
1 *cup corn*	3 *ounces sherry*
1 *cup ripe olives*	½ *cup grated Parmesan cheese*

Slice the tamales crosswise into 1-inch lengths and use to line a heat-proof casserole. Combine 1 cup of tomato paste, 1 cup of corn, 1 cup of ripe olives, pitted and chopped, ¼ cup of seedless raisins, 2 teaspoons of chili powder, 2 cups of the boned chicken, 1 cup of consommé, and 3 ounces of sherry. Pour this mixture over the tamales, sprinkle with ½ cup of grated Parmesan cheese, and bake in a moderate oven (350 degrees) for 1 hour.

My nomination for the Number 1 luncheon dish is Plantation Chicken Shortcake. A good many years ago it was a specialty at the College Inn, located in the Sherman Hotel in Chicago. At that time I was a member of an advertising agency which handled the College Inn account, and I used to eat there at least three times a week, for free! And I never had anything but Plantation Chicken Shortcake. It got so that the waiter wouldn't even bother to take my order—he'd bring me the specialty, along with iced coffee, automatically.

You don't have to hie yourself down to a southern plantation to enjoy this dish. All you need is some cooked or boned chicken (the brand the College Inn Foods put out is tops), some corn bread mix, some mushrooms, and a little grated Parmesan cheese.

PLANTATION CHICKEN SHORTCAKE

Sliced breasts cold chicken	1 *cup cream*
Slices baked ham	2 *tbsp. sherry*
Cornbread squares	1 *tbsp. flour*
½ pound mushrooms	*Salt*
3 *tablespoons butter*	*White pepper*
Grated Parmesan cheese	

First make a mushroom sauce. Clean ½ pound of small mushrooms (or large ones cut in quarters) and lightly brown them in a saucepan with 2 tablespoons of butter. Add 1 cup of cream and 2 tablespoons of sherry, and cook 6 to 8 minutes. Thicken with about a tablespoon of butter mixed with a tablespoon of flour, and season with ½ teaspoon of salt and a little white pepper.

Now take pieces of cornbread about 3 inches square (you can buy the cornbread at the corner bakery, or you can make it yourself out of a prepared cornbread mix so easily you won't believe it) and split and butter them. Place them in a large shallow baking dish, and lay on each piece a thin slice of baked ham. Over the ham lay a slice of cold chicken (preferably white meat). Next, pour your mushroom sauce over the combination, sprinkle grated Parmesan cheese over the top, and put the dish under the broiler and let it cook until it is hot and bubbly.

One of the delights of epicures is the immortal Falstaff's panegyric to "Sherris-Sack," which we know as sherry:

A good sherris-sack hath a twofold operation in it. It ascends me into the brain; dries me there all the foolish and dull and crudy vapours which environ it; makes it apprehensive, quick, forgetive, full of nimble, fiery, and delectable shapes; which deliver'd o'er to the tongue, which is the birth, become excellent wit. The second property of your excellent sherris is, the warming of the blood; makes it course from the inwards to the parts extreme.

But sherry has a third property which Falstaff neglected to mention. It probably is the most serviceable wine for cooking that there is. Many delectable dishes can be made even more delectable with it. Take this superb ham and chicken wedding, as composed by Pierre Borbey, who was, and perhaps still is, maître d'hôtel at the Mount Royal Hotel in Montreal.

CHICKEN BORBEY

3 *cups cooked chicken*   8 *tbsp. rich cream*
Butter   4 *slices Virginia ham*
4 *tbsp. chopped mushrooms*   *Paprika*
3 *ounces sherry*

For each portion mince ¾ cup of cold chicken and 1 tablespoon of mushrooms sautéed in 2 tablespoons of pure cream. Over a hot flame, sear in another pan one slice of Virginia ham per portion for 2 minutes, having the ham sprinkled well on both sides with paprika. Put in ¾ ounce of sherry for each slice of ham, and let simmer, turning the ham constantly until the gravy becomes reduced to a rich sauce. Remove the ham and stir the creamed chicken gently into the sauce. Add 1 teaspoon of butter per portion. When well mixed, place the slice of ham on a piece of toast and top with the wine-creamed chicken. (Serves 4.)

I guess I'm just an old sentimentalist, because I never stand before the regal, golden brown splendor of a roast turkey without my thoughts going back to the Pilgrim Fathers. I can see them taking down their fowling pieces from the walls of their log cabins and bravely venturing forth in search of food. And, after their return with a wild turkey or two, I can see the family gathered around a table, with heads bowed in thanks for the bounty of the strange new world in which they lived.

The appreciation of turkey was not limited to our forefathers. Jean Brillat-Savarin, French lawyer and gastronome, who came to America in 1793, later wrote in his famous book, *The Physiology of Taste:* "The turkey is certainly one of the most beautiful presents which the New World has made to the Old . . . It was imported to Europe by the Jesuits, and in familiar speech throughout France, the turkey is called a 'Jesuit.' " And speaking of the roast turkey, which he himself had shot earlier on a farm near Hartford, Connecticut, he said, "It was charming to look upon, delightful to smell, and delicious to taste; and so, until the last morsel was eaten, you could hear all around the table, 'Very good! Excellently good!' and 'O my dear sir, what a glorious bit!' "

There are no doubt many people, who like myself, become a little taste-tired of the standard breadcrumbs, sausage, and sage stuffing. So when, about 3 years ago, a friend of mine sent me a recipe for a pecan and mushroom combination stuffing, I told the Little Woman that I would prepare and stuff the turkey, and she was delighted to get that job off her hands. However, she watched the preparation, and when it was ready to go into the bird, she said, "What, no sage or poultry seasoning?" When I said no, she tch-tch-tch'd. But when she tasted the finished product, her praise was heartwarming, and after the Christmas dinner, I found an extra present from her under the Christmas tree.

Would you, too, like to find an extra present under your tree this Christmas? Then let me point the way with

PECAN AND CORN BREAD STUFFING

Turkey giblets	*2 cups chopped pecan meats*
3 cups crumbled cold corn bread	*5 hard boiled eggs*
	4 ounces butter
1 teaspoon nutmeg	*1½ cups chopped mushrooms*
4 tbsp. chopped parsley	*1 large mild onion*
½ tsp. thyme	*½ cup chopped celery*
½ tsp. marjoram	*Salt*
¼ tsp. ground mace	*Freshly ground pepper*

⅔ cup sherry

Parboil the turkey giblets in enough salted water to cover.

To 3 cups of crumbled cold corn bread add 1 teaspoon of nutmeg, 4 tablespoons of chopped parsley, ½ teaspoon each of thyme and marjoram, ¼ teaspoon of ground mace, 2 cups of chopped pecan meats, and 5 hard-boiled eggs, chopped. Blend all these well.

Put 2 ounces of butter in a saucepan, and when hot add 1½ cups of coarsely chopped mushrooms, and the drained and chopped giblets. Sauté these for about 6 or 7 minutes.

In another saucepan put 2 ounces of butter, and when hot add 1 large mild onion, peeled and chopped, and ½ cup of chopped celery. When the onion is tender, mix with the mushrooms and giblets, and then transfer this mixture to the corn bread and pecan mixture. Season with salt and freshly ground pepper to taste, add about ⅔ cup of sherry, and blend well. The stuffing should just nicely hang together, but it should not be wet or pasty. Transfer the stuffing to the turkey, and roast in the usual way.

The following Thanksgiving, my much better half asked, a touch wistfully, whether I wanted to stuff the turkey again for Thanksgiving. I think she feared that I would say "No," but I took her gently by the hand, led her into the living room, placed the vaccum cleaner at her disposal, and retired to the kitchen. She didn't know it, but I had stacked away the necessary ingredients for another terrific stuffing. This time it was a brandied chestnut stuffing.

BRANDIED CHESTNUT STUFFING

2 lb. chestnuts	1 tsp. chopped chives
1 cup cooking oil	½ tsp. thyme
2 cups consommé	½ tsp. marjoram
2 tbsp. butter	1 large bay leaf
6 little green onions	Salt
2 stalks celery	Pepper
¾ lb. sausage meat	2 cups soft breadcrumbs
1 tbsp. chopped parsley	Madeira

½ cup brandy

Pick over enough chestnuts to have 2 pounds of sound nuts. With a sharp and pointed knife cut an "X" on the flat side of the chestnuts. Heat 1 cup of cooking oil in a heavy skillet, and put in the chestnuts. Let them heat over a fast flame for about 3 minutes, shaking the pan and stirring the chestnuts all the while. Remove, drain, and the minute they can be handled, remove the shells and the inner skin. Put the shelled and skinned nuts into a saucepan with 2 cups of consommé, and let them cook until they are tender.

In a skillet melt 2 tablespoons of butter, and when the butter is hot add 6 little green onions (bulbs and tops), chopped, and 2 stalks of celery, chopped. When the onions begin to take on a little color add ¾ pound of sausage meat, 1 tablespoon of chopped parsley, 1 teaspoon of chopped chives, ½ teaspoon each of thyme and marjoram, and 1 large bay leaf, finely crumbled. Salt and pepper to taste, and sauté the whole for about 4 minutes, stirring constantly with a fork to break up the sausage meat and to blend the whole thoroughly.

Moisten 2 cups of soft breadcrumbs with a little Madeira and add them, along with ½ cup of brandy, to the contents of the skillet. Mix well, and then add the chestnuts, which have been coarsely chopped. Again stir the mixture, and then stuff the turkey with it. Put the turkey in a roaster, adding a basting mixture of 1 cup of water and 1 cup of dry American white wine. Roast in a moderate oven (325-350 degrees) until the turkey is tender— about 15 to 20 minutes to the pound for 12- to 16-pound birds.

While the turkey is truly an American bird, other countries have come to appreciate its succulent supremacy, and they pay tribute to it on many festive occasions. In Italy, stuffed turkey, called *Il Tacchino Ripieno,* is a great dish on feast days and other special occasions, and it can be bought already prepared in nearly all poultry shops at Christmas time. Due to the ingredients in the stuffing, it has one of the most unusual flavors I have ever tasted. For a new flavor thrill, I recommend it highly.

IL TACCHINO RIPIENO

Turkey giblets	4 *little green onions*
½ *cup cooked veal*	*Salt*
½ *cup cooked ham*	*Pepper*
½ *cup cooked salcissa*	¼ *tsp. nutmeg*
(*Italian pork sausage*)	¼ *cup grated Parmesan cheese*
1 *cup chestnuts*	1 *tbsp. strained honey*
½ *cup cooked prunes*	*Dry white wine*
½ *cup mushrooms*	2 *tbsp. olive oil*

2 *eggs*

Blanch and trim the gizzard, liver, and heart of the turkey, then put them through the meat grinder with ½ cup each of cooked veal, ham, and *salcissa*, 1 cup of chestnuts, which previously have been boiled and shelled, ½ cup of cooked prunes, ½ cup of mushrooms, and about 4 little green onions, bulbs and tops. Season this mixture with salt and freshly ground pepper to taste, and add ¼ teaspoon of nutmeg and ¼ cup of grated Parmesan or Romano cheese. Moisten with about 1 tablespoon of strained honey and just enough dry American white wine to be absorbed. Mix thoroughly, and cook in 2 tablespoons of olive oil for a few minutes. Then add 2 eggs, beaten, to bind everything together, and stuff Mr. Turkey. Don't press the stuffing in the cavities; rather pick up the bird and shake down the stuffing so that it settles itself.

In Russia no buffet supper is complete without a turkey. The birds usually come from the Ukraine, and they are of the finest quality. One of the favorite Russian stuffings is made with walnuts and liver, and imparts to the turkey a delicious and different flavor.

WALNUT AND LIVER STUFFING

1 *lb. calf's liver*	*Salt*
4 *tbsp. butter*	*Pepper*
1 *lb. shelled walnuts*	*Dash cayenne pepper*
2 *cups soft breadcrumbs*	*Pinch mace*
Madeira	4 *eggs*

In 4 tablespoons of butter sauté 1 pound of calf's liver for about 7 minutes, and then put it through the meat grinder.

Scald 1 pound of shelled walnuts, remove the skins, and put them through the meat grinder twice.

Combine the chopped liver and the ground walnuts, then add to them 2 cups of soft breadcrumbs, which have been moistened with Madeira. Season with salt and freshly ground pepper to taste, add a dash of cayenne pepper, a pinch of mace, and 2 whole eggs. Stir this mixture together thoroughly, then stuff the turkey with it. If you have a larger bird than 10 to 12 pounds, increase the ingredients by about one half.

There are scores of ways to fix left-over turkey, but the Russians have one of the most unusual methods. Their name is rather formidable—*inieka s vishniovim sousom*—but it means simply breasts of cooked turkey with cherry sauce, and it's unbelievably good.

TURKEY BREASTS WITH CHERRY SAUCE

Slices of turkey breast	Powdered cinnamon, cloves,
1 large can of black, pitted	ginger, nutmeg
cherries	2 tbsp. sugar
2 tbsp. cherry juice	Salt
1 tsp. of mixture in equal	Freshly ground pepper
parts of —	3 ounces Madeira

For the sauce, use 1 large can of black pitted cherries. Put them into a saucepan, with 2 tablespoons of their juice, 1 teaspoon of the mixed spices, and 2 tablespoons of sugar. Cook very slowly until they are reduced practically to pulp, and rub them through a sieve. At the same time, slice the breast of the turkey into firm, thin slices. Salt and pepper them, then sauté them in a mixture of bubbling butter and Madeira (about 2 tablespoons of butter and 3 ounces of wine). Turn the slices at least once, and when they are hot, remove to a heated dish, in the center of which reposes the cherry sauce. In serving the slices of breast, place some sauce on each dish. This dish rates chilled champagne as a beverage.

In the Near East from Greece to Asia Minor, the combination of eggplant with other foods is quite common. In Greece, the Balkans, Turkey, Persia, and India, eggplant is usually combined with lamb. Stuffed eggplant is also a favorite dish. I have already mentioned Eggplant Caviar in the chapter on hors d'oeuvres, and the famous Greek dish utilizing eggplant, *Moussak à la Grecque,* in the chapter on meats.

Eggplant combined with turkey, however, is rather unusual, but I can assure you that the following combination is quite delightful, and is another most delicious way of using left-over turkey.

COOKED TURKEY, SPANISH STYLE

Slices of turkey breast	*Pinch oregano*
1 *large eggplant*	1½ *cups tomato paste*
1 *clove garlic*	1½ *cups cream*
2 *tbsp. olive oil*	4 *ounces dry sherry*
Slices baked ham	*Salt*
	Pepper

Take a large eggplant and cut it into thin slices. Crush a large clove of garlic in 2 tablespoons of olive oil in a skillet, and brown the eggplant. Drain on paper, then place the slices in a large shallow baking dish. Cover the eggplant with slices of turkey breast, and then add another layer of eggplant slices and sprinkle with a pinch of oregano. On top of the second layer place thin slices of baked ham, and top with a third layer of eggplant. Now mix well 1½ cups of thick tomato paste, 1½ cups of cream, and 4 ounces of dry sherry, season with salt and pepper, and pour it over the layers of eggplant, turkey, and ham. Bake in a moderate oven for about 30 minutes.

There are so many ways of preparing tasty dishes with left-over turkey that you will wish the bird would last longer than it does. The following dish, Turkey à la Reine, is really fit for a queen. It comes from the South, and calls for a delightful ingredient—preserved chestnuts—which the French call *marrons glacés*. To my way of thinking, and tasting, this whole combination tops all cooked turkey dishes.

TURKEY À LA REINE

2 *cups cooked turkey*	1 *tsp. grated lemon rind*
Yolks of 2 hard-boiled eggs	*Salt*
1 *tbsp. butter*	*Pepper*
2 *tbsp. flour*	*Dash nutmeg*
1 *cup turkey gravy (or consommé)*	*Medium-sized can mushrooms*
3 *ounces dry Madeira*	4 *preserved chestnuts*
1 *tsp. Worcestershire sauce*	1 *tbsp. chopped parsley*
	Chopped whites of 2 hard-boiled eggs

Rub the yolks of 2 hard-boiled eggs smooth with 1 tablespoon of butter. Add 2 tablespoons of flour, 1 cup of turkey gravy or consommé, 3 ounces of dry Madeira, 1 teaspoon of Worcestershire sauce, 1 teaspoon of grated lemon rind, salt and pepper, and a dash of nutmeg. Cook 5 minutes on a medium fire. Now put in 2 cups of diced cold turkey and the contents of a can of mushrooms, sliced, and transfer all to the top of a double boiler, cooking over hot water for 10 to 15 minutes. Just before serving, add 4 preserved chestnuts, well drained and chopped, 1 tablespoon of chopped parsley, and the chopped whites of 2 hard-boiled eggs. Serve with hot biscuits.

Here is the fourth Cantonese recipe—this time for chicken.

BALI BALI FRIED CHICKEN

1 2½- to 3½-lb. fryer	12 pea pods
Boiling water	4 water chestnuts
3 tbsp. Cantonese bead	1½ cups sliced fresh
molasses	mushrooms
Ac'cent	1 cup chicken broth
1½ tsp. salt	1 tbsp. cornstarch
Pepper	1 tbsp. water
Sugar	1 tbsp. soy sauce
Peanut oil	Little green onions

Disjoint a 2½- to 3½-pound fryer, and place pieces in enough boiling water to cover, to which have been added 3 tablespoons of Cantonese bead molasses (this can be obtained in jar form in almost any first-class grocery store), 1 tablespoon of Ac'cent, 1 teaspoon of salt, ¼ teaspoon of pepper, and 1 teaspoon of sugar. Boil for about 15 minutes. The chicken should have a brownish appearance upon removal. Drain and pat dry with a paper towel.

In a deep skillet place enough peanut oil to cover the bottom of the pan to a depth of ½ inch. When hot, fry the chicken until it is a uniform deep brown on all sides, then remove it and place it on a hot platter while sauce is being made.

Pour off all but 3 tablespoons of the peanut oil from the skillet the chicken was browned in, and add to the pan 12 pea pods, 4 water chestnuts, sliced, and 1½ cups sliced fresh mushrooms.

Mix these vegetables thoroughly over a hot flame, then add 1 cup of chicken broth, lower the flame, cover the pan, and simmer for about 1½ minutes. Then add the following mixed seasonings: 1 tablespoon of cornstarch, diluted in 1 tablespoon of water, ½ teaspoon of salt, 1 teaspoon of Ac'cent, a dash of pepper, ½ teaspoon of sugar, and 1 tablespoon of soy sauce. Mix this sauce gently, but thoroughly, then cover and simmer over a moderate flame for 1 minute. Then pour it over the chicken, and serve, garnished with slivered little green onions.

((9)) VEGETABLES, POTATOES, AND RICE

There have been times, in private homes, clubs, and restaurants, when I have viewed the approach of vegetable dishes at luncheons or dinners with a jaundiced eye, have regarded them as they were set before me, with mingled pain and amazement, and have partaken of a few mouthfuls only under the compulsion of good manners and a horror of hurting the feelings of my host or hostess. That this should be so is a sad commentary on the preparation and cooking by the average person of some of the most delectable of nature's delicacies.

There is scarcely anything more tempting to the eye and appetite than the natural colors and flavors of fresh vegetables, or even the frozen vegetables. (I'd like to insert a word of warning at this point regarding the use of baking soda added to the water in which vegetables are cooked. Many people do this to retain the color, but baking soda destroys Vitamin C. A little lemon juice added to the cooking water will help to retain the color and flavor.) A properly prepared vegetable dish can raise the finest meal to undreamed-of heights, but vegetables served after a long exposure to a swimming pool of cooking water can ruin the efforts of the most expert chef.

The overcooking of vegetables is a cardinal sin, and one of the commonest. Only a very few vegetables (such as cabbage, turnips, and cauliflower) should be actually boiled. If vegetables have to be cooked in water, use very little, or steam them. Baking and braising are excellent methods. And don't forget that herbs tend to point up the flavor of legumes.

The possible combinations of wines and vegetables, or sauces and vegetables, are almost endless, and would fill a fair-sized book. Such combinations offer a fertile field for the adventuresome and imaginative cook. The following recipes will give you an idea of what can be done with wine and vegetables, and I hope will stimulate you to further experimentation.

ARTICHOKES AU VIN BLANC

6 *small artichokes*	1 *small onion*
1 *tbsp. olive oil*	*Pinch savory*
1 *clove garlic*	2 *tsp. salt*

1 *cup dry white wine*

Trim the tops from 6 small artichokes, as well as the stems, and remove a few of the outer leaves.

In a pot or deep casserole put 1 tablespoon of olive oil, 1 minced clove of garlic, 1 small onion, minced, a pinch of savory, and 2 teaspoons of salt. Place the artichokes upright in the pot or casserole, and pour over them 1 cup of dry American white wine. Cover tightly, and simmer slowly for 45 minutes, adding a little more wine and a touch more of olive oil, if necessary. When the hearts are tender, remove, and serve with the sauce poured over them.

ASPARAGUS IN WHITE WINE, AU GRATIN

1 *bunch asparagus* (*about*	*Salt*
2 *lb.*)	*Pepper*
3 *ounces butter*	2 *ounces grated Parmesan*
2 *ounces dry white wine*	*cheese*

Wash 1 bunch of asparagus, about 2 pounds, and cut off the tough ends. Have salted water boiling in a fairly deep saucepan, and stand the asparagus, retied in a bunch, upright in it. Let cook and steam for about 15 minutes. Then remove, untie, and place in a baking dish. Pour 3 ounces of melted butter over the asparagus, and 2 ounces of dry American white wine. Salt and pepper lightly, and sprinkle generously with grated Parmesan cheese, about 2 ounces. Place in a hot oven (425 degrees) for about 10 minutes, or until the cheese lightly browns. Remove, and serve.

GREEN BEANS PARISIENNE

1 *lb. young green beans*	*Freshly ground pepper*
4 *tbsp. butter*	½ *tsp. lime juice*
Salt	3 *ounces white wine*

Wash 1 pound of young green beans, nip off the ends of their pods, and cut them in thin, diagonal slices. Put them in a saucepan with cold water, and bring slowly to a boil. Then remove them and drain thoroughly.

In a heavy saucepan melt 4 tablespoons of butter. Add salt and freshly ground pepper to taste, ½ teaspoon lime juice, and 3 ounces of American white wine. Then put in the beans. Cover the pan tightly, and simmer very gently, stirring occasionally, until the beans are just tender, and the liquid has evaporated—about 20 minutes. Remove to a hot dish, dot with butter, and serve.

BRUSSELS SPROUTS AND CHESTNUTS

1 *lb. green brussels sprouts*	*Dash nutmeg*
1 *lb. large chestnuts*	*Consommé*
Salt	*Dry Madeira*
Pepper	*1½ tbsp. flour*

2 *tbsp. butter*

Get 1 pound of fresh, green brussels sprouts. Trim the ends slightly, remove any yellow or imperfect leaves, and wash them well, watching out carefully for any wild life. Then let them stand for about 10 minutes in lukewarm, salted water.

In the meantime, cover 1 pound of large, sound chestnuts with cold water, bring to a boil, and boil for 2 or 3 minutes. Then shell them and remove the skin.

Place the sprouts and the chestnuts in a greased casserole, lightly salt and pepper to taste, add a dash of nutmeg, and cover with equal parts of consommé and dry Madeira. Cover the casserole, and bake in a slow oven (300 degrees) for about 2 hours. When ready to serve, thicken the stock and wine with 1½ tablespoons of flour blended with 2 tablespoons of soft butter.

The one bad feature of onions is what it does to one's breath. But cooked onions obviate this unpleasant feature, as Dean Swift wrote:

> This is every cook's opinion,
> No savory dish without an onion,
> But lest your kissing should be spoiled,
> Your onions must be thoroughly boiled.

If you have a yen for onions, yet fear you have to forego them because you're taking Dream Boat out dancing, try onions in sauterne.

ONIONS IN SAUTERNE

24 *tiny onions*	*Salt*
American sauterne	1 *tbsp. butter*
	Paprika

Peel 24 tiny onions, parboil them for 10 minutes in salted water, then drain. Cover the onions with an American sauterne, salt to taste, and add 1 tablespoon of butter. Continue simmering until onions are tender. Drain and sprinkle with paprika.

I don't imagine many people would think of sauerkraut as an epicurean dish, worthy of gracing the tables of discriminating gourmets. It is best known in its more humble aspects, married to pigs knuckles, pork shanks, frankfurters, ham hocks, or spareribs. Actually, however, sauerkraut has a place on the most luxurious of tables when it is combined with duck, goose, fried oysters, or partridge, or when it is cooked with white wine or champagne.

Sauerkraut—which is merely shredded white cabbage combined with salt, packed in a wooden tub, and allowed to ferment in its own juices—was known even back in the days of Babylon. I have been told that there are references to it in Homer and in the writings of Confucius. In the modern world, it reigns supreme among all the vegetables used in Germany; the Italians make a most savory dish of sauerkraut, wine, and sausage; Poland's Hunters' Stew, called *Bigos* (the recipe for which has already been chronicled), is one of the most delicious dishes I have ever tasted; France makes two popular dishes of it, *Choucroute au Vin Bourgogne* and *Choucroute au Vin Blanc*.

Russians consume enormous quantities of sauerkraut, and Hungarians think nothing is too good to go with their pickled cabbage, so they cook it in champagne and call the dish *Savanyu Kaposzta Osztrigaval* (please don't ask me how to pronounce that!).

One of the great Alsatian dishes is *Choucroute Alsacienne*. It was a specialty at the Alsatian Café in Paris, and a rare treat at several inns throughout Alsace. To me, it is sauerkraut raised to the nth degree of deliciousness.

CHOUCROUTE ALSACIENNE
(Sauerkraut)

2 *lb. sauerkraut*	6 *juniper berries*
1 *onion*	*Salt*
2 *carrots*	4 *thin slices smoked ham*
1 *large sweet apple*	*Butter*
Lean bacon	1 *cup consommé*
10 *peppercorns*	1 *cup champagne*

Wash 2 pounds of sauerkraut in several changes of water and drain well, pressing to remove all water.

Chop 1 onion and 2 carrots fine and pare, core, and slice I large sweet apple.

Cover the bottom of an earthenware casserole with slices of lean bacon. Then add a layer of sauerkraut. Cover the sauerkraut with a layer of chopped onions, chopped carrots, and apple slices (about half the quantity of each), and sprinkle over the chopped vegetables about 10 bruised peppercorns and 6 bruised juniper berries, and salt lightly. Then add another thin layer of sauerkraut, and over that place 2 thin slices of smoked ham (Prosciutto ham is perfect). Next, comes a thin layer of sauerkraut, another layer of the chopped vegetables and apple slices, another thin layer of sauerkraut, 2 more slices of the thin ham, and a topping layer of the sauerkraut. Dot with butter, and pour over the contents of the casserole 1 cup of consommé and 1 cup of domestic champagne.

Cover the casserole tightly, and let cook slowly for about 4 hours. If more moistening is needed, add a little more champagne.

Maybe spinach *suprème* isn't a dish you'd think of serving to Junior, but anyone with a true appreciation of delicious flavors will love it.

SPINACH SUPRÈME

2 *lb. fresh spinach*	*Salt*
4 *tbsp. butter*	*Freshly ground pepper*
1 *tsp. Worcestershire sauce*	½ *cup sour cream*
1 *tsp. lime juice*	¼ *lb. fresh mushrooms*
¼ *cup Madeira wine*	

Wash 2 pounds of fresh spinach quickly in warm water (not hot) to release any sand, then wash several times in cold water. Discard any wilted leaves. Put the washed spinach in about ½ cup of salted water, cover, and cook over a low heat for about 10 minutes, or until tender. Remove the spinach, and drain, then put it through the meat grinder, using the finest blade.

Put the chopped spinach in a saucepan with 2 tablespoons of butter, add 1 teaspoon of Worcestershire sauce, 1 teaspoon of lime juice, ½ cup of sour cream, and salt and freshly ground pepper to taste. Beat all this well together, and keep warm.

In a separate saucepan melt 2 tablespoons of butter, and sauté ¼ pound of fresh mushrooms, thinly sliced, for about 7 or 8 minutes. Then add the sautéed mushrooms to the spinach and sour cream, and add ¼ cup of Madeira. Mix all well, and simmer for 2 or 3 minutes over a medium flame. Serve at once.

ACORN SQUASH WITH ANISE

1 *acorn squash*	2 *tsp. Anis del Mono*
2 *tsp. butter*	Salt
Freshly ground pepper	

For two persons, cut acorn squash in half lengthwise, and remove the seeds. In each cavity place a dab of butter (about 1 teaspoonful), and 1 teaspoon of *Anis del Mono* (Spanish anise liqueur). Salt and pepper lightly.

In the bottom of a shallow baking pan place about ½ inch of water, set the squash halves in, and bake in a moderate oven (350 degrees) for from 45 minutes to 1 hour, or until the squash is tender. One half squash is served to each person.

Bananas are usually thought of, not as vegetable, but as a fruit, as indeed they are. Yet they are a staple food in nearly all regions adjacent to the equator, and it is said that bananas alone will sustain life for a long period of time. Contrary to opinion, they are not indigestible if they are eaten when fully ripe.

I can't think of anything that goes better with a duck or game dinner than fried bananas.

FRIED RUM-SOAKED BANANAS

6 *firm bananas*   1 *egg*
Light rum   ¾ *cup fine breadcrumbs*
             Fat or cooking oil

Peel firm, all-yellow bananas, and cut them crosswise in pieces about 1 inch in length. Soak the pieces in a light rum for about ¾ of an hour, turning the pieces occasionally.

When ready to cook, dip the banana pieces in slightly beaten egg, then roll in fine breadcrumbs. Have 1 inch of melted fat or cooking oil in a frying pan, and heat it to 375 degrees. (You can determine this temperature, if you haven't a cooking thermometer, by dropping an inch cube of bread into the fat. At 375 degrees the bread will brown in about 40 to 45 seconds.)

Fry the crumbed banana pieces in the fat for about 2 minutes, or until brown and tender. Drain well on absorbent paper toweling, and serve very hot.

There is nothing that can beat properly prepared Boston Baked Beans, unless it is beans baked in the Brittany manner, or the way they bake frijole beans out in the great open spaces of the Southwest. However, at the risk of being banned in Boston, I'm going to give you an authentic Boston Baked Bean recipe with what I think is a slight improvement over the usual one.

After tasting these marvelous beans, I don't think you'll even speak of the Cabots or Lodges!

BOSTON BAKED BEANS

1½ *lb. navy beans*   ½ *to* ⅔ *cup molasses*
Bouquet garni   ¼ *cup brown sugar*
   1 *bay leaf*   2 *tsp. dry mustard*
   2 *sprigs celery leaves*   2 *tsp. salt*
   10 *sprigs fresh parsley*   ¼ *tsp. pepper*
   1 *sprig thyme*   1 *medium-sized onion*
½ *lb. salt pork*   1 *cup sherry*

Pick over 1½ pounds of navy beans (or any other variety that you fancy), cover with cold water, and let soak overnight, or for

12 hours. Cover with additional water, into which a *bouquet garni* of 1 bay leaf, 2 sprigs of celery leaves, about 10 sprigs of fresh parsley, and a sprig of thyme has been put. Cook over a low heat until the skins break if you blow on them—about 1 to 1½ hours. Drain the beans, reserving the liquid. Slice ½ pound of salt pork in ¼-inch slices. Put the beans and half of the sliced pork, in alternate layers, in a 2-quart bean pot or casserole. Now score remainder of the pork slices, and put them on top of the beans, in the center.

Next, mix ½ to ⅔ cup of molasses, ¼ cup of brown sugar, 2 teaspoons of dry mustard, 2 teaspoons of salt, ¼ teaspoon of pepper, and 1 minced medium-sized onion with 2 cups of the liquid you have drained off the beans, and pour the mixture over the beans. Cover and bake in a slow oven (250 degrees) for 6 to 8 hours. And now comes the *pièce de résistance*. One hour before the baking is finished, pour 1 cup of sherry over the beans, put the cover back on, and let bake the remaining hour.

It does take a lot of time and work to bake beans in your own home, but fortunately there are many excellent brands of baked beans on the market put up in cans or jars. I am excluding those canned varieties put up in a gooey tomato sauce. Take this recipe for canned baked beans done in the Argentine manner. It makes an excellent main dish, and has a titillating flavor.

BAKED BEANS ARGENTINE

2 *cans baked beans*	1 *tsp. dry mustard*
4 *strips bacon*	1 *tbsp. brown sugar*
1 *chopped onion*	3 *ounces curaçao*
	1 *orange*

Fry 4 strips of bacon until very crisp and place them on a strip of paper toweling until all the grease has been absorbed. Now add to 2 cans of any good variety of baked beans, 1 chopped onion, 1 teaspoon of dry mustard, 1 tablespoon of brown sugar, 3 ounces of curaçao, and the 4 strips of bacon broken up into small pieces. Mix all these ingredients gently, and put the resulting mixture into a baking dish, and cover with slices of 1 orange, skin and all. Bake in a moderate oven for 30 minutes.

The potato has one of the most interesting histories of any item of food. It is a native of the Americas, although its origin is lost in antiquity, But it is a known fact that the Spanish conquistadores, when they invaded South America in 1524, found a large number of varieties and species of potato under cultivation. But who first took them to Europe is lost in a maze of claims and counter-claims. Some aver that Sir Walter Raleigh took the potato back from Virginia in 1585. The only trouble with this statement is that the true potato did not reach Virginia until one hundred years later. Sir John Hawkins is credited with having introduced the potato into Europe in 1565, but what he took was the sweet potato. And then there is Sir Francis Drake. In Offenburg, Germany, there is, or was, a monument to Drake with the inscription on it, "Sir Francis Drake, introducer of the potato into Europe in the year of our Lord, 1580."

Actually, the Spaniards probably gave the potato to Europe, one Hieronymous Cardan, a monk, having taken the potato from Peru to Spain. From Spain it passed to Italy, from there to Austria, then to Germany, and from Germany to Switzerland to France, and then, I suppose to England and Ireland. Ironically, the potato didn't show up in North America until the English colonists brought it back to Virginia and Carolina. According to the most reliable sources, the first potatoes grown in what is now the United States were at Londonderry, New Hampshire, in 1719, from stock brought from Ireland. So the white potatoes, natives of the Americas, are known even today as "Irish potatoes!" And in 1847 the Irish had become so dependent on this article of food that when a blight hit the potato crop, over a million and a half Irish emigrated to America to escape starvation.

One of the favorite ways, especially in small towns and rural districts, of preparing potatoes is baking them, sliced, in a casserole with cream. This dish is usually known as Scalloped Potatoes. They're always good, but they're even better done in this unusual way.

ESCALLOPED POTATOES DE LUXE

1 *lb. raw potatoes*	*French mustard*
¼ *lb. Gruyère cheese*	½ *cup dry white wine*
1 *lb. onions*	¼ *cup fine breadcrumbs*
Salt	¼ *cup grated Parmesan cheese*
Pepper	4 *tablespoons butter*

Butter a baking dish well, and put a layer of peeled and sliced raw potatoes on the bottom. Sprinkle with salt and pepper, then top the layer of potatoes with thin slices of Gruyère cheese, and very lightly smear some French mustard over the cheese slices. On top of the cheese slices put a layer of thin onion slices. Repeat these layers until the dish is full. Press down well, and pour over ½ cup of dry American white wine. Sprinkle fine breadcrumbs over the top, then sprinkle over the breadcrumbs some grated Parmesan cheese. Dot with butter, and cover with a well-buttered piece of wax paper. Place in a moderate oven (350 degrees) for 30 to 35 minutes. After the potatoes have been baking about 20 minutes, remove the paper, and let the top brown. Serve very hot.

Pommes de terre Soufflées, or Balloon Potatoes, as they are sometimes called by the uninitiated, never fail to bring forth exclamations of delight whenever they are served. They seldom appear on the menus of any but the most exclusive restaurants, and they are seldom prepared in the home, because they are thought to be very difficult to cook so that the potatoes arrive at the table really looking like little oblong-shaped balloons.

I have heard or read a number of stories about their origin. The most often repeated, and probably the true version, is that they were due to the tardiness of the important guests at a banquet to celebrate the initial run in 1837 of the first railroad between Paris and St. Germain.

One version of the story has it that the train bearing officials, important guests, and King Louis Philippe himself, was delayed. Another version states that the train was on time, but that the King, travelling by carriage rather than risk his neck on those new-fangled choo choo trains, was the tardy one.

Anyhow, *pommes de terre frites* (fried potatoes to you) were on the menu to accompany a fillet of beef. The chef, going on schedule, put the slices of potatoes in the deep fat. After they were in, he was informed of the delay (of the train, or the King), and he took them out of the fat and let them drain. About 15 minutes later he was advised that the guests (or King) were arriving, and he returned the partially cooked potatoes to the fat again, which had continued to heat, and was hotter than when he had first put the potatoes into it. He was a little apprehensive of the result, but imagine his surprise and delight when he saw the potatoes puff out into golden brown, crisp balloons. He salted them, and sent them into the banquet, and thus a new dish was born.

There is really nothing mysterious about *pommes de terre soufflées,* and they shouldn't be too hard to make. But certain precautions must be taken: New potatoes cannot be used, oldish potatoes of a mellow texture are best; the slices must be very thin, not over an eighth of an inch thick; and the fat they are cooked in must be of two different degrees of heat. But let's get on to making them.

POMMES DE TERRE SOUFFLÉES

Peel the raw potatoes, and cut into slices not to exceed ⅛ inch in thickness. The slices must be of uniform size and thickness, trimmed to the shape of a flattened football. Put the slices in ice water for a few minutes, or run very cold water over them to remove any extra starch. Then they should be dried.

Heat a kettle of fat (lard is the best) to a temperature just below the boiling point, or just as it begins to smoke. Keep the full heat under the pot, as the cold potatoes cool the fat slightly. Let the slices cook until they begin to show a pale gold color, and the edges show faint signs of puffing. This should take about 3 minutes. Then remove the slices, drain them well in a collander or strainer, and allow to cool for about 5 minutes.

Most chefs insist upon 2 kettles of fat, the first one having a moderate temperature, just below boiling, and the other a high temperature, boiling and smoking. But it is possible to get by, I am told, with one pot of fat. After the initial immersion of the potatoes in the fat with a moderate temperature, turn the heat up and, while the potatoes are cooling, bring the fat to a boiling and smoking temperature.

When the potatoes have cooled, put a few slices at a time in the really hot fat, using a frying basket or a coarse sieve. It will probably be necessary to experiment with one or two before you learn the moment when they should be removed. This second frying is very quick, a matter of seconds rather than minutes. The potatoes should be properly crisp and brown, but not burned, when they are taken out. Drain them on absorbent paper, sprinkle with salt, and serve very hot.

Sweet potatoes are of two types: one has pale yellow flesh, which cooks dry and mealy; and the other has a deeper orange flesh, which is sweeter and more moist. The latter is called a yam commercially, although it isn't actually a yam. The true yam is a native of Africa.

Sweet potatoes seem to lend themselves to more exotic preparation than the white, or Irish potato. This dish can well be the *pièce de résistance* at any dinner, and it seems to go best with pork dishes.

SWEET POTATOES IN SHELLS

6 *sweet potatoes*	2 *ounces butter*
Bacon fat	*Pinch freshly ground pepper*
3 *ounces rum*	1 *tsp. salt*
3 *ounces brandy*	*Powdered cinnamon*

Wash 6 medium to large sweet potatoes, rub their skins with bacon fat, and bake in a hot oven (450 degrees) until tender—about 40 minutes.

Cut each potato in half, lengthwise, and remove the pulp, being careful not to break the shells.

Mash the potato pulp, then add 3 ounces of rum, 3 ounces of brandy, 2 ounces of butter, 1 teaspoon of salt, and a pinch of freshly ground pepper. Whip this mixture until it is smooth and fluffy, and put it back in the sweet potato shells. Sprinkle the tops with a little cinnamon, and place in the oven to brown.

Rice is the staple food of probably the majority of the world's inhabitants. It is the most important food of most of the Oriental peoples, including those of India. In the United States there are three types of rice produced—long grain, medium grain, and short grain. Rice is also classified under the head of brown rice, unpolished white rice, and polished white rice. Within recent years a new type of white rice has appeared on the markets called converted rice, and it is said that this type of rice is the easiest to cook. But for some reason rice, which is a true cereal, is a damn hard item to cook well. One method is to bring the rice to a boil in only its own weight of cold water. Then let it simmer very slowly, covered, until the rice has absorbed the water and is cooked. This is very similar to the Chinese method, only the latter, as a rule, uses two cups of water to two cups of rice, and let it cook about 40 minutes.

Another method of cooking rice is to cook it in a double boiler. Then there are those who advocate 2 quarts of rapidly boiling water to 1 cup of rice, cooking it for about 18 to 20 minutes and then pouring hot water through the rice in a colander until the water runs clear. Of course, in all methods the rice before cooking should be washed in several waters until the washing water is not cloudy.

I have obtained real success by cooking rice in the following manner, and I don't believe anyone can make a mistake with it.

BOILED RICE

For each cupful of rice have 3 quarts of briskly boiling water to which has been added the juice of half a lemon and 3 teaspoons of salt. Pour the washed rice in slowly, and if you must stir, use a wooden fork. After 12 minutes or so, when the rice is soft all through, pour into the boiling water a pint of *ice water* as you turn off the heat. Then pour the rice into a coarse sieve, and when drained, put into a shallow baking dish, lightly greased with butter, and place in a *warm* oven. In a short time the rice will be nicely dried, properly swollen, and each grain separate. Don't be surprised if your guests surreptitiously peek under tables and into closets to discover where you've hidden your Chinese cook.

I suppose the Latins are more addicted to the use of rice than any of the other Occidental peoples. *Arroz con Polo* and *Paella* are practically national dishes in Spain, and the Italians are famous for their *Risottos*.

The best *Risotto Milanaise* I've ever eaten is that which is prepared by a captain in Riccardo's Restaurant in Chicago, Alex Pucci. He makes it with loving care, and the finished dish is perfection. He is very meticulous about his work, and he spent an hour one evening giving me the recipe and explaining it to me. If you'll follow the directions, I know you can turn out this delicious dish.

RISOTTO MILANAISE À LA PUCCI

1½ *cups uncooked long-grain rice*

¼ *lb. butter*

1 *large Bermuda onion*

½ *lb. diced Italian ham*

3 *ounces dry white wine*

4¼ *cups chicken broth*

Salt

Pepper

¼ *cup chopped mushrooms*

Pinch nutmeg

¼ *tsp. powdered saffron*

½ *cup grated Parmesan cheese*

In a large heavy iron skillet melt ¼ pound of butter. When it is hot, but not brown, add 1 large Bermuda onion, peeled and chopped fine, and ½ pound of diced Italian ham (again, Prosciutto ham is the best, but ordinary ham will do). Sauté the onion and ham gently for about 10 minutes. Then add 1½ cups of long-grain rice, which has previously been thoroughly washed in cold running water and later completely dried. Stir constantly with a wooden fork until the rice begins to brown, which should be about 20 minutes. Then add 3 ounces of dry American white wine. Still stirring the rice, let it absorb the wine, which will take about 2 minutes. Then add 4 cups of boiling hot chicken broth, a little salt and pepper, a tiny pinch of nutmeg, and ¼ cup of chopped fresh mushrooms. Stir thoroughly with a wooden fork or spoon, then cover, and let simmer over a very low flame for about 20 minutes.

Dissolve ¼ teaspoon of powdered saffron in ¼ cup of hot chicken broth. Add this to the rice, along with ½ cup of grated Parmesan cheese. Stir gently but thoroughly, and cook for 10 minutes more. Remove from the fire, let stand for a couple of minutes, and serve.

The peoples of the Near East are also devotees of rice. Their most popular way of serving it is in a pilaf, and this has about the same place in the menu as potatoes have in America. The Near Easterners have as many ways of making a pilaf as Americans have of cooking potatoes. A pilaf is naturally more highly seasoned than boiled rice—in other words, it's rice with "oomph" in it.

RICE PILAF

1 *cup uncooked long-grain rice*	*Salt*
3 *tbsp. olive oil*	*Pepper*
2 *tbsp. chopped onion*	*Consommé*
	Grated Parmesan cheese

To make the rice pilaf, put 3 tablespoons of olive oil (or fat) in a heavy pan and add 2 tablespoons of chopped onion. Cook briskly for 1 minute, then add 1 cup of raw long-grain rice, and salt and pepper to taste. Cook very slowly for 3 minutes, stirring all the time. Cover the rice with enough consommé to reach ½ inch above the rice, cover the pan with wax paper, put on the lid, and cook in a 375-degree oven for 20 to 25 minutes. Remove the lid, stir in a very little grated Parmesan cheese, and the rice pilaf is ready to receive its blanket of whatever curry is being served, or eaten as is.

Another way of adding glamor to rice is to cook it with saffron. Saffron is manufactured from the dried parts of the purple crocus.

Saffron has long been cultivated in Persia and Kashmir. The Arabs, when in Spain, cultivated it as early as the tenth century. It was used as an ingredient in many of the complicated medicines of early times. As a perfume it was strewn in Greek halls, courts, and theaters, and in the Roman baths. When Nero made his entry into Rome, the streets were sprinkled with saffron.

Saffron is expensive, and during the late war was very difficult to get. The easiest form to use is the powdered saffron, which can be obtained now in the better food stores or in drug stores. It not only adds a delightful flavor to certain foods, but also colors them. Its yellow was a royal color in Greek times. Well, enough history! Here's the recipe given me by Walter Drannan, one of the members of the Streeterville and Sanitary Canal Gourmet and Study Society.

SAFFRON RICE

1 *cup long-grain rice*	1 *small onion*
2 *tbsp. butter*	⅛ *tsp. saffron*
	2 *cups chicken broth*

Melt 2 tablespoons of butter in a heavy kettle, and add 1 small onion, chopped very fine, and ⅛ teaspoon of saffron. Simmer slowly for a few minutes (do not burn or brown), then add 1 cup of uncooked rice. Stir and mix, then add 2 cups of boiling chicken broth. Mix well with a wooden spoon and bring to a fast boil. Cover tightly, reduce flame to the lowest possible point, and let simmer for twenty minutes. The liquid should be entirely absorbed and the rice grains whole. Place the rice in a shallow bowl or pan for a few minutes to allow the steam to escape, then serve.

(10) SALADS, SALAD DRESSINGS, AND SAUCES

SALADS

One of the most controversial issues in the field of gastronomy deals with the making of salads. Many writers and authorities aver that women have no business messing around with the making of salads. Having a great admiration for the gentle sex, and being a married man, I am going to be a middle-of-the-road guy. In all fairness, I must admit that many women have perverted the art of salad making and turned out some of the most impossible and atrocious salads of which the mind can conceive. In one book of salads written by a woman is a recipe for a salad which is called beautiful but very rich, and, believe it or not, the ingredients are: canned pears, canned pineapple and its syrup, canned cherries, maraschino cherries and their syrup, dates, pecans, sugar, cream cheese, lemon juice, sweet fruit salad dressing, and whipped cream! Personally, I think this salad should be garnished with Milk of Magnesia tablets, Bisodol, and Tums.

On the other hand, I have known a great many women who were literally magicians when it came to whipping up salads; and, again on the other hand, a cook book by a man gives a recipe for a salad using 39 ingredients. A footnote to this recipe suggests that the salad can be varied by using raw vegetables one time and cooked vegetables the next.

Actually, salads can be as simple or as complicated as you want them, and a complicated salad does not necessarily mean an impossible salad from the standpoint of a gourmet. Charles H. Baker, Jr., in his wonderful cook book, *The Gentleman's Companion,* gives a recipe for a magnificent Damascus Green Salad which is a thing of beauty to look at, and a joy to eat.

The rules for making an acceptable salad are few and simple. The ingredients should be strictly fresh, thoroughly chilled, and absolutely dry. The dressing, which is the final touch contributing

to a salad's perfection, should be carefully compounded. Harsh
vinegars are to be avoided, and only the finest olive oil should be
used. I have found Old Monk olive oil uniformly excellent. Both
red and white wine can be used with profit in French dressings
and in Roquefort dressing. To my mind, garlic is absolutely
essential in many salads, but the use of that delightful gift to
mankind can be varied according to taste. If you want just a
delicate flavor of garlic, rub the salad bowl with a cut clove, or
use a *chapon,* which is a crust of bread rubbed with garlic, and
put it in the bottom of a bowl of green salad.

Herbs are very important. The sweet herbs, such as chervil,
basil, chives, tarragon, parsley, and marjoram, go particularly well
with salads. Summer savory, sorrel, thyme, fennel, and dill can also
be used. In certain salads I am very partial to oregano, but it
must be used judiciously.

Probably the most popular salad, at least among men, is a tossed
green salad. Such a salad is simple to make, and all sorts of edible
greens, in almost any combination, can be used. Lettuce is
usually a "must"—head, leaf, or romaine. Then there are escarole,
curly endive, Belgian endive, chicory, and water cress. Beet tops,
young green spinach, and dandelion leaves are fine. And a real
touch of intriguing flavor can be obtained by adding a few young
nasturtium leaves. Green peppers, carefully trimmed of white ribs
and seeds, and sliced into rings or coarsely chopped, are desirable.
And, while they are not green, tender, young, crisp radishes,
sliced or cut in half, add to a green salad.

Here, for instance, is a delectable salad of mixed greens.

SALAD OF MIXED GREENS

Escarole	*Salt*
Lettuce	*Pepper, freshly ground*
Spinach leaves	*Clove garlic*
Dandelion leaves	*Lowry's salt*
Romaine	*French dressing*
Water cress	*Mustard*
Worcestershire sauce	

Thoroughly wash and dry escarole, lettuce, spinach leaves, dandelion leaves, romaine, and water cress. Place them in the icebox
to chill thoroughly.

Sprinkle a wooden salad bowl with salt, then rub it with a cut clove of garlic. (The salt acts as an abrasive agent.) Put in equal amounts of the six greens. Sprinkle with Lowry's salt and freshly ground pepper, and then add a French dressing to which has been added dry mustard and Worcestershire sauce. Toss until all the leaves are thoroughly coated with the dressing, and serve.

Another simple green salad I'm very fond of is made up of firm lettuce, water cress and *finocci,* an Italian anise-flavored species of celery.

A GREEN SALAD

½ *head crisp lettuce*	*Salt*
1 *bunch water cress*	*Garlic*
1 *stalk finocchi*	*Red wine dressing à la Wood*

Generously sprinkle a wooden salad bowl with salt. Then rub it with a cut clove of garlic.

Break up ½ good-sized head of firm lettuce, and slice 1 stalk of *finocchi.* Put these in the salad bowl, together with 1 bunch of fresh water cress, which is broken up. Toss everything with a wooden fork and spoon until the greens are thoroughly mixed. Then add the red wine dressing à la Wood, which has been thoroughly chilled, toss again, and serve.

Usually tomatoes have no part in a tossed green salad. They are wonderful in their place, but in a tossed salad they not only tend to obliterate other flavors, but, when quartered or cut, they just swamp the salad and weaken a carefully and thoughtfully wrought dressing. However, one night, in the Athens Café on Halsted Street in Chicago, I had a special Greek salad that used tomatoes and that was out of this world. I managed to wangle the recipe out of Apostle Paul Flabouras, the proprietor, and am delighted to pass it on.

GREEK SALAD

½ head crisp lettuce
18 medium-sized radishes
½ cup chopped parsley
6 little green onions
Generous pinch oregano

Freshly ground pepper
¼ lb. Feta cheese
French dressing
2 small tins of fillets of
    anchovies

2 medium-sized tomatoes

Tear about ½ small head of crisp lettuce into small pieces and put in a wooden salad bowl. Then add 18 medium-sized radishes, cut in half, ½ cup of chopped parsley, 6 little green onions (bulbs and tops), chopped, 2 medium-sized tomatoes cut into small pieces, a generous pinch of oregano, freshly ground pepper to taste, 2 small tins of fillets of anchovies (leave them whole), and ¼ pound of Feta cheese crumbled into small pieces (this is a Greek cheese, something like cottage cheese, but very firm, which can be purchased in almost any Greek grocery store).

Toss the whole mixture very gently, then cover with wax paper, and thoroughly chill in the refrigerator. When ready to serve, sprinkle on a French dressing (it should be made with the usual herbs and seasonings, but the proportion of pure olive oil to tarragon vinegar should be 3 to 1 respectively).

For some reason Caesar Salad seems to have become unusually popular. Almost everyone I meet who is interested in food has a recipe to offer. But here's my own version which I had for a Streeterville and Sanitary Canal Gourmet and Study Society dinner one night.

CAESAR SALAD

5 bunches romaine
3 slices bread, toasted
Cloves garlic
Red wine French dressing

2 eggs
2 small tins anchovy fillets
Freshly ground pepper
Grated Parmesan cheese

Separate the leaves from 5 bunches of romaine, wash, dry thoroughly, then place in the refrigerator to chill for about 1 hour.

Toast 3 slices of bread (which has been slightly dried out in the oven) to a golden brown, then stroke them on both sides with cloves of garlic, and cut them into small cubes.

Put the romaine leaves in a large salad bowl and thoroughly mix with a red wine French dressing. Then add the garlic-impregnated cubes of toast to the romaine, and toss again. Add 2 eggs, which have been boiled for only 30 seconds, and again mix everything. Next add the contents of two tins of anchovies (each fillet having been cut in two), and freshly ground pepper to taste, and give the salad a final mixing.

In serving, sprinkle over each portion some grated Parmesan cheese.

Romaine is a type of lettuce which is distinguished not only by its cylindrical and elongated head and coarser leaf, but its delightful flavor. One night Max Guggiari, of the Imperial House in Chicago, fixed me a romaine salad, the only other ingredient of which was sautéed cubes of garlic toast. The dressing was a Roquefort one.

ROMAINE SALAD

Romaine	*Butter*
Toast	*Salt*
Garlic	*Freshly ground pepper*
	Roquefort dressing

Thoroughly wash, dry, and chill romaine.

Toast bread, rub on both sides with a cut clove of garlic, cut into cubes, and fry lightly in butter.

Break the romaine leaves in half and put in a salad bowl, seasoning them with salt and freshly ground pepper to taste. Add the sautéed cubes of garlic toast, and mix well with the romaine. Then pour on Roquefort dressing, toss, and serve.

The avocado, which is often misnamed "alligator pear," has a delicate buttery flavor that is particularly pleasant in a salad. Epicures like to eat the avocado *au naturel,* with just a touch of a simple dressing filling the cavity. Even delicate wine or herb vinegars are too pungent to combine with the avocado, so the following dressing utilizing a light rum in place of vinegar, is delightful.

AVOCADO AU NATUREL

Ripe avocado

Lettuce

1 tbsp. lime juice

3 tbsp. pure olive oil

1 tsp. finely minced chives

1 tbsp. light rum

Salt

Freshly ground pepper

Cut a chilled ripe avocado in two and, after removing the seed and the inner dark skin next to it, nest the halves on a bed of lettuce.

Blend together 1 tablespoon of lime juice, 3 tablespoons of pure olive oil, 1 teaspoon of finely minced chives, 1 tablespoon of light rum, and salt and freshly ground pepper to taste. Chill, and pour this dressing into the cavities, and serve.

Avocados are rather oily in themselves, so the dressing should not be made with as much oil as is normally called for in a French dressing. Here is a deservedly popular salad of avocado combined with grapefruit segments, again using a milder French-type of dressing with rum.

AVOCADO AND GRAPEFRUIT

Avacado slices

Grapefruit segments

Lettuce

2 pimento strips

3 tbsp. olive oil

1 tbsp. lemon juice

1 tbsp. light rum

1 tsp. minced little green
  onion

1 tsp. minced parsley

¼ tsp. dry mustard

Dash Worcestershire sauce

Salt

Freshly ground pepper

Peel an avocado, remove the seed, and slice lengthwise.

Divide a grapefruit into segments, and remove the membrane.

On crisp lettuce alternate the avocado slices and the grapefruit segments, and top with 2 pimento strips laid crosswise.

Blend together 3 tablespoons of pure olive oil, 1 tablespoon of lemon juice, 1 tablespoon of light rum, 1 teaspoon of finely minced little green onion, 1 teaspoon of finely minced parsley, ¼ teaspoon of dry mustard, a dash of Worcestershire sauce, and salt and freshly ground pepper to taste. Chill, and pour over the salad.

In the following recipe the avocado is mashed, and it makes a very piquante salad.

SPANISH AVOCADO

2 *tomato slices*   1 *slice canned pimento*
1 *avocado*   1 *tsp. sherry*
Lettuce   *Pinch chili powder*
¼ *clove garlic*   *Salt*
1 *tsp. minced parsley*   *Freshly ground pepper*
1 *little green onion*   *French dressing*

Cut 2 center slices from a large, peeled tomato, and remove the pulp, or center, from each slice. Put the tomato slices individually on beds of lettuce, and chill.

Peel a ripe avocado, remove the seed, and mash the meat in a bowl. Add ¼ clove of garlic, finely minced, 1 little green onion (bulb and top), finely minced, 1 teaspoon of parsley, finely minced, 1 slice of canned pimento, minced, 1 teaspoon of sherry, a pinch of chili powder, and salt and freshly ground pepper to taste. Mix all this well together, form into 2 round balls, and chill.

Place the avocado balls in the tomato rings, and pour over them a herb French dressing.

Belgian endive is a great salad delicacy. It's grown from specially selected chicory roots. The white heads are formed of a number of thick, fleshy leaves, anywhere from 4 to 6 inches long and 2 inches wide.

I have called the following salad *Blanche et Verte* because of the color combination of white endive and green avocado and cucumber slices. This salad is appealing both to the appetite and to the eye.

BLANCHE ET VERTE SALAD

2 *stalks Belgian endive*   ½ *cucumber*
1 *ripe avocado*   *Romaine*
             Wine Roquefort dressing

Cut 2 stalks of Belgian endive in halves.

Peel an avocado, halve, remove the seed, and divide each half into thirds, slicing lengthwise.

Peel half a firm cucumber, cut in half across, and quarter the half lengthwise.

On a bed of romaine place, in a row, half an endive, an avocado slice, a cucumber slice, an avocado slice, a cucumber slice, an avocado slice, and an endive half.

Pour over this a wine Roquefort dressing, and serve.

One of my favorite comestibles are chestnuts, and they combine beautifully with endive.

ENDIVE AND CHESTNUT SALAD

1 *Belgian endive*	*White wine French dressing*
Water cress	¼ *clove garlic, minced*
Chopped cooked chestnuts	1 *slice canned pimento*
Grated Parmesan cheese	

For each portion halve a Belgian endive, and place the split halves on a bed of water cress. Sprinkle over the endive 2 tablespoons of coarsely chopped cooked chestnuts.

Add to a white wine French dressing ¼ clove of garlic, minced, 1 slice of canned pimento, chopped, and a little grated Parmesan cheese. When well mixed, pour the dressing over the endive and chopped chestnuts, and serve well chilled.

I don't believe there is a man in America who knows more about salads than Arnold Shircliffe, manager of the Wrigley Building Restaurant in Chicago, and noted steward, gastronomer, author, and bibliophile. His *Edgewater Salad Book* is a bible for chefs, restaurateurs, and gourmets. It contains several hundred recipes for salads and salad dressings, and also has 32 four-color plates showing just how some of the special salads should look when they are ready for the table.

One of the most popular salads at the Wrigley Building Restaurant is called "My Salad." And how it got its name is an interesting little story. Eddie Guest, one of America's best-known poets, frequently ate at that restaurant when he was in Chicago for his radio show. His favorite luncheon dish was Miramar salad, made with julienne lettuce and turkey, with Thousand Island dressing with Roquefort or blue cheese, and garnished with strips of bacon.

As Mr. Guest, however, preferred quartered hard-boiled eggs as a garnish, it was always served to him that way. So, when he came in for luncheon—always in a hurry—he'd say to the waiter, "Bring me that salad I like—you know, my salad." And "My Salad" it has been ever since.

MY SALAD

1½ cups cooked chicken
3 cups shredded lettuce
1 cup mayonnaise dressing
1 tbsp. tarragon vinegar
2 tbsp. chili sauce

1 tbsp. chopped green pepper
1 tbsp. chopped pimento
6 ounces Roquefort (or blue) cheese
Lettuce leaves

Mix 1½ cups of chicken (or turkey) cut in julienne strips with 3 cups of shredded lettuce.

To 1 cup of thick mayonnaise dressing add 1 tablespoon of tarragon vinegar, 2 tablespoons of chili sauce, 1 tablespoon of chopped green pepper, 1 tablespoon of chopped pimento, and 6 ounces of Roquefort (or blue) cheese, crumbled. Blend well.

Add this dressing to the chicken and lettuce, mix gently, and place the whole mixture in a bowl lined with lettuce leaves.

Like "My Salad," Singapore salad is really a light luncheon entrée. The influence of the Far East is indicated by the use of chutney.

SINGAPORE SALAD

3 cups cooked chicken
1 small head cabbage
1 green pepper
1 sweet red pepper
3 stalks celery
Salt
Clove garlic
1 cup mayonnaise
3 tbsp. Major Gray's chutney

Juice ½ lemon
1 tbsp. Madeira
1 tbsp. chopped chives
1 tsp. salt
1 tsp. Worcestershire sauce
½ tsp. paprika
Dash cayenne pepper
Lettuce leaves

Sprinkle a little salt in a wooden salad bowl, and rub the bowl with a cut clove of garlic.

Into the bowl put 1 small head of cabbage, shredded, 1 green pepper, seeded and shredded, 1 sweet red pepper, seeded and shredded, 3 stalks of celery, chopped, and 3 cups of chicken, cut in julienne strips.

Mix together in a separate bowl 1 cup of mayonnaise, 3 tablespoons of Major Gray's chutney, juice of ½ lemon, 1 tablespoon of Madeira, 1 tablespoon of chopped chives, 1 teaspoon of salt, 1 teaspoon of Worcestershire sauce, ½ teaspoon paprika, and a dash of cayenne pepper. When the dressing is well blended, add it to the vegetables and chicken, and mix all together thoroughly.

Serve on lettuce-lined plates.

Cucumbers and radishes combine perfectly with a sour cream dressing. This is a very easy salad to prepare and goes particularly well with rich entrées.

CUCUMBER AND RADISH SALAD WITH SOUR CREAM DRESSING

Small radishes   *Slender firm cucumbers*
                    Sour cream dressing

Wash little tender radishes and slice thin. Slice a slender, firm cucumber thin, but do not peel. Put the radish and cucumber slices in a bowl half filled with cracked ice.

A moment before serving, remove the radish and cucumber slices and shake very dry in a clean linen towel. Then add them to a bowl of sour cream dressing, stir gently, and serve on lettuce leaves.

The easiest salad of all to prepare and serve is sliced tomatoes with just salt and pepper or with a basic French dressing. The following salad is a variation of the familiar theme, and is very intriguing.

MINTED TOMATO SALAD

6 *firm tomatoes*	1 *cup fresh mint leaves*
Salt	*White wine French dressing*
Slice onion	*Hearts of lettuce*

Peel and slice 6 tomatoes.

Sprinkle a little salt in a wooden salad bowl, and rub it with the slice of an onion. Then place the tomatoes, sliced, in the bowl with 1 cup of fresh mint leaves, chopped fine. Add a white wine French dressing, and toss lightly.

Serve on individual salad plates on crisp hearts of lettuce.

As a rule I don't care for fruit salads. This is the one salad utilizing fruit that the Little Woman and I are very fond of and have quite frequently.

STUFFED PEAR SALAD

Pear halves (fresh or canned)	1 *tbsp. sour cream*
	1 *tbsp. chopped chives*
1 *pkg. Philadelphia cream cheese*	1 *tbsp. sherry*
	Lorenzo dressing

Blend 1 package of Philadelphia cream cheese with a tablespoon of sour cream, 1 tablespoon of chopped chives, and 1 tablespoon of sherry. Mould into balls.

On a bed of lettuce place half a cored fresh pear, per person (or half a canned pear), flat side up. Place a cheese ball in the cavity, and pour Lorenzo dressing (page 307) over the salad.

SALAD DRESSINGS

Of mordant mustard add a single spoon,
Distrust the condiment that bites too soon;
But deem it not, thou man of herbs, a fault,
To add a double quantity of salt;
Four times the spoon with oil of Lucca crown,
And twice with wine vinegar procured from town;
True flavor needs it, and your poet begs,
The pounded yellow of two well boiled eggs.

Let onion's atom lurk within the bowl,
And scarce suspected, animate the whole;
And lastly, in the flavored compound toss
A magic spoonful of anchovy sauce.

Sidney Smith, canon of St. Paul's Cathedral in London well over one hundred years ago, could not only make a good salad, but could put the recipe for the salad dressing into verse! You see, he recognized the fact that the dressing is the most important part of a salad.

According to Arnold Shircliffe, there are five basic salad dressings: French dressing, sour cream dressing, mayonnaise dressing, animal-fat dressing, and cooked dressing. All other dressings are variations of these basic five.

As there is only one Sarah Bernhardt, one Shakespeare, and one Babe Ruth, so there is only ONE French dressing—3 parts of olive oil, 1 part of wine vinegar, salt and freshly ground pepper to taste. This recipe may be legitimately varied by adding sweet herbs, but technically such additions make the dressing an herb dressing. Garlic is not a part of a true French dressing, but it can be added to the salad by rubbing the salad bowl with garlic, using a *chapon,* or by using toasted bread which has been stroked by garlic and cubed. Another way of getting a slight garlic flavor is to add a dash of Worcestershire sauce, but this addition takes it out of the true French dressing class.

Here is the recipe for 1 cup of real French dressing. This recipe is hereinafter referred to as a basic French dressing.

BASIC FRENCH DRESSING

6 *ounces olive oil* 1 *tsp. salt*
2 *ounces vinegar* ½ *tsp. freshly ground pepper*

The second basic dressing is a sour cream dressing. Blend the following ingredients together.

SOUR CREAM DRESSING

1 *cup thick fresh sour cream* *Salt*
1 *tbsp. chopped chives* *White pepper (or cayenne*
2 *tbsp. tarragon vinegar (or* *pepper)*
  lemon juice) ⅓ *tsp. sugar*

The third basic dressing, mayonnaise, is rather difficult for the amateur to make in that it is likely to curdle. There are good brands of mayonnaise on the market, but if you wish to make your own, here's how it's done.

MAYONNAISE

2 *raw egg yolks*
½ *tsp. salt*
Few grains cayenne pepper

½ *tsp. dry mustard*
2 *tbsp. tarragon vinegar*
1 *cup pure olive oil*

Beat the yolks of 2 fresh raw eggs with a wire egg beater until they are light. Then whip in ½ teaspoon of salt, a few grains of cayenne pepper, ½ teaspoon of dry mustard and 2 tablespoons of tarragon vinegar. (If you use a strong acid vinegar, it will partially coagulate the eggs and cause them to lose their effectiveness.)

Now add the very purest olive oil very, very slowly, and continue whipping until you have added 8 ounces, or 1 cup of oil. Remember, don't stop beating until all the oil has been added.

The easiest way I know of to make a perfect mayonnaise is to use a Waring blender. This household item belongs in the kitchen of every cook whether of professional or amateur status. It is just what its name implies—a blender. It consists of a chromium base which houses a small motor, and a strong, heavy glass mixing unit of 1-quart capacity. In the bottom of the latter are mounted steel blades something on the order of an airplane propeller. When the glass mixing unit is set on the base, the motor shaft automatically engages the base of the blender spindle. The blender eliminates such tasks as rubbing ingredients through a fine sieve. It is absolutely necessary in the making of a Green Goddess salad dressing. Cut up seedless oranges in quarters and put them in the blender, and in no time you have the finest orange juice you ever tasted. The blender is an indispensable piece of equipment at all bars, and you can't make a Frozen Daiquiri without it.

The fourth basic dressing is the animal-fat dressing, used for wilted salads and often for potato salads.

ANIMAL-FAT DRESSING

6 *slices bacon*   *Salt*
½ *cup vinegar*   *Pepper*
          ½ *tsp. sugar*

Finely dice 6 slices of bacon and put in a skillet. Let the fat render out, remove the skillet from the fire, and add slowly ½ cup of vinegar in which has been dissolved salt and pepper to taste and ½ teaspoon of sugar. While combining, whip thoroughly. This dressing should be poured over the salad while warm and served immediately.

The fifth basic dressing is a cooked one, and is used with vegetable, meat, or fish salads.

COOKED DRESSING

¼ *cup mild vinegar*   1 *tsp. salt*
½ *cup water*   1 *tbsp. lemon juice*
3 *ounces melted butter*   ¼ *tsp. paprika*
¼ *tsp. dry mustard*   1 *tsp. sugar*
          Yolks 4 *eggs*

Mix ¼ cup of mild vinegar, ½ cup water, 3 ounces of melted butter, ¼ teaspoon of dry mustard, 1 teaspoon of salt, 1 tablespoon of lemon juice, ¼ teaspoon of paprika, and 1 teaspoon of sugar together and bring to a boil. Remove from fire, allow to cool partly, then place in the top of a double boiler and whip in the yolks of 4 eggs. Whip over the fire until the sauce thickens, and remove.

The following dressings use a French dressing base.

Many recipes for red wine French dressings call for catsup as an ingredient. There may be a large number of people who like such recipes, but for myself I violently object to them. Catsup contains pungent spices, and it certainly tends to mask any delicate wine and herb flavors in the dressing. So I give you my version. (If you like your dressing with more olive oil in it, govern yourself accordingly.)

RED WINE DRESSING À LA WOOD

5 *ounces olive oil*   *Freshly ground pepper*
1 *ounce red wine vinegar*   ½ *tsp. Worcestershire*
2 *ounces dry red wine*   *sauce*
½ *tsp. mustard*   *Pinch basil*
1 *tsp. salt*   *Pinch tarragon*
                    1 *tsp. sugar*

Into an earthenware bowl put 5 ounces of pure olive oil, 1 ounce of red wine vinegar, 2 ounces of dry American red wine, ½ teaspoon of dry mustard, 1 teaspoon of salt, freshly ground pepper to taste, ½ teaspoon of Worcestershire sauce, a pinch each of basil and tarragon, and 1 teaspoon of sugar. Stir this until everything is well blended, and then set bowl in a container of ice to chill.

WHITE WINE FRENCH DRESSING

4 *tbsp. olive oil*   *Freshly ground pepper*
2 *tbsp. dry white wine*   *Dash cayenne*
½ *tsp. lemon juice*   *Dash onion juice*
½ *tsp. salt*   *Pinch sugar*
              Pinch dry mustard

Blend together and then chill.

ANCHOVY-CAPER DRESSING

To 1 cup of basic French dressing add:

3 *tsp. chopped anchovy*   2 *tsp. chopped parsley*
1½ *tsp. chopped capers*   4 *drops Tabasco*

CHUTNEY DRESSING

To 1 cup of basic French dressing add:

3 *tbsp. Major Gray's chutney*   3 *tbsp. walnut catsup*
                1 *tsp. chervil*

BRANDY DRESSING

To 1 cup of basic French dressing add:

2 *ounces brandy*	1 *tsp. tarragon*

This is a dressing that really needs a Waring blender.

CURRY SALAD DRESSING

To 1 cup of basic French dressing add:

3 *hard-boiled egg yolks*	¼ *clove garlic*
½ *tsp. curry powder*	*Dash Worcestershire sauce*
	3 *tbsp. cream*

Put the yolks of 3 hard-boiled eggs in a Waring blender. Add ½ teaspoon curry powder, ¼ clove of garlic, finely minced, a dash of Worcestershire sauce, and 3 tablespoons of cream. Blend these ingredients into a smooth paste, and whip 1 cup of basic French dressing into the paste.

HERB SALAD DRESSING

To 1 cup of basic French dressing add:

> ¼ *cup chopped herbs:*
>
> | | |
> |---|---|
> | *Marjoram* | *Chervil* |
> | *Rosemary* | *Savory* |
> | *Tarragon* | *Chives* |

LORENZO DRESSING

To 1 cup of basic French dressing add:

¼ *cup chili sauce*	¼ *cup chopped water cress*
	¼ *teaspoon paprika*

MARGUERY DRESSING

To 1 cup of basic French dressing add:

¼ *cup chili sauce*	¼ *cup chopped water cress*
	⅛ *teaspoon curry powder*

ROQUEFORT CHEESE DRESSING

To 1 cup of basic French dressing add:

½ cup crumbled Roquefort cheese

With a Waring blender, the Roquefort cheese alone can be added to the basic French dressing, and it will become completely emulsified. If you haven't a blender, then make a paste of the Roquefort cheese by adding 3 tablespoons of 40% cream. Simply mix the cream into the cheese, add the basic French dressing, and blend.

WINE ROQUEFORT DRESSING

To 1 cup of Red Wine French dressing add:

½ cup crumbled Roquefort cheese

VINAIGRETTE DRESSING

To 1 cup of basic French dressing add:

1½ *tsp. chopped green olives*	1½ *tsp. chopped gherkins*
1½ *tsp. chopped capers*	1½ *tsp. chopped parsley*
1½ *tsp. chopped chives*	1½ *tsp. chervil*

Some people like a lemon-flavored mayonnaise dressing.

MAYONNAISE BASIC DRESSING WITH LEMON JUICE

2 *fresh egg yolks*	½ *tsp. salt*
½ *tsp. dry mustard*	½ *tsp. sugar*
2 *tbsp. lemon juice*	1 *cup pure olive oil*

Beat the yolks of 2 fresh eggs with a wire egg beater, until they are light. Then whip in ½ teaspoon of dry mustard and 1 tablespoon of lemon juice at the same time. Add the oil very slowly, beating all the while. When all the oil has been added, beat in ½ teaspoon of sugar and ½ teaspoon of salt which have been thoroughly dissolved in 1 tablespoon of lemon juice.

The following dressings use the basic mayonnaise dressing as a base.

ANCHOVY DRESSING II

To 1 cup of basic mayonnaise, or mayonnaise with lemon, add:

1 *tbsp. chopped anchovies*   1 *tbsp. chopped gherkins*
1 *tsp. finely chopped chives*

BRANDY MAYONNAISE

To 1 cup of basic mayonnaise with lemon add:

1 *tsp. dry white wine*   1 *tsp. brandy*
1 *tbsp. whipped cream*

CAVIAR DRESSING

To 1 cup of basic mayonnaise dressing with lemon add:

1 *generous tablespoon caviar*   1 *tsp. chopped chives*
1 *tsp. chopped parsley*

This is somewhat similar to a Russian dressing, in that both call for caviar. But this is a more delicate dressing than the Russian.

For really luxurious eating, try this dressing on a lobster salad sometime when you've made a killing at the races, or at bridge, or gin rummy—or just a killing . . . period!

The Palace Hotel in San Francisco has become famous for the following dressing, which is indeed wonderful. But my good friend, and fellow-member of the Streeterville and Sanitary Canal Gourmet and Study Society, Walter Drennan, has certainly improved the original recipe, and you'd be surprised at the number of dinner invitations he receives, not only because he's excellent company, but also because he will whip up his Green Goddess salad dressing at the drop of a cocktail napkin.

GREEN GODDESS DRESSING

To 1 cup of basic mayonnaise dressing add:

3 *tbsp. finely chopped anchovies*	1 *tbsp. lemon juice*
3 *tbsp. chopped chives (or little green onions)*	3 *tbsp. tarragon wine vinegar*
	⅛ *cup chopped parsley*
1 *clove garlic, grated*	*Salt*
	Freshly ground pepper

½ *cup heavy cream*

Put the above ingredients in an electric blender for 20 seconds, chill, and pour over mixed greens. This dressing is wonderful over limestone or Bibb lettuce.

The following dressing also has caviar in it, but don't get the idea that it is common throughout Russia, or that it was even in the old days of the Czars. Even in Russia, caviar is a gourmet luxury.

RUSSIAN DRESSING

To 1 cup of basic mayonnaise dressing with lemon add:

3 *tbsp. diced green pepper*	3 *tbsp. chili sauce*
3 *tbsp. of diced sweet red pepper*	3 *tbsp. caviar*
	Dash cayenne pepper

Following is one of the most popular of the salad dressings using a basic mayonnaise dressing. It's excellent with seafood or poultry salads, and makes a plain head of lettuce salad something very tasty.

The addition of a cup of whipped cream makes a very creamy dressing. This, however, is optional.

THOUSAND ISLAND DRESSING

To 1 cup of basic mayonnaise dressing add:

3 *tbsp. chili sauce*	1 *tsp. chopped chives*
1 *tbsp. chopped green pepper*	1 *cup whipped cream*
1 *tsp. chopped pimento*	*(optional)*

SAUCES

You will find many gastronomical authorities who will insist that, while almost anyone can learn to boil, broil, bake, fry, or roast, a sauce maker must be born.

That may have been true hundreds of years ago, when the great chefs were inventing sauces. Then, and even today, in the sharply drawn class lines of professional chefs, the *saucier* heads the aristocracy. But in this advanced age, almost any cook who has a respect for recipes, who is careful and painstaking, and who uses only the best ingredients, can become an excellent sauce maker.

Sauces are, of course, of tremendous importance in cooking. But even more important is the choice of exactly the right sauce for the dish with which it is to be served. It should not disguise the flavor of food, but enhance it. And a sauce should be smooth, light, without being too thin, glossy to the eye, and decided as to taste.

There are five basic sauces which are the foundation for most sauces. These sauces are Béchamel and Velouté, which are white, or blonde, sauces; sauce Espagnol, a brown sauce; mayonnaise; and Hollandaise.

Béchamel sauce is a cream sauce made with scalded milk. It can be kept in the refrigerator almost indefinitely. It is said that Louis de Béchamel, the Maître d'Hotel of Louis XIV, invented this sauce.

BÉCHAMEL SAUCE

2 *tbsp. butter*	1 *small bay leaf*
2 *tbsp. flour*	6 *peppercorns*
1 *medium-sized onion*	1 *tsp. salt*
	2 *cups milk*

Melt 2 tablespoons of butter in a saucepan, and add 2 tablespoons of flour, 1 medium onion, peeled and chopped fine, 1 small bay leaf, 6 peppercorns, and 1 teaspoon of salt. Simmer very slowly over a low flame for about 10 minutes, blending well. Then add very slowly 2 cups of scalded milk, stirring constantly, and let cook about 20 minutes over a low flame. Remove and strain.

Velouté sauce is also a cream sauce, but it can be varied for different dishes. Fish, meat, game, chicken or vegetable stock is used instead of milk.

VELOUTÉ SAUCE

2 *tbsp. butter*
2 *tbsp. flour*
1 *medium-sized onion*
1 *small bay leaf*
6 *peppercorns*

1 *tsp. salt*
2 *cups stock (courtbouillon, chicken, vegetable, game or veal)*

Melt 2 tablespoons of butter in a saucepan, and add 2 tablespoons of flour, 1 medium-sized onion, peeled and chopped fine, 1 small bay leaf, 6 peppercorns, and 1 teaspoon of salt. Simmer very slowly over a low flame for about 10 minutes, blending well.

Next add 2 cups of stock, the kind of stock depending on what the velouté sauce is to be used with. If fish, use 2 cups of court-bouillon; if chicken, 2 cups of chicken broth; if vegetables, 2 cups of the water vegetables have been cooked in; if game, 2 cups of the game stock; or, for meat, 2 cups of veal stock. The stock should be added to the *roux* very slowly, stirring constantly, and the whole should cook about 20 minutes over a very low flame. Then remove and strain.

Sauce Espagnol is the great brown sauce and is the basis for practically all brown sauces. It may appear to be rather difficult to make, or perhaps, I should say a lot of work; but this sauce, too, can be stored in the refrigerator and kept almost indefinitely. The addition of the meat bones as directed below not only adds color to the sauce, but also adds flavor and substance.

SAUCE ESPAGNOL

Butter
⅔ *cup chopped carrots*
⅔ *cup chopped onions*
¼ *cup chopped turnip*
½ *lb. lean ham*
½ *lb. lean veal*
2 *cloves garlic*
4 *tbsp. chopped parsley*
1 *tsp. thyme*
1 *tsp. majoram*
¼ *cup chopped celery*
2 *bay leaves*

6 *peppercorns*
1 *lb. beef bones*
1 *lb. veal bones*
Veal knuckle
1 *ham bone*
2 *cups canned tomatoes*
2 *whole cloves*
½ *tsp. allspice*
8 *cans beef bouillon*
6 *cups water*
¾ *cup flour*
1 *cup dry Madeira*

Melt 4 ounces of butter in a large saucepan or kettle, and when hot add ⅔ cup each of chopped carrots and chopped onions, ¼ cup chopped turnip, ½ pound each of lean ham, chopped, and lean veal, chopped, 2 cloves of minced garlic, 4 tablespoons of chopped parsley, 1 teaspoon each of dried thyme and marjoram, ¼ cup of chopped celery, 2 bay leaves, and 6 peppercorns. Sauté these briskly until light brown. Then pour off the butter and save.

In the meantime, spread out in a flat pan about 1 pound each of beef and veal bones, a ham bone, and a veal knuckle. Place the pan in a moderately hot oven (400 degrees) and let the bones cook until they are well browned.

Add the cooked bones to the sautéed vegetables and herbs, along with 2 cups of canned tomatoes, 2 whole cloves, ½ teaspoon of allspice, 8 cans of beef bouillon, and 6 cups of water. Simmer for 3 hours, skimming occasionally. At the end of 3 hours, skim and strain through a fine sieve or cheesecloth.

Add enough melted butter to the butter saved from sautéing the vegetables to make ¾ cup of butter. Put this in a saucepan over a very low fire, and stir in ¾ cup of flour, blending well. Let this become a golden brown. Then add, very slowly, the strained broth, mixing and stirring well. When all the broth is added, let it boil up, and then simmer over a low flame until it is reduced to the desired sauce consistency. Stir in 1 cup of dry Madeira, and let cool, stirring occasionally. Store the sauce in the refrigerator, to be used as necessary. It will keep almost indefinitely.

The recipe for mayonnaise will be found under the salad dressing section of this chapter.

There are a number of commercially made and bottled mayonnaise dressings, but if they are used, they should not be sweet. Many of the very finest restaurants use Old Monk mayonnaise, which is made with the purest ingredients. If you are hesitant about attempting to make a mayonnaise, I can highly recommend the Old Monk.

Another sauce that many people are afraid to attempt is a Hollandaise sauce. It can go wrong very easily, but if you are careful and follow the recipe exactly, you should be able to make a perfect Hollandaise sauce. Most professional cooks use a wire whisk in the preparation of a Hollandaise sauce. It seems to blend the ingredients much better than a slotted spoon or an egg beater. A wire whisk can be purchased at any hardware store.

HOLLANDAISE SAUCE

6 *egg yolks*	12 *ounces butter*
1 *tbsp. water*	¼ *tsp. salt*
1 *tbsp. lemon juice*	

Put enough water in the bottom of a double boiler to reach about 1 inch below the bottom of the top part of the double boiler. Bring the water almost to the boiling point, *but do not let it boil at any time.*

Put the yolks of 6 eggs and 1 tablespoon of water in the top of the double boiler. Beat with a wire whisk (or a slotted spoon) until creamy. Now add, bit by bit, the butter, beating or stirring constantly. Have each addition of butter thoroughly blended before the next is added. Add about ¼ teaspoon of salt, still beating or stirring gently with the whisk (or spoon), until the sauce is thick. At the very end, add 1 tablespoon of lemon juice. This will make approximately 2 cups of sauce.

Sauce Bernaise is a variation on the Hollandaise theme. It is one of the leading sauces served with fish, steak, eggs, and so forth.

SAUCE BERNAISE

½ *tsp. chopped tarragon*	2 *tbsp. dry white wine*
½ *tsp. chopped chervil*	2 *tbsp. tarragon vinegar*
8 *peppercorns*	1 *tsp. salt*
2 *tbsp. minced little green onions*	*Tiny pinch cayenne pepper*

In a small saucepan put ½ teaspoon each of chopped tarragon and chopped chervil, about 8 peppercorns, slightly bruised, 2 tablespoons of minced little green onions, 2 tablespoons of dry American white wine, and 2 tablespoons of tarragon vinegar. Let this simmer gently until nearly dry.

Proceed with a Hollandaise sauce as directed above, only add the above paste to the egg yolks after they are creamy, and blend thoroughly. Then proceed as with the making of the Hollandaise sauce. Strain and add 1 teaspoon of salt and a tiny pinch of cayenne pepper. Serve hot.

Another well known sauce, based on the sauce Espagnol, is sauce Bordelaise, which is excellent over broiled meats.

SAUCE BORDELAISE

2 *tbsp. butter*	1 *small piece bay leaf*
2 *little green onions*	½ *cup dry red wine*
½ *tsp. chopped parsley*	2 *tbsp. beef marrow*
1 *cup Sauce Espagnol*	

Melt 2 tablespoons of butter in a saucepan, add 2 little green onions, ½ teaspoon of chopped parsley, a small piece of crumbled bay leaf, and sauté gently until the onions begin to brown. Then add ½ cup of dry American red wine (claret type) and simmer over a low flame until it has reduced to about ¼ of its original quantity. Then add 1 cup of sauce Espagnol, and let the whole thing boil gently for about 10 minutes. Just before serving, add 2 tablespoons of beef marrow, which has been diced and placed in warm water for a couple of minutes, and then drained.

I presume that Creole Sauce originated in the South. It is suitable for service with a great many foods, such as eggs and fish and is a great sauce for left-over dishes of meat, poultry, and game.

CREOLE SAUCE

2 *tbsp. butter*	½ *cup dry white wine*
1 *clove garlic*	½ *cup tomato paste*
2 *tbsp. chopped onion*	*Pinch cayenne pepper*
2 *tbsp. chopped green pepper*	1 *cup sauce Espagnol*
¼ *cup sliced fresh mushrooms*	6 *green olives*

Melt 2 tablespoons of butter in a saucepan, and add 1 clove of garlic, crushed and minced, 2 tablespoons each of chopped onion and chopped green pepper, ¼ cup sliced fresh mushrooms. Sauté for about 5 minutes, until the vegetables and mushrooms are tender, but not brown. Then add ½ cup of dry American white wine, ½ cup of tomato paste, a pinch of cayenne pepper, salt to taste, a cup of sauce Espagnol, and 6 green olives which have been pitted and chopped. Simmer gently, stirring, until the sauce reduces to the proper consistency.

This is a wonderful sauce to serve over cold cuts, smoked meats, and any kind of game, particularly goose, duck, guinea hen, or other game birds.

CUMBERLAND SAUCE

1 *lump sugar*	5 *tbsp. port*
Dry white wine	5 *tbsp. orange juice*
Peel of 1 orange	2 *tbsp. lemon juice*
2 *tbsp. dry mustard*	1 *tsp. powdered ginger*
½ *cup currant jelly*	*Tiny pinch cayenne pepper*
	Salt

Rub a lump of sugar over the outside of an orange until the lump becomes saturated with the oil of the orange. Then moisten the sugar with 1 tablespoon of dry American white wine.

Peel off the skin of the orange as thin as possible and, after removing every particle of the white inner skin, cut the peel into thin, match-like strips.

Mix 2 tablespoons of dry mustard with enough dry American white wine to form a paste.

In the top of a double boiler melt ½ cup of currant jelly. Cool, then add the dissolved lump of sugar, the orange peel slivers, the mustard paste, 5 tablespoons of port, 5 tablespoons of orange juice, 2 tablespoons of lemon juice, 1 teaspoon of powdered ginger, a tiny pinch of cayenne pepper, and salt to taste. Bring to a boil, then lower the flame and simmer for a few minutes.

This sauce can be served either hot or cold. If served cold, allow to cool, then chill in the refrigerator until very cold.

The following sauce is wonderful with any meat, fowl or game, and it uses a sauce Espagnol for a base.

MADEIRA SAUCE

2 *tbsp. butter*	*Freshly ground pepper*
1 *cup chopped fresh*	¼ *cup tomato paste*
mushrooms	4 *ounces Madeira*
½ *tsp. salt*	1 *cup sauce Espagnol*

1 *tsp. chopped parsley*

Melt 2 tablespoons of butter in a saucepan, and add 1 cup of chopped fresh mushrooms, about ½ teaspoon of salt, freshly ground pepper to taste, and cook until the mushrooms are brown —about 10 minutes. Then add ¼ cup of tomato paste, 4 ounces of Madeira, and 1 cup of sauce Espagnol. Let this boil gently for about 6 to 8 minutes, then add 1 teaspoon of chopped parsley, and blend.

Mornay sauce uses a base of béchamel sauce, and is used on fish or vegetables. If used on fish, use a fish stock (courtbouillon); if used on vegetables, use a vegetable stock.

MORNAY SAUCE

1 *cup béchamel sauce*	3 *tbsp. of grated Parmesan*
3 *tbsp. stock (courtbouillon*	*cheese*
for fish, or vegetable stock	1 *tbsp. butter*
for vegetables)	2 *slightly beaten egg yolks*

To 1 cup of hot béchemel sauce add 3 tablespoons of stock (court bouillon for fish, vegetable stock for vegetables), 2 slightly beaten egg yolks, and 3 tablespoons of grated Parmesan cheese. Blend well, and at the very last add 1 tablespoon of butter, bit by bit, stirring it in with a whisk. Serve hot.

Here is one of the finest sauces for game, particularly venison.

POIVRADE SAUCE

¾ lb. butter	2 bay leaves
½ medium-sized onion, chopped	4 ounces Burgundy
	1 pint sauce Espagnol
½ ounce crushed peppercorns	Salt
½ ounce crushed juniper berries	Dash Worcestershire sauce

Place ¼ pound of butter in a casserole with ½ medium-sized onion, chopped; brown a little, add ½ ounce each of crushed peppercorns and juniper berries, 2 bay leaves, and 4 ounces of Burgundy. Boil to a dry consistency, then add 1 pint of sauce Espagnol and boil for 20 minutes. Strain the sauce. Remove from the fire and add ½ pound of butter, whipping the sauce until the butter is completely invisible. Season to taste, and add a dash of Worcestershire sauce.

A white wine sauce can be made very easily by adding 2 ounces of white wine to a béchemel sauce. However, here is a rather unusual white wine sauce for fried fish.

WHITE WINE SAUCE FOR FISH

3 tbsp. butter	1 tbsp. lemon juice
1 green onion, minced	1 cup dry white wine
½ tsp. dry mustard	Salt
½ tsp. sugar	Pepper
½ cup solid-pack canned (or diced fresh) tomatoes	1 tbsp. sweet pickle relish

Sauté 1 little green onion (top and bulb), minced, in 3 tablespoons of butter until tender. Add ½ teaspoon of dry mustard, ½ teaspoon of sugar, ½ cup of canned tomatoes, 1 tablespoon of lemon juice, and 1 cup of dry American white wine. Season to taste with salt and pepper, and let simmer from 15 to 20 minutes. Add 1 tablespoon of sweet pickle relish, heat again, and serve in a gravy boat.

There are almost as many versions of barbecue sauce as there are barbecues. Everyone who owns a barbecue outfit has or devises his or her own special sauce, and that is just as it should be. In Hollywood, nearly every film star has his or her own special sauce. Rochester, the shining light on Jack Benny's program, has an excellent one, as has Dick Cromwell. But the finest, and most intriguing barbecue sauce I have ever tasted was devised by Ken Churchill, one of the top music arrangers in this country. If anyone can top his sauce for piquancy, I'd like to know about it.

BARBECUE SAUCE

2 *lbs. onions*	1 *tsp. garlic salt*
6 *large cloves garlic*	1 *tbsp. oregano*
½ *cup bacon fat*	2½ *tbsp. paprika*
½ *cup catsup*	½ *tsp. red pepper*
½ *cup chili sauce*	¼ *tsp. marjoram*
10 *ounces tomato purée*	1½ *ounces chili powder*
28 *ounces tomatoes*	1½ *tsp. salt*
12 *ounces tomato juice*	3 *bay leaves*
½ *cup light vinegar*	2 *tsp. celery salt*
½ *cup dark vinegar*	2 *tsp. onion salt*
¼ *cup rum*	1 *tbsp. brown sugar*
2 *tbsp. Beau Monde seasoning*	6 *dashes Tabasco*

½ *tsp. ground cloves*

Brown 2 pounds of onions, finely chopped, and 6 large cloves of garlic, minced, in ½ cup of bacon fat. Then add the rest of the ingredients, mixing well.

Here is a wine barbecue sauce which is excellent to brush over broiled steaks, chickens, or chops. It may be kept for several days in the refrigerator.

WINE BARBECUE SAUCE

1 *cup dry red wine*	1½ *tbsp. salt*
¼ *cup vinegar*	1 *tsp. pepper*
1 *cup olive oil*	*Dash cayenne pepper*
2 *large onions, grated*	*Pinch thyme*
2 *crushed cloves of garlic*	*Pinch marjoram*

Combine the above ingredients, stirring until the salt is dissolved. Let it stand for several hours, or overnight. Use to baste or brush over broiling steaks, chickens, or chops, applying frequently and generously during broiling. Sauce may be kept for several days; in such case, it is best to remove the garlic after the first 24 hours.

One of the things I am fondest of is spaghetti—"express" spaghetti, cooked, *al dente,* to your individual order. Plain (*al burro*) with Parmesan cheese sprinkled over it, sailor style (*marinara*), or with a rich meat sauce, it is, in my opinion, a food for the gods. I am almost (but not quite) as fond of macaroni, which is oversized spaghetti with a hole through it.

The majority of people associate spaghetti and macaroni exclusively with Italy. Yet nearly four thousand years ago the Chinese made out of wheat flour a paste that could be shaped and dried. In the latter part of the eighteenth century a club of London exquisites was called the Macaroni Club, the name having been adopted, it is said, because macaroni was their favorite dish. And don't forget Yankee Doodle, who "stuck a feather in his cap and called it macaroni."

Probably the most complete book ever published on the Italian pastas is *Macaroni Manual,* by the late Crosby Gaige. It is a veritable encyclopedia of spaghetti, macaroni, and noodle dishes, containing some 200 different ways of preparing these foods, and about 50 recipes for sauces. You'll find ways not only of cooking the pastas in soups, with meats, with poultry, fish, and seafoods, with eggs and vegetables, but of using them in salads, and, believe it or not, in desserts.

I think the tops in meat sauces for spaghetti is contained in Mr. Gaige's book. It is similar to the recipe I wangled out of an old Italian friend, who in turn had filched it from his mother. However, Mr. Gaige's recipe has a touch, or two or three, that should be an improvement, so I combined the recipes. It's rich—but then, who ever heard of a spaghetti sauce that was *maigre* (lean or thin)?

Before the recipe, a word about cooking spaghetti. First, never break it or chop it into small lengths either before or after cooking, and second, use plenty of boiling salted water. I cook mine 10 to 12 minutes, which leaves it *al dente* (firm enough to be felt under the teeth). I do not put it in a colander and run cold or hot water over it. I pick up a bunch with a wooden fork and spoon, hold it above the kettle until the water has drained from it, and then place it directly on the plate. Then a very generous portion of the sauce is ladled over the spaghetti, and it is sent to the table. Freshly grated Parmesan cheese is sprinkled over the whole, and it is eaten immediately, accompanied by crusty Italian bread, which has been spread with garlic butter and toasted in the oven. In ordering spaghetti in an Italian restaurant, ask for "express spaghetti" (cooked to your individual order). And everything is washed down with copious quantities of good Chianti. A tossed green salad is a mighty fine accompaniment. Man, O man, what a meal!

SPAGHETTI MEAT SAUCE DE LUXE

¼ cup butter	1½ cans tomato paste
1 tbsp. olive oil	½ #2 can tomatoes
½ lb. ground chuck beef	½ tbsp. Worcestershire sauce
½ lb. ground round steak	½ tbsp. Angostura bitters
½ lb. ground veal	½ tbsp. sugar
½ green pepper, chopped	½ cup dry red wine
4 cloves garlic, minced	Salt
1 large onion	Pepper
½ lb. fresh mushrooms,	½ tsp. celery salt
chopped	2 bay leaves

Dash cayenne pepper

In a large kettle heat ¼ cup of butter and 1 tablespoon of olive oil, and in this brown ½ pound each of ground chuck beef, ground round steak, and ground veal. Then add ½ green pepper, chopped, 4 cloves of garlic, minced, 1 large onion, chopped, ½ pound of fresh mushrooms, chopped, 1½ cans of tomato paste (get this at an Italian grocery), ½ large can of tomatoes, ½ tablespoon of Worcestershire sauce, ½ tablespoon of Angostura bitters, ½ tablespoon of sugar, ½ cup of good dry American red wine (Chianti type), salt and pepper to taste, ½ teaspoon of celery salt, 2 crumbled bay leaves, and a generous dash of cayenne pepper. Cover this nectar, and cook very slowly for at least 3 hours.

Spaghetti with *marinara* sauce is really spaghetti, sailor style. The true *marinara* sauce contains garlic, tomatoes, onions, and anchovies, because garlic, canned tomatoes, onions, and anchovies were always to be found among a ship's stores. But I made a sauce which I call a *marinara* sauce, only I add minced clams to it in place of the anchovies. I have never had any complaints about the sauce from Italians, so I guess they found it pretty good. I think it's terrific.

MARINARA SAUCE

4 *tbsp. olive oil*	24 *soft clams*
2 *cloves garlic*	*Salt*
2 *medium-sized onions*	*Pepper*
1 *large can tomatoes*	¼ *tsp. sugar*
½ *cup dry red wine*	¼ *tsp. oregano*

Grated Parmesan cheese

Put 4 tablespoons of pure olive oil in a heavy saucepan, and when it is hot add 2 cloves of garlic, crushed, and 2 medium-sized onions, peeled and sliced. Sauté for about 5 minutes, or until the onions are soft. Then add 1 large can of tomatoes and cook rapidly for about 5 minutes. Then lower the flame, add ½ cup of dry American red wine (Chianti type), and simmer for 1 hour.

In the meantime, clean, steam, and drain 24 soft clams. Chop them up, and add them to the tomato- and onion-mixture after it has simmered for an hour. Season the whole with salt and pepper to taste, add ¼ teaspoon of sugar, and let it cook slowly for about 10 minutes more. Then add ¼ teaspoon of oregano, stir, and keep hot over a low flame until ready to serve. Pour over spaghetti, sprinkle with grated Parmesan cheese, and serve.

((111)) EGGS AND CHEESE

Once upon a time (don't stop here, because this isn't a fairy story), the Egg wore blue denim jeans, and usually was seen in company wtih porkers. He was a fellow of low habits, most of the time being boiled or fried. He met few prominent people because he retired from the scene right after breakfast, and didn't come out of his shell again until the next morning.

But things are different now! He can be piquant in the morning; smart and dashing at noon, in his French habiliments; elegant after dark, in white tie and tails; and—Ooh, la la!—you ought to see him after midnight when he consorts with caviar and champagne! So let's look in on the egg during some of his most intriguing moments, starting with breakfast.

Of all the recipes I have, the one most people frequently ask for is what I call Eggs Parmesan. One of my most enthusiastic boosters is a very old and dear friend who manufactures batteries by day, and at night lives to eat. Ward Perry, wherever he goes, spreads the gospel of gracious living. He is not a cook, yet he makes one dish to perfection, eggs Parmesan, and wherever he goes he either gives out the recipe or, with great enthusiasm, gives a demonstration.

Eggs Parmesan is the perfect breakfast dish. But don't serve it with bacon or sausage, but just with toast or muffins, so that alien flavors will not detract from its deliciousness.

EGGS PARMESAN

2 *eggs*	*Salt*
2 *tbsp. butter*	*Freshly ground pepper*
2 *ounces sherry*	2 *tbsp. grated Parmesan cheese*

Lightly brown 2 tablespoons of butter in a skillet, and as the butter takes on color, add 2 ounces of sherry. When the liquid begins to bubble, break 2 eggs into it. As the white begins to set,

323

remove the skillet from the fire and sprinkle 2 tablespoons of grated Parmesan cheese over the eggs, after having seasoned them to taste with salt and freshly ground pepper.

Put the skillet under the broiler, and when the whites set and the cheese begins to brown, remove and serve. But watch the eggs carefully while they are under the broiler. The yolks should not be allowed to become hard, nor the cheese to burn.

Another extremely easy breakfast dish to make is eggs scrambled in anchovy butter. Scrambled eggs seem to go exceedingly well with salt fish, such as bloaters and herring, but in the following dish, the flavor of the anchovies is not too pungent.

SCRAMBLED EGGS WITH ANCHOVY BUTTER

4 *eggs*
1 *tbsp. dry white wine*

Freshly ground pepper
1 *tsp. grated Parmesan cheese*
2 *ounces anchovy butter*

Anchovy Butter

½ *cup butter*

½ *cup anchovy paste*
4 *dashes paprika*

First make the anchovy butter, combining ½ cup of butter at room temperature with ½ cup of anchovy paste and about 4 dashes of paprika. Work together until well blended with a wooden spoon.

Lightly beat together 4 eggs with a tablespoon of dry American white wine and 1 teaspoon of grated Parmesan cheese, and freshly ground pepper to taste.

Put 2 ounces (4 tablespoons) of the anchovy butter in a skillet, and when hot, add the beaten eggs, and scramble them. Serve hot.

One of the most delightful meals of the week, to my mind, is Sunday morning breakfast. It can be a leisurely meal, with every delicious mouthful savored to the utmost, and steaming hot coffee lingered over. In winter, it is fun to set up a card table in front of the fireplace, and in summer there can be no more attractive place to eat Sunday morning breakfast than in your garden, if you have one. Or serve it in the dining room or the dinette, but make the table a little gayer than usual, with colored china and a bowl of flowers.

Bacon and eggs, or ham and eggs, or boiled or scrambled eggs, are the usual breakfast fare. But on Sunday, why not try something different—something special in the way of egg dishes? The Italians have something pretty fine when they scramble eggs with ripe olives and Parmesan cheese; eggs poached in Burgundy are a French delicacy; the English have a most unusual dish called Devonshire eggs; scrambled eggs, Bombay style, are an Indian dish; *Lesco* is a Hungarian dish combining eggs and frankfurter; eggs New Orleans are a southern version of eggs Benedict; and eggs baked with a chestnut purée are something out of this world.

BAKED EGGS WITH CHESTNUT PURÉE

4 *eggs*	*Salt*
1 *lb. chestnuts*	*Pepper*
½ *cup cream*	8 *slices fried bacon*
6 *ounces dry red wine*	*Cayenne pepper*
4 *tbsp. melted butter*	1 *tbsp. chopped chives*

Get 1 pound of sound chestnuts, and cut an "X" on the flat side of each nut. Place the nuts in a pan of cold water and bring to a boil. Boil for 30 minutes, then allow the nuts to cool just to the point where they can be handled. Remove the shells and inner skins, and put through the food chopper, using a coarse blade. To the chopped chestnuts add ½ cup of hot cream, ½ cup of dry American red wine which has been heated, 1 tablespoon of melted butter, and salt and pepper to taste. Mix well, and put the chestnut purée into the bottom of a buttered casserole or baking dish.

Fry 8 slices of bacon until done, but don't let them become too crisp. Lay the bacon slices on top of the chestnut purée, and then break 4 eggs into the casserole, being careful not to break the yolks. Sprinkle over the eggs a pinch of cayenne pepper and 1 tablespoon of finely chopped chives. Mix together 3 tablespoons of melted butter and 4 tablespoons of dry American red wine, and pour over the eggs. Place the casserole in a moderate oven (350 degrees) and bake until the eggs are set.

To consume a breakfast of fish, bacon and eggs, sausage, a cold cut of ham, toast, marmalade, and tea is really throwing a handsome matutinal knife and fork, so to speak. But when that repast has been preceded somewhat earlier by a half-pound of cold steak and a pint of beer, it seems to me that the height of something or other is reached. Nevertheless, such a meal was not out of the ordinary for a young British subaltern on active duty.

Maj. Reginald Hargreaves, M.C., gives some interesting data on breakfasts in a recent gastronomical quarterly of the London Wine and Food Society. Other breakfasts of which he partook were:

Bread and butter, and a hunk of blue Vinney cheese, washed down with a draft of cider; freshly caught trout grilled over a fire on the bank of a stream from which they had just been lifted, accompanied by freshly turned bannocks (oatmeal or barley cakes baked on a griddle), and coffee; in Egypt, a handful of dates, washed down with a bowl of unsweetened mint tea; in Arabia, olives and maize bread; in Abyssinia, a bowl of strongly spiced millet porridge, accompanied by a sort of mead; in India, curried prawns or kedgeree, rounded off with excellent fruit; and, finally, in the home of the late Lord Lonsdale, a couple of peaches and a bottle of Niersteiner.

But regardless of climate and custom, the average American breakfast probably is the most satisfying and sensible of any throughout the world. A menu composed of fresh fruits in the summer or stewed fruits or fruit juices in the winter, light, easily digested cereals, eggs in various forms, or combined with bacon, ham, or sausages, toast or hot breads, and fresh, properly brewed coffee, starts the day off in a mighty pleasant and satisfactory manner.

One of the most delightful breakfast dishes I know is Eggs Omar Pasha. It is a favorite with Adolphe Menjou.

If you have little individual casseroles, use them because they're effective on either the breakfast table or the luncheon table. If you haven't any, Eggs Omar Pasha can be made in an ordinary casserole.

EGGS OMAR PASHA

Eggs   *Butter*
Chopped onion   *Grated Parmesan cheese*

Tomato Sauce

3 *slices bacon*   *Pinch summer savory*
1 *onion*   4 *peppercorns.*
2 *tbsp. carrots, chopped*   ½ *clove garlic*
1 *#2 can tomatoes*   ¼ *tsp. sugar*
Bay leaf   1 *tbsp. flour*
Pinch thyme   ¼ *cup consommé*
Pinch marjoram   2 *ounces sherry*
Pinch basil   1 *tbsp. butter*

Sauté 1 tablespoon of chopped onion (per person) in butter until tender, but not brown. Line each individual casserole with the chopped onion, then break an egg over the onion, and sprinkle with 1 teaspoon of grated Parmesan cheese. Put the casseroles into a fairly hot oven (400 degrees) and let the eggs cook until they are firm, but not hard. Then take them out, pour tomato sauce over the eggs, sprinkle with chopped parsley, and serve.

To make the tomato sauce, chop 3 slices of bacon and put them in a saucepan. When they are browned, but not crisp, add 1 onion, peeled and chopped, and 2 tablespoons of carrots, finely chopped. When the onion is tender, but not brown, add 1 large can of tomatoes, a crumbled bay leaf, a pinch each of thyme, marjoram, basil, and summer savory, 4 peppercorns, slightly bruised, ½ clove of garlic, crushed, ¼ teaspoon of sugar, 1 tablespoon of flour mixed with ¼ cup of consommé, and 2 ounces of sherry. Simmer for about 45 minutes, then strain the sauce into another saucepan, rubbing the vegetables through the sieve. Heat, add 1 tablespoon of butter, and it is ready for use.

Now, let's meet our friend, the egg, in the midst of black patent leather boots, red coats, dogs straining on the leash, eager horses, and "Tantivy!" At a hunt breakfast, this is the perfect dish.

SCRAMBLED EGGS À LA CHASSEUR

4 *eggs*	1 *tsp. chopped chives*
4 *chicken livers*	*Salt*
4 *ounces butter*	*Pepper*
8 *mushrooms*	1 *tbsp. flour*
1 *little green onion*	3 *ounces consommé*
1 *tbsp. chopped parsley*	3 *tbsp. Madeira*

Rinse 4 chicken livers in cold water, dry, and cut each one into quarters.

Melt 2 ounces of butter in a saucepan, and when hot add the chicken livers. Sauté gently for about 4 minutes, stirring frequently, then add 8 mushrooms, coarsely chopped, 1 little green onion (bulb and top), chopped, 1 tablespoon of chopped parsley, 1 teaspoon of chopped chives, salt and pepper, freshly ground, to taste, and sprinkle in 1 tablespoon of flour. Blend all these ingredients well, then add 3 ounces of consommé and 3 tablespoons of Madeira. Cover, and let simmer very gently for about 15 minutes.

Scramble 4 eggs lightly in 2 ounces of butter. Put them on a hot platter, pour the sauce over, and serve hot.

I have found, over a period of several years of experimenting, that you can scramble eggs with almost any comestible and nine times out of ten come up with a masterpiece. That epicure of the army, Col. Frank Dorn, even bakes eggs in beer. But one of the most delicious egg dishes is his scrambled eggs and almonds, which I have altered slightly, certainly not to its detriment.

SCRAMBLED EGGS AMANDINE

4 *eggs*	*Dash tabasco*
½ *cup rolled almonds*	½ *tsp. chili powder*
1 *medium-sized onion*	½ *cup chopped cooked*
½ *cup cream*	*chicken*
Salt	¼ *cup consommé*
Pepper	¼ *cup dry white wine*
4 *tbsp. butter*	

Melt 4 tablespoons of butter in a skillet, and add ½ cup of rolled almonds (rolled fine with a rolling pin), 1 medium-sized onion,

EGGS AND CHEESE 329

chopped fine, ½ cup of cream, salt and pepper to taste, a dash of Tabasco, ½ teaspoon of chili powder, ½ cup of finely chopped cooked chicken, ¼ cup of consommé, and ¼ cup of dry American white wine. Cook this mixture until brown, stirring constantly (it will burn easily if not stirred). The mixture should have just enough liquid to boil. When it becomes brown, pour in 4 lightly beaten eggs, and continue stirring until the eggs are thoroughly cooked and blended into the mixture.

I have been told that at the celebrated Cordon Bleu Cooking School in Paris it is a cardinal sin to scramble eggs in any way except in a double boiler. I remember one day, after a column of mine on scrambled eggs had appeared in the *Chicago Daily Tribune,* a friend of my mother's went to her and said, "My dear, I think your son's columns are delightful, but he certainly doesn't know how to scramble eggs. Imagine scrambling eggs in a skillet." I should have been covered with confusion and humiliated, but I wasn't. I like to scramble my eggs in plenty of butter, among other things, and as to scrambling them in a double boiler, I say to hell with it!

If you hold with the Cordon Bleu theory, go ahead and scramble your eggs *l'Indienne* in a double boiler. If not, do it my way.

SCRAMBLED EGGS À L'INDIENNE

6 *eggs*	*Salt*
2 *tsp. curry powder*	*Pepper*
Dry white wine	1 *tbsp. finely chopped tart*
Cream	*apple*
3 *tbsp. butter*	

Make a smooth paste of 2 teaspoons of curry powder and an equal amount of dry American white wine and cream (about ½ teaspoon of each). The paste should be on the thin side rather than on the thick.

Beat 6 eggs thoroughly, add salt and pepper to taste, then add the curry paste and blend well.

Melt 3 tablespoons of butter in a skillet, and when hot, add the eggs and curry, and scramble them. When the eggs are about half done, add about a tablespoon of finely chopped tart apple. Finish the scrambling to your taste, and serve.

Egg dishes are, of course, international. I don't suppose there is a country in the world that doesn't eat eggs in one form or another. In the wilds of Borneo they are highly regarded, and in highly civilized England plover eggs are a great delicacy. I have a friend who'll eat nothing but duck's eggs and who raises ducks principally for their eggs. In Turkey, eggs are boiled for 12 hours in olive oil and Turkish coffee. Believe it or not, they're delicious. In Mexico, they poach eggs in a sauce made of mashed green chilis, onions, and garlic, and their *Huevos con Hongos* (eggs with mushrooms) are pretty terrific.

SCRAMBLED EGGS MEXICAN

6 *eggs*	1 *medium-sized onion*
4 *tbsp. butter*	½ *tsp. chili powder*
½ *cup sliced fresh mush-rooms*	½ *tsp. salt*
	Small pinch oregano
2 *ounces sherry*	3 *tbsp. cream*
Triangles of buttered toast	

Put 2 tablespoons of butter in a saucepan, and when hot, add ½ cup of thinly sliced mushrooms. Sauté gently until tender—about 10 minutes. Then blend in 2 ounces of sherry, and keep warm.

Put 2 tablespoons of butter in a skillet, and when hot, add 1 medium-sized onion, peeled and chopped, and blend in ½ teaspoon of chili powder. Sauté until onions are tender, then add the mushrooms and sherry from the saucepan. Now add 6 lightly beaten eggs to the onion and mushroom mixture, together with about ½ teaspoon of salt, a small pinch of oregano, and 3 tablespoons of cream. Scramble the eggs until just set, then serve on triangles of buttered toast.

Eggs combine beautifully with cheese as well as olives. Add a bit of sherry, and you have a delectable combination.

EGGS SCRAMBLED WITH CHEESE AND OLIVES

4 *eggs*	2 *ounces sherry*
12 *ripe olives*	*Salt*
1 *cake Philadelphia cream*	*Pepper*
cheese	2 *tbsp. butter*
3 *tbsp. olive oil*	1 *little green onion*

1 *tbsp. chopped parsley*

Pit and coarsely chop 12 ripe olives.

In a mixing bowl mash 1 cake of Philadelphia cream cheese, then add 3 tablespoons of pure olive oil, the chopped olives, 2 ounces of sherry, salt and pepper to taste, and 4 eggs, lightly beaten. Mix these ingredients thoroughly.

Melt 2 tablespoons of butter in a heavy skillet, then add 1 little green onion (bulb and top), chopped, and 1 tablespoon of parsley, chopped. Cook about 3 minutes, then add the cheese-and-egg mixture. Cook over a low flame, stirring constantly, until the eggs are cooked to the desired consistency.

The Hungarians like to combine eggs with other ingredients to make lusty breakfast dishes. I have found that a great many Americans enjoy the Magyar food from the very first bite, largely because it is sufficiently different from American food to be piquant and exciting. Eggs *Lesco* is a typical egg dish.

EGGS LESCO

4 *eggs*	1 *tbsp. paprika*
3 *fresh frankfurters*	*Salt*
3 *tbsp. butter*	*Pepper*
1 *sweet onion*	1 *large ripe tomato*
2 *tbsp. chopped green pepper*	2 *ounches sherry*

In a skillet melt 3 tablespoons of butter, and when hot, add 1 sweet onion, peeled and chopped, 2 tablespoons of chopped green pepper, and 3 fresh frankfurters, cut into ½-inch pieces. Sprinkle over the contents of the skillet 1 tablespoon of paprika, salt and pepper to taste, and sauté for about 5 minutes. Then add 1 large ripe tomato, peeled and cut into eighths, and 2 ounces of sherry. Let all simmer gently for about 15 to 20 minutes, then break 4 eggs into the skillet, and scramble all together until the eggs are just set. Serve hot.

There's not much of a trick to poaching eggs. Add plenty of salt and just a few drops of vinegar to the water in which they're poached.

Unless people are experimentally minded, they are likely to fall into the habit of cooking eggs in one of three ways: frying, boiling, or scrambling. But eggs are one of the most versatile of foods, and can be prepared in almost endless ways. I thought I knew most of the tricks with eggs, but I ran across a new one, a year or so ago, that I had never heard of and, of course, had never sampled. So I tried it one morning, and was it good, to say nothing of being quick and simple—eggs poached in mushroom soup.

EGGS POACHED IN MUSHROOM SOUP

2 *eggs*	*Dry white wine*
1 *can condensed cream of*	*Salt*
mushroom soup	*Pepper*
	Buttered toast slices

Empty a can of condensed cream of mushroom soup into a shallow saucepan. Then add enough dry American white wine (between ¼ and ½ cup) to make it of sauce consistency. Heat over a low flame until the liquid simmers, then break 2 eggs into the sauce, season with salt and pepper to taste, and cover the pan and simmer for about 3 minutes, or until the whites of the eggs set. Carefully remove the eggs to buttered toast slices, and pour the sauce over them.

Eggs can be poached very profitably in white wine or in sherry, but it seems like a waste of good spirits unless the wine can be combined with other ingredients and used as a sauce to pour over the poached eggs.

Some people claim that red wine does not go well with eggs, yet one of the great gourmet dishes, particularly in the Burgundy district of France, is eggs poached in a red wine sauce. It really is a delightful gastronomic experience.

POACHED EGGS IN RED WINE SAUCE

Eggs	*Small bay leaf*
Buttered toast slices	*Salt*
3 tbsp. butter	*Pepper*
Tiny sliver garlic	*Pinch thyme*
1 white onion	*2 cups dry red wine*
2 tbsp. chopped celery	*1 tsp. flour*

Put 2 tablespoons of butter in a heavy saucepan, and a tiny sliver of garlic. When the butter is hot, add 1 white onion, peeled and chopped, and 2 tablespoons of chopped celery. Sauté these until tender (but not brown) and then add a small bay leaf, salt and pepper to taste, and a tiny pinch of thyme. Simmer together for about 10 to 12 minutes.

While the sauce is simmering, toast as many slices of bread as there are persons to be served. Cut a circle about 2 inches in diameter out of the center of each slice, which should then be buttered and kept warm.

After the sauce has simmered the required length of time, break 1 egg per person on the edge of the saucepan and slip it carefully into the simmering sauce. Poach for from 2 to 3 minutes (depending upon the desired consistency of the eggs), and carefully remove with a skimmer to the toast slices. Strain the sauce through a fine sieve into another saucepan, thicken with blended 2 teaspoons of butter creamed with 1 teaspoon of flour, heat, and pour over the poached eggs. Serve immediately.

One of the classical egg dishes is eggs Benedictine, or eggs Benedict, as it is more often called. The recipe is more or less standard —a thin slice of ham is placed on an English muffin, and is topped by a poached egg. Then the whole is covered with a Hollandaise sauce.

I've often wondered how and where the dish got its name. Was it evolved by the Benedictine monks, who, hundreds of years ago, were really gourmets? If not, why is the dish called eggs Benedictine, when there is no Benedictine in the recipe? I've searched through many source books, but to date I haven't found the answer. So, I decided to experiment, and here's the recipe for this well-known dish which does contain Benedictine!

EGGS BENEDICTINE

4 *eggs*   *Butter*
2 *English muffins*   4 *thin slices ham*
                   Benedictine Hollandaise sauce

Benedictine Hollandaise Sauce

3 *egg yolks*   1½ *tbsp. dry white wine*
1 *tsp. water*   ½ *tbsp. Benedictine*
6 *ounces butter*   ⅛ *tsp. salt*

Split, toast, and butter 2 English muffins and keep warm.

Lightly sauté 4 thin slices of ham, about ⅛ inch thick and cut into pieces about 4 inches square, in a little butter until the ham is heated through. Place ham slices on the English muffin halves.

Poach 4 eggs, drain them, and put a poached egg on each ham-topped muffin half. Then pour over them a Benedictine Hollandaise sauce and serve immediately.

The Benedictine Hollandaise sauce is made thusly: Put enough water in the bottom part of a double boiler to reach about 1 inch below the bottom of the top part of the double boiler. Bring the water almost to the boiling point, *but do not let it boil.*

Put the yolks of 3 eggs and 1 teaspoon of water in the top of a double boiler. Beat with a wire whisk (or a slotted spoon) until creamy. Now add, bit by bit, the butter, beating or stirring constantly. Have each addition of butter thoroughly blended before the next is added. Continue beating or stirring gently, and add, little by little, 1½ tablespoons of dry American white wine with which has been mixed ½ tablespoon of Benedictine. When all the wine has been added, remove the top of the double boiler from the bottom part, to prevent further cooking, and add ⅛ teaspoon of salt.

This will yield approximately 1 cup of sauce.

If you've noticed throughout this book the type of cheese I most often specify is Parmesan cheese. I don't think its subtle and tangy flavor can be beaten. Yet for plain eating my favorite cheese is Swiss. This cheese seems to go particularly well in the following baked egg recipe.

SWISS EGGS

6 *eggs*   1 *tbsp. chopped parsley*
Butter   *Salt*
Thin slices Swiss cheese   *Freshly ground pepper*
1 *little green onion, chopped*   1 *cup cream*
                 ½ *cup dry white wine*

Generously butter the bottom and sides of a shallow fireproof baking dish. Line the sides and bottom with slices of Swiss cheese not over ⅛ inch thick. Sprinkle over the cheese on the bottom of the casserole 1 little green onion (top and bulb), finely minced, and 1 tablespoon of chopped parsley. Now drop in 6 eggs, being careful not to break the yolks, and distributing the eggs evenly over the bottom of the casserole. Add salt and freshly ground pepper to taste, 1 cup of cream, and ½ cup of dry American white wine.

Place in a 300-degree oven, and cook for 10 to 15 minutes. Remove, stir the mixture in the casserole, and serve from the casserole.

My friend, Olive Chester, whom I mentioned as being such a terrific fish cook, bakes eggs with chicken livers. This is another example of red wine combined with eggs to delight the palate.

BAKED EGGS WITH CHICKEN LIVERS

8 *eggs*   *Salt*
1 *lb. chicken livers*   *Pepper*
2 *ounces butter*   ¼ *cup cream*
              ¼ *cup dry Madeira*

Sauté 1 pound of chicken livers in 2 ounces of butter for about 8 minutes. Then season with salt and pepper to taste.

Beat 8 eggs together with ¼ cup cream and ¼ cup of dry Madeira. Pour the eggs into a well-buttered baking dish or casserole, add the livers, and bake in a slow oven (325 degrees) for about 25 minutes, covered. Serve hot.

For my money, there is a great deal of balderdash about the making of an omelet. One chef is said to have one secret, another is alleged to have a different one. Then there are those abominations—the one-dish amateur chefs, who, if their specialty happens to be the making of an omelet, try to surround the preparation (and sometimes even the cooking) with a tremendous air of mystery.

There seems to be two schools of omelet-makers (the serious ones, I mean). One group say to beat the whites and the yolks of the eggs separately, then combine them. This makes for a very fluffy omelet, almost a soufflé. The other school beats the entire egg.

The most famous place in the world for omelets is Mont-Saint-Michel, a tiny islet off the coast of France between Saint-Malo and Avranches, in the Gulf of St. Malo. There is a very old and very famous monastery on Mont-Saint-Michel, and on the winding street that leads up to the monastery there are about a dozen restaurants. The specialty of all of them is the omelet. But one of them, Saint-Michel la Tête d'Or, was owned by Mother Poulard, who is regarded as the mother of the omelet.

There are really only a few simple rules for the making of a good omelet. The skillet should be very hot before the eggs are put in. Although it may seem very silly, the skillet used for making an omelet should never be washed with water. I must admit to having a heavy iron skillet, 8 inches across, that I keep for making omelets, and it is never washed. When I have finished with it, I wipe it very carefully with paper toweling, and put it away.

The eggs (for 4 people use 5 eggs) should be beaten thoroughly and well. The more they are beaten (with a fork, not an egg beater), the lighter the omelet will be. Then the eggs are seasoned with salt and pepper to taste. As I said, the skillet (or pan) should be very hot. Put in enough butter to cover the bottom of the pan (about 1 tablespoon) and when it gives off a characteristic nutty smell, put in the eggs quickly. Stir briskly with a fork in order to heat the whole mass evenly, then press the edges back toward the center, so that the soft part will run immediately to fill the vacant spaces. When the eggs do not run easily, but are still soft, press the handle of the pan downward, and let the omelet slide toward it. When a third of the flat omelet has slid up the side of the pan, fold this third over with the aid of a spatula or knife. Then raise the handle of the pan to slide the omelet in the opposite direction,

and when that third is all the way up of the edge of the pan
farthest from you, hold a heated dish under it, and as the rim of
the omelet touches the dish, raise the handle of the pan more and
more until the pan is turned upside down. And, *voila!* you have an
oval-shaped, golden-brown omelet.

There are gadgets on the market which allegedly make certain
types of egg cookery very easy. One which I don't particularly
object to and have used on occasion myself is an individual egg
poacher. But when it comes to omelet pans, I draw the line.
In the first place, they take all the fun out of making omelets,
and I think the use of an omelet pan isn't quite cricket. Furthermore, I never yet have seen an omelet that was made in this
mechanical contrivance that was worthy of the name.

Here is an omelet that makes a pretty terrific dinner dish—
a lobster omelet. In its easiest form, it is made with canned lobster
meat, but fresh cooked lobster meat makes it even more delicious.

LOBSTER OMELET

5 *eggs*	1 *cup medium cream*
Salt	2 *tbsp. sherry*
Freshly ground pepper	1 *egg yolk*
Butter	1 *tbsp. milk*
1 *tbsp. flour*	*Pinch paprika*
1 *cup chicken broth*	1 *tsp. chopped parsley*
1 *can lobster meat*	

Melt a tablespoon of butter in a medium-sized saucepan, then
blend in a tablespoon of flour until the mixture is quite smooth.
Next add 1 cup of chicken broth, 1 cup of coffee cream, and
2 tablespoons of sherry. When the mixture is thick, remove the
saucepan from the fire, and stir in 1 egg yolk mixed with 1 tablespoon of milk. Season with salt and pepper to taste; add a
generous pinch of paprika and a teaspoon of chopped parsley.
Have ready 1 can of lobster meat cut in medium-sized pieces (or
an equal amount of fresh cooked lobster). Sauté these in butter
until thoroughly hot, then add them to the sauce. Put the saucepan
on a mat over the lowest possible flame (you just want to keep it
hot, don't even let it simmer) while you make your omelet. In
making the omelet, allow 1 egg per person plus 1 extra egg (for

4 people, use 5 eggs). When the omelet is done, pour the lobster sauce over it, and serve.

One of the fanciest omelets I have ever eaten is a creation of the fabulous Colonel Frank Dorn. Its name, *Tortilla Pomposo,* is misleading. *Tortillas,* which are Mexican paper-thin cakes made from corn meal, and baked on a griddle, are not used. This dish is an omelet made in a special Dorn manner, with a magnificent sauce. It is a perfect luncheon dish, or a *pièce de résistance* at a late supper party. The use of chocolate is typically Mexican.

TORTILLA POMPOSO

Eggs (2 per person)	Dash Tabasco
4 strips bacon	½ tsp. peppercorns
2 green peppers	½ tsp. sage
2 onions	1 cup dry red wine
6 bay leaves	2 cups sliced mushrooms
2 tbsp. chili powder	Cornstarch
½ cup unsweetened chocolate	1 tbsp. rich cream (per egg)
Pinch salt	Butter
	Almond paste

Brown 4 strips of chopped bacon, 2 green peppers, chopped, 2 onions, chopped, and 6 bay leaves in a saucepan. Then add 2 tablespoons of chili powder, ½ cup of Mexican (or unsweetened) chocolate, ground and made into a paste, a pinch of salt, a dash of Tabasco, ½ teaspoon of whole peppercorns, ½ teaspoon of sage, and 1 cup of American dry red wine (claret type), and when the mixture comes to a boil stir for 15 minutes. Add enough cornstarch to bring the mixture to the consistency of thin gruel. Then add 2 cups of sliced fresh mushrooms, and allow the sauce to simmer for 10 minutes.

In the meantime, prepare an omelet, allowing 2 strictly fresh eggs per person. Beat the whites separately, using 1 tablespoon of heavy sweet cream per egg. Then fold in the beaten yolks. Pour the entire mixture into a frying pan containing enough butter to cover the entire bottom and sides of the pan, let it raise on top of the stove, then place in a slow oven (300 degrees) for 15 minutes. Finally, pour the sauce over the omelet, and serve with strips of dry toast spread with almond paste. Sauce should serve four people.

SPANISH OMELET

5 *eggs*	*Salt*
1 *tbsp. butter*	*Freshly ground pepper*

Spanish Sauce

2 *tbsp. butter*	2 *cups canned tomatoes*
1 *clove garlic*	*Pinch coriander*
1 *onion*	*Cayenne pepper*
½ *green pepper*	1 *tsp. salt*
6 *green olives*	2 *ounces sherry*

Put 2 tablespoons of butter in a sancepan, and add 1 clove of garlic, chopped. When the butter is hot, add 1 onion, peeled and chopped, ½ green pepper, chopped, and 6 green olives, pitted and chopped coarsely. Sauté these for a few minutes, until the onions and pepper are tender. Then add 2 cups of canned tomatoes, a pinch of coriander, a slight sprinkling of cayenne pepper, 1 teaspoon of salt, and 2 ounces of sherry. Simmer until the moisture has nearly evaporated.

Make an omelet with 5 eggs. Before folding it, add 2 tablespoons of the Spanish sauce in the center. Then complete the omelet, place on a hot platter, and pour the rest of the sauce over it.

Would you ever guess that there is a right and a wrong way to hard-boil eggs? I didn't, for a long time. But when I found out the right way, I've used it ever since.

The wrong way is to put eggs into boiling water, let them boil furiously for several minutes, and then take out of the water, cool —if they are to be used for garnish—or shell them as soon as they can be handled if they are to be used warm.

The right way is to have your water just below the simmering point. Put the eggs in, and leave them in for 15 to 20 minutes, keeping the water "smiling," as the French say. Then remove them, cover them with cold water, and put them away in the refrigerator if they are to be used as a garnish, or let them cool sufficiently to handle if they are to be used warm.

I suppose everyone remembers that fascinating wench, Du Barry. She had a way, I understand, with Louis XV, of France. And she must have had a way, too, with our friend the egg. I don't know whether or not she invented the following dish, or whether it was named after her by an admirer. But I do know the result is delicious.

EGGS DU BARRY

6 *eggs*	1 *cup light dry red wine*
1 *tbsp. butter*	½ *cup consommé*
¾ *cup lean raw ham*	*Salt*
6 *small mild onions*	*Pepper*
8 *medium-sized mushrooms*	½ *tsp. sugar*
1 *tbsp. flour*	*Pinch marjoram*
½ *clove garlic*	*Pinch thyme*

Melt a generous tablespoon of butter in a heavy saucepan, and when it is sizzling hot, add ¾ cup of lean raw ham cut in strips, and 6 small mild onions, quartered. Sauté these until they are light brown, and then add 8 medium-sized mushrooms, quartered. Cook for about 2 minutes, then sprinkle a level tablespoon of flour into the mixture, and stir well while it browns. Pour in 1 cup of light dry American red wine and ½ cup of consommé. Add salt and pepper to taste, ½ teaspoon of sugar, ½ clove of garlic, and a pinch each of marjoram and thyme. Bring the mixture to a boil, then cover and simmer for about 20 minutes.

While the sauce is cooking, hard-boil 6 eggs. When the eggs are done, cool them just enough so that they can be handled, remove the shells, and halve them. Put on rounds of buttered toast, and pour the sauce over them.

Cheese and wine are the best companions in the gastronomic world. One of the best desserts it is possible to serve is fruit, cheese, and wine, all in their natural state.

Perhaps a dissertation on cheese belongs in the chapter on desserts, but there are so many uses to which cheese can be put in every type of cooking that I'd like to list some of the great cheeses.

By and large, America makes wonderful cheeses. Although it isn't seen very often nowadays, an aged Herkimer County (New York) cheese was right at the top of all cheeses, domestic or imported. Wisconsin today makes many great cheeses, some of them equalling, or even surpassing, their imported counterparts.

There are some imported cheeses, however, that Americans don't seem able to duplicate, such as Parmesan, Roquefort (although I have tasted an Oregon blue cheese that came damn near an imported Roquefort), French Brie, Bel Paese, and Strachino de Milano. I have never seen a domestic Mozzarella, a moist, smooth, white, unsalted Italian cheese with a very delicate flavor. And I've never tasted the domestic counterpart of an aged Stilton cheese.

One of the greatest delicacies in the world is cheese with wine in it. For years certain cheeses imported into the United States were filled with wine, but their cost was such that only plutocrats could afford them. But you can easily do the same trick right in your own home. Just cut four cylindrical plugs in a cheese, remove them and cut about an inch from each end. Replace the short plugs in the hole, fill the holes with wine, and replace the top plugs. Let the cheese remain intact for about two weeks, changing the position of the cheese every day or so, in order that the wine may permeate every part of the cheese. And what wine? Well, port for Stilton, sherry or Madeira for Gorgonzola, sauterne for Edam or Cheddar cheeses.

No mention of cheese would be complete without including two cheeses which have recently appeared upon the market—garlic cheese and anchovy cheese. These are put up in cellophane-wrapped cylinders, and are out of this world when spread on crackers and served with cocktails.

There is something intimate and gay about chafing dish suppers —and chafing dish breakfasts, for that matter. They give a lift to the host, too, for he holds the center of the stage. Things seem to taste better when served direct from the chafing dish to the plate, for there is no cooling-off process such as there is bound to be when food has to come to the table from the kitchen.

Welsh rabbit is the classic chafing dish recipe, and to my mind, there is only one thing to make it with—stale ale or beer. My father was a master at making Welsh rabbit, and here's how he did it.

WELSH RABBIT

1 *bottle stale ale*	1 *tbsp. dry mustard*
1 *lb. sharp American cheese*	1 *tbsp. Worcestershire sauce*
1 *tbsp. butter*	*Dash cayenne pepper*
Dash paprika	

In the morning he opened a bottle of ale and allowed it to stand all day; also, a pound of sharp American cheese was cut into small dice. Then, at night, when the guests were seated round the table after a game of five hundred or whist, the spirit lamp under the chafing dish was lighted, and a tablespoon of butter was melted in the pan. Next, the cheese was added, and melted very slowly. One tablespoon of dry mustard, a tablespoon of Worcestershire sauce, and a dash of cayenne pepper were mixed with a tablespoon of ale in a cup. As the cheese melted, the seasonings were added and stirred in, and then the ale was added very slowly as the mixture was being stirred constantly in one direction only. When everything had blended (be careful that the cheese never bubbles), it was poured over slices of toast, a dash of paprika added, and everyone fell to without delay. Of course, the beverage was cold ale, or beer.

One of the specialties of Savoie and Switzerland is a fondue made with butter, Swiss cheese, and white wine. It has the consistency of cheese custard, and can be flavored in a number of different ways.

A favorite dish of King Edward VII, who lived most of his life as the Prince of Wales and all of his life as a prince of gourmets, was Neufchâtel Fondue. Like Welsh Rabbit, the fondue should be made in a chafing dish. But unlike the Welsh rabbit, it should not be spread over toast or crackers, but should be eaten from the chafing dish. Crusty French bread is served with it. Each guest breaks pieces from the bread, puts the piece of bread on a fork, and "dunks" the bread in the fondue, giving it a stir as he or she does so. This is a dish that is not only delightful and delectable, but one that you can have fun serving. There's nothing that breaks the ice at any party (outside of cocktails, of course) like everybody "dunking" in the same dish.

SWISS FONDUE

1 *lb. Swiss cheese, grated*	1 *cup very dry white wine*
3 *tbsp. flour*	*Salt*
Garlic	*Freshly ground pepper*
2 *tbsp. butter*	*Pinch nutmeg*
3 *tbsp. chopped chives*	2 *ounces kirsch*

Mix together 1 pound of Swiss cheese, grated, and 3 tablespoons of flour.

Put 2 tablespoons of butter in the top of a chafing dish, which has been lightly rubbed with a split clove of garlic. When the butter is hot, add 3 tablespoons of finely chopped chives, and sauté them for 1 minute. Then add 1 cup of very dry American white wine, and bring the liquid just up to the boiling point, but do not allow to boil. Keep it simmering and add the cheese and flour mixture slowly, and stir constantly in one direction until the cheese is melted. Continue to stir while adding salt and freshly ground pepper to taste and a pinch of nutmeg.

When the mixture starts to bubble (you're still stirring), add 2 ounces of kirsch (the Swiss Kirsch Dettling Superior Vieux, if you can get it), and when the kirsch has been added, serve immediately.

I have been wondering where to put the following recipe, inasmuch as there is no chapter on breads, rolls, biscuits, and so forth. So, because the recipe calls for an egg, I am including here the recipe for Hush Puppies.

This is not only a very delicious item, but it has an interesting story behind it, which was furnished me by the *Corn Belt Farm Dairies*. It seems that in the old days of the deep South, fish fries were one of the leading social events. Families, friends, children, and hound dogs attended in full force. Suspended over a roaring fire there was always a big kettle of deep fat in which the fish were fried, notably cat fish. The batter was prepared, the cat fish were dipped in it, and then dropped into the kettle of boiling fat. If you've ever attended a fish fry, you know what tantalizing odors impregnate the surrounding atmosphere. People could do something about it, but all the hound dogs could do was to yowl a hungry appeal. So the cooks would drop spoonfuls of the batter into the fat and when they were a golden brown, they would take them out and toss them to the hungry dogs, saying "Hush, puppies. Hush puppies." And it seemed to work like a charm. Allegedly, on one fish fry, a cook decided to sample one of these magic morsels. He tasted the cooked tidbit, smacked his lips in approval, and gave it the name which had been used in addressing the hounds—"Hush, Puppies." And, ever since, it has become a necessary complement to fish fries and a delight to southern gourmets. If you attended the Chicago Railroad Fair in 1949, and ate in the Illinois Central all-electric dining car, you tasted hush puppies prepared exactly in the following manner. Everyone voted them marvelous!

HUSH PUPPIES

1 *egg*	1½ *tsp. baking powder*
1 *cup cornmeal*	¼ *tsp. black pepper*
1 *tbsp. flour*	1 *large mild onion*
½ *tsp. salt*	½ to ¾ *cup sweet milk*

Sift together 1 cup of cornmeal, 1 tablespoon of flour, ½ teaspoon of salt, 1½ teaspoons of baking powder, and ¼ teaspoon of black pepper. Then add 1 large mild onion, peeled and chopped fine, and 1 egg. Mix and beat well, and then add, a little at a time, about ½ to ¾ cup of sweet milk. Beat the batter well until it is smooth, and drop, by tablespoons, from the side of the spoon into at least 2 inches of hot fat (375 degrees) and fry until golden brown. Dip the hush puppies out with a perforated spoon, let them drain a moment, and then serve them sizzling hot.

(12) DESSERTS

Of all the desserts ever devised, none is more delicious, more effective, or swankier to serve than *Crêpes Suzette*. These glorified pancakes, so thin and delicate, combined with a rich *crêpe* butter and pungent liqueurs, have the most delectable flavor imaginable. Their final preparation at the table, with blue flames dancing above the chafing dish, brings an air of enchantment to the most simple setting. And although they are supposed to be quite expensive (and are in top bracket restaurants), they are not too costly to serve in the home occasionally.

There are many stories about the origin of *Crêpes Suzette*. Henri Charpentier, one of the great showmen chefs in America for the last 40 years, told me one afternoon in his restaurant on North Dearborn Street in Chicago that he originated them by accident in Paris while serving the celebrated gourmet, King Edward VII of England.

As Henri was preparing *crêpes* for the king, the sauce accidentally caught fire. For a moment he was horrified, then had an inspiration. He carried the flaming pan in which the crêpes were immersed to the table, and when the fire had died out, he served the little pancakes to the king and his party. Edward pronounced them delicious and asked what Henri called them. "They have just been invented, sir," Henri replied, "and they shall be called 'Crêpes Princesse.'" The king smiled, but shook his head. "Where is your gallantry, Henri?" he asked. Then, indicating the young daughter of his host, he announced, "They shall be called Crêpes Suzette, in mademoiselle's honor."

On the other hand, there is a well-known story which credits the origin of *Crêpes Suzette* to a chef in the reign of Louis XV, of France. According to the story, Princess Suzette de Carignan was infatuated with the king, and one afternoon when she was entertaining him and a group of his fellow huntsmen in the forest of

Fontainebleau, she ordered her chef, Jean Reboux, to create an unusual dish. *Crêpes Suzette* were the alleged result.

But let's go right into your own home and whip up some *Crêpes Suzette,* exactly as good as Henri's or Reboux's.

CRÊPES SUZETTE

1½ cups sifted flour	¼ cup melted butter
¼ cup powdered sugar	2 tbsp. orange curaçao
Generous pinch salt	1 tsp. grated lemon rind
1 cup milk	5 eggs

Crêpe Butter

½ cup sweet butter	Grated rind 1 small lemon
1 cup powdered sugar	½ cup orange juice
Grated rind 1 orange	2 ounces yellow chartreuse

Crêpe Sauce

1 jigger Grand Marnier	1 jigger kirsch

1 jigger brandy

Combine in a mixing bowl 1½ cups of sifted flour, ¼ cup of powdered sugar, and a generous pinch of salt. Stir in slowly 1 cup of milk, ¼ cup of melted butter, 2 tablespoons of orange curaçao, and 1 teaspoon of grated lemon rind. Next add 5 well-beaten whole eggs, and beat the mixture vigorously until it is very smooth and of about the consistency of cream. Cover and let stand for about half an hour.

Grease a 5- or 7-inch skillet well with butter and when it is hot, put in enough batter to cover the bottom of the skillet with a thin layer (this will be about 2 or 3 tablespoons, depending on the size of the pan). Let the batter fry for a few seconds, then lift the pan from the flame and tilt it from side to side so that the cakes will be of uniform thickness. Cook until one side is brown (about 1 minute), then turn and fry the second side until brown. Take out the *crêpe,* roll up, and set aside. Continue this procedure until all the *crêpes* are made, keeping them warm.

To make the *crêpe* or Suzette butter, cream ½ cup of sweet butter in a bowl until light, then add 1 cup of powdered sugar, the grated rinds of 1 orange and 1 small lemon, ½ cup of orange juice, and 2 ounces of yellow chartreuse, poured in very slowly. Continue to beat until thoroughly blended.

For the final preparation, put a portion of the Suzette butter in a chafing dish, melting it over the low flame. Add as many of the rolled *crêpes* as the pan will comfortably hold, turn them so that they will heat through, then pour over them in the pan about a jigger each of Grand Marnier, kirsch, and brandy. Set them alight, and, tilting the top of the chafing dish from side to side, let the pan blaze for a moment. Then spoon out the *crêpes* and the liquid to individual plates. Repeat until all the *crêpes* are used, then stand up to take bows!

CRÊPES MONTE CARLO

Crêpes are prepared exactly as for *Crêpes Suzette*. But instead of rolling them, lay them flat on a hot plate, stacking about 5 of them. As they are stacked, pour about a pony (¾ ounce) of a different flavored liqueur over each one.

For instance, pour over the first *crêpe* curaçao, over the second Crème de Cacao, over the third yellow chartreuse, over the fourth Benedictine, and over the fifth crème de violette, or vary any other liqueurs to your taste.

I never feel quite satisfied with a dinner, no matter how good, unless it is topped by a sweet of some sort. Even a bit of jelly with cream cheese, or a sharp and pungent cheese accompanied by a fairly sweet liqueur, suffices nicely. I am very fond of ice cream combinations, fruits marinated in wine or liqueurs, and pies, particularly apple, mince, cherry, and that out-of-this-world concoction of the Little Woman, Florida lime pie. But when it comes to cake, I take a run-out powder whenever I can without offending my hostess. The only exception I can think of is chocolate layer cake—when the chocolate icing and layers are at least half inch thick. Even then, I eat all of the chocolate and leave a good share of the cake!

Early in 1949 I had the pleasure of dining with that grand young man of 70-odd years, Karl Eitel, head of the Bismarck Hotel, in Chicago. The occasion was the opening of the delightful Swiss Chalet room, a room that brings a bit of Switzerland right into the Middle West. After serving a succession of delicious German dishes, accompanied by bottles of Piesporter, a Moselle of subtle dryness and flowery bouquet, the waiter set before me a piece of cake! Inwardly shrinking, I took a bite. I was entranced! In fact, so much so, that I unblushingly accepted a second slice and consumed it to the last crumb. Later I obtained the recipe from Walter Striedieck, the pastry chef, and now I'm passing it on to you. It's called Swiss Napoleon cake.

SWISS NAPOLEON CAKE

Puff Paste

2 *cups bread flour*	¾ *cup cool water*
8 *ounces butter*	¼ *tsp. salt*

Pastry Cream

1 *pint milk*	4 *ounces sugar*
1 *ounce Grand Marnier*	1 *ounce cornstarch*
Pinch salt	3 *egg yolks*

Whipping Cream

½ *pint whipping cream* (32%)	3 *ounces sugar*

Icing

4 *ounces powdered sugar*	1 *drop orange coloring*
1 *drop pink coloring*	4 *tbsp. water*

Butter Cream

2 *ounces butter*	1 *ounce shortening*
3 *ounces powdered sugar*	1 *tsp. crème de violette*

The procedure for making the puff paste is as follows: Mix 2 cups of bread flour, ¼ teaspoon of salt, and about ¾ cup of cool water. The dough should be of medium consistency (not too soft and not too firm). If the dough is sticky, add only enough more flour to facilitate kneading. Put it in the refrigerator for 1 hour. Then take it out, roll it out into a 12-inch-square piece. Place ⅓ of the 8 ounces of butter in the center of the rolled-out dough. Fold in all four sides toward the center. Roll it out again, fold all four sides into the center. Roll it out a third time, and fold all four sides into the center. Now again put the dough into the refrigerator, and let it remain for 1 hour. The above constitutes *one* rolling.

Repeat the above directions for the second rolling, using the second third of the 8 ounces of butter. Replace dough in the refrigerator for 1 hour.

Repeat the above directions for the third rolling, using the remaining third of the 8 ounces of butter.

The last step is to divide the dough into 3 parts, roll each part into the size of a 10-inch round cake form, and bake for 15 minutes in a 350-degree oven. Watch it carefully, as it should not be allowed to become too dark in color.

To make the pastry cream, bring ¾ pint of milk to the boiling point; add 1 ounce of Grand Marnier, pinch of salt, 4 ounces of sugar, and 1 ounce of butter. Mix ¼ pint of milk with 1 ounce of cornstarch and 3 egg yolks, and pour into boiling milk while stirring. Let cool.

Prepare whipping cream by adding 3 ounces of sugar to ½ pint of 32% cream, and whip slowly until stiff.

For the icing, mix into a smooth paste 4 ounces of powdered sugar, 1 drop each of pink coloring and orange coloring, and 4 tablespoons of water.

To put the cake together, spread pastry cream on a layer of puff paste, add another layer of puff paste and spread the whipping cream on top of this. Then cover with the third layer of puff paste and pour icing all over and let the cake dry before decorating.

To decorate (at the Bismarck they form edelweiss flowers, but you can use any design you choose), make a butter cream of 2 ounces of butter, 3 ounces of powdered sugar, 1 ounce of shortening, and 1 teaspoon of crème de violette. Whip these ingredients well, place in a pastry bag, and go to it on the decoration.

A swell dessert that's a quickie to prepare is what I call brandy cake. It is light, as it utilizes sponge cake.

BRANDY CAKE

Individual sponge cake	*2 tbsp. blackberry jelly*
3 tbsp. rum	*½ cup brandy*

For each portion, hollow the center of an individual sponge cake, place the cake on a plate, and pour over it 3 tablespoons of rum. Put 2 tablespoons of blackberry jelly, or your favorite jelly, in the center cavity. Around the edge of the cake pour ½ cup of brandy, ignite, and serve.

Cheesecake has a totally different meaning to a newspaper man from what it has to a gourmet. In City Room parlance, cheesecake is another name for leg art. When a gorgeous and curvaceous celebrity arrives anyplace by (a) boat, (b) train, (c) just arrives, the photographers will importune the G. and C. celebrity to display a little cheesecake, i.e., dress lifted at least to the knees. But I have never been able to understand why the name of a delectable dessert should be given to leg art.

Cheesecake *is* a delectable dessert. I was first introduced to it at Jensen's Hofbrau in New York a good many years ago. And I've been a cheesecake enthusiast ever since. (I'm still talking about the dessert, although God knows I'm not against cheesecake in the newspaper sense.) California has done amazing things with cheesecake, topping it with all manner of fruits, and so forth. But I still like this old-fashioned kind best.

CHEESECAKE

¾ *pkg. Zwieback*	*Pinch salt*
11 *ounces sugar*	2 *tbsp. flour*
½ *cup melted butter*	4 *eggs*
1 *tsp. powdered cinnamon*	1 *tsp. grated orange rind*
2 *lb. Philadelphia cream cheese*	1 *tsp. grated lemon rind*
2 *tbsp. Madeira*	2 *cups sour cream*

Mix together ¾ package of Zwieback, finely crushed, ¼ cup of sugar, ½ cup of melted butter, and 1 teaspoon of powdered cinnamon. When thoroughly mixed and blended, line a 10-inch spring-form cake pan on the bottom and sides with ¾ of this mixture.

The cheese filling is made as follows: Cream 2 pounds of Philadelphia cream cheese with 9 ounces of sugar. Add 2 tablespoons of flour, a pinch of salt, 1 tablespoon of Madeira, the well-beaten yolks of 4 eggs, and 1 teaspoon each of grated orange rind and grated lemon rind. Mix well, then add 2 cups of sour cream.

Fold in 4 stiffly beaten egg whites, and when all is blended, pour the filling into the lined cake pan. Bake in a moderate oven (375 degrees) for about 30 minutes. Then cover the top with the remaining Zwieback mixture, sprinkle with about 1 tablespoon of Madeira, and put back in the oven, turning it up to 400 degrees, and bake for another 15 minutes or so. Cool, and then place in the refrigerator for several hours. Remove about an hour before serving.

To my mind one of the greatest desserts ever devised by man, if not the greatest, is trifle. It is as English as Piccadilly, the Tower of London, and Buckingham Palace all rolled into one.

When I was living in Los Angeles, I used to eat at the Cock 'n Bull down at the end of the strip on Sunset Boulevard. Trifle there was well-nigh perfect. And then I moved out to Tarzana. Imagine my delight on finding, about a block from my house, on the corner of Tampa Street and Ventura Boulevard, a little wayside restaurant run by an English couple who served the most delicious trifle I have ever tasted! About three nights a week we'd cook dinner at home, *sans* dessert, and walk down to the corner to have trifle. But I never got my fill of it, and it never palled.

One of the favorite Italian desserts, which Ric Riccardo mentioned in his preface, is *Zuppa Inglese,* which is very similar to the English trifle. *Zuppa* literally means soup in Italian, but *Zuppa Inglese* is simply cake soaked with rum and covered with a custard. It's good, but I still prefer English trifle.

ENGLISH TRIFLE

1 *sponge cake*	*Macaroons*
Lady fingers	*Raspberry jam*

1 *cup Madeira*

2 *cups milk*	¼ *tsp. salt*
6 *egg yolks*	*Grated rind* ½ *lemon*
½ *cup sugar*	2 *ounces brandy*

½ *tsp. vanilla extract*

½ *tsp. lemon extract*	2 *tbsp. dry white wine*
3 *tbsp. maraschino cordial*	2 *cups heavy whipping cream*

Sugar to taste

Slivered almonds	*Candied cherries*

Line the sides of a glass bowl, or china salad bowl, with halved lady fingers standing upright, the flat side of the lady fingers resting against the sides of the bowl. Cover the bottom of the bowl with a 1½-inch layer of sponge cake, not too fresh. Spread a generous layer of raspberry jam over the sponge cake, and over the jam place a layer of macaroons. Pour over all 1 cup of Madeira—or enough to saturate the cake, macaroons, and lady fingers thoroughly. Put in a cold place until wanted.

Make a boiled custard, as follows: Scald 2 cups of milk. Combine 6 egg yolks, lightly beaten with ½ cup of sugar, the grated rind of ½ lemon, and ¼ teaspoon of salt. Slowly add the scalded milk to the egg mixture, stirring constantly. Put the whole into the top of a double boiler, and cook over hot water, stirring constantly, until the mixture thickens and will coat a spoon. Cool, and add 2 ounces of brandy and ½ teaspoon of vanilla extract. Beat well, and set the custard in the refrigerator to chill.

In a glass bowl, which has been set in a larger bowl filled with cracked ice, mix together ½ teaspoon lemon extract, 3 tablespoons of maraschino cordial, 2 tablespoons of white wine, 2 cups of heavy whipping cream, and sugar to taste. Have the beater well chilled also. Whip the cream until stiff, then place in the refrigerator for a couple of hours.

To complete the trifle, pour the custard into the bowl containing the sponge cake, ladyfingers, and macaroons, put the whipped cream over the custard, building it up. Sprinkle slivered almonds over the whipped cream, decorate with candied cherries, and serve.

There are a number of cream-and-custard desserts, most of which I am not enthusiastic about. But there are two which stand out, to my way of thinking, as real gourmet desserts. One of these is *Crème Brule.*

Literally translated *crème brule* is "burned cream" and is nothing more than a custard topped with caramelized sugar. But the following is no ordinary custard. It's made with Grand Marnier.

CRÈME BRÛLÉ, GRAND MARNIER

3 *whole eggs*	2 *cups rich cream*
2 *tbsp. sugar*	2 *tbsp. Grand Marnier*
3 *egg yolks*	*Sifted brown sugar*

Beat 3 whole eggs and 3 egg yolks with 2 tablespoons of sugar until creamy and light, and put in the top of a double boiler.

Heat 2 cups of rich cream, to which has been added 2 tablespoons of Grand Marnier.

Pour the cream into the egg mixture very slowly and carefully, beating constantly. Cook in the double boiler until the mixture thickens and will coat the back of a wooden spoon. Then pour into a shallow glass baking dish of a size to allow the mixture to be about 2 inches thick. Place in the refrigerator and thoroughly chill.

About 2 hours before serving, cover the surface of the cream with about ¼-inch layer of sifted brown sugar, so that none of the cream shows. Place the dish in a larger dish with crushed ice in it, and place the whole thing under the broiler until the top of the brown sugar melts and forms a hard glaze. Watch carefully during this process. Then put the baking dish back in the refrigerator to chill again before serving.

The other cream dessert that I am passionately fond of is *Zabaglione,* the famous Italian dessert. It is perfect at the conclusion of almost any dinner because it is light and most flavorsome. It, too, is really a custard, but its consistency is such that you can almost drink it. The following recipe is the way Max Guggiari of the Imperial House in Chicago, prepares it.

ZABAGLIONE GUGGIARI

5 *egg yolks*	9 *tsp. sugar*
5 *ounces Marsala*	1½ *ounces brandy*

In the bottom of a double boiler have the necessary amount of water (to come within an inch of the bottom of the top part) at a temperature of between 90 and 100 degrees. Put the double boiler over a medium flame, and into the top part put the yolks of 5 eggs, 5 ounces of Marsala, 9 teaspoons of sugar, and 1½ ounces of brandy. With a wire whisk, whip this, without stopping, until the amount has increased to 4 times what it was at the start. Then pour into glass compotes and serve at once. The *Zabaglione* should be creamy, but just a little too thick to pour. Don't delay serving this dessert, because it will "fall" quickly and curdle if permitted to stand.

There was a time when bananas were restricted to the box lunch, or were sliced and served with cream for breakfast. And then along came *Chicquita Banana* in the pages of newspapers, magazines, and on the radio, and now bananas serve not only as a breakfast dish or a lunch-box item, but also as a vegetable and as the base for delectable desserts. The following is a delectable of delectables.

BANANAS FLAMBÉ

6 *ripe bananas*	*Lime juice*
3 *ounces butter*	½ *tsp. powdered cloves*
½ *cup sifted brown sugar*	½ *tsp. powdered nutmeg*
½ *tsp. powdered cinnamon*	1½ *tsp. grated orange rind*

½ *cup medium rum*

Peel 6 ripe bananas, cut them in half lengthwise, and brush with lime juice.

Melt 3 ounces of butter in a shallow fireproof baking dish that can be brought to the table. Place the split bananas in the baking dish, and put in a 450-degree oven for about 15 minutes.

Mix together ½ cup of sifted brown sugar, ½ teaspoon each of powdered cinnamon, nutmeg, and clove, and 1½ teaspoons of grated orange peel.

Take the bananas out of the oven, and sprinkle each piece with the above mixture. Return the bananas to the oven for a few moments, until the sugar has melted. Take them out of the oven, pour in around them ½ cup of medium rum, set it alight, and bring the dish to the table as it blazes.

Fresh fruits are a great boon to harassed hosts and hostesses when they are stuck for a dessert. Any number of fruits can be combined in any number of ways with any number of wines and liqueurs, and the result is always tops. One could devote almost an entire book to fruits as desserts. I am going to limit myself in this chapter to only a few of the outstanding ones.

BING CHERRIES WITH BRANDY AND CURRANT JELLY

1 *lb. fresh Bing cherries* 4 *ounces red currant jelly*
     2 *ounces brandy*

Pit a pound of fresh Bing cherries and place them in a bowl with 4 ounces of red currant jelly. Mix, and then set in the refrigerator for several hours, until they are very cold. When you serve them, pour 2 ounces of brandy over the cherries and jelly. The brandy cuts the sweetness of the jelly, and the flavor of the whole is pretty wonderful.

Here's a dessert that's swanky, suave, and swell, to say nothing of being simple. In any smart restaurant it will cost you anywhere from a dollar and a half to two dollars a copy, but you can make it in your own home at a fraction of the cost with canned cherries and you'll never know the difference.

CHERRIES JUBILEE

1 *large can Bing cherries* 3 *ounces Cointreau*
5 *ounces brandy*   3 *ounces kirsch*
    Vanilla ice cream

Drain ¾ of the juice from a can of Bing cherries. Put the cherries and the remaining juice in a bowl, and add 3 ounces each of brandy, Cointreau and kirsch. Allow the cherries to marinate in this mixture for a couple of hours.

Just before serving, warm the cherries and their marinade.
Serve out individual portions of vanilla ice cream in deep dishes. Put 2 ounces of brandy in a ladle, warm it, and set it alight, and with the blazing brandy ignite the cherries and their marinade. Mix while blazing, and ladle the cherries and their marinade over the ice cream.

A very effective dessert to serve, especially after a heavy meal, is wine-frosted grapes. You may have eaten them and wondered how in hell they were prepared. If so, wonder no longer.

WINE-FROSTED GRAPES

1 *large bunch white grapes*	1 *tbsp. dry white wine*
2 *egg whites*	*Finely granulated sugar*

Select large, perfect white grapes. Divide up the bunch into small clusters of a few grapes each.

Add 1 tablespoon of dry white wine to 2 egg whites, and beat them lightly, but not to a foam. Dip the grapes in this, and immediately sprinkle with very fine granulated sugar. Place in the refrigerator to chill and harden, and serve cold.

I have never been an advocate of serving melon as a dessert, although I admit that is a purely personal prejudice and one that won't hold water. I love melons for breakfast, and I had always thought that was the only meal at which they should be served until I discovered Stuffed Persian Melon. Now I've tossed my prejudices out of the window.

STUFFED PERSIAN MELON

1 *large, firm, ripe Persian melon*	*Strawberries*
	Blueberries
Cubes fresh pineapple	*Powdered sugar*
Black raspberries	2 *ounces Anis del Mono*

Select a rather large, ripe Persian melon that is still firm. Cut a slice off the bud end so that the melon will stand upright. Then cut about a 3-inch-square plug out of the top, with the stem in the center. Carefully remove the seeds and any juice, and then, with a melon ball scoop, scoop out the flesh from the melon, being careful not to remove the meat too close to the rind.

In a bowl mix the melon balls with ½ as much of the following fresh fruits: small cubes of fresh pineapple, black raspberries, halved strawberries, and blueberries. Sprinkle powdered sugar over the fruit, mix gently, and put it back in the melon. Pour into the melon 2 ounces of *Anis del Mono,* and replace the plug in the top. Thoroughly chill in the refrigerator for 24 hours, and serve.

Many years ago, in my simple and naïve way, I disliked fruit compotes either as a first course or as a dessert. I still don't like fruit cocktails as a first course (with the exception of the minted fruit cup mentioned in the second chapter), but I've learned to do tricks with fruits and liqueurs in my more mature years. Here's one compote that is simple, easy, and delicious.

FRUIT COMPOTE WITH RUM

1 *ripe cantaloupe*	5 *ounces rum*
1 *quart strawberries*	½ *pint whipping cream*
1 *can sliced pineapple*	*Sugar*
	Kirsch

Cut a cantaloupe in half, and with a melon ball scoop, scoop out the meat. Combine this with 1 quart of fresh strawberries, and 1 can of sliced pineapple cut into about ¾-inch squares. Pour 5 ounces of light rum over the mixed fruit, sprinkle with powdered sugar, and place it in the refrigerator to chill.

Whip ½ pint of heavy whipping cream which has been sweetened with sugar and flavored with kirsch. (Add the sugar to the cream, whip until the cream becomes stiff, and add the kirsch very slowly while whipping the cream. It should take about 1 tablespoon of kirsch.)

Put the fruit mixture into individual compotes, top with the flavored whipped cream, and serve.

For some reason, nobody seems to have discovered the origin of a peach. It was known and appreciated by the ancient Greeks and Romans. Its Latin name was *prunus Persica,* meaning plum from Persia. In case you're interested, there are 2,000 varieties of peaches.

Brillat-Savarin, the gourmet philosopher, believed that taste gives rise to sensations of three different orders, namely: direct sensation, complete sensation, and reflex sensation. In applying that theory, he used the peach as an example:

He who eats a peach, for example, is at first agreeably struck by the odour which emanates from it; he puts it in his mouth, and feels a sensation of freshness and of sourness which induces him to continue; but it is only at the moment when he swallows it, and when the mouthful passes under the nasal fossa, that the perfume is revealed to him. This completes the sensation which a peach ought to produce. Finally, it is only when it has been swallowed that, considering what he has just experienced, the taster says to himself, "How delicious!"

Delightful as the flavor of the fresh peach is, it can be enhanced to delight not only the taste, but also the eye.

PÊCHE FLAMBÉ

1 *ripe peach per person*   1½ *ounces brandy per person*
Sugar

Peel a whole ripe peach, sprinkle it with sugar, and pour 1½ ounces of brandy over it. Set it alight, and serve.

Fresh peaches combine beautifully with champagne, and the following is probably the most unusual dish you have ever tasted. You soak the peach slices in champagne while you are drinking it, and then fish out the peach afterwards for dessert.

FRESH PEACHES IN CHAMPAGNE

Ripe peaches   *Iced champagne*

Peel ripe peaches, and remove the pits. Cut into ½-inch slices, and fill tall 14-ounce glasses about ½ full. Thoroughly chill the fruit and glasses.

Fill the glasses with iced dry American champagne, and drink with dinner. Then eat the fruit afterwards.

Peaches sliced and put over ice cream make a delightful dessert, but sometime try reversing the process by first poaching the peaches in white wine and then putting ice cream on the peaches.

FRESH PEACHES POACHED IN WINE

8 *fresh peaches*   2 *tbsp. sugar*
4 *ounces dry Madeira*   4 *peach pits*
4 *ounces port*   1 *tbsp. currant jelly*
1 *quart vanilla ice cream.*

Scald 8 fine, fresh peaches, peel off the skins, cut in halves, and remove the pits. In a flat pan heat 4 ounces of dry Madeira and

4 ounces of American port with 2 tablespoons of sugar. Add 4 of the peach pits. Gently place the peach halves in the pan and simmer slowly for 20 minutes. Take out the pits. Lay the peach halves on a dish and chill in the refrigerator. Cook the juice and wine to a thick syrup, adding a little more sugar and about 1 tablespoon of currant jelly. Chill this sauce.

For 8 portions, use 1 quart of vanilla ice cream. Fill the peach halves with ice cream and pour on the wine sauce.

Of all the desserts I have ever served, I have received more raves and more requests for the recipe for *Stuffed Peaches* than for any other. They're not so difficult to prepare as they appear to be.

STUFFED PEACHES

7 *ripe peaches*	½ *tbsp. chopped candied citron*
3 *macaroons*	2 *ounces curaçao*
½ *tbsp. chopped candied orange peel*	½ *cup dry white wine*
	1 *tbsp. brandy*

Select 7 peaches that are ripe, but firm. Cover with boiling water for 20 to 30 seconds, then drain, and cover with cold water. Remove, and the skins will slip off easily. Halve the peaches, and remove the pits.

Crumble 3 macaroons, and mix with them ½ tablespoon each of chopped candied orange peel and chopped candied citron, and 2 ounces of curaçao. Mash ½ peach to a pulp, and mix this with the crumbled macaroon mixture.

Pack the cavities of the peaches with the stuffing, and put each of the two halves together, securing them with toothpicks. Place the peaches in a baking dish, pour over them ½ cup of dry American white wine, and bake in a moderate (350 degree) oven for about 15 or 20 minutes, basting frequently with the white wine.

To serve, remove a peach to each plate, pour its share of the wine sauce over it. Warm a tablespoon of brandy, set it alight, and pour over the peach.

It is said that the sister of that immortal epicure, Brillat-Savarin, made the most heroic single gesture known in the history of eating.

When a fatal stroke caught her midway through a magnificent meal, she cried out to the cook, "Rush the dessert!"

History did not record what the dessert was, but, of course, she knew. And if the same thing happened to me, and I knew the dessert was baked pineapple as it is served in Hawaii, I, too, would cry out, "Rush the dessert!"

You don't need a grass skirt, a surf board, or a *lei* to concoct this delectable finale to a dinner. Just obtain a large pineapple— sun-ripened—and get out of your liquor closet a bottle of rum and a bottle of brandy.

BAKED PINEAPPLE

1 *large pineapple*	4 *ounces light rum*
½ *cup blanched almonds*	¼ *cup sugar*
1 *large ripe peach*	1 *ounce brandy*
	Butter

Cut off the top of a large, sun-ripened pineapple, saving the top for later use.

Scoop out the meat from the pineapple, using a curved grape-fruit knife that is sharp, being very careful not to puncture the skin of the pineapple. Discard any tough or pithy meat, and cut the rest into about ½-inch cubes.

Shred ½ cup of blanched almonds and add to the pineapple meat.

Peel 1 large ripe peach, remove the pit, and cut into pieces about the size of the pineapple cubes. Combine the pineapple meat, the peach, and the almonds, and pour over the mixed fruit 4 ounces of light rum. Sprinkle with ¼ cup of sugar, and toss lightly.

Put the combined fruit back into the pineapple in layers, dotting each layer with butter. Put the top of the pineapple back on and bake in a moderate oven (350 degrees) until the inside fruit is tender.

Serve on a platter, pouring 1 ounce of warm brandy over the pineapple, and setting it alight.

Another excellent fresh pineapple dish, utilizing the whole pineapple, is pineapple surprise. This is a lovely hot weather dessert.

PINEAPPLE SURPRISE

1 *large ripe pineapple*   1½ *cups domestic champagne*
3 *fresh peaches*   1 *cup sugar*
                1½ *tsp. Fraisette or kirsch*

Take a ripe pineapple and cut it in half lengthwise, leaving the
leaves on. Scoop out the meat, leaving a ½-inch shell, and being
careful not to puncture it. Discard the tough or pithy meat, and
chop the rest, together with 3 fresh peaches. Put the chopped
pineapple and peaches back in the shell.

Take 1½ cups of domestic champagne and heat it, but do not
let it even simmer. Add to the champagne about 1 cup of sugar
(less, if you don't want too sweet a sauce), and when the sugar
has dissolved, remove the champagne from the fire and let it cool
to just about lukewarm. Then add 1½ teaspoons of *Fraisette* if
you have it or can get it (a cordial made from a specially prepared
alcoholic syrup and strawberries, with a dry white wine added)
or the same amount of kirsch. Mix well, then pour the syrup over
the chopped peaches and pineapple in the pineapple boat, and set
the boats in the refrigerator and thoroughly chill.

I have run across many recipes for strawberries Romanoff, but
they all failed to use the one ingredient which is typically Russian,
namely vodka. I first had this in the home of a White Russian
friend of mine. In writing it out for me, he gave the strawberries
their Russian name, which you can use if you want to be high hat. It
is pronounced just as it's spelled.

KLOOBNIKA ROMANOFF
(Strawberries Romanoff)

1 *quart strawberries*   1½ *ounces curaçao*
½ *cup powdered sugar*   1½ *ounces rum*
1½ *ounces vodka*   1 *cup whipping cream*
                1 *tbsp. kirsch*

Wash and hull 1 quart of fresh strawberries, and toss them with
about ½ cup of powdered sugar. Then put them in a bowl suitable
for serving at the table, and pour over them a mixture of 1½

ounces each of vodka, curaçao, and rum. Place in the refrigerator to chill.

Serve very cold, with the strawberries topped with 1 cup of heavy cream whipped with 1 tablespoon of kirsch.

I shall never forget a disaster that occurred at the Maison Wood one evening. Six of us were to partake of that king of dishes, *Boeuf Bourguignon,* with garlic bread and a special tossed salad with Roquefort cheese dressing. For dessert my much better half had prepared the *pièce de résistance,* a Florida lime pie. Taking time by the forelock, I had made the *Boeuf Bourguignon* the day before (for some reason the second and third heating of a carefully prepared ragout seems to make it even more delectable), and the Little Woman had made her pie twenty-four hours in advance and placed it in the refrigerator.

The guests were scheduled to arrive at six o'clock. I was in the kitchen preparing an *aperitif,* and my wife opened the refrigerator to get out some cubes of ice; and that's when it happened! You guessed it. As the refrigerator door swung open, out slid the lime pie, landing top side down on the kitchen floor, with the glass pie plate breaking into a hundred pieces! My helpmate sat down on a chair and stared, and, while she didn't burst into tears, if she had moved her foot, she would have kicked her chin.

I scraped up the mess aind deposited it in the incinerator. I wasn't happy either, because I am fond of lime pie. Then, in a voice issuing from the depths of her despair, my wife said: "They'll be here in fifteen minutes. What shall we do?" I could have said, paraphrasing Marie Antoinette, "Let 'em eat candy," but instead I dived for the refrigerator and got together quickly a mélange of what fresh fruit there was and doused it with rum. But it couldn't replace the lime pie.

Here's the way the lime pie was made, and I can assure you the above disaster has never occurred a second time.

FLORIDA LIME PIE

1 *can Eagle brand sweetened condensed milk*	*Prebaked pie shell*
⅓ *cup fresh lime juice*	1 *cup whipping cream*
	Sugar to taste
3 *eggs*	1 *tbsp. rum*

Mix together 1 can of Eagle brand sweetened condensed milk, ⅓ cup of fresh lime juice, and the beaten yolks of 3 eggs. Then fold in the well-beaten whites. Place the mixture in a good, flaky pie shell, already baked, and bake in the oven for 10 minutes at 250 degrees. When cool, place in the refrigerator until ready to serve. When serving, top each piece of pie with slightly sweetened whipped cream to which has been added a little rum. This recipe makes a pie that will serve six sparingly. But the odds are that four will finish the pie, because it's that good.

Back in the chapter on game one of the items on the menu of the early American dinner was New England rum pie. It's one of those pies that men will probably take delight in making because it is impossible to have a failure with the crust.

NEW ENGLAND RUM PIE

Crust

18 *graham crackers*	⅓ *cup sugar*
¼ *lb. butter*	*Dash cinnamon*

Filling

4 *small pkgs. cream cheese*	2 *eggs*
½ *cup sugar*	1 *tbsp. rum*

Topping

1 *cup sour cream*	3 *tbsp. sugar*
	1 *tbsp. rum*

Make a crust of 18 graham crackers, crumbled, ¼ pound of butter, melted, ⅓ cup of sugar, and a dash of cinnamon. Line a pie tin with this. For the filling, mix together 4 small packages of cream cheese, ½ cup of sugar, 2 beaten eggs, and 1 tablespoon of rum. When thick as cream, pour the filling into the crust and bake in a 375-degree oven for 20 minutes. In the meantime, mix together 1 cup of sour cream, 3 tablespoons of sugar, and a tablespoon of rum. Spread this mix on the baked pie and cook 5 minutes more in the 375-degree oven.

The Hungarians have a delightful dessert which will appeal to anyone who's fond of chestnuts. I can't pronounce the Hungarian name for chestnuts, but it doesn't detract from the dessert in any way to call it just plain Chestnut Pudding.

GESZETENYE PURÉE
(Chestnut Pudding)

1 *lb. chestnuts*	1 *cup heavy cream*
½ *tsp. vanilla extract*	*Juice* 1 *orange*
2 *ounces rum*	1 *tbsp. curaçao*
1 *tsp. powdered sugar*	*Currant jelly*

Boil 1 pound of chestnuts (imported Italian chestnuts if you can get them) for 20 to 30 minutes. Peel and remove inner skin, and press through a ricer while still hot. Add ½ teaspoon of vanilla extract, 2 ounces of rum, and 1 teaspoon of powdered sugar (more, if you prefer more sweetness). Mix this well, and chill.

Beat 1 cup of heavy cream until stiff and add gradually the juice of 1 orange and 1 tablespoon of curaçao. Now add the puréed chestnuts, and beat all together thoroughly. Put back in the refrigerator until cold, and serve with a teaspoon of currant jelly over the top.

I don't suppose there is anyone who hasn't heard of cointreau, a liqueur which was made famous by the Sidecar cocktail. Cointreau is somewhat similar to white curaçao, but is usually sweeter. They are both prepared from a principal base of fine brandy and orange peel. The following recipe is from Jacques Mercier Cointreau and it is a soufflé par excellence.

SOUFFLÉ AU COINTREAU

¾ *cup milk*	7 *eggs*
1 *tbsp. sugar*	4 *ounces Cointreau*

Boil ¾ cup of milk and 1 tablespoon of sugar, adding the yolks of 7 eggs. Then allow the mixture to cool in the refrigerator. Beat the whites of the 7 eggs to a stiff froth, mixing in 4 ounces of Cointreau. Now add this mixture lightly to the other ingredients, and pour the whole into a baking dish with a very flat and even bottom. Place in a very hot oven (450-500 degrees) for approximately 10 to 15 minutes. Serve immediately, so that the lightness of the soufflé is not lost. And that, Messieurs and Mesdames, is truly ambrosial.

There have been occasions when dinner time came around and somebody neglected to think of a dessert. However, that is never too much of a tragedy because a few pieces of good candy will serve very well as the final sweet touch to a meal.

I don't know anything about candy making, so there are no recipes for candy in this book; but there are two confections I can and do make which may serve to satisfy one's sweet tooth.

In the Vienna that used to be, there was a Christmas delicacy that was in tremendous demand during the holiday season. It was called Chocolate Truffles, and hardly a home was without them. They are not hard to make, and they call for no hard-to-get ingredients.

CHOCOLATE TRUFFLES

5 *tbsp. granulated sugar*	1 *tbsp. kirsch*
5 *tbsp. ground almonds*	½ *beaten raw egg*
1 *drop bitter almond extract*	1 *tbsp. water*
1 *tsp. powdered cocoa*	½ *lb. grated chocolate*

Powdered chocolate

To 5 tablespoons of granulated sugar add the same quantity of finely ground blanched almonds. Then add 1 drop of bitter almond extract, 1 teaspoon of powdered cocoa, and a tablespoon of kirsch. Combine these ingredients with ½ beaten raw egg, and shape into small round balls about the size of a large cherry. Now put 1 tablespoon of water in about ½ pound of grated chocolate and bring it to a boil. Then, keeping it over hot water, dip the cakes into this, let them cool, roll in powdered chocolate, and dry in a very slow oven.

The recipe for the second confection was given to me by Teresa Heraty, secretary to Arnold Shircliffe of the Wrigley Building Restaurant. Miss Heraty is what I would call a gourmette, if such a word can be used. She knows almost as much about fine foods as her genial boss does. Knowing my predilection for sweets, she dug this recipe out for me, and I found that I could make it almost with my eyes closed.

RUM BALLS À LA HERATY

½ lb. vanilla wafers	1 cup finely chopped pecans
1 cup confectioner's sugar	½ cup light corn syrup
2 tbsp. cocoa	¼ cup rum

Grind or roll ½ pound of vanilla wafers very fine. Mix with them 1 cup of confectioner's sugar and 2 tablespoons of cocoa. Then add 1 cup of finely chopped pecans, ½ cup of corn syrup, and ¼ cup of rum. Stir until stiff.

Coat hands with confectioner's sugar, and roll the above mixture into balls about the size of a walnut and let them stand for about an hour to dry somewhat. Then roll the balls in confectioner's sugar, and store in a tin container. They will keep well for several weeks.

This is in the nature of a last word—something that has been the birthright of Little Women since time began, and which mere men rarely enjoy.

When you consult the index, you will note that there are no recipes in this book for breads, cookies, jams, preserves, only one for baking a cake, and two for pies. Personally, I am of the firm opinion that these dishes should be the sole prerogative of the Little Woman of the household. As far as the bachelor is concerned, there are excellent breads on the market, notably Pepperridge Farm Bread, which, for my money, tops anything that can be baked in the home. As to rolls, biscuits, etc., these can be purchased either from your favorite bakery, in frozen form, or, if you must whip up something, there are a large variety of already-prepared biscuit- roll- and muffin-mixes on any grocery shelves. In the field of pies, I have eaten some excellent frozen pies, and again, there are piecrust-mixes on the market that are said to be foolproof. As for cakes, I have never eaten a really good store-bought cake. Serve something else.

A final word of warning. When you are acquiring the status

of an amateur chef, it will be wise to have a recipe before you and follow it exactly the first time. If you are invited out to cook a meal at friends' homes (and believe me you will be) take the written recipe along with you, unless you have graduated from a memory course, and can keep several of your best recipes in your head. As you progress, and acquire confidence, to say nothing of a knowledge of what goes well with what, and a respect for the materials used, you can begin to experiment with your written, proven recipes. Sometimes this will provide a big thrill, and sometimes it may prove to be disastrous. But, in any event, it will be fun.

So, have fun, boys and girls!

INDEX

369